The Regionalization
of the World Economy

A National Bureau
of Economic Research
Project Report

The Regionalization of the World Economy

Edited by Jeffrey A. Frankel

The University of Chicago Press

Chicago and London

JEFFREY A. FRANKEL is professor of economics at the University of California, Berkeley, and a research associate of the National Bureau of Economic Research, where he is also director of the program in International Finance and Macroeconomics. After this project was completed, he took leave to serve on the Council of Economic Advisers.

The University of Chicago Press, Chicago 60637
The University of Chicago Press, Ltd., London
© 1998 by the National Bureau of Economic Research
All rights reserved. Published 1998
Printed in the United States of America
07 06 05 04 03 02 01 00 99 98   1 2 3 4 5
ISBN: 0-226-25995-1 (cloth)

Library of Congress Cataloging-in-Publication Data

The regionalization of the world economy / edited by Jeffrey A.
   Frankel
       p.   cm. — (National Bureau of Economic Research project
   report)
    Includes bibliographical references and index.
    ISBN 0-226-25995-1 (cloth : alk. paper)
 1. Trade blocs.   2. Regionalism.   3. International trade.
 4. International economic integration.   I. Frankel, Jeffrey A.
 II. Series.
 HF1418.7.R447 1998
 337.1—DC21   97-15325
                                                                  CIP

Relation of the Directors to the
Work and Publications of the
National Bureau of Economic Research

1. The object of the National Bureau of Economic Research is to ascertain and to present to the public important economic facts and their interpretation in a scientific and impartial manner. The Board of Directors is charged with the responsibility of ensuring that the work of the National Bureau is carried on in strict conformity with this object.

2. The President of the National Bureau shall submit to the Board of Directors, or to its Executive Committee, for their formal adoption all specific proposals for research to be instituted.

3. No research report shall be published by the National Bureau until the President has sent each member of the Board a notice that a manuscript is recommended for publication and that in the President's opinion it is suitable for publication in accordance with the principles of the National Bureau. Such notification will include an abstract or summary of the manuscript's content and a response form for use by those Directors who desire a copy of the manuscript for review. Each manuscript shall contain a summary drawing attention to the nature and treatment of the problem studied, the character of the data and their utilization in the report, and the main conclusions reached.

4. For each manuscript so submitted, a special committee of the Directors (including Directors Emeriti) shall be appointed by majority agreement of the President and Vice Presidents (or by the Executive Committee in case of inability to decide on the part of the President and Vice Presidents), consisting of three Directors selected as nearly as may be one from each general division of the Board. The names of the special manuscript committee shall be stated to each Director when notice of the proposed publication is submitted to him. It shall be the duty of each member of the special manuscript committee to read the manuscript. If each member of the manuscript committee signifies his approval within thirty days of the transmittal of the manuscript, the report may be published. If at the end of that period any member of the manuscript committee withholds his approval, the President shall then notify each member of the Board, requesting approval or disapproval of publication, and thirty days additional shall be granted for this purpose. The manuscript shall then not be published unless at least a majority of the entire Board who shall have voted on the proposal within the time fixed for the receipt of votes shall have approved.

5. No manuscript may be published, though approved by each member of the special manuscript committee, until forty-five days have elapsed from the transmittal of the report in manuscript form. The interval is allowed for the receipt of any memorandum of dissent or reservation, together with a brief statement of his reasons, that any member may wish to express; and such memorandum of dissent or reservation shall be published with the manuscript if he so desires. Publication does not, however, imply that each member of the Board has read the manuscript, or that either members of the Board in general or the special committee have passed on its validity in every detail.

6. Publications of the National Bureau issued for informational purposes concerning the work of the Bureau and its staff, or issued to inform the public of activities of Bureau staff, and volumes issued as a result of various conferences involving the National Bureau shall contain a specific disclaimer noting that such publication has not passed through the normal review procedures required in this resolution. The Executive Committee of the Board is charged with review of all such publications from time to time to ensure that they do not take on the character of formal research reports of the National Bureau, requiring formal Board approval.

7. Unless otherwise determined by the Board or exempted by the terms of paragraph 6, a copy of this resolution shall be printed in each National Bureau publication.

(Resolution adopted October 25, 1926, as revised through September 30, 1974)

Contents

Acknowledgments

This volume's papers and corresponding discussants' comments examine regionalism in international economic policy. They were originally presented at a conference held in Woodstock, Vermont, on 21–22 October 1995. A preconference, held in Cambridge, Massachusetts, in July 1995, helped to keep the authors on track.

On behalf of the National Bureau of Economic Research, I would like to thank the Ford Foundation for its financial support of this project. I would also like to thank Martin Feldstein for asking me to undertake the project, and the participants for obeying a rigorous time schedule that allowed timely publication of the volume.

Introduction

Jeffrey A. Frankel

One has a choice of events with which to date the beginning of the current surge in regional economic arrangements. Europe has been in the forefront of this movement, so one could choose as the starting point the decision of the European Community around 1986–87 to adopt the Single Market Initiative. Alternatively, one could argue that the key event was the decision by the United States, which became manifest in the negotiation and adoption of a free trade area (FTA) with Canada in 1988–89, to abandon its long-standing opposition to regionalism. Or, thirdly, one could emphasize the spread of FTAs to the developing countries, the years 1990–91 seeing important regional initiatives in the Andean Pact, Mercosur, and the Association of Southeast Asian Nations.

In any case, regionalism is with us. The subject offers ample new territory for research, empirical as well as theoretical. We want to study a country's raising or lowering of trade barriers, not vis-à-vis the world at large, but rather vis-à-vis particular neighbors.

Most international trade research in the past has ignored the geographic dimension. International trade models, whether empirical or theoretical, whether based on small-country or large-country assumptions, and whatever else their attributes, tended until recently to have one curious thing in common: they treated countries as disembodied entities that lacked a physical location in geographical space. There are, to be sure, some things one can say about FTAs even without the geographic dimension, provided one is at least willing to include three countries in the model. But many of the most interesting aspects of regional trading arrangements require the introduction of a geographic dimension. Without it, one can hardly claim to be studying regionalism.

Jeffrey A. Frankel is professor of economics at the University of California, Berkeley, and a research associate of the National Bureau of Economic Research, where he is also director of the program in International Finance and Macroeconomics. After this project was completed, he took leave to serve on the Council of Economic Advisers.

This volume addresses several large questions. Why do countries adopt FTAs and other regional trading arrangements? To what extent have existing regional arrangements actually affected patterns of trade? What are the welfare effects of such arrangements? It is worth spelling out this third question more fully from the outset. In most economic models, whether classical or new-fangled, economic welfare is maximized by worldwide free trade. The difficult questions arise when one assumes that this first-best solution is not attainable politically. Which is second-best: a system of most-favored nation (MFN), that is, nondiscriminatory tariffs? or a system where groups of countries deviate from the MFN principle in order to form FTAs, which eliminate trade barriers internally while keeping them externally? Both systems contain distortions. Choosing between them is an exercise in the theory of the second-best.

This volume focuses on trade. The issue of regional currency arrangements enters tangentially into two of the chapters, by way of their effects on trade. Other aspects of regional integration, however, such as optimum currency areas, financial issues, foreign direct investment, and fiscal federalism, have been excluded from the volume, in order to keep it focused.

Several of the chapters, particularly where the effects of regional arrangements are explored econometrically, make extensive use of the gravity model of bilateral trade. This model is a standard by which to judge what is the normal pattern of trade between pairs of countries, and thereby to judge when regional arrangements are having an extra effect on trade. The book thus begins with a chapter by Alan Deardorff, exploring the theoretical foundation for the gravity model.

Until recently, it was said of the model that, although it fit the data well, it was sorely lacking in theoretical foundations. During the past fifteen years, the theory of trade in imperfect substitutes and increasing returns to scale has been developed, to the point where it is accepted as a theoretical foundation for the gravity equation. The empirical success of the equation has been adduced as evidence in favor of the imperfect-substitutes theory, in comparison, for example, with the Heckscher-Ohlin theory of trade based on international differences in factor endowments. Now Deardorff shows in chapter 1 that the gravity equation can be derived from the Heckscher-Ohlin theory, almost as easily as from the imperfect-substitutes theory. The equation has thus apparently gone from an embarrassing poverty of theoretical foundations to an embarrassment of riches! Those who debate the proper theory of trade will now have to reckon with the Deardorff paper. Those of us who wish to use the gravity equation as a tool for considering other questions can in any case proceed, with our heads held high.

The first of three chapters that use the gravity equation to study the effects of regional trading arrangements is by Barry Eichengreen and Douglas Irwin, who take a historical perspective in chapter 2. The idea is that the effects of regional arrangements can be imputed only to intraregional concentrations of trade that exceed what can be explained by the economic fundamentals: country size, income per capita, and distance between the pair of countries in question. In many such studies, a tendency for trading patterns to change relatively slowly over time has been observed, even when the change in regional trading arrangements or political links is sudden. Eichengreen and Irwin take the bull by the horns and include lagged values of bilateral trade in their gravity estimates for the period from 1928 to 1965. They find, for example, that trade links among British colonies in 1954 and 1964, which might otherwise be attributed to Commonwealth preferences, are in fact simply the lagged effects of trade flows of 1949, when the countries belonged to the British Empire. Evidently, effects such as established marketing channels and brand-name loyalty last long after the original reasons for initiating them may have vanished. The authors conclude that one should always include lagged variables in the gravity equation.

In chapter 3, John Whalley provides the book's review of recent regional initiatives, summarized in table 3.1. He then considers the motives behind countries' decisions to participate. The motives include the use of regional agreements to underpin domestic policy reforms, the desire to achieve more assured market access with large trading partners, a link between trade agreements and security arrangements, the use of agreements to strengthen collective bargaining power in multilateral trade negotiations, and the use of regional negotiations as a threat to driving multilateral negotiations forward.

Chapter 4, by Jeffrey Frankel, Ernesto Stein, and Shang-Jin Wei, serves two purposes. First it uses the gravity model to examine the effect that explicit and implicit regional trading arrangements have had on trade. It takes up where chapter 2 leaves off, in the sense that the period covered is 1970–90. It finds an intraregional bias to trade in each of three continental blocs: the European Community, the Western Hemisphere, and East Asia.

The chapter then develops a theoretical framework for considering the welfare implications of this regionalization of trade. It builds on Paul Krugman's idea (1991b) that, in the presence of intercontinental transport costs, a world of three FTAs can be an improvement over the status quo of MFN, provided the FTAs are drawn along the *natural* geographic lines of the three continents. The chapter develops the idea that there is an *optimal degree of regionalization,* which is determined by the magnitude of transportation costs. If the margin of intrabloc preferences exceeds this optimal level, then it enters what we call the *supernatural* zone. We find that existing regional initiatives, such as the European Union, are indeed in danger of entering the supernatural zone, that is, of exceeding the extent of regional preferences that can be justified on natural geographic grounds. This judgment leaves many factors out. Perhaps most importantly, it takes the worldwide level of tariffs as fixed exogenously.

Chapter 5, by Antonio Spilimbergo and Ernesto Stein, addresses a critique that has been made against the results of Krugman (1991a, 1991b) and of chapter 4, namely that they depend on the assumption that trade is based on imperfect substitutes rather than on differences in factor endowments. At stake is whether a move from many small blocs to a few large blocs raises or lowers welfare. In the Spilimbergo-Stein model, trade is based on both imperfect substitution and factor endowments. They first look at the case where transportation costs are zero, which is the traditional assumption. The Krugman (1991a) result once again emerges, provided the elasticity of substitution parameter is not too high, that is, consumers' love for variety is not too low: welfare reaches a minimum at three large blocs. The world would be better off with larger numbers of smaller blocs. If the love for variety is very low, however, then welfare is monotonically decreasing in the number of blocs, justifying the skeptics. In this case, the model behaves like the factor-endowments model. The conclusion, which is that economic welfare is monotonically increasing in the size of the blocs, would then offer a more optimistic outlook for regionalism. If 60 countries combine into 12 blocs of 5 countries each, and then combine into 6 blocs of 10 each, followed by 3 blocs of 20 each, economic welfare is improved at every step of the way. This suggests that FTAs can be stepping stones toward the ultimate goal of one bloc of 60 countries, also known as worldwide free trade. The authors go on to consider the effects of blocs formed between rich and poor countries, as compared to blocs among the rich and among the poor.

Particularly interesting is what Spilimbergo and Stein find when they allow for intercontinental transport costs. Notwithstanding the introduction of differences in factor endowments as a determinant of trade, the results are qualitatively the same as in the model laid out in chapter 4 of this volume. Specifically, the three most important results continue to hold. (1) FTAs put the world into the supernatural zone (for a wide range of intercontinental costs). We are now able to see, however, that the effect is quite different in rich countries than in poor countries. The latter are likely to be better off from a move to four continental blocs, even though the rich are worse off. (2) Preferential trading arrangements can raise welfare, even for rich countries, provided the margin of preferences is not set too high. (3) The optimal margin of preferences rises with the level of intercontinental costs. Unless intercontinental costs exceed 0.25 of trade value, however, the optimal margin of preferences is in the range of 20 to 30 percent. Anything above that level enters the zone of negative returns to regionalization, and anything over 60 percent enters the supernatural zone.

It would probably be unwise, not to say monotonous, to rely exclusively on the gravity model's analysis of trade quantities, for our information on the extent to which the influences of geography versus regional economic policy arrangements determine trading patterns. Charles Engel and John Rogers in chapter 6 offer an alternative approach: they examine prices rather than quantities. There are excellent reasons to gauge international integration by the ability of arbitrage to eliminate price differentials for similar goods, particularly where the null hypothesis is perfect integration between two markets.

They examine the behavior of final goods prices for eight goods (plus aggregate consumer price indexes) measured in twenty-three countries and eight North American cities. Deviations from the law of one price are large; the question is what they have to tell us about regional influences. The authors find that the log of distance has a statistically significant effect on relative price variability for seven out of nine sectors tested. For all goods combined, the estimate implies that a 1 percent increase in distance raises the monthly standard deviation of relative prices by .00000789. The annualized impact of a 1 percent increase in distance is an increase in the standard deviation of .0000273, nearly identical to the effect that Engel and Rogers (1995) found in an earlier study using U.S. and Canadian city data. Even after allowing for the effect of distance, however, there is a tendency for arbitrage to work better within regions than across regions. (Sharing a common border reduces relative price variability across countries as well.)

This residual regionalization could be due either to currency factors, regional trading arrangements, or other influences. Other influences include linguistic and political links. The authors introduce a theoretical model, in order to highlight the importance of an integrated network of distribution and marketing within nations and within regions. Currency links are tested by including bilateral exchange rate variability in the regression equation. Exchange rate variability has a statistically significant positive effect on relative price variability in all regressions, with the relationship close to one to one. Even after holding constant for proximity and currency links, regional effects remain for North America and Europe (less so for Asia). It appears that all four elements matter—distance, currency links, regional groupings, and an unidentified residual that could be due to integrated distribution networks.

Chapter 7, by Frankel and Wei, picks up a number of threads. Again, we lead with the gravity model. Extensions relative to earlier work include updating the results to 1992, estimating imports and exports separately, and including an effect for remoteness. (This last twist was inspired by the specification derived by Deardorff in chapter 1.) We also present some estimates of the role that currency links may have played in promoting intragroup trade, as in chapter 6.

The welfare analysis in chapters 4 and 5 took the level of tariffs against nonmembers as exogenously fixed. The bulk of chapter 7 relaxes that assumption. Others have made various political-economy arguments regarding regionalism, either to the effect that it can undermine more general liberalization or to the effect that it can help build political momentum for multilateral liberalization. We present a simple model of our own that is in the latter category: it illustrates one possible beneficial effect of trade blocs as a political building block to further trade liberalization. The result could as easily go the other way, however. Is regionalism a building block to global free trade or not? The trade-diversion estimates of the gravity model provide a tentative assessment.

One of the ways that the political economy of FTAs can set back trade liberalization is when special interests are able to influence the terms of an agreement in their favor (as Bhagwati 1993 has emphasized). An example is when a politically powerful industry manages to get itself exempted from the elimination of protective tariff barriers. Article XXIV of the General Agreement on Tariffs and Trade (GATT) requires that liberalization within an FTA apply to all sectors. Even when this rule is obeyed, however, favored industries can win the establishment of long, drawn-out periods during which protection against the partner is phased out. This was the case with the North American Free Trade Agreement (NAFTA) and is the subject of chapter 8, by Carsten Kowalczyk and Donald Davis. They find that American industries that have been able to win higher duties in the past tend to get longer periods of adjustment in NAFTA. The same pattern does not seem to hold for Mexican industries, however. The speed of U.S. phase-out for a sector seems to affect the speed of Mexican phase-out, suggesting reciprocity in the negotiations within narrow categories. The authors conclude that slow phase-outs were a concession that Mexico granted the United States, because it wanted the agreement more badly (as suggested in chapter 3 and in Grossman and Helpman 1995).

The book concludes with an overview of the papers by Anne Krueger. This overview, like the comments on each of the papers, places the chapters in perspective and helps to round out the discussion.

References

Bhagwati, Jagdish. 1993. Regionalism and Multilateralism: An Overview. In Jaime de Melo and Arvind Panagariya, eds., *New Dimensions in Regional Integration*. New York: Cambridge University Press.

Engel, Charles, and John Rogers. 1995. How Wide Is the Border? University of Washington. Manuscript.

Grossman, Gene, and Elhanan Helpman. 1995. The Politics of Free Trade Agreements. *American Economic Review* 85 (September): 667–90.

Krugman, Paul. 1991a. Is Bilateralism Bad? In Elhanan Helpman and Assaf Razin, eds., *International Trade and Trade Policy*. Cambridge: MIT Press.

———. 1991b. The Move toward Free Trade Zones. In Federal Reserve Bank of Kansas City, *Policy Implications of Trade and Currency Zones,* 7–42. Kansas City: Federal Reserve Bank.

1 Determinants of Bilateral Trade: Does Gravity Work in a Neoclassical World?

Alan V. Deardorff

1.1 Introduction

It has long been recognized that bilateral trade patterns are well described empirically by the so-called gravity equation, which relates trade between two countries positively to both of their incomes and negatively to the distance between them, usually with a functional form that is reminiscent of the law of gravity in physics. It also used to be frequently stated that the gravity equation was without theoretical foundation. In particular, it was claimed that the Heckscher-Ohlin (HO) model of international trade was incapable of providing such a foundation, and perhaps even that the HO model was theoretically inconsistent with the gravity equation. In this paper I will take another look at these issues. It is certainly no longer true that the gravity equation is without a theoretical basis, since several of the same authors who noted its absence went on to provide one. I will briefly review their contributions in a moment. Since none of them build directly on an HO base, it might be supposed that the empirical success of the gravity equation is evidence against the HO model, as at least one researcher has implied by using the gravity equation as a test of an alternative model incorporating monopolistic competition. I will argue, however, that the HO model, at least in some of the equilibria that it permits, admits easily of interpretations that accord readily with the gravity equation. At the same time, developing these interpretations can yield additional insights about why bilateral trade patterns in some cases depart from the gravity equation as well.

There are two keys to these results, which once stated may make the rest of

Alan V. Deardorff is professor of economics and public policy at the University of Michigan.

The author has benefited greatly from comments and conversations with Don Davis, Simon Evenett, Jeffrey Frankel, Jon Haveman, David Hummels, Jim Levinsohn, and Bob Stern, as well as from the comments of the discussants, Jeffrey Bergstrand and Gene Grossman.

the paper obvious to those well-schooled in trade theory. The two keys open doors to two different cases of HO-model equilibria, one with frictionless trade and one without.

With frictionless trade—that is, literally zero barriers to trade of all sorts, including both tariffs and transport costs—the key is that trade is just as cheap, and therefore no less likely, as domestic transactions. Therefore, instead of thinking as we normally do of countries first satisfying demands out of domestic supply and then importing only what is left, we should think of demanders as being indifferent among all equally priced sources of supply, both domestic and foreign. Suppliers likewise should not care about to whom they sell. The HO model (and other models based solely on comparative advantage and perfect competition) is usually examined only for its implications for net trade, and we then jump to the conclusion that gross trade flows are equal to net. But with no trade impediments, there is no reason for trade to be this small. If instead we allow markets to be settled randomly among all possibilities among which producers and consumers are indifferent, then trade flows will generally be larger and will fall naturally into a gravity-equation configuration, in a frictionless form without a role for distance. With identical preferences across countries, this configuration is particularly simple. With nonidentical preferences it is a bit more complex, but it is also more instructive.

The other key is to the case of trade in the presence of trade impediments. If there exist positive impediments to all trade flows, however small, then the HO model cannot have factor price equalization (FPE) between any two countries that trade with each other. For if they did have FPE, then their prices of all goods would be identical and neither could overcome the positive barrier on its exports to the other. Since we do observe trade between every pair of countries that we care about, it follows that the HO equilibria we look at with impeded trade should be ones without FPE between any pair of countries. If we assume also that the number of goods in the world is extremely large compared to the number of factors, it will be true that for almost all goods only one country will be the least-cost producer. With trade barriers this does not imply complete specialization by countries in largely different goods, but it makes such a case more plausible than might have been thought otherwise. In any case, motivated by this observation, I will study bilateral impeded trade under the assumption that each good is produced by only one country. With that assumption, bilateral trade patterns in the HO model are essentially the same as in other models with differentiated products, and it is no surprise that the gravity equation emerges once again. My contribution here will be to derive bilateral trade in terms of incomes and trade barriers in a form that may be more readily interpretable than before.

None of this should be very surprising, although I admit that this is much clearer to me now than it was when I started thinking about it. All that the gravity equation says, after all, aside from its particular functional form, is that bilateral trade should be positively related to the two countries' incomes and negatively related to the distance between them. Transport costs would surely yield the latter in just about any sensible model. And the dependence on incomes would also be hard to avoid. The size of a country obviously puts an upper limit on the amount that it can trade (unless it simply reexports, which one normally excludes), so that small countries necessarily trade little. For income not to be positively related to trade, it would therefore have to be true also that large countries trade very little, at least on average. Therefore, the smaller the smallest countries are, the less must all countries trade in order to avoid getting a positive relationship between size and trade. Looked at in that way, it would therefore be very surprising if some positive relationship between bilateral trade and national incomes did not also emerge from just about any sensible trade model. The HO model has some quirky features, but in this respect, at least, it turns out to be sensible.

As for the functional form, a simple version of the gravity equation—what I will call the standard gravity equation—is typically specified as

(1)
$$T_{ij} = A\frac{Y_i Y_j}{D_{ij}}$$

where T_{ij} is the value of exports from country i to country j, the Ys are their respective national incomes, D_{ij} is a measure of the distance between them,[1] and A is a constant of proportionality. While this particular multiplicative functional form may not be obvious, the easiest alternative of a linear equation clearly would not do, for trade between two countries must surely go to zero as the size of either goes to zero. None of this constitutes a derivation of the gravity equation, of course, but it does suggest why one would expect something like it to hold in any plausible model.

I turn in section 1.2 to a brief review of the literature, followed by the two cases just mentioned: frictionless trade in section 1.3 and impeded trade in section 1.4.

1.2   Theoretical Foundations for the Gravity Equation

As has been noted many times, the gravity equation for describing trade flows first appeared in the empirical literature without much serious attempt to justify it theoretically. Tinbergen (1962) and Pöyhönen (1963) did the first econometric studies of trade flows based on the gravity equation, for which they gave only intuitive justification. Linnemann (1966) added more variables and went further toward a theoretical justification in terms of a Walrasian general equilibrium system, but the Walrasian model tends to include too many

---

1. Clearly this measure should not go to zero for adjacent countries, or equation (1) would yield infinite trade between them. Empirical work typically uses distance between national capitals. For theoretical purposes below, it is convenient to use a measure that starts at one (such as one plus distance) to accommodate transactions of a country with itself.

explanatory variables for each trade flow to be easily reduced to the gravity equation. Leamer and Stern (1970) followed Savage and Deutsch (1960) in deriving it from a probability model of transactions. Their approach was very similar to what I will suggest below, but they applied it only to trade, not to all transactions, and they did not make any explicit connection with the HO model. Leamer (1974) used both the gravity equation and the HO model to motivate explanatory variables in a regression analysis of trade flows, but he did not integrate the two approaches theoretically.

These contributions were followed by several more formal attempts to derive the gravity equation from models that assumed product differentiation. Anderson (1979) was the first to do so, first assuming Cobb-Douglas preferences and then, in an appendix, constant-elasticity-of-substitution (CES) preferences. In both cases he made what today would be called the Armington assumption, that products were differentiated by country of origin. His framework was in fact very similar to what I will examine here with impeded trade, although I motivate the differentiation among products, as already noted, by the HO model's case of non-FPE and specialization rather than by the Armington assumption. Anderson modeled preferences over only traded goods, while I will assume for simplicity that they hold over all goods. Anderson's primary concern was to examine the econometric properties of the resulting equations, rather than to extract easily interpretable theoretical implications as I seek here.

Finally, Jeffrey Bergstrand has explored the theoretical determination of bilateral trade in a series of papers. In Bergstrand (1985) he, like Anderson, used CES preferences over Armington-differentiated goods to derive a reduced-form equation for bilateral trade involving price indexes. Using GDP deflators to approximate these price indexes, he estimated his system in order to test his assumptions of product differentiation. For richness his CES preferences were also nested, with a different elasticity of substitution among imports than between imports and domestic goods. His empirical estimates supported the assumption that goods were not perfect substitutes and that imports were closer substitutes for each other than for domestic goods.

In Bergstrand (1989, 1990) he departed even further from the HO model by assuming Dixit-Stiglitz (1977) monopolistic competition, and therefore product differentiation among firms rather than among countries. This was imbedded, however, in a two-sector economy in which each monopolistically competitive sector had different factor proportions, thus being a hybrid of the perfectly competitive HO model and the one-sector monopolistically competitive model of Krugman (1979). In the first paper Bergstrand used this framework to derive yet again a version of the gravity equation, and in the second he examined bilateral intraindustry trade.

Bergstrand's later work therefore serves to bring together the earlier Armington-based approaches to deriving the gravity equation with a second strand of literature in which gravity equations were derived from simple monopolistic competition models. Almost from the start of the new trade theory's attention to such models, it was recognized that they provided an immediate and simple justification for the gravity equation.[2] Indeed, Helpman (1987) used this correspondence between the gravity equation and the monopolistic competition model as the basis for an empirical test of the latter. That is, he interpreted the close fit of the gravity equation with bilateral data on trade as supportive empirical evidence for the monopolistic competition model. For this to be correct, of course, it would need to be true, as Helpman apparently believed, that the gravity equation does not also arise from other models. He remarked that "the factor proportions theory contributes very little to our understanding of the determination of the volume of trade in the world economy, or the volume of trade within groups of countries" (63), and he went on to demonstrate geometrically that the volume of trade under FPE in the $2 \times 2 \times 2$ HO model is independent of country sizes.[3] Helpman was, I would like to think, in good company. No less an authority than Deardorff (1984, 500–504) noted several of the empirical regularities that are captured in the gravity equation and pronounced them paradoxes, inconsistent with, or at least not explainable by, the HO model.

Helpman applied his test to data on trade of the Organization for Economic Cooperation and Development (OECD) countries, where most would agree that monopolistic competition is plausibly present. Hummels and Levinsohn (1995) decided to attempt a sort of negative test of the same proposition by looking for the same relationship in the trade among a much wider variety of countries, including ones where monopolistic competition is less plausibly a factor. To their surprise, they found that the test worked just as well for that group of countries, thus leading one to suspect that perhaps the relationship represented by the gravity equation is more ubiquitous, and not unique to the monopolistic competition model. It might be thought that the work by Anderson and Bergstrand cited above would have already suggested this, since they derived gravity equations from a variety of models other than the monopolistic one that Bergstrand eventually incorporated into his analysis. But in fact the versions of the gravity equation that Anderson and Bergstrand obtained were somewhat complex and opaque, and it was not obvious that they would lead to the success of the very simple gravity equation tested by Helpman.

My point in this paper, of course, is that one can get essentially this same

---

2. One such was apparently Krugman (1980), cited in Helpman (1987).

3. This argument appeared first in Helpman and Krugman (1984). I would argue that Helpman's locus for comparisons, which are along straight lines parallel to the diagonal of a Dixit-Norman-Helpman-Krugman factor allocation rectangle, is inappropriate. Along these straight lines, the differences in relative factor endowments of the two countries also change, becoming more pronounced (and leading to greater trade) at the same time that countries are becoming more different in size (leading to less trade). A better comparison would have been along a locus for which the percentage difference in factor endowment ratios remains constant. This would be a curve bowed out from the diagonal of the box, and along this curve the trade volume would be largest where country incomes are equal, just as in the gravity equation.

simple gravity equation from the HO model properly considered, both with frictionless and with impeded trade. This does not mean that the empirical success of the gravity model lends support to the HO model, any more than it does to the monopolistic competition model. For reasons I have already indicated, I suspect that just about any plausible model of trade would yield something very like the gravity equation, whose empirical success is therefore not evidence of anything, but just a fact of life.

1.3   Frictionless Trade

Consider now an HO model with any numbers of goods and factors. In fact, for most of what I will say in this section,[4] the argument is more general and could apply to any perfectly competitive trade model with homogeneous products, including a Ricardian model, a specific-factors model,[5] a model with arbitrary differences in technology, and so forth. For this model, consider a frictionless trade equilibrium—that is, an equilibrium with zero transport costs and no other impediments to trade—with each country a net exporter of some goods to the world market and a net importer of others. This equilibrium need not be unique, as it will not be in the HO model with FPE and more goods than factors. If the model is HO, then there may be FPE among some or all countries, but there need not be. We need merely have some vectors of production, consumption, and therefore net trade in each country that are consistent with maximization by perfectly competitive producers and consumers in all countries, facing the same prices (due to frictionless trade) for all goods, the vectors being such that world markets clear.

It is customary to note that patterns of bilateral trade are not determined in such a model, and indeed they are not. But the reason for this indeterminacy is itself important: both producers and consumers are indifferent, under the assumption of frictionless trade and homogeneous products, among the many possible destinations for their sales and sources for their purchases. Therefore, while it is true that a wide variety of outcomes is possible, we can get an idea of the average outcome by just allowing choices among indifferent outcomes to be made randomly.

Thus, having already found the equilibrium levels of production and consumption, let the actual transactions be determined as follows: producers in each industry put their outputs into a world pool for their industry; consumers then choose randomly their desired levels of consumption from these pools. If consumers draw from these pools in small increments, then the law of large numbers will allow us to predict quite accurately what their total choices will be by using expected values. In general, these expected values will be appro-

---

4. The only exception is the penultimate paragraph of this section, where bilateral trade is related to per capita incomes using an assumption about preferences and factor intensities of goods.

5. Of course the specific-factors model is just a special case of the HO model with many goods and factors.

priate averages of the wide variety of outcomes that are in fact possible in the model.

1.3.1   Homothetic Preferences

All of this works extremely simply if preferences of consumers everywhere are identical and homothetic, which I will now assume as a first case. Let x_i be country i's vector of production and c_i its vector of consumption in a frictionless trade equilibrium with world price vector p.[6] Its income is therefore $Y_i = p'x_i = p'c_i$, where I also assume balanced trade so that expenditure equals income. Now consider the value of exports from country i to country j, T_{ij}. With identical, homothetic preferences all countries will spend the same fraction, β_k, of their incomes on good k, so that country j's consumption of good k is $c_{jk} = \beta_k Y_j / p_k$. Drawing randomly from the world pool of good k, to which country i has contributed the fraction $\gamma_{ik} = x_{ik} / \Sigma_h x_{hk}$, country j's purchases of good k from country i will be $c_{ijk} = \gamma_{ik} \beta_k Y_j / p_k$. Let $x_k^w = \Sigma_i x_{ik}$ be world output of good k. Note that, with identical fractions of income being spent on good k by all countries, that fraction must also equal the share of good k in world income, Y^w: $\beta_k = p_k x_k^w / Y^w$. The value of j's total imports from i is therefore

$$T_{ij} = \sum_k p_k c_{ijk} = \sum_k \gamma_{ik} \beta_k Y_j$$

(2)
$$= \sum_k \frac{x_{ik}}{x_k^w} \frac{p_k x_k^w}{Y^w} Y_j = \sum_k p_k x_{ik} \frac{Y_j}{Y^w}$$

$$= \frac{Y_i Y_j}{Y^w}.$$

Thus with identical, homothetic preferences and frictionless trade, an even simpler gravity equation than (1) emerges immediately, with constant of proportionality $A = 1/Y^w$. Distance, of course, plays no role here since there are no transport costs, and I will call equation (2) the simple frictionless gravity equation. To get this, all that is needed is to resolve the indeterminacy of who buys from whom by making that decision randomly.

1.3.2   Arbitrary Preferences

If preferences are not identical and/or not homothetic, then the equilibrium may have each country spending a different share of its income on each good, and the simple derivation above does not work. Let β_{ik} now be the share of its income that country i spends on good k in the equilibrium, and also let α_{ik} be the share of country i's income that it derives from producing good k. The first and second equalities of equation (2) still hold, but with β_k replaced by β_{ik}. The value of world output of good k is $p_k x_k^w = \Sigma_i \alpha_{ik} Y_i$, and therefore the fraction of world output of good k that is produced by country i is $\gamma_{ik} = \alpha_{ik} Y_i / \Sigma_h \alpha_{hk} Y_h$.

---

6. All vectors are column vectors unless transposed with a prime.

Country j, again drawing randomly from the pool for good k an amount equal to its demand $\beta_{jk}Y_j$, will get that fraction from country i. Thus the value of sales by country i to country j of good k will be

(3)
$$T_{ijk} = \frac{\alpha_{ik}Y_i}{\sum_h \alpha_{hk}Y_h}\beta_{jk}Y_j.$$

Summing across goods k, we get

(4)
$$T_{ij} = \sum_k T_{ijk} = \sum_k \frac{\alpha_{ik}Y_i}{\sum_h \alpha_{hk}Y_h}\beta_{jk}Y_j = Y_iY_j\sum_k \frac{\alpha_{ik}\beta_{jk}}{p_kx_k^w}.$$

This is not the gravity equation, since the summation could be quite different for different values of i and j. As an extreme example, if country i happens to specialize completely in a good that country j does not demand at all, then T_{ij} will be zero regardless of Y_i and Y_j.

However, it is possible to simplify equation (4) further if one can assume that the fractions that exporters produce and that importers consume are in some sense unrelated. Let $\lambda_k = p_kx_k^w/Y^w$ be the fraction of world income accounted for by production of good k. Then

(5)
$$T_{ij} = \frac{Y_iY_j}{Y^w}\sum_k \frac{\alpha_{ik}\beta_{jk}}{\lambda_k}.$$

Clearly, since each country's good shares of both production (α_{ik}) and consumption (β_{jk}) sum to one, this will reduce to the simple frictionless gravity equation (2) if either the exporter produces goods in the same proportions as the world ($\alpha_{ik} = \lambda_k$) or if the importer consumes goods in the same proportion as the world ($\beta_{jk} = \lambda_k$, as was true in the case of identical, homothetic preferences), but not in general. If the λ_k were equal for all k, thus each being $1/n$ where n is the number of goods, we would also get back to equation (2) if α_{ik} and β_{jk} were uncorrelated. With goods having unequal shares of the world market, we can still get this if we define correlations on a weighted basis, using the λ_k as weights.

That is, let

$$\tilde{\alpha}_{ik} = \frac{\alpha_{ik} - \lambda_k}{\lambda_k}, \quad \tilde{\beta}_{jk} = \frac{\beta_{jk} - \lambda_k}{\lambda_k},$$

be the proportional deviations of country i's production shares and of country j's consumption shares from world averages. Then

(6)
$$\sum_k \lambda_k\tilde{\alpha}_{ik}\tilde{\beta}_{jk} = \sum_k \frac{1}{\lambda_k}\left(\alpha_{ik}\beta_{jk} - \lambda_k\beta_{jk} - \lambda_k\alpha_{ik} + \lambda_k^2\right)$$
$$= \sum_k \frac{\alpha_{ik}\beta_{jk}}{\lambda_k} - 1,$$

and we can rewrite equation (5) as

(7)
$$T_{ij} = \frac{Y_i Y_j}{Y^w}\left(1 + \sum_k \lambda_k \tilde{\alpha}_{ik} \tilde{\beta}_{jk}\right).$$

This is the main result of this section of the paper. The sign of the summation in equation (7) is the same as the sign of the weighted covariance between $\tilde{\alpha}_{ik}$ and $\tilde{\beta}_{jk}$. Thus, if these deviations of exporter production shares and importer consumption shares from world averages are uncorrelated, then once again the simple frictionless gravity equation (2) will hold exactly.

Perhaps more importantly, equation (7) also states simply and intuitively when two countries will trade either more or less than the amounts indicated by the simple frictionless gravity equation. If an exporter produces above-average amounts of the same goods that an importer consumes above average, then their trade will be greater than would have been explained by their incomes alone. On the other hand, if an exporter produces above average what the importer consumes below average, their trade will be unusually low. These statements presume that the simple frictionless gravity equation describes what is "usual." This is in fact the case here, since across all country pairs (i, j) the average of bilateral trade is equal to what the simple frictionless gravity equation prescribes.

(8)
$$\sum_{ij}\left(T_{ij} - \frac{Y_i Y_j}{Y^w}\right) = \sum_{ijk}\frac{Y_i Y_j}{Y^w}\lambda_k \tilde{\alpha}_{ik}\tilde{\beta}_{jk}$$

$$= \sum_{ik}\frac{Y_i}{Y^w}\tilde{\alpha}_{ik}\sum_j\left(Y_j \beta_{jk} - Y_j \lambda_k\right)$$

$$= \sum_{ik}\frac{Y_i}{Y^w}\tilde{\alpha}_{ik}\left(\sum_j c_{jk} - \lambda_k Y^w\right)$$

$$= 0$$

To sum up, with frictionless trade the values of bilateral trade are on average given by the simple frictionless gravity equation, $Y_i Y_j /Y^w$. If expenditure fractions differ across countries because preferences are not identical and/or not homothetic, then individual bilateral trade flows will vary around this frictionless gravity value. If one country tends to overproduce what another overconsumes, then exports of the former to the latter will be above that value, and if one tends to underproduce what another overconsumes, then these exports will be below that value.

It is important for these results that sales of a country to itself, T_{ii}, be included along with international trade. In this form the gravity equation holds on average even in the special case of countries who each demand only their own products. Their above average "exports" to themselves then offset their below average (zero) exports to each other to leave the average unaffected.

Combined with what we already know about the HO model and what we may suspect about preferences, this also leads us loosely to a corollary that I suspect could be made more formal with additional effort. Suppose that preferences are internationally identical but not homothetic, and suppose further that high-income consumers tend to consume larger budget shares of capital-intensive goods. Then capital-abundant countries will have higher than average per capita incomes and will therefore consume capital-intensive goods in disproportionate amounts. At the same time, from the HO theorem, they will also produce disproportionate amounts of these same goods. Therefore we would expect to find these countries trading more than average with each other and less than average with low-income labor-abundant countries. This is the same result that Markusen (1986) found in his "eclectic" model and for essentially the same reason. Although Markusen had increasing returns and monopolistic competition in his manufacturing sectors, these features served primarily to generate intraindustry trade. His volume-of-trade result was driven by a high income elasticity for capital-intensive goods.

Such a disproportionately high volume of trade among high-income countries happens to accord well with trade patterns in the real world. On the other hand, under the same circumstances the theory here also predicts that labor-abundant (hence poor) countries will trade disproportionately with each other as well. This is the same conclusion that Linder (1961) came to from a quite different theoretical model, but the empirical evidence in its favor is less clear.[7]

1.4   Impeded Trade

I turn now to the case of impeded trade, assuming instead that there not only exist barriers to trade, such as transport costs, but that these exist for every good. These barriers needn't be large, but I will assume them to be strictly positive on all international transactions. The case that I will consider will in addition have the property that every country produces and exports different goods. Indeed, this extreme specialization is the only property that I actually need in this section—the trade barriers are incidental.[8] I thought briefly that this case was the only one that could arise with positive transport costs, but I now realize that my thinking was flawed. I will nonetheless try to motivate the specialization assumption along the lines of that argument, but ultimately I can only claim to be considering a special case.

As mentioned in the introduction, the HO model has a striking implication in the presence of strictly positive transport costs: while in general the HO model permits equilibria with both FPE and non-FPE among groups of coun-

7. As I understand it, Jeffrey Frankel and co-authors have found in several studies, such as Frankel, Stein, and Wei (chap. 4 of this volume), that high-income countries trade disproportionately more than the gravity equation would suggest with all trading partners and not just among themselves, while low-income countries trade less.

8. Thus the results in this section would also obtain in an HO model with frictionless trade if factor endowments differed sufficiently to yield such specialization, as well as in a Ricardian model with specialization. They would also hold in any Armington model and any monopolistic-competition model, in both of which product differentiation in effect implies specialization.

tries, no two countries that have the same factor prices can trade with each other. The reason is that with identical factor prices (recall that the FPE theorem equates factor prices absolutely, not just relatively) they will have identical costs of production. With perfect competition neither country's producers could compete with domestic producers in the other's market, since the exporters would have to overcome the positive transport cost and domestic suppliers would not.

Now this is not a very appealing property of the HO model, I admit, and this by itself might be enough to make you prefer a model with some sort of imperfect competition. But it is a property of the HO model nonetheless, and I will take advantage of it. Since we do in the real world observe virtually every country trading with every other, if we are to give the HO model a chance to apply in the real world, we must assume unequal factor prices in each pair of countries.

Now suppose also that there are many more goods than there are factors, perhaps even an infinite number of goods as in Dornbusch, Fischer, and Samuelson (1977, 1980). If trade were frictionless, having unequal factor prices would severely limit the number of goods that any two countries could produce in common. With trade impediments this is no longer the case, since goods can become nontraded, and they can also compete in the same market if the difference in transport costs exactly equals the difference in production costs. But if transport costs for a given good are constant between any pair of countries (not varying with the amount transported), then I think the case can be made that only a negligibly small subset of all goods will be sold by any two countries to the same market. Thus for almost all trade, a country's consumers will be buying each good from only a single country's producers, either their own domestic industry or from the industry of a single foreign exporter.

This is not quite the same as saying that there exists only a single exporter of each good anywhere in the world, but that is nonetheless the case that I will consider. Indeed, I will go one step further and assume that each good is not only exported by only one country but is also produced only in that country. That being the case, the products of each country will be distinct in the eyes of consumers, not because of an Armington assumption that national origin matters, but because there really are different goods. One could argue that this is just as unrealistic as the case I dismissed above of countries not trading with each other at all, since for any industrial classification one observes production in multiple countries of goods that are classed the same. However, just as in the debate over the existence of intraindustry trade, where the phenomenon is sometimes argued to be an artifact of aggregation,[9] it may be that multiple producing countries may simply be producing different goods.

Suppose then that every good is produced by a different country in a particular international trading equilibrium. As long as we consider only that equilib-

---

9. See Deardorff 1984, 501, for a discussion.

rium, we can identify each good with the country that produces it and enter them into a utility function as imperfect substitutes. Let transport costs be of Samuelson's "iceberg" form, with the transport factor (one plus the transport cost) between countries i and j being t_{ij}. That is, a fraction $(t_{ij} - 1)$ of the good shipped from country i is used up in transport to country j.

With perfect competition, sellers from country i will not discriminate among markets to which they sell, and they will therefore receive a single price, p_i, for their products in all markets. Buyers, however, must pay the transport cost, and therefore the buyers' price in market j will be $t_{ij} p_i$.

What can we say about the pattern of bilateral trade? That depends on preferences, which I will assume first to be identical and Cobb-Douglas. That is, consumers in each country spend a fixed share, β_i, of their incomes on the product of country i. Let x_i be the output of country i. Country i's income, Y_i, is

$$(9) \qquad Y_i = p_i x_i = \sum_j \beta_i Y_j = \beta_i Y^w,$$

from which $\beta_i = Y_i/Y^w$. Trade can be valued either exclusive of transport costs (f.o.b.) or inclusive of transport costs (c.i.f.). On a c.i.f. basis we get immediately

$$(10) \qquad T_{ij}^{cif} = \beta_i Y_j = \frac{Y_i Y_j}{Y^w}.$$

With Cobb-Douglas preferences, therefore, we once again get the simple frictionless gravity equation for c.i.f. trade, with no role for transport costs or distance. On an f.o.b. basis, however, these flows must be reduced by the amount of the transport cost:

$$(11) \qquad T_{ij}^{fob} = \frac{Y_i Y_j}{t_{ij} Y^w}.$$

To the extent that transport cost is related to distance, this immediately gives a result very similar to the standard gravity equation (1), which includes distance.

This Cobb-Douglas formulation is nonetheless not very satisfactory, because the bilateral expenditures on international trade do not decline with distance. To allow for that to happen, and as the last model that I will consider, let preferences be instead CES. Let consumers in country j maximize the following CES utility function defined on the products of all countries i (including their own):

$$(12) \qquad U^j = \left(\sum_i \beta_i c_{ij}^{(\sigma-1)/\sigma} \right)^{\sigma/(\sigma-1)},$$

where $\sigma > 0$ is the common elasticity of substitution between any pair of countries' products. Facing c.i.f. prices $t_{ij} p_i$ of the goods, j's consumers, maximizing this function subject to their income $Y_j = p_j x_j$ from producing x_j, will consume

(13)
$$c_{ij} = \frac{1}{t_{ij}\,p_i} Y_j \beta_i \left(\frac{t_{ij}p_i}{p_j^I}\right)^{1-\sigma},$$

where p_j^I is a CES price index of landed prices in country j:

(14)
$$p_j^I = \left(\sum_i \beta_i t_{ij}^{1-\sigma} p_i^{1-\sigma}\right)^{1/(1-\sigma)}.$$

Therefore the f.o.b. value of exports from country i to country j is

(15)
$$T_{ij}^{fob} = \frac{1}{t_{ij}} Y_j \beta_i \left(\frac{t_{ij}p_i}{p_j^I}\right)^{1-\sigma}.$$

Note that the c.i.f. value of trade is this same expression multiplied by t_{ij}, which is therefore now decreasing in t_{ij} if $\sigma > 1$.

The parameter β_i is no longer country i's share of world income, as it was in the Cobb-Douglas case, so this does not reduce as easily to the standard gravity equation. However, if we let θ_i be country i's share of world income, we can relate it to β_i as follows, and then solve for β_i:

(16)
$$\begin{aligned}
\theta_i &= \frac{Y_i}{Y^w} = \frac{p_i x_i}{Y^w} \\
&= \frac{1}{Y^w} \sum_j \beta_i p_j x_j \left(\frac{t_{ij}p_i}{p_j^I}\right)^{1-\sigma} \\
&= \beta_i \sum_j \theta_j \left(\frac{t_{ij}p_i}{p_j^I}\right)^{1-\sigma},
\end{aligned}$$

from which

(17)
$$\beta_i = \frac{Y_i}{Y^w} \frac{1}{\sum_j \theta_j \left(\dfrac{t_{ij}p_i}{p_j^I}\right)^{1-\sigma}}.$$

Using this in equation (15) we get

(18)
$$T_{ij}^{fob} = \frac{Y_i Y_j}{Y^w} \frac{1}{t_{ij}} \left[\frac{\left(\dfrac{t_{ij}}{p_j^I}\right)^{1-\sigma}}{\sum_h \theta_h \left(\dfrac{t_{ih}}{p_h^I}\right)^{1-\sigma}} \right].$$

To simplify this and facilitate interpretation, first select units of goods so that each country's product price, p_i, is normalized at unity. Then p_j^I becomes a CES index of country j's transport factors as an importer, what I will call its average distance from suppliers δ^S:

(19)
$$\delta_j^s = \left(\sum_i \beta_i t_{ij}^{1-\sigma} \right)^{1/(1-\sigma)}.$$

What matters for demand along a particular route is the transport factor t_{ij} relative to this average distance from suppliers, what I will call the relative distance from suppliers ρ_{ij}:

(20)
$$\rho_{ij} = \frac{t_{ij}}{\delta_j^s}.$$

With this notation, the trade flow in equation (18) becomes

(21)
$$T_{ij}^{fob} = \frac{Y_i Y_j}{Y^w} \frac{1}{t_{ij}} \left[\frac{\rho_{ij}^{1-\sigma}}{\sum_h \theta_h \rho_{ih}^{1-\sigma}} \right].$$

This is the main result of this section of the paper. It says the following: if importing country j's relative distance from exporting country i is the same as an average of all demanders' relative distances from i, then exports from i to j will be the same as in the Cobb-Douglas case. That is, c.i.f. exports will be given by the simple frictionless gravity equation, while f.o.b. exports will be reduced below that equation by the transport factor from i to j, much as in the standard gravity equation with the transport factor (one plus transport cost) measuring distance. If j's relative distance from i is greater than this average, then c.i.f. (respectively f.o.b.) trade along this route will be correspondingly less than the simple frictionless (resp. standard) gravity equation, while if j's relative distance from i is less than this, trade will be correspondingly more. Since the transport factor for a country from itself is always unity and therefore less than any such average, countries' purchases from themselves will always be more than would appear warranted by the simple frictionless gravity equation.

The result also says that the elasticity of trade with respect to these relative distance measures is $-(\sigma - 1)$. Thus, the greater the elasticity of substitution among goods, the more trade between distant countries will fall short of the gravity equation and the more trade among close countries (and transactions within countries themselves) will exceed it.

Likewise, a general reduction in the transport factors themselves, such as might occur with an improvement in transportation technology, will pull trade closer to the amounts predicted by the simple frictionless gravity equation. This does not therefore mean that all bilateral trade flows will expand with a drop in transport costs. Rather, trade between distant countries will expand, while trade between close countries—neighbors—will contract, since the latter lose some of their advantage relative to distant countries. Of course a country is its own closest neighbor, and therefore purchases of a country from itself also contract. It follows that total international trade expands.

1.5 Conclusion

In this paper I have derived equations for the value of bilateral trade from two extreme cases of the HO model, both of which also characterize a variety of other models as well. The first case was frictionless trade, in which the absence of all barriers to trade in homogeneous products causes producers and consumers to be indifferent among trading partners, including their own country, so long as they buy or sell the desired goods. Resolving this indeterminacy with a random drawing, I derived expected trade flows that correspond exactly to the simple frictionless gravity equation whenever preferences are identical and homothetic. Generalizing the result to arbitrary preferences, I found that this gravity equation would still hold on average, but that individual trade flows would exceed or fall short of it depending on a weighted correlation between the exporter's and the importer's deviations from the world average supplies and demands. This in turn is suggestive of how particular nonhomotheticities in demand could interact with factor endowments and factor proportions to cause countries to trade excessively (compared to the simple frictionless gravity equation) with countries like themselves.

The second case considered was of countries that each produce different goods. This is also a possible equilibrium of the HO model, though of course it is a property as well of other models that have been used in the literature to derive the gravity equation, such as models with Armington preferences and models with monopolistic competition. Here I derived expressions for bilateral trade, first with Cobb-Douglas preferences and then with CES preferences. The former is almost too simple, yielding the simple frictionless gravity equation exactly for trade valued c.i.f. and the standard gravity equation, with division by a transport factor, for trade valued f.o.b. The CES case is more cumbersome, but it too reduces to something not all that different: bilateral trade flows are centered on the same values found in the Cobb-Douglas case, but they are smaller for countries that are a greater-than-average distance apart as measured by transport cost, and larger for countries that are closer than average. The latter includes purchases of a country from itself, which are increased above the Cobb-Douglas case by the greatest amount. The extent of these departures from the simple Cobb-Douglas gravity equation depends on the elasticity of substitution among goods, being larger the greater is that elasticity.

The lesson from all of this is twofold, I think. First, it is not all that difficult to justify even simple forms of the gravity equation from standard trade theories. Second, because the gravity equation appears to characterize a large class of models, its use for empirical tests of any of them is suspect.

References

Anderson, James E. 1979. A Theoretical Foundation for the Gravity Equation. *American Economic Review* 69 (March): 106–16.

Bergstrand, Jeffrey H. 1985. The Gravity Equation in International Trade: Some Microeconomic Foundations and Empirical Evidence. *Review of Economics and Statistics* 67 (August): 474–81.

———. 1989. The Generalized Gravity Equation, Monopolistic Competition, and the Factor-Proportions Theory in International Trade. *Review of Economics and Statistics* 71 (February): 143–53.

———. 1990. The Heckscher-Ohlin-Samuelson Model, the Linder Hypothesis, and the Determinants of Bilateral Intra-Industry Trade. *Economic Journal* 100 (December): 1216–29.

Deardorff, Alan V. 1984. Testing Trade Theories and Predicting Trade Flows. In Ronald Jones and Peter Kenen, eds., *Handbook of International Economics,* 1:467–517. New York: North-Holland.

Dixit, Avinash K., and Joseph E. Stiglitz. 1977. Monopolistic Competition and Optimum Product Diversity. *American Economic Review* 67:297–308.

Dornbusch, Rudiger, Stanley Fischer, and Paul A. Samuelson. 1977. Comparative Advantage, Trade, and Payments in a Ricardian Model with a Continuum of Goods. *American Economic Review* 67:823–39.

———. 1980. Heckscher-Ohlin Trade Theory with a Continuum of Goods. *Quarterly Journal of Economics* 95 (September): 203–24.

Helpman, Elhanan. 1987. Imperfect Competition and International Trade: Evidence from Fourteen Industrial Countries. *Journal of the Japanese and International Economies* 1:62–81.

Helpman, Elhanan, and Paul R. Krugman. 1985. *Market Structure and Foreign Trade: Increasing Returns, Imperfect Competition, and the International Economy.* Cambridge: MIT Press.

Hummels, David, and James A. Levinsohn. 1995. Monopolistic Competition and International Trade: Reconsidering the Evidence. *Quarterly Journal of Economics* 110 (August): 799–836.

Krugman, Paul R. 1979. Increasing Returns, Monopolistic Competition, and International Trade. *Journal of International Economics* 9:469–79.

———. 1980. Differentiated Products and Multilateral Trade. Mimeo.

Leamer, Edward E. 1974. The Commodity Composition of International Trade in Manufactures: An Empirical Analysis. *Oxford Economic Papers* 26:350–74.

Leamer, Edward E., and Robert M. Stern. 1970. *Quantitative International Economics.* Boston: Allyn and Bacon.

Linder, Staffan Burenstam. 1961. *An Essay on Trade and Transformation.* New York: Wiley and Sons.

Linnemann, Hans. 1966. *An Econometric Study of International Trade Flows.* Amsterdam: North-Holland.

Markusen, James R. 1986. Explaining the Volume of Trade: An Eclectic Approach. *American Economic Review* 76 (December): 1002–11.

Pöyhönen, Pentti. 1963. A Tentative Model for the Volume of Trade between Countries. *Weltwirtschaftliches Archiv* 90:93–99.

Savage, I. R., and K. W. Deutsch. 1960. A Statistical Model of the Gross Analysis of Transactions Flows. *Econometrica* 28 (July): 551–72.

Tinbergen, Jan. 1962. *Shaping the World Economy: Suggestions for an International Economic Policy.* New York: Twentieth Century Fund.

Comment   Jeffrey H. Bergstrand

For over thirty years, international trade economists have evaluated empirically the economic determinants of bilateral international trade flows using the "gravity equation." As Alan Deardorff notes, Jan Tinbergen (1962) provided one of the first sets of estimates of a gravity equation applied to international trade flows. He estimated a version very similar to this paper's equation (1), but allowing the right-hand-side variables' coefficients to vary from unity. Over the years, numerous trade economists have used gravity equations to explain statistically international trade flows with various ulterior economic motives, including but not nearly limited to the papers referenced in Deardorff's study.

Theoretical Foundations

Those thirty years have also witnessed a frustrating fascination of trade economists with the gravity equation. The fascination stems from the consistently strong empirical explanatory power of the model, with R^2 values ranging from 65 to 95 percent depending upon the sample, which has been a persuasive motivation for its usage. For many years, the frustration has stemmed from a so-called absence of formal theoretical foundations. Yet as Deardorff notes in section 1.2, there are several formal theoretical foundations for the gravity equation in international trade. Anderson (1979), Helpman and Krugman (1985), and Bergstrand (1985, 1989, 1990) motivate the multiplicative gravity equation assuming either products differentiated (somewhat arbitrarily) by origin or monopolistically competitive markets with (well-defined) product differentiation. Baldwin (1994, 82) aptly summarizes the state of theoretical foundations for the gravity model: "The gravity model used to have a poor reputation among reputable economists. Starting with Wang and Winters (1991), it has come back into fashion. One problem that lowered its respectability was its oft-asserted lack of theoretical foundations. In contrast to popular belief, it does have such foundations."

Despite these theoretical foundations, part of the frustration of trade economists with the gravity equation has been a lack of willingness to motivate the gravity equation in the context of *classical* theories, especially the Heckscher-Ohlin framework.[1] Deardorff's paper addresses this concern carefully and adeptly.

Frictionless Models

Before focusing upon classical issues though, Deardorff first challenges the reader to think of international trade unconventionally. Whereas classical mod-

---

Jeffrey H. Bergstrand is associate professor of finance and business economics at the University of Notre Dame.

1. As Deardorff notes, an exception is Bergstrand (1989), which imbeds monopolistically competitive product-differentiated markets in a two-sector economy with differing relative factor intensities between the two industries.

els typically consider export supplies as residual production after satisfaction of domestic demands, and conversely import demands as residual consumption beyond domestic production, Deardorff's first set of models—frictionless models—asks the reader to think of consumers and producers as being basically indifferent between domestic and foreign consumption and production, respectively. The essence of Deardorff's frictionless models can be reflected in the following simple framework. Suppose a country produced and consumed one homogeneous good under conditions of perfect competition. If the country's production and consumption were split into two equal economic "nations" (A and B), the representative consumer in A would be just as likely to consume A's output as B's output, and the representative producer in A would be just as likely to sell its output in the domestic market as in the foreign market.

The thrust of Deardorff's first frictionless model can be captured in three assumptions. (1) In each country, income (Y_i) equals production (PX_i) and consumption (PC_i), implying

$$(1) \qquad Y_i \equiv PX_i \equiv PC_i \equiv \sum_{j}^{N} PX_{ij}$$

and

$$(2) \qquad Y_j \equiv PX_j \equiv PC_j \equiv \sum_{i}^{N} PX_{ij},$$

where PX_{ij} is the flow of trade from i to j for all $i, j = 1, \ldots, N$ (including i to itself). (2) Tastes are identical across countries and homothetic, implying

$$(3) \qquad PX_{ij} = \gamma_i Y_j.$$

(3) The probability of country i exporting to country j is determined by the law of large numbers, implying

$$(4) \qquad \gamma_i = X_i / \sum_{j}^{N} X_j = Y_i / \sum_{j}^{N} Y_j = Y_i / Y^w,$$

where Y^w is world GDP ($\sum_{j}^{N} Y_j$) and is constant across country pairs. Substituting equation (4) into equation (3) yields a simple frictionless gravity equation:

$$(5) \qquad PX_{ij} = Y_i Y_j / Y^w.$$

This suggests that the gravity model can be derived under few assumptions and international trade can be generated without natural or acquired comparative advantages. Although one might consider little trade likely to be generated in this simple context, it is useful to see that the usual sources of international trade between nations—relative factor endowment differences or product diversity combined with increasing returns—are unnecessary for, but can be incorporated easily into, this simple trade framework.

Deardorff's model of frictionless trade under homothetic preferences in section 1.3 is not depicted quite so simply, because his ultimate motive in the section is rather to demonstrate that a slightly modified version of gravity equation (5) above is readily consistent with a Heckscher-Ohlin-type world, although one allowing nonhomothetic tastes. In the latter, consider a world with N countries where each country's share of production of commodity k can differ from the world's share (i.e., $p_k x_{ik}/Y_i = \alpha_{ik} \gtreqless \lambda_k = p_k x_k^W/Y^W$) and each country's relative demand for commodity k can differ from the world's relative demand (i.e., $p_k c_{jk}/Y_j = \beta_{jk} \gtreqless \beta_k = p_k c_k^W/Y^W$). Deardorff demonstrates that if the α_{ik} and β_{jk} are positively (negatively) correlated, then trade between countries i and j will exceed (fall short of) the simple frictionless gravity equation (5). The suggestion is that high real per capita income countries have high capital-labor ratios and tend to produce relatively capital-intensive goods. With nonhomothetic tastes, if capital-intensive goods are luxuries in consumption, high real per capita income countries will tend to trade more because of their tendency to produce and consume larger proportions of capital-intensive goods.

The main contributions of section 1.3 are to illustrate that the gravity model stands on its own, but also that Heckscher-Ohlin trade with nonhomothetic preferences can be generated within the context of and consistent with the gravity model. That the gravity model can evolve from an essentially Heckscher-Ohlin world (without any role for monopolistically competitive markets as in Bergstrand 1989) is a useful insight. Footnote 3 underscores the relevance of Deardorff's insight showing that—even in the absence of imperfectly competitive markets and increasing returns to scale—equal-sized countries in the Helpman and Krugman (1985) model (for instance, pp. 22–24) will tend to trade more *for given relative factor endowments.*

Models with Transportation Costs

What makes section 1.3's model interesting and novel is that the gravity model is derived in the *absence* of product differentiation, as in Leamer and Stern (1970). Section 1.4 considers trade in the *presence* of products differentiated by origin. While the first several pages attempt to motivate a rationale for why products are differentiated by origin from a non-factor-price-equalization context, the results in this section parallel earlier contributions to this literature more closely. The main result of section 1.4 is that the bilateral distance between i and j diminishes trade *and* that trade is influenced by the relative distance of importer j from exporter i (relative to other markets of i) relative to the average of all demanders' relative distances from i.

These notions have been present in one form or another in the earlier literature, similarly utilizing functions of constant elasticity of substitution; compare Anderson (1979) and Bergstrand (1985, 1989). For instance, Anderson showed that the trade flow was related to the bilateral i–j distance *and* to a complex "bracketed" term (as in this paper). In Anderson, the bracketed term was the ratio of a weighted average of importer j's distance from all markets to a weighted average of all countries' weighted average distances.

Bergstrand (1989) also used "iceberg" form transport costs as here. His gravity equation (12) can be rewritten to reflect the bilateral distance and the relative distance terms. Normalizing prices to unity and some algebraic manipulation yields trade flows as a function of (among other variables) the bilateral distance term (ignoring the industry superscript A in the original paper), $C_{ij}^{-(\sigma-1)/(\gamma+\sigma)}$, *and* the bilateral distance between i and j relative to the average distance of exporter i to all markets, $\{C_{ij}[\sum_n^N (1/C_{in})^{1+\gamma}]^{1/(1+\gamma)}\}^{-\gamma(\sigma-1)/(\gamma+\sigma)}$.

Deardorff's formulation is different because the relative distance term in his equation (21) isolates the distance of j from i relative to the average distance importer j faces for all suppliers from the average distance of i to all markets relative to all exporting countries. However, equation (21) is equivalent to equation (18), which specifies (after normalizing prices to unity) that the bracketed term reflect the distance between i and j relative to a weighted average of distances of exporter i to all markets, similar to Bergstrand (1989).

Nevertheless, an interesting common implication of all three studies is that the typical gravity equation specification with just the bilateral distance between i and j omits a potentially important explanatory variable, that is, the transport costs between i and j *relative* to some measure of "overall" transport costs.

It is interesting to note that the paper here, like Anderson's, normalizes all prices to unity to examine the importance of relative distances. However, suppose one considers the "frictionless" case where distances are normalized to unity but prices are not. In Deardorff's paper, equation (18) simplifies to

$$(6) \qquad T_{ij}^f = \{Y_i Y_j / Y^W\} \, [(p_i/p_j')^{1-\sigma} / \sum_h \theta_h (p_i/p_h')^{1-\sigma}].$$

Similarly, in the absence of the normalization of prices, Anderson's gravity equations would have included measures of relative prices. The importance of relative prices for suggesting the presence of product differentiation was emphasized in Bergstrand (1985). Bergstrand's model, under stronger assumptions, can be shown essentially equivalent to equation (6) above. Assuming the elasticities of substitution between imported and domestic products and that among imported goods are identical and the elasticities of substitution in production among export markets and between export and domestic are infinite (i.e., producers are indifferent between domestic and foreign markets and among foreign markets), the bilateral import demand function in Bergstrand can be written as

$$(7) \qquad X_{ij}^D = a_i (Y_j/P_{ij})(P_{ij}/P_j')^{1-\sigma}$$

or

$$(8) \qquad PX_{ij}^D = a_i Y_j (P_{ij}/P_j')^{1-\sigma}$$

The income constraint ensures

(9)
$$Y_i = \sum_{j}^{N} PX_{ij}^{S}.$$

In general equilibrium, $PX_{ij}^{S} = PX_{ij}^{D}$, so equation (8) can be substituted into (9) to yield

(10)
$$Y_i = \sum_{j}^{N} a_i Y_j (P_{ij}/P_j^I)^{1-\sigma}$$

or

(11)
$$a_i = Y_i / \sum_{j}^{N} Y_j (P_{ij}/P_j^I)^{1-\sigma}$$

Substituting equation (11) into (8) yields

(12)
$$PX_{ij} = Y_i Y_j [(P_{ij}/P_j^I)^{1-\sigma} / \sum_{j}^{N} Y_j (P_{ij}/P_j^I)^{1-\sigma}].$$

Equation (12) is similar to equation (6) above (and equation [18] in Deardorff) and suggests that relative prices, relative distances, relative tariffs, and so forth all matter in explaining departures of international trade flows from the basic gravity equation. Gravity equation practitioners have tended to ignore the importance of relative prices. Yet work by Kravis and Lipsey (1988) and Summers and Heston (1991) suggest that in cross-section prices differ considerably. In chapter 6 in this volume, by Charles Engel and John Rodgers, this view is lent further support. To the extent that measures of product differentiation, or distance of countries' products from their "ideal" variety (in the Hotelling-Lancaster sense), can be measured cross-sectionally, these factors need to be incorporated along with other asymmetries such as relative distance and relative tariffs in explaining departures from the basic frictionless gravity model. For completeness, in the case that goods are perfect substitutes ($\sigma = 1$), equation (12) simplifies to $PX_{ij} = Y_i Y_j / Y^W$, as in Deardorff's paper.

Conclusions

First, I agree with the paper's conclusion that simple forms of the gravity equation can be derived from standard trade theories. In fact, the author's first simple multiplicative frictionless gravity model can be derived *apart from* standard classical and the "new" trade theories. Second, I would agree more readily with the statement that the gravity equation appears to *be consistent with* a large class of models, rather than the gravity equation appears to "characterize" a large class of models. Third, the paper's conclusion that "its use for empirical tests of any of them is suspect" is correct; however, this statement is also misleading. Practitioners of the gravity equation over three decades have not—with the notable exception of Helpman (1987) and Hummels and Levinsohn (1995)—typically used the gravity equation to "test" trade theories. In most cases, the basic gravity model has been employed to capture statistically the bulk of trade variation to discern the marginal explanatory power of free trade pacts and/or exchange rate variability—additional variables appended to the basic frictionless model, without an aim to test one theory or another. Moreover, these contributions seem compatible with, and do not preclude, enhancements of the simple frictionless model to incorporate correlations between exporter relative factor endowments with importer relative goods demands, or the inclusion of distance and relative distance, as provided in this paper. Clearly, more work appears warranted on discerning further the gravity equation's empirical role in the context of international trade and trade theory, in step with the excellent enhancements and clarifications initiated in this paper.

References

Anderson, James E. 1979. A theoretical foundation for the gravity equation. *American Economic Review* 69:106–16.

Baldwin, Richard E. 1994. *Towards an integrated Europe.* London: Centre for Economic Policy Research.

Bergstrand, Jeffrey H. 1985. The gravity equation in international trade: Some microeconomic foundations and empirical evidence. *Review of Economics and Statistics* 67:474–81.

———. 1989. The generalized gravity equation, monopolistic competition, and the factor-proportions theory in international trade. *Review of Economics and Statistics* 71:143–53.

———. 1990. The Heckscher-Ohlin-Samuelson model, the Linder hypothesis, and the determinants of bilateral intra-industry trade. *Economic Journal* 100:1216–29.

Helpman, Elhanan. 1987. Imperfect competition and international trade: Evidence from fourteen industrial countries. *Journal of the Japanese and International Economies* 1:62–81.

Helpman, Elhanan, and Paul Krugman. 1985. *Market structure and foreign trade.* Cambridge: MIT Press.

Hummels, David, and James Levinsohn. 1995. Monopolistic competition and international trade: Reconsidering the evidence. *Quarterly Journal of Economics* 110:799–836.

Kravis, Irving B., and Robert E. Lipsey. 1988. National price levels and the prices of tradables and nontradables. *American Economic Review Papers and Proceedings* 78:474–78.

Leamer, Edward E., and Robert M. Stern. 1970. *Quantitative international economics.* Boston: Allyn and Bacon.

Summers, Robert, and Alan Heston. 1991. The Penn-World-Table (Mark 5). *Quarterly Journal of Economics* 106:327–68.

Tinbergen, Jan. 1962. *Shaping the world economy: Suggestions for an international economic policy.* New York: Twentieth Century Fund.

Wang, Z., and L. Alan Winters. 1991. The trading potential of Eastern Europe. Discussion Paper no. 610. London: Centre for Economic Policy Research, November.

Comment   Gene M. Grossman

This paper is vintage Alan Deardorff: crystal clear and elegant. Such papers are a pleasure to read but a nightmare to discuss.

Deardorff provides theoretical underpinnings for the so-called gravity equation, a simple equation explaining bilateral trade volumes as a function of the income levels of the two trading partners and the distance between them. This equation has been remarkably successful in innumerable empirical applications.

The "spin" that Deardorff puts on his findings is that the equation can readily be derived from a factor endowments model (such as Heckscher-Ohlin), whether there is universal factor price equalization or not. Thus, the empirical success of the gravity equation cannot be taken as evidence in favor of "new" trade models with imperfect competition and increasing returns to scale, as some previous authors may have suggested.

I will concentrate my remarks on the second part of the paper, as I don't find the first part (considering the case with no transport costs and factor price equalization) to be particularly compelling. When factor prices are equalized, production costs are the same in all countries. Then, as Deardorff notes, the location of production may be indeterminate and the gross volume of trade certainly will be so. He argues that, in this case, we may as well assume that consumers choose their supply sources randomly. In the event, the gravity equation drops out once we assume identical and homothetic preferences. But I would argue differently that, in cases of indeterminacy, ties must be broken by something. Perhaps this something is small, so small that we exclude it from our model. Nonetheless, it may well be systematic. Transport costs are just the candidate for tie-breaking here. And, indeed, this is the route that Deardorff follows in the second part of the paper.

I would give Deardorff's findings a slightly different spin. Only my emphasis would be different from his, as the points are ones that he himself makes. I would interpret his theoretical propositions as demonstrating that there is nothing at all surprising about finding that incomes Y_i and Y_j have substantial explanatory power in a regression for the bilateral trade volume T_{ij}. *Specialization* lies behind the explanatory power of these variables, and of course some degree of specialization is at the heart of any model of trade. Thus, the derivation of the gravity equation need not make reference to any particular trade model at all, as Deardorff points out in footnote 5. Specialization—and not new trade theory or old trade theory—generates the force of gravity.

The intuition is quite clear. If countries are specialized, then consumers in country i will want to buy things from country j that are not available, or not abundantly available, at home. The more things firms in j have to sell, the

Gene M. Grossman is the Jacob Viner Professor of International Economics at Princeton University and a research associate of the National Bureau of Economic Research.

more things consumers in i will want to buy. So country j's output enters into determining the trade flow. Also, the more income country i's residents have, the more of country j's goods they will be able to buy. So country i's output enters into determining the trade flow. With *complete specialization* (each good produced in only one country) and *identical and homothetic preferences*, the elasticity of bilateral trade with respect to each partner's income level will be one. This is true no matter what supply-side considerations give rise to the specialization, be they increasing returns to scale in a world of differentiated products, technology differences in a world of Ricardian trade, large factor endowment differences in a world of Heckscher-Ohlin trade, or (small) transport costs in a world of any type of endowment-based trade.

So I agree that there is nothing surprising about the statistical significance of log Y_i and log Y_j in a regression for log T_{ij}, nor that their coefficients are often found to be close to one. I also agree that there is nothing surprising about the estimated *sign* of the coefficient on log D_{ij} (the distance between countries i and j, in the same regression). What I do find surprising is the *size* of the estimated coefficient on the distance variable.

McCallum (1995) provides an interesting recent example. He estimates trade flows between and among different provinces of Canada and states in the United States. The estimated coefficients on the log of income in the exporting region is 1.21, that on the log of income in the importing region is 1.06. Both are in keeping with the gravity predictions. But the coefficient on the log of distance in McCallum's regression is -1.42. This means that two regions separated by 500 miles will, all also equal, trade more than 2.67 times as much as two regions separated by 1,000 miles. In the same spirit, Leamer's estimates (1993) imply that in 1985 West Germany's trade with a partner country located 1,000 miles away was on average 4.7 times as great as that with a country of similar income located 10,000 miles away. In a world of modest transport costs, these findings are unexpected to me.

At least as surprising are the recurrent findings that countries trade so much with themselves. Trefler (1995) reports that the net factor content of trade for thirty-three countries accounting for three-quarters of world trade is an order of magnitude smaller than what would be predicted based on observed differences in their factor endowments. McCallum finds, even more strikingly, that trade between two provinces in Canada is more than twenty times larger than trade between one of these provinces and a similarly sized state in the United States located the same distance away!

Deardorff provides one possible explanation for the large coefficient on log D_{ij} (though not for the overriding importance of national boundaries, after controlling for distance). If all pairs of goods have a constant elasticity of substitution σ, and if transport costs are of the "iceberg" variety, then the coefficient on the log t_{ij} (the ratio of shipments to arrivals) in a regression explaining f.o.b. trade volume ought to be close to $-\sigma$. However, few would consider the "iceberg" formulation of shipping costs as anything more than useful trick for models with constant demand elasticities, and possibly a good approximation to the technology for shipping tomatoes.

Suppose instead that to ship a unit of country i's output to country j has a constant cost τ_{ij}. This cost reflects both the type (and average weight) of the goods in which country i is specialized, and the distance between between i and j. Suppose further that consumers worldwide have Cobb-Douglas preferences and that τ_{ij} is related to weight and distance according to $\tau_{ij} = w_i D_{ij}^\alpha$, where w_i measures the per unit weight (and other characteristics relevant for shipping expense) of country i's output. Then, according to my calculations,

$$\frac{d \log T_{ij}^f}{d \log D_{ij}} = -\alpha \left(\frac{\tau_{ij}}{p_i + \tau_{ij}} \right).$$

I suspect that shipping costs are no more than perhaps 5 percent of the value of traded goods, on average. A plausible value for α is perhaps 0.6. So the coefficient on D_{ij} ought to be less than -0.03. Elasticities of substitution above unity would raise this somewhat, but it is hard to see how one can get to -1.42 by this route.

All this leads me to believe that something is missing from our trade models, be they of the Heckscher-Ohlin or Dixit-Stiglitz-Krugman variety. It seems we need models where distance (and common polity, and common language, and common culture) play more of a role. I suspect this is a model with imperfect information, where familiarity declines rapidly with distance. Perhaps it is a model with very localized tastes (as in Trefler's "home bias" [1995]), which are historically determined and change only slowly with experience. Perhaps it is a model where distribution networks play a more central role. In any event, while Deardorff can give us a convincing explanation for the existence of gravitational forces in trade, he cannot tell us why these forces are so strong.

References

Leamer, Edward E. 1993. U.S. manufacturing and an emerging Mexico. *North American Journal of Economics and Finance* 4:51–89.
McCallum, John. 1995. National borders matter: Canada-U.S. regional trade patterns. *American Economic Review* 85:615–23.
Trefler, Daniel. 1995. The case of the missing trade and other mysteries. *American Economic Review* 85:1029–46.

2 The Role of History in Bilateral Trade Flows

Barry Eichengreen and Douglas A. Irwin

2.1 Introduction

The rise of regionalism continues to pose challenges for specialists in international trade. One classic question is the aggregate welfare effects of regional trade liberalization. Another is the political economy of regionalism: how liberalization on a regional basis affects the welfare of nations and domestic interest groups, and how their self-interested actions shape the global trading system. A third question, with which we are concerned in this paper, is how important regional arrangements actually have been for the pattern of trade.

The gravity model of international trade has been the workhorse for empirical studies of this question to the virtual exclusion of other approaches.[1] Trade between two countries is posited to increase with their size (as proxied by their GDPs and populations) and to decline with transactions costs (proxied by the geographic distance between them and by whether or not they share a common border). While there is no close correspondence between the leading theoretical models of trade and the variables appearing in the gravity equation, a number of authors have suggested that the gravity-model framework is compatible both with the Heckscher-Ohlin model and with theories of trade in the presence of imperfect competition.[2] The attraction of the gravity model (no pun intended) is not simply lack of theoretical incompatibility, of course, but its

Barry Eichengreen is the John L. Simpson Professor of Economics and Political Science at the University of California, Berkeley. Douglas A. Irwin is professor of economics at Dartmouth College.

The authors thank Tam Bayoumi for providing the International Monetary Fund data and Nina Steinberg for assistance in organizing it. Jeffrey Frankel, Robert Lawrence, Tom Rothenberg, Paul Wonnacott, and participants at the Woodstock conference provided helpful comments. This paper was written while Irwin was visiting the American Enterprise Institute, whose hospitality is gratefully acknowledged.

1. Frankel (1995) is the most extensive compendium of research adopting this framework.
2. See Anderson (1979); Bergstrand (1985); and Deardorff (1984, chap. 1 of this volume).

ability to explain the variation in bilateral trade flows across a wide variety of countries and periods. Few aggregate economic relationships are as robust.

To analyze the effects of regionalism, investigators typically add dummy variables for participation in regional arrangements (Hamilton and Winters 1992; Frankel and Wei 1993). A positive coefficient on the dummy variable indicating that two countries, both of which participate in the same preferential arrangement, trade more with one another than predicted by their incomes, population, and distance is interpreted as suggesting that the arrangement is trade-creating for its members. A negative coefficient on a second dummy variable indicating when only one member of the pair participates in a particular preferential arrangement is taken as evidence of trade diversion vis-à-vis the rest of the world.

Empirically, dummy variables for regional arrangements sometimes show up as having substantial trade-creating effects. Two countries both of which are members of one of these regional groupings trade more with one another than would be predicted by their observable economic characteristics (GDP, population, distance from one another) and the average behavior of countries in the sample. Alarmingly, however, they often trade significantly more with one another than otherwise predicted even before the regional arrangement in question came into effect.[3] One can argue that this reflects the impact on trade of the anticipated implementation of a regional liberalization agreement: suppliers begin to reorient their exports in anticipation of future market opening. In addition, regional arrangements are often preceded by other arrangements that are less formal and less comprehensive in commodity coverage but that include many of the same countries: the European Economic Community was preceded by the European Coal and Steel Community, and the European Payments Union was preceded by the First Agreement on Multilateral Monetary Compensation and the Agreement for Intra-European Payments and Compensations, for example. But the fact that dummy variables for membership in a regional grouping can indicate substantial effects long before the preferential arrangement in question and even its predecessors came into operation, plus the fact that there is little sign of increases in the magnitude of the bloc variable when negotiations quicken or a successful conclusion is reached, gives grounds for skepticism that it is merely expectational effects at work.

Another interpretation of the persistent significance of bloc variables is that members of a regional trade arrangement differ systematically from other countries in ways that promote unusually high levels of intrabloc trade. Measures of bloc membership are thus contaminated by omitted-variables bias. One response to this problem has been to develop measures of the relevant omitted factors. Frankel and Wei (1993) take a step in this direction, adding common language in an effort to pick up cultural and political factors that may reduce transactions costs and encourage bilateral trade.

---

3. This appears to be the case, for example, in several of the interwar trade and payments arrangements considered in Eichengreen and Irwin (1995).

Another response, as in Bayoumi and Eichengreen (1995), is to estimate the gravity equation in first-difference form, which causes determinants of bilateral trade flows that are constant over time, including unobservable characteristics of countries affecting their propensity to trade, to drop out of the specification. Of course, this does not correct for omitted-variables bias caused by determinants of trade that vary with time. Nor is this procedure suited for samples in which membership in regional arrangements does not change, since the bloc variables will drop out of the differenced specification.[4]

In this paper we take another step by analyzing the impact of history on trade. The idea that past trade patterns influence current trade flows is intuitively plausible. Countries with a history of trading with one another—whether for reasons related to politics, policies, or other factors—generally continue doing so. Producers, having set up market-specific sales, distribution, and service networks that allow them to generate a level of exports greater than would be predicted by the scale and geographical distance of the destination market, should continue to generate a disproportionate level of exports over time. Thus, passing historical events that allow costs to be sunk can be associated with persistent increases in the level of trade. The events in question can be anything from a history of colonialism (in which case military means were used to install the infrastructure needed to support bilateral trade) to a history of migration (one thinks of Japanese migration to Brazil and Peru, which provides Latin America with linguistic and cultural capital that supports extensive trade with Japan) to purely chance events.

The recent theoretical and empirical literature suggests a number of other explanations for hysteresis in trade (the possibility that trade does not return to its previous value after a temporary shock).[5] The existence of economies of scale and scope in the production of goods and services can cause trade to flow in particular geographical channels for historical reasons; thus, a large share of South African exports has long been destined for Britain because economies of scale implied the existence of only one international gold market, which for historical reasons was located in London. A temporary tariff or exchange rate fluctuation that causes foreign firms to establish branch plants in overseas markets—one thinks of "transplant" production by Japanese automotive firms—may continue to influence trade in intermediate and final goods long after the disturbance is past. Current consumption may be influenced by the history of trade: manufacturers who use steel as an input may shun foreign supplies because they lack familiarity with its quality; a steel strike that interrupts domestic supplies, as happened in the United States in the 1960s and 1970s, may leave them no alternative to imports. As a result, they acquire familiarity with reliable foreign suppliers and consume a permanently higher share of imported

4. Thus, the specification of Frankel, Stein, and Wei (1993), who hold the composition of their European Community bloc constant over time, is not suited to this approach.

5. Hysteresis, strictly speaking, refers to the case where a passing shock to trade has permanent effects. For our purposes, all that is necessary is that a passing shock has effects with significant persistence.

steel even after the temporary interruption to domestic supplies has passed. Readers will be quick to think of other examples.

The common implication of these stories is that current trade flows should be a positive function of past trade flows even after controlling for the determinants of bilateral trade included in the gravity model. Insofar as other variables included in the gravity equation are correlated with past trade flows, omitting lagged trade will bias their estimated effects. In particular, there is reason to suspect that preferential trade arrangements are positively correlated with past trade flows. Some countries seek to insulate their important trade relations from shocks to the global trade regime by using preferential trade arrangements as safeguards.[6] Insofar as the creation of the preferential arrangements was itself a response to the unusual importance historically of intrabloc trade, gravity equations omitting lagged trade may overstate the effects of bloc membership.

This is not to suggest that such effects should be equally powerful in all times and places. The influence of past trade over current trade may vary with circumstances; a war, a depression, trade conflict, or an unusually successful global trade negotiation may disrupt established trade relations in ways that lift the heavy hand of history. Similarly, the correlation between past trade flows and regional arrangements will tend to vary with circumstances; the recent literature points to a number of reasons why countries have been attracted to the regional approach to liberalization in recent years. The importance of the factors on which we focus in this paper is ultimately an empirical question.

In practice, isolating the impact of lagged trade on current trade presents not inconsequential estimation problems. As in Griliches's classic article (1961), it may be difficult to distinguish the effects of lagged dependent variables from those of autocorrelated residuals. Although we estimate the model using cross-section rather than time-series data, a standard time-series result carries over: ordinary-least-squares (OLS) estimates of the effects of lagged trade on current trade flows may be biased in the presence of autocorrelated errors. We employ a variety of econometric techniques to address this problem, all of which fortunately tend to yield similar results.

The rest of the paper is organized as follows. Section 2.2 reviews the theoretical literature on hysteresis in trade, emphasizing contributions with potential relevance for the gravity model, and recounts some historical episodes designed to illustrate the applicability of those models. In section 2.3 we present an empirical analysis of historical factors in bilateral trade. Adding historical factors turns out to have important implications for the effects we ascribe to regional arrangements; we draw these out in the conclusion.

---

6. One motivation for the development of the British system of Commonwealth preferences, for example, was that the unusually extensive network of intra-Commonwealth trade that had developed over the years, as a result of British migration to the overseas regions of recent European settlement and the special protection afforded British investment in its overseas dependencies, was seen as warranting special protection against the corrosive effects of tariff protection in the 1930s.

2.2   Theoretical Literature and Historical Illustrations

Traditional trade theory provides little guidance on the question of how past trade patterns should affect current trade flows. Typically, current trade is related to current factor endowments and current technologies. There is no reason in these models why earlier factor endowments and technologies, much less earlier trade flows, should influence current trade patterns independent of current factor endowments and current technologies.

In contrast, new theories of trade in the presence of monopolistic competition suggest that initial conditions can influence trade flows in ways that introduce a role for history. These theories were developed to analyze, among other things, the possibility of hysteresis in trade. Baldwin (1988), Dixit (1989), Baldwin and Krugman (1989), and others focused on how a large but temporary real exchange rate shock could have permanent effects on the pattern of trade. These effects hinge on sunk costs of market entry and exit for domestic and foreign firms. Sunk costs are associated with the need to set up distribution and sales networks in the foreign markets prior to initiating export sales. A temporary appreciation of a country's currency can make the entry of foreign firms profitable, leading them to undertake a one-time investment in distribution capacity in the domestic market. Even if the currency depreciates back to its initial level, they have no incentive to exit, the up-front costs of distribution and marketing having been sunk. Thus, a temporary exchange rate shock can alter the structural relationship between imports and the exchange rate, permanently affecting the pattern of trade.

Although in this example exchange rate movements are the temporary shock permanently altering the pattern of trade, any number of factors can have such effects. Any temporary disruption to current trade patterns—due to war, depression, or temporary tariffs, for example—could provide an incentive for exporters to sink the fixed costs of penetrating foreign markets.

There is some empirical evidence consistent with these models. Bean (1988) finds evidence from the United Kingdom's trade in the 1980s which suggests structural change in the United Kingdom's export and import patterns as a result of the appreciation of sterling in the early 1980s. Roberts and Tybout (1995), using firm-level data from Colombia, examine the role of fixed costs in determining whether a firm exports or not. They find that previous export experience has a substantial effect on the probability of exporting, rejecting the view that sunk costs are unimportant.

Historical examples may also be useful for illustrating that these mechanisms can actually operate in practice. The point is not to demonstrate hysteresis in trade—that one-time changes in the direction of trade have *permanent* effects—since this is not necessary for our argument, only to show that changes in trade flows can have effects with significant persistence.

For simplicity, it may help to start with the case of a particular firm. An example is the impact on the exports of the Singer Sewing Machine Company of the temporary preferences extended by Australia to British sewing machines in 1907. While imports from other countries paid 10 percent duties, for a period of only a few months machines of British manufacture were admitted free. In response, Singer transferred its Australian business from its American to its British branch. British sewing-machine exports rose, while their U.S. counterparts fell. Importantly for our purposes, Singer's British branch having established the relevant contacts with Australian retailers, the source of exports to Australia did not shift back following the removal of the tariff not long thereafter. Britain, not the United States, remained the dominant source of Singer's exports to Australia (Saul 1960, 218–19). Thus, a one-time rise in British exports of sewing machines due to a purely transitory shock resulted in a persistent rise in British sales to Australia of the product.

It is not obvious, of course, that the effects of changes in the level of trade have comparable effects in the aggregate. Two sources of variation in the aggregate data capable of shedding light on this question are wars and depressions. Consider the effects of World War I on trade in the 1920s. The war was a severe disruption to the pattern of multilateral settlements inherited from the nineteenth century. Insofar as hostilities were concentrated in Europe, its most powerful impact was on intra-European trade and on the trade of European nations with other parts of the world. Because of the sudden shortage of shipping and the diversion of capacity to domestic military uses, the war disrupted exports from Britain to Asia, Africa, and Latin America. The Allies discouraged Latin American countries from exporting raw materials to Germany and maintained a blacklist of firms in Latin America that they believed to be under the control of German nationals. As a result, Latin American customers accustomed to purchasing manufactures from British and German sources suddenly found themselves starved of merchandise. U.S. manufacturers, in contrast, saw an opportunity in the Latin American market vacated by the British and Germans. They set up marketing, distribution, and after-sales service networks; having sunk the costs of entry during the war, they proved hard to dislodge after 1918.[7] As table 2.1 illustrates, the United Kingdom's share of the imports of every Latin American country fell between 1913 and 1928, while the share of the United States rose for every country but the Guianas. This change occurred despite the absence of significant changes in the relative tariff treatment of Latin American imports from the two sources.

World War I disruptions similarly provided Japan the opportunity to penetrate Asian markets long dominated by European producers. Japan constructed paper mills and factories for the manufacture of drugs, paints, and other products for sale in India and in other Asian markets temporarily vacated by the British. Its textile industry penetrated the Australian market for the first time. The cost of factory construction and distribution having been sunk, the Japa-

---

7. Moreover, wartime shipbuilding increased the export capacity of the United States and permitted U.S. goods to be transported more cheaply in the 1920s. Additional details beyond those presented here can be found in Kaufman (1974).

Table 2.1   **South American Imports from the United States and United Kingdom, 1913 and 1928 (percentage share)**

Imports of	1913 Imports			1928 Imports		
	U.S.	U.K.	Others	U.S.	U.K.	Others
Bolivia	7.3	20.0	72.7	29.7	17.2	53.1
Chile	16.9	30.4	52.8	30.8	17.8	52.8
Ecuador	32.2	30.0	37.8	45.7	16.0	38.3
Peru	30.0	26.7	43.3	40.9	15.9	43.2
Venezuela	41.2	27.1	31.7	62.2	12.2	25.6
Brazil	15.7	24.5	59.8	26.6	21.5	51.9
Colombia	26.7	20.4	52.9	40.6	11.7	47.7
Argentina	14.7	31.0	54.3	23.2	19.6	57.2
Paraguay	6.0	—	94	16.0	—	84
Uruguay	12.7	23.8	63.5	—	—	—
Guianas	23.4	56.3	20.3	12.1	55.0	32.9

Source: Mitchell 1993, 418–93.

nese did not withdraw from these new markets when British exports came on stream again in the 1920s. In the aggregate, then, the wartime change in the volume of exports from Britain and the United States to Latin America and from Britain and Japan to southern Asia had persistent effects throughout the 1920s.

A further example is the impact of the breakdown of the pattern of multilateral settlements in the 1930s on the post–World War II direction of trade.[8] The destruction of multilateral trade in the 1930s is too well known to be rehearsed here. Tariffs and nontariff barriers were applied to restrict trade to a series of relatively self-contained trade blocs. Germany in particular used bilateral clearing arrangements and exchange controls to limit its trade to Central and Eastern European countries in its sphere of influence. But the phenomenon was general: as tariffs were raised, countries extended preferences to their overseas territories and to countries associated with them in a monetary area. Thus the share of the exports of Western Europe (including Britain) that flowed to the overseas sterling area rose from 26.8 percent in 1928 to 28.5 percent in 1938, whereas the share of Western European imports drawn from this area rose from 22.1 to 25.0 percent. Meanwhile, the share of Western European imports drawn from the overseas territories of the continental European countries rose from 4.9 to 8.7 percent (Dewhurst et al. 1961, 655). Increasingly, direct foreign investment flowed through these same channels, with new British factories set up in the sterling area importing capital equipment and suitable raw materials from British sources, and new factories set up by continental European countries in their overseas dependencies doing likewise (Dewhurst et al. 1961, 658).

8. Eichengreen and Irwin (1995) provides references to the literature in which this phenomenon is discussed.

Thus, the share of Britain's and continental Europe's trade conducted with the sterling area and the overseas territories, respectively, remained high in the wake of World War II. This would appear to be another instance where changes in the pattern of trade in the 1930s, by leading producers to sink fixed costs, had effects on the pattern of trade that were still evident decades later.

It is important to note that this last example admits to an alternative interpretation. Intra–sterling area trade and trade between continental Europe and its colonies could have remained high not because of the impact of sunk costs on trade but because the changes in commercial policy that brought about this shift in the 1930s were not fully reversed in the 1950s. While European countries rolled back their tariffs in early General Agreement on Tariffs and Trade (GATT) rounds (Geneva in 1947, Annecy in 1949, Torquay in 1950–51), many countries in Latin America and Asia were not yet GATT members and did not participate. Thus relatively high tariffs held over from the 1930s could have been responsible for the diversion of trade into imperial channels. Moreover, Britain, when imposing its general tariff in 1932, at the same time extended preferential treatment to its empire; because tariffs were rolled back incompletely in the 1950s, imperial preferences remained. It could have been the persistence of these changes in commercial policy, rather than persistence in trade itself, in other words, that explains this link from the 1930s to the 1950s.

Ultimately, the relative importance of lagged trade and current commercial policy in explaining the pattern of trade is an empirical question, to which we now turn.

2.3   Empirical Analysis

2.3.1   Data and Estimation

The typical gravity-model specification relates bilateral trade to income, population (or per capita income, as here), contiguity, and distance between the trading partners. Thus the value of bilateral trade between countries i and j in a given year is considered to be a (natural) log-linear function of the independent variables as in the following expression:

$$\beta_0 + \beta_1 \ln (Y_i Y_j) + \beta_2 \ln (P_i P_j) + \beta_3 \ln (DIST_{ij}) + \beta_4 (CONT_{ij}) + \varepsilon_{ij},$$

where $Y_i Y_j$ is the product of the two countries' national incomes (the so-called gravity variable), $P_i P_j$ is the product of the two countries' per capita incomes, $DIST$ is the straight-line distance (in kilometers) between the economic centers of gravity of the two countries, $CONT$ is a dummy variable indicating whether the two countries are contiguous (taking a value of 1 if they share a common border), and ε is a randomly distributed error term. As trade is expected to increase with size, per capita income, and contiguity, and to decline with distance, β_1, β_2, and β_4 should be positive, while β_3 should be negative.

Most applications specify the gravity model in double-log form, expressing the dependent variable as log ($TRADE_{ij}$), where $TRADE_{ij}$ is the value of bilateral trade (exports plus imports) converted into millions of U.S. dollars, and estimate the equation by OLS. The double-log specification permits coefficients to be interpreted as elasticities but omits country pairs for which trade is zero. This is undesirable insofar as the omitted observations contain information about why low levels of trade are observed. One solution is to express the dependent variable in levels and estimate the equation using Tobit, but the results are difficult to interpret because the constant elasticity relationship is lost.

Another approach preserves the double-log form but yields results similar to Tobit. The dependent variable is expressed as log ($1 + TRADE$). For large values of $TRADE$, ln ($1 + TRADE$) $\cong$ ln ($TRADE$), preserving the double-log relationship, while for small values ln ($1 + TRADE$) $\cong TRADE$, approximating the semilog Tobit relationship. The equation can be estimated by scaled OLS, in which the least-squares estimates are multiplied by the reciprocal of the proportion of the observations in which $TRADE$ does not equal zero (Greene 1993, 697).[9]

In the empirical work that follows, we fit the gravity model to our data using each of these specifications and estimators. In addition, we estimate the double-log specification in first differences in order to control for unobservable determinants of trade that are constant over time. Reassuringly, the alternative estimators and specifications yield quite similar results. We therefore focus for simplicity on the scaled-OLS estimates.

We estimate the model using data on interwar and postwar trade flows. Interwar trade data from 1928 and 1938 are available from Hilgert (1942). Data for national income in these years, drawn from sources described in the appendix to Eichengreen and Irwin (1995), are converted to millions of U.S. dollars using the exchange rates provided by Hilgert.[10] The limited availability of national income data reduces the interwar data set to thirty-four countries, yielding 561 bilateral trade observations. Our postwar trade data are drawn from the International Monetary Fund's *Direction of Trade Statistics,* while national income and population data are from the IMF's *International Financial Statistics.* We gathered data for the immediate postwar period in order to concentrate on the effects of interwar trade patterns for the postwar development of trade. We selected data from 1949, 1954, and 1964; 1949 is just after the first GATT negotiating round and a time when postwar trade routes were still being reestablished, while 1954 and 1964 are, respectively, prior to and after the forma-

---

9. If any of the independent variables are correlated with the disturbance term, OLS will produce biased estimates. In particular, there is reason to worry that if trade is measured with error, national income will be measured with error as well, since trade is a component of income. In Eichengreen and Irwin (1995) we estimated the basic specification by both OLS and instrumental variables. For the interwar years considered there, the use of instruments made little difference for the results. Below we report some instrumental variables estimates implemented in a different fashion.

10. This appendix also describes the sources from which interwar population figures were drawn.

Table 2.2   **Basic Determinants of Bilateral Trade, 1928 and 1938**

	1928			1938		
Estimation Method	OLS Logs	OLS Scaled	Tobit	OLS Logs	OLS Scaled	Tobit
Mean dependent variable	2.49	2.01	42.34	2.22	1.85	27.27
Constant	−4.93	4.19	−8.71	−6.24	4.86	−10.79
	(6.85)	(5.76)	(7.93)	(8.53)	(6.66)	(9.91)
National incomes	0.90	0.91	1.14	0.86	0.77	1.11
	(20.50)	(27.58)	(17.62)	(19.73)	(23.65)	(17.42)
Per capita national	0.89	0.33	1.30	0.73	0.16	1.04
incomes	(16.30)	(6.28)	(15.96)	(16.59)	(3.62)	(16.64)
Distance	−0.51	−0.78	−0.56	−0.37	−0.53	−0.33
	(8.67)	(12.63)	(6.34)	(6.79)	(8.64)	(4.08)
Contiguity	0.47	0.79	1.38	0.30	0.45	1.19
	(2.02)	(2.94)	(3.75)	(1.37)	(1.69)	(3.55)
R^2	0.59	0.69	0.33	0.58	0.62	0.31
Standard error	3.08	3.20	1.91	2.58	2.61	1.64
N	419	561	561	426	561	561

Source: Eichengreen and Irwin 1995, 11.
Note: T-statistics are in parentheses.

tion of the European Economic Community; these dates are well suited, therefore, for analyzing the effects of regional and global liberalization initiatives. The postwar sample consists of thirty-eight countries, yielding 703 bilateral observations in each year. In addressing whether interwar trade patterns still affect postwar trade patterns, we augment the prewar trade data with additional observations on bilateral trade from Hilgert to match the larger postwar sample.

2.3.2   Results

To analyze the impact of historical factors, we proceed in steps, starting with the standard gravity-model specification, adding lagged trade, and then turning to the effects of blocs.

Basic Specification

Table 2.2 summarizes the findings from our earlier paper regarding interwar trade patterns. This provides a basis for comparison with the present paper's results for the postwar period. All of the arguments of the standard gravity model reported in table 2.2 enter with their expected signs and differ significantly from zero at standard confidence levels. In addition, the alternative estimators deliver very similar results.[11]

Table 2.3 provides analogous estimates for 1949, 1954, and 1964. Again, the

---

11. The coefficient on per capita incomes is somewhat smaller when the model is estimated scaled OLS than when plain-vanilla OLS is used.

alternative estimators and specifications deliver broadly similar results.[12] In contrast to table 2.2, for the early postwar period the coefficient on per capita incomes is not sensitive to the substitution of log $(1 + TRADE)$ for log $(TRADE)$ and the use of scaled OLS rather than regular OLS.

In conjunction with table 2.2, table 2.3 allows us to trace the evolution of the coefficients over time. The coefficient on the product of national incomes, for example, declines slightly between the 1920s and 1930s but recovers to 1920s levels after World War II. An interpretation is that trade restrictions imposed in the 1930s reduced the elasticity of trade with respect to national income but that this trend was reversed after the war.

The same basic pattern is evident for per capita incomes, except that the coefficient on this variable is small and statistically indistinguishable from zero in 1949. This coefficient is typically interpreted in terms of intraindustry trade: richer economies consume a wider variety of differentiated products than poorer countries, and many of those differentiated varieties are produced abroad; hence, richer countries should engage in more intraindustry trade than their poorer counterparts. The insignificance of this coefficient in 1949 is consistent with the notion that intraindustry trade was depressed in the aftermath of World War II by the slow progress of reconstruction in Europe, which prevented the countries of that continent from exporting the traditional level of manufactures to the United States, and by the dollar gap, which prevented Europe from importing much from the United States other than essential raw materials and capital goods. (For details see Eichengreen 1993.)

The scaled-OLS estimates indicate that the effect of per capita incomes had been restored by 1954, suggesting that the prewar pattern of intraindustry trade had been successfully reestablished by the midfifties. But estimating the model in first differences continues to yield an insignificant coefficient on this variable in 1954, suggesting that this restoration was delayed until somewhat later.[13]

The coefficient on distance is greater in size and significance in 1949 than in other years, perhaps reflecting the difficulty of reestablishing and reconstructing transportation networks, especially over long distances, in the aftermath of World War II. More generally, however, it exhibits little trend. This is not to say that there was no decline in transportation costs over time. If there is "distance-neutral" technological progress in the provision of transportation services, then the cost of transporting goods over various distances will decline proportionately, and we will observe no change in the magnitude of the distance coefficient. Only if technical progress is "distance saving," in the sense that it reduces the cost of transporting goods over long distances more than the cost of transporting them over short ones, would we expect to see the magni-

12. An exception is the first-difference specification, whose use alters the coefficients on per capita incomes in 1954 and national incomes in 1964. We return to this point below.

13. We find the same thing when we use Hatanaka's method to estimate a variant of the gravity model including lagged trade in quasi-differenced form, as described below.

Table 2.3 — Basic Determinants of Bilateral Trade, 1949, 1954, and 1964

	1949				1954					1964				
	OLS Levels	OLS Logs	OLS Scaled	Tobit	OLS Levels	OLS Logs	OLS Scaled	Tobit	First Difference	OLS Levels	OLS Logs	OLS Scaled	Tobit	First Difference
Mean dependent variable	48.86	2.18	1.95	39.72	80.29	2.47	2.35	78.72	0.40	152.63	3.05	2.86	149.3	0.51
Constant	34.84	5.52	6.86	8.48	101.10	5.23	6.19	9.29	0.34	137.15	4.94	5.63	9.12	−0.17
	(3.02)	(9.05)	(11.44)	(7.22)	(4.56)	(9.17)	(11.93)	(8.12)	(7.76)	(4.80)	(9.22)	(11.13)	(8.29)	(1.48)
National incomes	0.14	0.89	1.00	1.09	−0.03	0.87	0.91	1.15	0.31	0.06	0.87	0.92	1.19	0.14
	(17.57)	(23.76)	(28.66)	(19.39)	(0.48)	(24.80)	(29.91)	(20.34)	(3.19)	(22.41)	(27.44)	(31.90)	(21.87)	(0.69)
Per capita national incomes	−0.00	0.05	0.05	0.13	0.01	0.29	0.33	0.93	−0.02	−0.01	0.36	0.38	1.01	0.52
	(1.98)	(0.72)	(0.88)	(1.20)	(0.36)	(6.46)	(8.29)	(7.29)	(0.69)	(2.48)	(9.34)	(11.17)	(8.92)	(3.01)
Distance	−0.00	−0.82	−0.95	−0.63	−0.01	−0.70	−0.76	−0.45	—	−0.01	−0.76	−0.81	−0.40	—
	(1.56)	(11.38)	(13.64)	(4.31)	(1.98)	(10.22)	(12.32)	(3.59)		(3.30)	(12.05)	(13.67)	(2.99)	
Contiguity	242.01	0.21	0.37	0.92	464.52	0.34	0.41	0.98	—	1037.8	0.19	0.25	1.01	—
	(7.85)	(0.62)	(1.11)	(1.92)	(8.05)	(1.06)	(1.40)	(2.14)		(13.58)	(0.65)	(0.91)	(1.89)	
R^2	0.39	0.59	0.63	0.28	0.12	0.64	0.71	0.30	0.02	0.54	0.73	0.77	0.31	0.19
Standard error	142.1	1.35	1.11	1.25	259.87	1.31	1.05	1.40	0.78	351.73	1.20	1.02	1.39	0.65
N	703	545	703	703	703	595	703	703	703	703	611	703	703	703

Notes: R^2 in the Tobit regression is the squared correlation between the actual and fitted value of the dependent variable. T-statistics are in parentheses.

Table 2.4   **Basic Determinants of Bilateral Trade, Including Lagged Trade**

	1949	1954	1964
Constant	4.06	1.36	2.52
	(7.26)	(3.66)	(7.80)
National incomes	0.50	0.25	0.27
	(10.77)	(6.64)	(9.77)
Per capita national incomes	0.06	0.15	0.20
	(1.19)	(5.81)	(9.02)
Distance	−0.54	−0.13	−0.30
	(8.11)	(2.80)	(7.64)
Contiguity	−0.03	−0.03	−0.01
	(0.09)	(0.17)	(0.06)
Trade in 1954	—	—	0.94
			(23.69)
Trade in 1949	—	0.70	−0.02
		(22.38)	(0.59)
Trade in 1938	0.34	0.22	−0.09
	(6.60)	(5.08)	(2.43)
Trade in 1928	0.15	0.03	0.09
	(2.09)	(0.75)	(0.64)
Implied long-run income elasticity	1.0	2.6	4.5
R^2	0.72	0.88	0.92
Standard error	0.97	0.68	0.62
F-statistic	299.44	717.29	974.50

Notes: Estimated by scaled OLS, where the dependent variable is ln $(1 + TRADE)$. T-statistics are in parentheses.

tude of this coefficient decline; there is no evidence of this across our sample years.

Adding Lagged Trade

Table 2.4 shows the effect of adding lagged trade to this basic specification. The first column presents the results for trade in 1949, with lagged dependent variables for 1928 and 1938.[14] Current incomes and distance still help to predict current trade, but the magnitude of their coefficients is reduced. Trade in both 1938 and 1928 exerts independent and statistically significant effects on trade in 1949 and significantly raises the share of the variation in the dependent variable accounted for by the model. These estimates suggest that an extra dollar of trade in 1938 and 1928 raised the predicted value of 1949 trade by 50 cents. The influence of past trade patterns on current trade flows diminishes with time: the coefficient on 1938 trade is greater than that on 1928 trade by a factor of two. One might have anticipated that 1928 trade would have had a

14. We adjust the lagged values of trade by the change in the U.S. wholesale price index between these years and the year of interest in the regression, to have comparable nominal values of trade. This permits the lagged coefficients to be interpreted more easily.

stronger impact than 1938 on the direction and volume of postwar trade; that component of 1928 trade not strongly correlated with relative incomes and geographic distance plausibly reflected unobservable economic characteristics of countries that encouraged them to trade disproportionately with one another—characteristics that should have continued to influence the direction of trade after World War II. In contrast, 1938 trade was strongly shaped by the transitory trade restrictions of the 1930s and, absent strong hysteresis effects, should not have continued to exert the stronger role after World War II. It is striking, therefore, that the value for 1938 continues to exert the stronger effect in 1949. This is consistent with our interpretation of the lags as capturing hysteresis effects rather than merely as proxies for unobservable structural characteristics.

In this augmented specification, the coefficients on the standard arguments of the gravity model can be interpreted as short-run, or impact, effects. To derive the implicit long-run elasticities, we divide through by one minus the sum of the coefficients on the lagged dependent variables. In the standard regression, the coefficient on national incomes is approximately unity; a doubling of income implies a doubling of trade. The estimates for 1949 in table 2.4 suggest that, while the short-run increase in trade due to a doubling of income is on the order of 50 percent, the estimated long-run elasticity of trade with respect to income is about one, close to the results from the specification that does not include lagged trade.

The column for trade in 1954 tells a similar story that differs in one important particular. The coefficients on national incomes, per capita national incomes, and distance are smaller than in the specification that excludes past trade but remain statistically significant at standard confidence levels. Those on lagged trade (included here for 1949, 1938, and 1928) exhibit the same decaying pattern over time as in the regression for 1949. The coefficients on the first two lags differ significantly from zero at standard confidence levels, but not that for 1928. The sum of the coefficients on lagged trade sum to about 0.9. By these calculations, the estimated long-run income and per capita income effects are significantly higher in the augmented specification than when the standard gravity model is estimated. While the short-run impact of an increase in incomes on trade is estimated to be 0.25, the long-run impact is closer to 2.5. These results are consistent with the observation that trade has grown more quickly than income over the postwar period.

In 1964, in contrast, only 1954 trade and not the values for 1949, 1938, and 1928 has its anticipated positive effect. Perhaps after twenty years the postwar recovery and the GATT process had sufficiently changed the orientation of trade that its own footprints dominated those of earlier years.[15] Like the results obtained for 1954, the coefficient on lagged trade is about 0.94. This implies that, while the short-run impact of incomes on trade is only 0.27, the long-run

---

15. We analyze this hypothesis explicitly in the next subsection.

impact is 4.5. The large coefficients on lagged trade suggest a high degree of persistence in trading patterns and imply that small changes in current trade patterns can end up having quite large long-run effects.[16]

Here as elsewhere, the interpretation of lagged dependent variables is problematic. On the one hand, a large coefficient on lagged trade could indicate that a greater propensity to trade in the past actually has the economic effect of encouraging greater trade in the present; on the other, the lagged dependent variable could simply be picking up the effects of random factors which cause some country pairs to trade more than others. Some bilateral trade flows may be unusually high, in other words, because of persistent error terms rather than hysteresis in trade per se. And the combination of autocorrelated errors and lagged dependent variables introduces the possibility of biased coefficient estimates due to the correlation between the lagged variable and the error term.

A standard approach to estimation in this case is to instrument lagged trade (Liviatan 1963). Since by assumption the instrumental variables are uncorrelated in the probability limit with the disturbance, substituting the instrumented value of lagged trade will yield consistent estimates (although those estimates will not be efficient since the adjustment has not dealt with the autocorrelation of the disturbance terms). Obvious instruments are the arguments of the gravity model (lagged incomes, lagged incomes per capita). Intuitively, including only the predicted, or systematic, component of lagged trade enhances the plausibility of our interpretation that the lagged value is picking up hysteresis in trade rather than simply persistent random effects.

The second column of table 2.5 reports the results employing fitted values of lagged trade. (For comparison, the first column shows the same regressions estimated by OLS.) Lagged trade continues to have an economically important and statistically significant impact on current trade flows in both 1949 and 1954, although its magnitude is somewhat reduced, as expected. In the equation for 1949, the coefficient on lagged trade declines from 0.68 to 0.41 when the fitted value is substituted for the actual one. In the equation for 1954, it declines from 0.83 to 0.60. In 1964, it declines from a relatively large 0.89 to essentially zero.

Another approach to this question is Hatanaka's two-step method. This uses instrumental variables to obtain a consistent estimate of the autocorrelation coefficient, adds both the fitted value of lagged trade and the residual from that first-stage regression to the gravity model, and reestimates the equation in quasi-differenced form. Thus this approach deals both with the problem of obtaining consistent estimates and with that of autocorrelated residuals. An

---

16. This strong persistence implies that lagged trade is an excellent predictor of current trade in the postwar sample. For example, a regression of 1964 trade on a constant and 1954 trade and no other explanatory variables yields a coefficient on lagged trade of 1.04 with a standard error of 0.01 and an R^2 of 0.89. Explaining 1954 trade by 1949 trade and a constant yields a coefficient of 0.96 (with a standard error of 0.02) and an R^2 of 0.83. By contrast, explaining postwar trade from interwar trade typically yields coefficients of less than 0.9 with less explanatory power.

Table 2.5   Basic Determinants of Bilateral Trade, Including Fitted Values of Lagged Trade

	1954			1964		
Constant	1.87	2.80	1.58	2.51	5.05	4.45
	(4.87)	(3.11)	(2.55)	(7.79)	(7.33)	(11.07)
National incomes	0.31	0.44	0.29	0.25	0.86	0.57
	(10.72)	(4.14)	(3.92)	(9.70)	(9.73)	(11.07)
Per capita national	0.14	0.37	0.15	0.20	0.47	0.15
incomes	(5.15)	(9.29)	(5.05)	(9.55)	(8.80)	(4.79)
Distance	−0.20	−0.28	−0.17	−0.29	−0.70	−0.62
	(4.41)	(2.28)	(2.04)	(7.49)	(7.25)	(10.97)
Contiguity	0.12	0.25	0.14	0.05	0.25	0.08
	(0.62)	(0.85)	(0.72)	(0.33)	(0.89)	(0.48)
Actual trade in	0.83	—	—	0.04	—	—
1949	(28.48)			(1.16)		
Fitted trade in 1949	—	0.60	0.85	—	0.31	0.34
		(4.56)	(9.32)		(2.44)	(4.24)
Residual from fitted	—	—	0.81	—	—	0.01
trade, 1949			(27.94)			(0.45)
Actual trade in	—	—	—	0.93	—	—
1954				(23.94)		
Fitted trade in 1954	—	—	—	—	0.23	0.78
					(1.53)	(8.08)
Residual from fitted	—	—	—	—	—	0.93
trade, 1954						(25.26)
R^2	0.86	0.72	0.86	0.92	0.78	0.92
Standard error	0.71	1.03	0.71	0.62	1.01	0.59
F-statistic	888.7	349.9	747.9	1279.3	401.5	1053.7

Note: See table 2.4 notes.

economic argument for including both the fitted values of lagged trade and the residual from the first-stage equation is that changes in lagged trade due to both systematic (observable) and random (unobservable) factors will tend to influence current trade patterns, although the magnitude of their effects may differ.

We show the results in the third and sixth columns of table 2.5. These estimates again reduce the magnitude of the coefficient on the lagged dependent variable, although it remains statistically significant at standard confidence levels for both cross-section years.[17] They produce a pattern of coefficients on lagged trade that decline over time, as if the heavy hand of interwar commercial history was gradually lifted over the postwar years. The coefficient on the residual from the first-stage regression is consistently less significant and important than that on the fitted value of trade, as if movements in trade due to systematic factors associated with the gravity model have a more persistent

17. Thus, where estimation by instrumental variables yielded a zero coefficient on the lagged dependent variable in 1964, Hatanaka's method yields a statistically significant coefficient of 0.10.

impact on future trade patterns than idiosyncratic fluctuations in trade. Only in 1954 does the coefficient on the first-stage residual differ significantly from zero at the 90 percent confidence level.

The use of Hatanaka's method enhances the importance of continuity in 1954, and it lengthens (through 1954) the postwar period over which our intraindustry-trade proxy (per capita incomes) fails to regain its effect. By reducing the magnitude of the coefficient on the lagged dependent variable, it no longer suggests a long-run elasticity of trade with respect to income greater than unity (or greater than the scaled-OLS estimates). Otherwise, the coefficients on the other variables remain essentially unchanged.

Thus, estimating the extended gravity model using a variety of alternative approaches does not fundamentally alter the results. It does not undermine our interpretation of the lagged dependent variable in terms of the economic effects of lagged trade flows on current trade patterns, operating through channels like those highlighted in recent models of hysteresis in trade. For simplicity and in the interest of comparability with other studies, in the remaining subsections we concentrate on our scaled-OLS results.

Trade and Financial Bloc Variables

Table 2.6 adds dummy variables designed to capture the impact of the two principal trade liberalization initiatives of the early postwar period, GATT and the European Economic Community (EEC). GATT was initiated in 1947, when twenty-three participating countries agreed to exchange tariff reductions and to extend to one another most-favored-nation (MFN) trading status.[18] The EEC was formed in 1958 when six European countries agreed to establish a customs union.[19]

Including dummy variables is the standard way of assessing the impact of such trade arrangements in the gravity-model framework. In our regressions, one dummy variable for each arrangement takes a value of 1 when a pair of countries both participate in GATT or the EEC. A positive coefficient on this variable indicates "trade creation," or that the two countries trade more with each other than would be predicted by their incomes, populations, and geographical location and the average behavior of countries in the sample. A second set of dummy variables takes on a value of 1 if only one of the two countries participates in the trade arrangement in question. This variable captures the "external effect" of the grouping on trade with nonmembers. A positive coefficient indicates greater trade with nonmembers, a negative one "trade diversion," or a reduction in trade with nonmembers.

Previous assessments of trade blocs and regional arrangements utilizing this

18. Twenty-nine of the thirty-four members of GATT in 1949 are in our sample; thirty-four of forty-one members of GATT are in our 1954 sample; and thirty of sixty-nine members of GATT are in our 1964 sample.

19. Each of the founding members of the EEC—Belgium-Luxembourg, France, Germany, Italy, the Netherlands—is in our sample.

Table 2.6   Determinants of Bilateral Trade, Including Lagged Trade and Commercial Initiatives

	1949		1954		1964	
Constant	7.00	5.03	5.62	1.68	4.46	1.89
	(12.10)	(9.27)	(10.43)	(3.83)	(7.48)	(5.84)
National incomes	0.85	0.48	0.85	0.30	0.87	0.21
	(23.59)	(10.91)	(26.78)	(10.09)	(28.92)	(9.36)
Per capita	0.00	0.00	0.30	0.14	0.37	0.18
national incomes	(0.02)	(0.03)	(7.59)	(5.27)	(10.77)	(9.66)
Distance	−0.98	−0.67	−0.70	−0.14	−0.74	−0.23
	(14.40)	(10.34)	(11.05)	(3.02)	(12.23)	(6.59)
Contiguity	0.49	0.04	0.53	0.21	0.30	−0.10
	(1.51)	(0.12)	(1.80)	(1.07)	(1.05)	(0.63)
EEC	−0.22	−0.31	0.18	0.38	0.63	0.49
	(0.47)	(0.73)	(0.40)	(1.28)	(1.54)	(2.23)
EEC-X	0.37	0.05	0.59	0.46	0.48	0.11
	(2.90)	(0.45)	(4.96)	(5.71)	(4.27)	(1.71)
GATT	1.84	1.50	0.19	−0.27	0.72	0.06
	(10.55)	(9.33)	(1.19)	(2.40)	(2.37)	(0.36)
GATT-X	0.61	0.55	0.00	−0.15	0.72	0.15
	(5.42)	(5.46)	(0.01)	(1.46)	(2.31)	(0.88)
Lagged trade	—	0.61	—	0.84	—	0.77
		(12.89)		(28.51)		(33.85)
R^2	0.69	0.75	0.71	0.87	0.78	0.92
Standard error	1.02	0.92	1.02	0.69	1.00	0.61
F-statistic	194.3	232.3	222.6	519.7	310.9	859.5

Notes: T-statistics are in parentheses. Lagged trade for 1949 is trade in 1938, for 1954 trade in 1949, and for 1964 trade in 1954. EEC equals unity when both countries are EEC members, while EEC-X equals unity when one of the two countries is an EEC member. GATT equals unity when both countries are GATT members, while GATT-X equals unity when one of the two countries is a GATT member.

approach have failed to control for past trade patterns and relationships. Insofar as countries with a tendency to trade disproportionately with one another for historical reasons not otherwise captured by the gravity model also have a tendency to negotiate preferential trade arrangements to lock in those high levels of trade, there may be a tendency to spuriously attribute to the bloc variable the effects of historical factors. As already noted, we found in Eichengreen and Irwin (1995) that dummy variables for preferential arrangements often suggested statistically significant trade-creating effects even before the actual formation of those blocs. This suggests that controlling for previous trade patterns may diminish the estimated impact of trade policies on trade flows.

There is no evidence in table 2.6 that in 1949, nearly a decade prior to the formation of the EEC, the prospective members of that regional grouping traded more extensively with one another than would be predicted by their economic characteristics (incomes, per capita incomes, distance, and contiguity) and the typical behavior of countries in the sample (as captured by the gravity model).[20] The regression in the first column of the table suggests, curiously, a tendency for prospective EEC members to trade disproportionately with countries that were *not* among the founding six in 1949. This paradox evaporates when lagged trade is added to the equation, however. An interpretation is that countries like France, Belgium, and the Netherlands traded disportionately with their current and former overseas dependencies for historical reasons not readily captured by the standard arguments of the gravity model; in the standard specification, this shows up as an EEC effect—as a tendency for prospective EEC members to trade disproportionately with countries not among the founding six—where it is properly attributable to the effects of history.

GATT members appear to have traded significantly more with one another than would be predicted by the standard arguments of the gravity model as early as 1949. This is consistent with the fact the initial GATT negotiating round in 1947 succeeded in cutting the tariffs of members quite significantly.[21] Strikingly, trade between GATT members and nonmembers does not appear to have been discouraged; indeed, there is evidence of a statistically significant positive effect, albeit a smaller one than that for trade between pairs of countries both of which belonged to the GATT.[22] This could reflect the fact that GATT members continued to respect treaties with nonmembers that contained MFN clauses and that the Geneva tariff cuts were extended to them.

In 1954, four years prior to the formation of the EEC, there is again no evidence that the future founding members of Europe's customs union traded more heavily with one another than can be accounted for by the standard arguments of the gravity model and the typical behavior of countries in the sample. If anything, the soon-to-be founding members of the EEC tended to trade unusually heavily with countries that did not become members of the EEC in 1958. Interestingly, this effect is no longer absorbed with the addition of lagged trade, either for 1949 (as reported in the table) or even including 1938 (in results we do not report).

In 1954 GATT no longer appears to have had significant trade-creating or trade-diverting effects. This is consistent with the lack of progress toward additional multilateral trade liberalization in the 1950s and the failure of GATT to attract new members. In the regression including lagged trade (for 1949), GATT members actually appear to have traded less with one another than would be expected given their other characteristics, although this lower trade does not fully erase the positive impact apparent in 1949.

---

20. In addition, there is the curious result that EEC members tended to trade more heavily with nonmembers. The absence of any tendency for EEC members to trade unusually heavily with one another prior to EEC formation cannot be attributed to contiguity because, in results we do not report, the exclusion of that variable does not affect the coefficient on the EEC.

21. For a discussion of the impact of early GATT activities on trade policies in Europe and elsewhere, see Irwin (1995a, 1995b).

22. This effect fails to disappear when a control for previous trade patterns is introduced.

The EEC's impact is evident in the regressions for 1964, when it exerts a modestly positive effect on trade with nonmembers. While GATT appears to have had positive trade-creating effects for trade both among members and between GATT signatories and the rest of the world, these effects disappear when lagged trade is accounted for. This does not mean that GATT was unimportant; insofar as earlier GATT rounds were trade creating, they stimulated lagged trade in ways that, according to the last equation in table 2.3, continued to encourage trade in 1964. But the two equations for 1964 suggest that any positive effects arising from the Dillon Round of GATT negotiations from 1960–61 were in fact largely the effects of earlier liberalization initiatives.

Our previous paper suggested that both commercial and monetary arrangements had impacts on the pattern of trade in the 1930s. To explore this same question for the early postwar years, table 2.7 adds dummy variables to capture the effects of the leading regional monetary arrangement of the period, the European Payments Union (EPU). The EPU, created in 1950, was a generalization of previous postwar efforts to establish a framework for multilateral clearing among European countries; its participants included most of Europe (other than Spain), their overseas dependencies, and Turkey. Countries participating in the EPU agreed to adopt the Organization for Economic Cooperation and Development (OECD) Code of Liberalization committing them to remove controls and quantitative restrictions on trade with one another according to a predetermined schedule. By providing short-term credits and reestablishing a system of multilateral clearing within Europe, the EPU economized on the need for foreign exchange reserves and may have encouraged trade with the rest of the world.

Table 2.7 confirms the importance of the EPU. As in Eichengreen (1993) we find that EPU membership encouraged trade both with other EPU partners and with the rest of the world. The estimated effects of EPU membership are diminished somewhat, however, when lagged trade is included in the specification. The interpretation is that EPU members traded disproportionately with one another not just because of their preferential arrangement but also because those countries that chose to join the EPU had a disproportionate tendency to trade in the past and a special desire to rebuild their commercial relations after World War II. Once again, our results point to the importance of considering past trade as a determinant of current bilateral flows when attempting to assess the impact of preferential and regional agreements.

Former Colonial Relationships

Most colonial relationships between the European powers and developing regions persisted until the mid–twentieth century. While these relationships are known to have had an important impact on trade, it is uncertain how quickly the ties that bound a colony to its "mother country" dissolved upon independence. We provide a partial assessment of this question by analyzing trade relationships among several countries that at one time had colonial relation-

Table 2.7   **Determinants of Bilateral Trade, Including Lagged Trade and Commercial and Monetary Initiatives**

	1949		1954		1964	
Constant	5.07	3.56	4.68	1.36	4.15	2.25
	(7.57)	(5.66)	(7.26)	(2.93)	(6.05)	(5.27)
National incomes	0.85	0.53	0.88	0.31	0.88	0.24
	(25.07)	(12.57)	(27.84)	(10.45)	(29.26)	(9.06)
Per capita	−0.12	−0.09	0.21	0.12	0.31	0.21
national incomes	(2.25)	(1.91)	(5.21)	(4.32)	(8.32)	(8.99)
Distance	−0.81	−0.57	−0.63	−0.14	−0.73	−0.27
	(10.80)	(7.86)	(8.74)	(2.65)	(10.44)	(5.89)
Contiguity	0.74	0.25	0.67	0.27	0.36	−0.11
	(2.41)	(1.13)	(2.29)	(1.32)	(1.29)	(0.62)
EEC member	−0.99	−0.87	−0.20	0.29	0.45	0.61
	(2.15)	(2.08)	(0.45)	(0.97)	(1.07)	(2.34)
Non–EEC	−0.23	−0.38	0.24	0.36	0.25	0.14
member	(1.68)	(3.02)	(1.81)	(3.96)	(2.24)	(1.77)
GATT member	1.91	1.58	0.11	−0.29	0.70	0.05
	(11.53)	(10.26)	(0.69)	(2.54)	(2.29)	(0.26)
Non–GATT	0.64	0.57	−0.05	−0.17	0.69	0.15
member	(6.09)	(5.80)	(0.32)	(1.62)	(2.21)	(0.78)
EPU member	1.43	1.14	0.78	0.18	0.38	−0.07
	(6.35)	(5.53)	(3.52)	(1.18)	(1.77)	(0.55)
Non–EPU	0.97	0.70	0.66	0.18	0.39	−0.03
member	(8.38)	(6.39)	(5.76)	(2.32)	(3.47)	(0.47)
Lagged trade	—	0.46	—	0.81	—	0.87
		(11.54)		(27.52)		(33.47)
R^2	0.72	0.77	0.73	0.87	0.78	0.92
Standard error	0.97	0.89	1.00	0.69	1.00	0.62
F-statistic	181.1	208.2	189.8	430.3	253.6	705.3

Notes: See table 2.4 notes. Lagged trade for 1949 is trade in 1938, for 1954 trade in 1949, and for 1964 trade in 1954.

ships. We first consider trade after World War II among the countries that had composed the British Empire and were within the British Commonwealth. Our sample of British colonies is more broadly defined than the British Commonwealth, which retained within-group trade preferences even after the war, and includes such areas as Palestine (Israel), Ireland (which quit the Commonwealth in 1948), and British Malay (Malaysia, which joined the Commonwealth in 1957), as well as Commonwealth members Canada, Australia, India, New Zealand, Pakistan, South Africa, and the United Kingdom.

Table 2.8 reports the coefficients on the variable denoting pairs of bloc members and that denoting trade between members and nonmembers.[23] All the summary statistics and other coefficients are comparable to those found on the

23. The regressions exclude other blocs, such as GATT and the EEC, but our results are robust to their inclusion.

Table 2.8　　　　**Coefficients on Former Colonial Relationships**

		Basic Specification	Including Lagged Trade
British colonies	1949	0.86	0.13
		(3.82)	(0.81)
		0.00	−0.11
		(0.01)	(1.13)
	1954	0.19	−0.33
		(0.95)	(2.49)
		−0.34	−0.34
		(3.39)	(5.16)
	1964	0.00	−0.14
		(0.00)	(1.26)
		−0.41	−0.13
		(4.50)	(2.19)
British Commonwealth	1949	1.83	1.13
		(5.77)	(3.97)
		0.13	0.15
		(1.17)	(1.52)
	1954	0.89	−0.25
		(3.22)	(1.31)
		0.34	−0.33
		(3.27)	(5.62)
	1964	0.65	−0.01
		(2.86)	(0.08)
		−0.35	−0.12
		(3.59)	(2.34)
United States– Philippines	1949	2.44	1.77
		(2.16)	(1.81)
		0.12	0.36
		(0.83)	(2.70)
	1954	1.32	−0.21
		(1.25)	(0.29)
		−0.31	−0.30
		(2.24)	(3.21)
	1964	1.73	0.08
		(1.69)	(0.12)
		0.11	0.08
		(0.89)	(0.12)
Netherlands– Indonesia	1949	3.30	1.85
		(2.99)	(1.89)
		−0.33	−0.38
		(2.36)	(3.16)
	1954	3.66	0.63
		(3.53)	(0.89)
		0.35	0.24
		(2.73)	(2.71)
	1964	2.51	−0.43
		(2.47)	(0.69)
		0.24	−0.10
		(1.92)	(1.31)

Note: See table 2.4 notes.

other tables. The result for 1949 obtained from estimating the standard gravity-model specification suggests that countries that had once been members of the British Empire continued to trade unusually heavily with one another immediately after World War II. As the reader will by now be well aware, this effect could reflect either Commonwealth preferences (which were maintained until the United Kingdom entered the EEC in the early 1970s) or the persistent influence of past trade on current trade. The second column in table 2.8 points to the latter interpretation: former British colonies traded disproportionately more with one another in 1949 not because of the trade-creating effects of Commonwealth preferences but because of the effects of history.

For 1954 and 1964 the standard specification suggests no trade-creating effects among the former colonies but some trade diversion. Adding lagged trade suggests, strikingly, that members of the British Commonwealth and Britain's former colonies tended to trade less than predicted by the standard arguments of the gravity model, both with one another and with the rest of the world, once the effects of history are taken into account. This is consistent with historical accounts (viz. Schenk 1994) suggesting that Britain failed to reorient its trade toward continental Europe and other parts of the world in the 1950s. This is also suggestive of an unraveling of the trade and transportation networks that had once bound these disparate regions together. Countries of the empire appear to trade less with others than would have been anticipated, even when accounting for past trade patterns. A possible interpretation is that, as colonial networks dissolved, the former colonies lost access to the British "hub" (wherein Britain acted as an entrepôt and reexported colonial goods) that allowed the colonies to maintain trading ties with countries they might normally not trade with.

The results for the British Commonwealth suggest that these countries traded unusually heavily with one another in 1949, even when controlling for the pattern of trade in 1938. This effect disappears in 1954 and 1964 once lagged trade is included, although the negative effect on trade with nonmembers is still apparent.

We also examined trade ties between the United States and the Philippines and between the Netherlands and Indonesia. The results suggest that larger-than-expected trade flows between these countries are properly attributed to the effects of history, except in 1949.

2.4   Conclusions and Implications

Our goal in this paper has been to make a simple point. We have argued that both theory and evidence suggest that history plays a role in shaping the direction of international trade. The standard gravity-model formulation, which neglects the role of historical factors, suffers from omitted-variables bias. Because there are reasons to anticipate a positive correlation between the predominant direction of trade flows in the past and membership in preferential arrangements in the present, there may be a tendency to spuriously attribute to preferential arrangements the effects of historical factors and to exaggerate the influence of the former.

We have illustrated these points by analyzing the evolution of trade between 1949 and 1964. We found that lagged trade exercises an important effect even after controlling for the arguments of the standard gravity model. While it is always appropriate to interpret the coefficients on lagged dependent variables with caution, our findings are robust to the use of instrumented values in place of actual values of lagged trade to better distinguish persistent effects of trade from persistent random effects (where the gravity model conveniently furnishes the logical instruments). Among our substantive findings are that the omission of historical factors overstates the trade of the countries of continental Europe with its former colonies after the late 1940s, that it exaggerates the trade-creating effects of the EPU, and that it overstates the importance of the Dillon Round of the early 1960s.

The implication is that we will never run another gravity equation that excludes lagged trade flows. If our paper is successful (and widely read), neither will other investigators.

References

Anderson, James E. 1979. A Theoretical Foundation for the Gravity Equation. *American Economic Review* 69:106–16.

Baldwin, Richard E. 1988. Hysteresis in Import Prices: The Beachhead Effect. *American Economic Review* 74:773–85.

Baldwin, Richard E., and Paul Krugman. 1989. Persistent Trade Effects of Exchange Rate Shocks. *Quarterly Journal of Economics* 104:635–54.

Bayoumi, Tamim, and Barry Eichengreen. 1995. Is Regionalism Simply a Diversion? Evidence from the Evolution of the EC and EFTA. International Monetary Fund and University of California, Berkeley. Manuscript.

Bean, Charles R. 1988. Sterling Misalignment and British Trade Performance. In Richard C. Marston, ed., *Misalignment of Exchange Rates: Effects on Trade and Industry.* Chicago: University of Chicago Press.

Bergstrand, J. H. 1985. The Gravity Equation in International Trade: Some Microeconomic Foundations and Empirical Evidence. *Review of Economics and Statistics* 67:474–81.

Deardorff, Alan. 1984. Testing Trade Theories and Predicting Trade Flows. In Ronald Jones and Peter Kenen, eds., *Handbook of International Economics,* 1:467–517. Amsterdam: Elsevier.

Dewhurst, J. Frederic, John O. Coppock, P. Lamartine Yales, and associates. 1961. *Europe's Needs and Resources.* New York: Twentieth Century Fund.

Dixit, Avinash. 1989. Hysteresis, Import Penetration, and Exchange Rate Pass Through. *Quarterly Journal of Economics* 104:205–28.

Eichengreen, Barry. 1993. *Reconstructing Europe's Trade and Payments.* Manchester: Manchester University Press; Ann Arbor: University of Michigan Press.

Eichengreen, Barry, and Douglas A. Irwin. 1995. Trade Blocs, Currency Blocs, and the Reorientation of Trade in the 1930s. *Journal of International Economics* 38:1–24.

Frankel, Jeffrey. 1995. *Regional Trade Blocs.* Washington, DC: Institute for International Economics.

Frankel, Jeffrey, Ernesto Stein, and Shang-Jin Wei. 1993. Continental Trading Blocs: Are They Natural or Supernatural? NBER Working Paper no. 4588. Cambridge, MA: National Bureau of Economic Research, June.

Frankel, Jeffrey, and Shang-Jin Wei. 1993. Trade Blocs and Currency Blocs. In Centre for Economic Policy Research, *The Monetary Future of Europe.* London: Centre for Economic Policy Research.

Greene, W. H. 1993. *Econometric Analysis.* 2d ed. New York: Macmillan.

Griliches, Zvi. 1961. A Note on the Serial Correlation Bias in Estimates of Distributed Lags. *Econometrica* 29:65–73.

Hamilton, Carl, and L. Alan Winters. 1992. Opening Up International Trade in Eastern Europe. *Economic Policy* 14:77–117.

Hilgert, Folke. 1942. *The Network of World Trade.* Geneva: League of Nations.

Irwin, Douglas A. 1995a. The GATT in Historical Perspective. *American Economic Review Papers and Proceedings* 85:323–28.

———. 1995b. The GATT's Contribution to Economic Recovery in Post-War Europe. In Barry Eichengreen, ed., *Europe's Postwar Growth, Revisited.* New York: Cambridge University Press.

Kaufman, Burton I. 1974. *Efficiency and Expansion: Foreign Trade Organization in the Wilson Administration, 1913–1921.* Westport, CT: Greenwood Press.

Liviatan, N. 1963. Consistent Estimation of Distributed Lags. *International Economic Review* 4:44–52.

Mitchell, Brian R. 1993. *International Historical Statistics: The Americas, 1750–1988.* 2d ed. New York: Stockton Press.

Roberts, Mark J., and James R. Tybout. 1995. The Decision to Export: An Empirical Model of Entry with Sunk Costs. Georgetown University. Mimeo.

Saul, S. B. 1960. *Studies in British Overseas Trade, 1870–1914.* Liverpool: Liverpool University Press.

Schenk, Susan. 1994. *Britain and the Sterling Area: From Devaluation to Convertibility.* London: Routledge.

Comment   Robert Z. Lawrence

In this paper, Eichengreen and Irwin argue that traditional gravity models are incompletely specified because they fail to take account of the likelihood that trade patterns will be influenced by history, that is, previous trade. In principle, this could seriously bias the estimates obtained on the independent variables in traditional models if these are correlated with variables that are omitted. Eichengreen and Irwin argue that this is in fact the case and present evidence that shows how the coefficients on traditional variables are dramatically altered when a lagged dependent variable is introduced into the estimation. On the

Robert Z. Lawrence is the Albert L. Williams Professor of International Trade and Investment at the Kennedy School of Government, Harvard University, and a research associate of the National Bureau of Economic Research.

basis of these results, they promise never again to run gravity models that exclude historical trade flows, and advise other modelers to do the same.

I think the paper does succeed in raising some important questions about the use of these models, but I'm not sure where it leaves us. I take away the message that it is important to interpret these models with great care, although I am not convinced that simply introducing a lagged dependent variable will suffice. In my view, there is no substitute for including both current and lagged exogenous determinants of trade flows explicitly in the equation.

An important question is what do the estimated parameters in the model actually mean when estimated together with the lagged dependent variable? Should these coefficients be viewed simply as historical descriptions of the relationship between the variables or can they be thought of as time-related structural parameters? The authors seem to be on both sides of this issue. In the introduction to the paper, they note that "the influence of past trade over current trade may vary with circumstances"—in other words this influence is not stable or structural—and this observation is supported by the results reported in table 2.4, which indicate that past trade has variable effects. However, in their discussion of table 2.4 the authors imply that these coefficients are structurally stable when they infer effects such as the implied long-run income elasticity. I doubt this practice gives us very good answers. It is noteworthy that the coefficient on the contemporaneous income variable is virtually unchanged between 1954 and 1964 at 0.25 and 0.27 respectively; the implied long-run elasticity increases dramatically from 2.6 to 4.5. These results suggest that income operates on trade with extremely long lags—and while most macrotrade equations do suggest lagged effects, they do not indicate these are felt for more than a year or two.

The structural interpretation using a lagged dependent variable constrains the timing of adjustment to all independent variables to be the same. But I find this implausible. We know from macrotrade equations, for example, that price effects generally operate more slowly than income effects. In this case, the full effects of concluding a free trade area, for example, are likely to take much longer than an increase in income. It would be interesting therefore if the lagged income variables, rather than (or in addition to) the lagged dependent variable, were included in the regression.

Another hint of the problems in providing a structural interpretation comes in table 2.6. Suppose you want to use table 2.6 to know what being a member of the European Community (EC) does to trade. Is the answer 0.49, the dummy on the EC in 1964, or should the coefficient be taken in conjunction with the lagged dependent variable of 0.77 to obtain estimates that are six times as large? In this case, the lagged variable is estimated using trade from 1954 when countries were not even members of the EC.

As is the case in time-series analysis, the appearance of lagged dependent variables with large coefficients can be rationalized as lagged adjustment, but it may also indicate serious misspecification. The best approach, therefore, is not simply to drop the lagged dependent variable into the equation but to try explicitly to capture the truly exogenous variables that affected lagged trade.

The issue of exogeneity may also be an important problem when dummy variables are used to estimate the effects of free trade areas. Free trade areas may well be an endogenous variable—that is, a response to, rather than a source of, large trade flows. Frankel and Wei and others have used gravity models to determine which groups of countries form "natural" trading blocs. Presumably, such groups are more likely to form free trade areas, since the benefits outweigh the costs. Similarly, it is argued that in Asia, in particular, formal agreements are following the market, whereas in Europe it seems more likely that these arrangements have tended to lead. If we find a large coefficient on a particular free trade area, is that an indication the agreement has strong effects or simply that the countries that have formed the agreement have chosen well?

Comment   Paul Wonnacott

As we have come to expect, Eichengreen and Irwin have presented a careful and interesting paper on a current topic, adding a historical perspective. Their main point, that past trade patterns continue to influence current trade flows, is, as they note, "intuitively plausible." They present empirical evidence supporting this plausible viewpoint. In the introductory section, they also present historical examples, of which I find South African exports to the London gold market to be one of the more compelling. Indeed, South Africa is perhaps one of the more interesting examples one can think of: not only can the gold market be cited, but South African exports of diamonds to the Netherlands likewise show the importance of history and established commercial relationships in determining current trade patterns.

In any paper with such a broad scope, there are always points on which additional information could be brought in, or additional hypotheses tested. I have no quarrel with the choices of Eichengreen and Irwin from the options open to them; their choices seem reasonable and well motivated. And, to keep the paper manageable, they were forced to follow Yogi Berra's advice: when you come to a fork in the road, take it. I would, nevertheless, like to suggest some alternative ideas that might be worth considering. I will pass over the issues raised by the general tendency for lagged variables to be relatively powerful explanatory variables, and concentrate on the more specific issues raised by the paper.

First, and perhaps most important, is what one makes of the persistence of historical trade patterns. The emphasis of their paper is on historical accidents,

Paul Wonnacott is the Alan R. Holmes Professor at Middlebury College.

such as empires or wars, that lead to new trade patterns. Once costs are sunk in developing new markets, the resulting trade pattern generally persists, in large part because of economies of scale.

Without questioning the validity of this conclusion, I would like to suggest an additional explanation for the persistence of historical patterns of trade. Trade is driven not just by the variables in the gravity model and by historical accident, but also by the traditional idea of comparative advantage. While comparative advantage can change, it generally does so only slowly. Thus, for example, temperate countries with fertile prairie lands are quite likely to export wheat to heavily populated countries with poor soil, and this trading pattern is likely to persist. Similarly, one would explain Japanese imports from the Persian Gulf by the large supplies of oil there, and the thirst of Japanese industry for that oil. Likewise, bauxite is shipped from countries that have bauxite mines to those that have plentiful supplies of electric power, most notably cheap hydropower, and both the bauxite supplies and the hydropower are likely to last for an extended period of time.

What difference, it might be asked, does this make? Why should we care whether persistent trade patterns are the result of historical accidents—such as war or empire—or whether they are the result of things that might be classified under the concept of comparative advantage? It matters quite a bit in terms of the main topic of this conference—namely, regional arrangements. If, prior to the establishment of a free trade association, countries are close trading partners because of fundamental economic forces—those of classical comparative advantage and geographical proximity—then I would argue that the case for a free trade agreement is strengthened. The countries are natural trading partners, and discrimination against outsiders that any such agreement entails is likely to have relatively weak trade-diverting effects.

In contrast, if the high level of trade is explained on the basis of historical accident, then discrimination against outsiders is more questionable. Sunk costs are of course real costs, and cutting across traditional lines of commerce—such as between the South African and London gold markets or the South African and Dutch diamond markets—can inflict real losses. But fortifying traditional ties by discriminating against new outside competitors strikes me as less desirable than fortifying the natural advantages that come from geographical proximity or from comparative advantage in the traditional sense.

Second, Eichengreen and Irwin struggle with a puzzle, that dummy variables for regional arrangements often show up even before the regional agreement comes into effect, sometimes long before. Perhaps there is a relatively straightforward explanation for this advanced effect. Comprehensive regional arrangements are often preceded with more limited agreements. For example, the Treaty of Rome was preceded by the European Coal and Steel Community (ECSC). In addition, the European Union (EU) was preceded by the dollar shortage and the European Payments Union (EPU), which gave preference to intra-European trade even before the Treaty of Rome. There were also powerful noneconomic objectives at work, both in ECSC and the Treaty of Rome. An objective of ECSC was to integrate so thoroughly the French and German coal and steel industries that a fourth Franco-Prussian war would become impossible. For the Treaty of Rome, a significant political objective was to develop a strong integrated unit that would be able to withstand challenges from the east. These political objectives could also have led to greater intra-European trade even before the Treaty of Rome. Political objectives were of course also the reason for U.S. support for the European Community (EC), even though we would be discriminated against. For details on the pre-Rome increase in trade within Western Europe, I defer to Eichengreen, as he has already done extensive research with Bayoumi (1995).

In North America, there were likewise preliminary steps that increased trade prior to the signing of the Canada-U.S. Free Trade Agreement and North American Free Trade Agreement (NAFTA). The Canada-U.S. FTA was preceded by more than two decades by the Auto Pact of 1965, which led to a very rapid increase in the trade of manufactures between the two countries.

On the Mexican side, the maquiladora industries had special access to the U.S. market prior to beginning of NAFTA negotiations.

On the broader issue of "anticipation" of a regional agreement, the three cases I have cited—Europe, United States, Canada, and NAFTA—seem quite different. U.S.-Canadian free trade was a topic off and on for well over a hundred years, dating back to the Reciprocity Treaty that preceded the Canadian Confederation. A free trade agreement was negotiated in 1911, but rejected at the polls. A preliminary secret agreement was reached shortly after the Second World War, but Prime Minister King got cold feet and withdrew. From the 1960s on, there was a major shift in Canadian business opinion, away from import protection, and toward assured and open access to the U.S. market as a goal.

The European case seems to me to fall into the middle—laying aside attempts by Napoleon and Hitler to unify the continent with the sword. There was a period of about ten years of growing attention before the Treaty of Rome was signed. The Mexican period of anticipation was much shorter; the 1990 approach was the result of a very rapid change in Mexican politics.

In short, all three comprehensive regional agreements were preceded by limited special arrangements. But the degree of anticipation of the comprehensive agreements varied sharply among the three cases.

It is possible that mutual causation was at work, helping to explain the apparent advanced effect of regional arrangements. Nations that are increasingly trading with one another may gradually begin to consider a free trade association or customs union. This fits into my first point: insofar as countries are naturally growing together, the economic case for a regional arrangement is strengthened. The problem here, however, is that the case is muddied by the special arrangements made along the way. For example, the preferential Auto Pact was a significant contributor to the growth of U.S.-Canadian trade after

1965, and this trade should be discounted in any attempt to quantify whether the United States and Canada were becoming natural trading partners.

Third, let me touch on a potpourri of small points in the Eichengreen-Irwin paper.

It is puzzling that the Asia-Pacific Economic Cooperation (APEC) shows up as having substantial trade-creating effects, since it provides no preferences, although it does constructive work in such things as customs clearance procedures. I find it hard to believe that people have much confidence that an APEC free trade association will actually come into effect within the next decade, in spite of official pronouncements. Perhaps there are alternative explanations for the increase in trade. The APEC area is the center of economic dynamism; rapidly growing countries may have a tendency to trade intensively with other rapidly growing countries—even more than one would expect simply on the basis of national product or per capita national product. Is there a case for putting the rate of growth of per capita income as an argument in gravity models? Do the high and rising income elasticities of trade in table 2.4 of the Eichengreen-Irwin paper suggest that the answer to this question might be yes?

In dealing with the possible alternative explanations for the postwar persistence of trade within the Commonwealth and between continental Europe and its colonies, perhaps it would be worth considering monetary arrangements. The discriminations involved in, say, the sterling area may have been as important as traditionally defined commercial policies.

Finally, with the authors, I am puzzled by lack of trend in the distance coefficient (tables 2.2 and 2.3: -0.78 in 1928 to -0.81 in 1964). One would have thought that the decline in transportation costs over time would have caused a trend. But two interesting changes did occur in the coefficient—a substantial decline in the absolute size of the coefficient during the 1930s, and an even bigger increase in the 1940s. Was the fall of the absolute size of the distance coefficient in the 1930s the combined result of the general strangling of trade, together with the rise of importance of preferential trade in the far-flung British Empire? Was the increase in absolute size of the coefficient in the 1940s the result of the postwar financial mess, and the tendency to make bilateral and regional financial arrangements in the face of the "dollar shortage"?

These are some of the questions that arose as I read the Eichengreen-Irwin paper. I congratulate them on an interesting and thought-provoking paper.

Reference

Bayoumi, Tamim, and Barry Eichengreen. 1995. Is Regionalism Simply a Diversion? Evidence from the Evolution of the EC and EFTA. International Monetary Fund and the University of California, Berkeley. Manuscript.

3 Why Do Countries Seek Regional Trade Agreements?

John Whalley

3.1 Introduction

This paper argues that a wide range of considerations enter when countries seek to negotiate regional trade agreements. Some see trade agreements as providing underpinnings to strategic alliances, and hence implicitly form part of security arrangements (as in Europe). Smaller countries see trade agreements with larger partners as a way of obtaining more security for their access to larger country markets (as in the Canada-U.S. Free Trade Agreement [CUSTA]). Some countries have tried to use regional (and multilateral) agreements to help lock in domestic policy reform and make it more difficult to subsequently reverse (Mexico in North American Free Trade Agreement [NAFTA]). Other countries' use of regional trade agreements reflects tactical considerations; conscious efforts to use prior regional agreements to influence subsequent multilateral negotiation (services in CUSTA and in NAFTA). Regional trade arrangements around the world are thus different one from another, not the least because countries have different objectives when they negotiate them.

As a result, a wide range of differences have to be taken into account in analyzing them. Much of the recent literature on regionalism implicitly assumes that regional trade agreements are similar. This is partly because in analytical discussion it is common to analyze the symmetric case in which countries are of equal size (Krugman 1991; Haveman 1992; Krugman 1993). If any differentiation is noted, it is usually that some agreements (such as the Euro-

John Whalley is professor of economics at the University of Western Ontario and a research associate of the National Bureau of Economic Research.

The author is grateful to Jeff Frankel and participants both at the preconference meeting held in Cambridge, 19 July 1995, and at the conference in Woodstock for helpful comments. Later sections draw on joint work with Carlo Perroni.

pean Union [EU]) are customs unions, while others (such as NAFTA) are free trade areas. Yet some are part of a process headed toward eventual deeper integration (European Community [EC] in the 1960s), some are consciously stand-alone, more shallow agreements (NAFTA), some are simple in structure while others are more complex, and these differences go well beyond differences between customs unions (CUs) and free trade areas (FTAs).

The line of argument offered is that these differences need to be factored into both an analysis of the effects of any given regional trade agreement, and any balanced discussion of the threat that regionalism now poses for the future evolution of the trading system. An implication is that the gain or loss to any country from a regional agreement needs to be evaluated relative to the appropriate counterfactual, which itself may be difficult to specify analytically. In this paper, I discuss how such considerations can change conventional analyses of the impacts of regional trade agreements, and summarize what is known about the significance of some of the factors involved in some specific cases.

3.2   Recent and Longer-standing Regional Trade Agreements in the Trading System

That regional trade agreements have been present in the multilateral trading system since its early days, and that they have grown in coverage and scope recently is hardly news. But the number and range of these agreements is now quite extraordinary.

Table 3.1 lists the regional trade agreements notified to General Agreement on Tariffs and Trade/World Trade Organization (GATT/WTO) and in operation as of 1 January 1995, and included in a recent WTO volume on regionalism.[1] This long list includes the formation of the European Free Trade Association, the bilateral arrangements between Canada and the United States under the Auto Pact of 1965 and the 1988 Canada-U.S. Free Trade Agreement; and other more recent initiatives including Community Association Agreements, Community Enlargement, NAFTA, Mercosur, the Australia–New Zealand Closer Economic Relationship (CER), and others.

Besides the more prominent regional arrangements involving the United States and the EC, an increasing number of these arrangements are between smaller countries. These usually attract less attention because the trade covered by them is relatively small. Earlier examples include the Latin American Free Trade Association of 1960, the Central American Common Market of 1960, and the (now defunct) East African Common Market of the same period. More recently, there have also been various bilateral agreements not notified to

1. Also see Stoeckel, Pearce, and Banks (1990, 24), for a detailed listing of various trading arrangements, as well as Schott (1989), appendix A, which lists all preferential trade agreements notified to GATT. Regional trade arrangements are also discussed in two recent volumes, one sponsored by GATT (Anderson and Blackhurst 1993), and the other by the World Bank (de Melo and Panagariya 1993).

Table 3.1   **Regional Integration Agreements Notified to GATT/WTO and in Force as of January 1995**

Reciprocal Regional Integration Agreements

Europe

European Community (EC)

Austria	Germany	Netherlands
Belgium	Greece	Portugal
Denmark	Ireland	Spain
Finland	Italy	Sweden
France	Luxembourg	United Kingdom

EC free trade agreements with

Estonia	Latvia	Norway
Iceland	Liechtenstein	Switzerland
Israel	Lithuania	

EC association agreements with

Bulgaria	Hungary	Romania
Cyprus	Malta	Slovak Rep.
Czech Rep.	Poland	Turkey

European Free Trade Association (EFTA)

Iceland	Norway	Switzerland
Liechtenstein		

EFTA free trade agreements with

Bulgaria	Israel	Slovak Rep.
Czech Rep.	Poland	Turkey
Hungary	Romania	

Norway free trade agreements with

Estonia	Latvia	Lithuania

Switzerland free trade agreements with

Estonia	Latvia	Lithuania

Czech Rep. and Slovak Rep. Customs Union

Central European Free Trade Area

Czech Rep.	Poland	Slovak Rep.
Hungary		

Czech Rep. and Slovenia Free Trade Agreement

Slovak Rep. and Slovenia Free Trade Agreement

North America

Canada-U.S. Free Trade Agreement (CUFTA)

North American Free Trade Agreement (NAFTA)

Latin America and the Caribbean

Caribbean Community and Common Market (Caricom)

Central American Common Market (CACM)

Latin American Integration Association (LAIA)

Andean Pact

Southern Common Market (Mercosur)

Middle East

Economic Cooperation Organization (ECO)

Gulf Cooperation Council (GCC)

Asia

Australia–New Zealand Closer Economic Relationship (CER)

Bangkok Agreement

Common Effective Preferential Scheme for the ASEAN Free Trade Area

Lao People's Dem. Rep. and Thailand Trade Agreement

Other

Israel-U.S. Free Trade Agreement

Nonreciprocal Regional Integration Agreements

Europe

EEC-association of certain non-European countries and territories (EEC-PTOM II)

EEC cooperation agreements with

Algeria	Lebanon	Syria
Egypt	Morocco	Tunisia
Jordan		

ACP-EEC Fourth Lomé Convention

Asia

Australia–Papua New Guinea Agreement

South Pacific Regional Trade Cooperation Agreement (SPARTECA)

Source: WTO 1995.

GATT/WTO; examples are the Chile-Mexico bilateral trade agreement concluded in 1991 and the 1992 Chile-Venezuela bilateral agreement. As well, there are wider-ranging agreements besides those in table 3.1; in the United Nations Conference on Trade and Development (UNCTAD), for instance, a negotiation on trade preferences among developing countries, the Generalized System of Trade Preferences (GSTP), is still ongoing, although not with any marked vigor.[2]

Thus, and as the chronology from Hamilton and Whalley (1996) shows (table 3.2), regional trade arrangements have been a central feature in the development and evolution of the postwar trading system rather than the exception, and this has been despite the growth in importance of GATT/WTO. Furthermore, as this chronology also clearly shows, the number of regional trade agreements has grown substantially in the trading system in the last few years. Most of the chronology is devoted to arrangements since 1991, with a wide range of bilateral and minilateral arrangements recently entering the system. Indeed, despite the presence of multilateral rules and disciplines in the system, it is still the case that most GATT/WTO contracting parties are now parties to at least one regional trade arrangement.

But these trade agreements, numerous as they are, also vary substantially one from another. These differences include the coverage of the agreements, the balance of concessions between the parties to the agreement, and whether the agreement forms part of an ongoing process of wider economic integration. Differences in coverage relate to such issues as whether or not freer factor flows are included (as in the EU), whether agreements seek to go beyond the coverage of GATT at the time (services in CUSTA; environment and labor standards in NAFTA); whether financial transfers are included; whether industrialization objectives (including production-sharing agreements) are included; and whether payments arrangements are a central feature of the agreement. And these all go beyond the widely noted differences between FTAs and CUs noted above.

De La Torre and Kelley (1992) list some of these differences for a sample of agreements between developing countries, reproduced here as table 3.3. While this table relates to only a subset of developing-country arrangements, the diversity among the agreements covered is immediately apparent. Some have provisions aiming to provide freer factor movements; some have payments arrangements, while others do not; some use a positive-list approach, in reaching agreed disciplines, and others a negative-list approach.

A similar range of differences can be found in regional arrangements among developed countries. For example, trade agreements in North America have special dispute-settlement procedures for anti-dumping and countervailing duties, trade provisions relating to the environment and labor standards, and com-

---

2. See the cautionary discussion of the GSTP scheme in Hudec (1989), who argues that negotiating preferences in a regime of unbound tariffs (as most developing-country tariffs are) is virtually doomed to failure. More details on the GSTP scheme can be found in UNCTAD (1987).

Table 3.2   **A Chronology of the Growth of Regionalism in the Postwar Trading System and Its Acceleration in Recent Years**

1947	GATT agreed to by 23 countries, with article XXIV, which allows formation of CUs and FTAs under certain conditions.
1957	Treaty of Rome establishes the European Economic Community (EEC), a CU between Belgium, Luxembourg, France, the Netherlands, Germany, and Italy. Treaty in force 1 January 1958.
1959	Stockholm Convention establishes the European Free Trade Association (EFTA) in effect 1 July 1960. Members include Austria, Denmark, Norway, Portugal, Sweden, Switzerland, and the United Kingdom.
1960	Montevideo Treaty establishes Latin American Free Trade Association (LAFTA) comprising Brazil, Chile, Peru, Uruguay, Argentina, Mexico, and Paraguay.
	Central American Common Market (CACM) formed; includes Costa Rica, El Salvador, Guatemala, Honduras, and Nicaragua.
1963	Yaoundé Convention between the EEC and former French, Belgian, and Italian colonies in Africa gives these countries preferential access to the EC and sets up the European Development Fund.
1965	Canada and the U.S. sign Automobile Products Trade Agreement (Auto Pact).
1969	Yaoundé Convention extended.
1973	EC enlarged to include Britain, Ireland, and Denmark.
1975	Yaoundé Convention superseded by Lomé Convention, extends preferential arrangements to include former colonies of Britain, and is widened to include countries in the Caribbean and Pacific.
1977	Association of Southeast Asian Nations (ASEAN) formed; includes Indonesia, Malaysia, Philippines, Singapore, and Thailand.
1981	Greece joins the EC.
1983	Australia and New Zealand form Closer Economic Relationship to provide for an FTA.
1984	U.S. implements Caribbean Basin Economic Recovery Act to extend duty-free treatment to 21 beneficiary countries in the region for 12 years.
1985	Israel-U.S. Free Trade Agreement enters into force. Over a 10-year period, all tariffs between the two countries to be eliminated.
1986	Portugal and Spain join the EC. Single European Act signed to provide for full European integration in 1992.
1989	Canada-U.S. Free Trade Agreement enters into force. Under agreement, by 1998 all items should be traded duty-free between the two countries.
1990	EC and EFTA undertake discussions on a European Economic Area (EEA) to provide for freer movement of goods, services, capital, and people between the two associations.
	U.S. announces Enterprise for the Americas Initiative to explore a hemispheric-wide free trade zone between countries of North, Central, and South America.
1991	U.S., Mexico, and Canada enter discussions on a North American FTA, leading eventually to the signing of NAFTA.
	Andean Pact members (Bolivia, Colombia, Ecuador, Peru, and Venezuela) sign accord to implement free trade zone by the end of 1995.
	Treaty of Asuncion signed by Brazil, Argentina, Uruguay, and Paraguay to form Mercosur (the South American Common Market). Aim is to create a duty-free common market by the end of 1994.

(continued)

Table 3.2   (continued)

	Chile and Mexico sign free trade accord. All nontariff barriers to be eliminated. Common tariff of 10 percent to apply to 95 percent of trade as of January 1992. Tariff to be reduced to 0 over 4 years.
	Turkey and EFTA sign a free trade agreement to go into force Janaury 1992. EFTA to eliminate duties on imports of industrial goods (excluding textiles) and processed farm products.
	EC and EFTA finalize EEA to go into effect in 1993.
	ASEAN Free Trade Agreement (AFTA) formed. Group agrees to 15-year period in which to create a single ASEAN market.
	EFTA signs trade cooperation accords with Bulgaria, Romania, and three Baltic states.
	EC signs association accords with Poland, Hungary, and Czechoslovakia. Agreements to result in free trade within 10 years.
1992	El Salvador, Guatemala, and Honduras agree to form a free trade zone. The countries agree to allow unrestricted movement of most goods and capital, and work toward establishing uniform tariffs on imports.
	NAFTA (U.S.-Mexico-Canada) negotiations concluded. Agreement provides for the elimination of tariffs in stages over a period of no more than 15 years, and in 10 years in some cases, including a phase-out of tariffs on textiles and apparel. Side agreements later negotiated on labor and environment. The agreement goes into effect 1 January 1994.
	Implementation of EEA (due to go into effect 1 January 1993) delayed when Switzerland voted against joining.
	Poland, Hungary, Slovakia, and the Czech Republic establish a regional trade zone. Aim is to gradually eliminate tariffs over next 17 years and become more compatible with the EC and EFTA.
1993	Hungary and EFTA conclude a free trade agreement. Extends free trade in a range of goods, including processed agricultural goods, industrial goods, and fish.
	Bulgaria and EFTA conclude free trade agreement. Extends free trade in industrial goods, processed farm goods, and fish products.
	Chile and Venezuela sign a free trade agreement. Import tariffs expected to be eliminated on 90 percent of products by 1997.
	Chile and Bolivia sign a bilateral agreement to reduce tariffs.
	South Asian Preferential Trading Agreement established with the aim of forming a common market between Bangladesh, Bhutan, India, Maldives, Nepal, Pakistan, and Sri Lanka.
	Nicaragua, Honduras, El Salvador, and Guatemala reach an agreement to liberalize trade. Barriers to trade in textiles, shoes, and leather goods will be reduced.
	Group of Three (Mexico, Venezuela, and Colombia) sign a free trade agreement to go into effect June 1994. Agreement covers market access, rules of origin, investment, government procurement, and intellectual property.
	Chile and Colombia sign a free trade agreement. Most nontariff barriers eliminated and tariffs reduced.
	Guatemala, Honduras, El Salvador, Nicaragua, Costa Rica, and Panama sign an agreement toward freer trade and increased integration.
	Turkey and the EC negotiate a timetable leading to CU between Turkey and the EC by 1995.

Table 3.2	(continued)

1994	EEA comes into effect, creating an FTA between the EU (EC) and the EFTA countries of Austria, Finland, Norway, Sweden, and Iceland.
	Sweden, Finland, Austria, and Norway negotiate full membership in the EU.
	Mexico and Costa Rica conclude a free trade agreement to go into effect January 1995. Tariffs and most nontariff barriers to be eliminated. Provisions included on national treatment for investment, intellectual property rights, labor mobility, and dispute settlement.
	Andean Pact members agree to a common external tariff. Four-tier tariff to go into effect January 1995.
	Colombia and Caricom conclude a free trade agreement to go into effect January 1995. Colombia to gradually reduce tariffs on Caricom products over 3-year period; Caricom to take 5 years.
	Mercosur members reach a compromise agreement on a common tariff structure allowing CUs to become effective January 1995.
	APEC members agree to accelerate the liberalization of trade and investment measures within the group. Members will begin liberalizing tariff and other barriers in 2000 and developed-country members will achieve an open market by 2010. The developing countries will have until 2020 to complete their liberalization. APEC consists of Australia, Brunei Darussalam, Canada, Chile, Hong Kong, Indonesia, Japan, Malaysia, Mexico, New Zealand, Papua New Guinea, People's Republic of China, Philippines, Singapore, S. Korea, Taiwan, Thailand, and U.S.
	Chile formally invited to begin negotiations to join NAFTA. At the Summit of the Americas held in Miami (9–11 December) the 34 countries located in North, Central, and South America, and the Caribbean jointly agree to negotiate an FTA of the Americas by the year 2005.
1995	The EU and Turkey agree on a CU accord. Tariffs will be eliminated and a common tariff established on products from outside the CU. Some EU agriculture restrictions will still apply to Turkish exports. The CU goes into effect 1 January 1996.
	Chile begins negotiating with the members of NAFTA (Mexico, Canada, and the U.S.). Negotiations are expected to be completed by end of 1995.
	Estonia, Lithuania, and Latvia sign association agreements with the EU. The agreements provide trade and cooperation deals and possible future EU membership.
	Vietnam joins ASEAN and is given longer implementation periods to fulfill ASEAN liberalization timetables.

Source: Hamilton and Whalley 1996, table 6.1.

plex sectoral arrangements in autos and textiles; while European arrangements instead have much more extensive sectoral arrangements in agriculture and steel, interregional resource transfers through social and regional funds, free labor mobility provisions, and other provisions not found in North American trade agreements.

It is also clear that these regional agreements embody much more than discriminatory trade-barrier reduction as it is common to represent them in the

Table 3.3   **Differences among Selected Regional Trade Arrangements between Developing Countries**

	CACM	ASEAN	LAFTA/ LAIA	Andean Pact	ECOWAS	PTA	GCC
Tariff elimination	0	0	0	0	0	0	0
Nontariff elimination	0	0		0	0	0	
Positive list		0			0	0	
Negative list				0			
Rules of origin		0			0	0	0
Common external tariff	0			0	0		0
Special timetable for liberalization	0			0	0	0	0
Free trade in services							0
Free movement of labor					0		0
Free movement of capital					0	0	0
Promotion of industrialization	0	0	0	0	0	0	0
Compensation fund					0	0	0
Promotion of other trade objectives		0		0	0		
Accompanying payments arrangement	0		0		0		

Source: De La Torre and Kelley 1992.

Notes: CACM denotes the Central American Common Market; ASEAN, the Association of Southeast Asian Nations; LAFTA/LAIA, Latin American Free Trade Area; ECOWAS, the Economic Community of West African States; PTA, the Preferential Trade Agreement in Eastern and South Africa; and GCC, the Gulf Cooperation Council.

literature, whether in explicit tariff form or in the form of ad valorem equivalents. Factor mobility as well as goods mobility is involved to some degree in more agreements. Moves toward harmonized regulatory arrangements are at issue in financial services, transportation, and other service sectors. And in moving ahead of the GATT/WTO into such areas as environment and labor standards, agreements such as NAFTA have moved into areas where there is an explicit linkage drawn between trade and nontrade objectives, with trade policy potentially becoming the policeman to be used to achieve nontrade objectives. The diversity in regional arrangements therefore also implies that analyzing them simply as preferential reductions in ad valorem equivalent trade barriers can be potentially misleading.

3.3   Country Objectives Underlying Regional Trade Agreements

These differences in content and form among regional trade agreements, in large part, reflect sharp differences in the objectives of the countries seeking them. Hence the rationale for the paper: why do countries seek regional trade agreements?

In some cases, there are multiple country negotiating objectives that drive participation in regional trade agreements; in other cases, one or two objectives tend to be dominant. It is also the case that objectives frequently reflect only the interests of narrower subgroups within countries, rather than a wider country interest, as with sectoral arrangements in textiles, agriculture, autos, or other areas perceived to be politically sensitive. Nonetheless, once the reasons that countries seek these arrangements are understood, the form that the eventual agreement takes becomes more explicable.

3.3.1   Traditional Trade Gains

Perhaps the most conventional objective thought to underlie a country's participation in any trade negotiation is the idea that through reciprocal exchanges of concessions on trade barriers there will be improvements in market access from which all parties to the negotiation will benefit. The reasons for participating in a regional negotiation rather than any other type, including multilateral, are usually that key trading partners are involved, that the chances of success are seen as high because the number of countries is small, or there has been a prior history of frustration with negotiating failures at the multilateral level.[3] In reality, however, and as is well known from the research literature on regional trade arrangements, gains may not accrue to countries forming a CU since trade may also be diverted to higher-cost suppliers within the integrating area (Viner 1950); that is, trade-diversion losses may outweigh trade-creating gains.

Despite this, this idea of trade gains from regional integration was the key economic objectives behind the creation of the EC in the late 1950s, although probably not the central objective, which, as discussed below, was strategic. The notion that gains follow from increased regional trade has also motivated much of the postwar support for other regional trade agreements, which has in turn stimulated extensive literature on the effects of CUs and FTAs.

3.3.2   Strengthening Domestic Policy Reform

Yet another objective countries have in seeking regional trade agreements is the idea that a regional trade treaty can underpin domestic policy reform and make it more secure; that is, by binding the country to the masthead of an international trade treaty, any future reversal of domestic policy reform becomes more difficult to implement.

In reality, this can be an objective in either bilateral or multilateral negotiation and need not be an objective solely for regional trade agreements. However, this was a central preoccupation behind the Mexican negotiating position on NAFTA. As such, it led to the outcome that Mexican negotiators were less concerned to secure an exchange of concessions between them and their nego-

---

3. These were all key factors in Canada's decision to pursue bilateral negotiations with the United States in the mid-1980s, but prior to this the argument had been that the security of multilateral disciplines were needed around any bilateral arrangement with such a dominant trading partner to ensure the enforcement.

tiating partners, and were more concerned to make unilateral concessions to larger negotiating partners with whom they had little negotiating leverage as part of the bilateral negotiation. The idea was clearly to help lock in domestic policy reform through this process.

Pursuit of this objective by one of the parties to a negotiation, however, makes it likely that the concessions made by the parties in the negotiation are asymmetric (as was the case in the NAFTA negotiation and in the Canada-U.S. negotiations).[4] The relative size of the countries involved in both of the North American negotiations meant that the negotiating outcome was one-sided, especially in the NAFTA negotiation, since one of the parties was, in effect, using a negotiation on a regional trade agreement for nontrade purposes.

3.3.3   Increased Multilateral Bargaining Power

A further objective for countries that adopt regional trade agreements is to increase their bargaining power with third countries by negotiating an agreement with common external barriers (i.e., through a CU rather than a FTA). This idea was shared by the countries involved in the formation of the EC in the late 1950s. At the time, the notion was that individually European countries might have limited leverage in a negotiation with the United States, including multilaterally, but if all the European countries acted cooperatively in using a common trade policy, they would increase their leverage.

Indeed, one argument sometimes heard is that it was the creation of the EC that propelled GATT negotiations, first in the Dillon Round (1959–61), then in the Kennedy Round (1963–67), and subsequently in the Tokyo Round (1973–79). These rounds were initiated by the United States, who sought to deal with issues of access to a unified European market with individual European countries adopting common external (third-country) barriers. This objective of increasing negotiating power has also been present in some of the Latin American arrangements (such as Mercosur) where the argument has been that groups of countries will have more leverage in accession negotiations to NAFTA than will individual countries. Similar arguments were also made in Eastern Europe after 1989, where it was argued that a prior regional negotiation between Hungary, Poland, and Czechoslovakia (as it then was) would give increased combined leverage to these countries in EC accession negotiations.

3.3.4   Guarantees of Access

An objective present in recent large-small country trade negotiations, beginning with the Canada-U.S. agreement, is to use a regional trade agreement to make access to the larger country market in the region more secure for the smaller country. In the Canada-U.S. case, the Canadian aim was to achieve a regional trade agreement that gave Canadians some degree of exemption from the use of anti-dumping and countervailing duties by the U.S. producers. They

---

4. See also the discussion of NAFTA and CUSTA in Whalley (1993).

also sought special bilateral arrangements that would limit the application of U.S. safeguard measures to Canada (a form of escape from most-favored nation [MFN]).

These arrangements were secured by implicit side payments in the form of domestic policy disciplines undertaken by Canada and favorable to the United States. Special bilateral policy disciplines were agreed to as part of the trade agreement on energy and investment policies, which effectively prevented the return in Canada to older policies adverse to the United States under the Canadian Energy Policy and the former Canadian Foreign Investment Review Agency. Canada also made changes in pharmaceutical protection laws parallel to the trade agreement, and limited special Canadian protection for wine and beer. This idea of achieving access guarantee objectives for the smaller country in a regional trade agreement was also there in the Mexican case, with investment and energy provisions in the agreement, different from but related to those present in the Canadian case; although this was probably a less significant objective than that of underpinning domestic policy reform.

3.3.5   Strategic Linkage

A further country objective in negotiating regional trade agreements is that such agreements can help underpin security arrangements among the integrating countries, a central theme in early European integration in the 1950s. The idea was that a postwar regional trade agreement that produced enhanced trade flows between Germany and France would help prevent a fresh outbreak of European war, especially in light of Franco-Prussian relations between 1870 and 1945. As such, strategic linkage (helping prevent further European war) became the dominant consideration in the negotiation of European trade arrangements, overriding all other integration objectives because the issues at stake were so important.

This is also a key difference between European and recent North American trade agreements, in that strategic linkage is largely missing as a country objective in the latter group of regional arrangements. European integration has been able to move progressively toward ever deeper integration, because the political commitment to it is so strong, almost to the point of agreement to found a European federation to partially supersede arrangements between the individual nation-states in Europe. This is reflected in the fact that European integration provides for both an ongoing process of integration and an institutional framework to support ever deeper integration, including a European court structure. More recent North American economic integration, as reflected in NAFTA, stands, in contrast, as a series of one-off agreements, and provides no road map for ongoing and more extensive integration.

3.3.6   Multilateral and Regional Interplay

A final set of objectives that enters into country calculations of whether and or how to negotiate regional trade agreements involves the actual or potential use of regional agreements for tactical purposes by countries seeking to achieve their multilateral negotiating objectives. The opposite can also be true in that ongoing multilateral negotiations can be used to influence the outcome of regional negotiations, since multilateral negotiations create regional opportunities.

Hence, during the Uruguay Round, it was widely thought that it was to the U.S. advantage to have regional trade negotiations under way, so that in dealing with recalcitrant multilateral negotiating partners, the United States could threaten or actually play the bilateral card, and engage in active discussions with prospective regional partners. If multilateral partners were slow to react, initiation of regional negotiations would be the result.

In turn, it was also widely believed during the round that smaller countries consciously used multilateral and regional interplay as a way of improving their negotiating leverage in regional arrangements with the larger countries. Hence, Canada consciously offered the United States the possibility of negotiating regional arrangements in services, which was then an emerging issue in multilateral negotiation, with the idea that a prior regional agreement would give the United States more leverage in subsequently multilateralizing their preferred services agreement. The Canadian hope was that this could then enable Canada to obtain improvements elsewhere in the package of issues making up the regional agreement. In the Canada-U.S. negotiation (with the outcome also echoed in NAFTA), tactical interplay between regional and multilateral trade negotiations also provided a reason for a number of seemingly largely contentless chapters in the final agreement. These were offered for multilateral agenda-shaping purposes by the smaller country, and helping establish them in this way on the agenda for future multilateral negotiations was one of the benefits to the larger country.

3.4   Assessing the Importance of Country Objectives in Regional Trade Negotiations

Assessing the relative importance of the various objectives set for regional trade agreements by individual countries is difficult, since the quantitative orders of magnitude are often hard to pin down. They also clearly vary in importance from agreement to agreement, and from country to country. Table 3.4 sets out a schematic representation illustrating the importance of various objectives for particular agreements, denoting them as strong or weak objectives. This table largely summarizes the discussion in the earlier section but usefully illustrates the diversity in objectives involved.

To go beyond this, however, quantitative work is needed even if it is only to provide an assessment of the relative importance of some of these objectives. A calibrated general equilibrium model of world trade and protection, on which I have recently worked jointly with Carlo Perroni (Perroni and Whalley 1994) provides some insights as to the considerations involved in a number of these cases, indicating where large or small effects are at stake, and offering an as-

Table 3.4   **Assessing the Importance of Country Objectives for Particular Regional Agreements**

Country Objectives	Regional Trade Agreement			
	EC	NAFTA	Canada-U.S.	Mercosur
Traditional trade gains	W			W
Strengthening domestic policy reform		S (Mexico)		
Increased multilateral bargaining power	W			W (Bargaining power in NAFTA)
Access guarantees		W	S (Canada)	
Strategic linkage	S			
Multilateral and regional interplay		W (U.S.)	W (Canada, U.S.)	S

Notes: S = strong objective; *W =* weaker objectives.

sessment of the net effect, when two partially offsetting considerations are involved. These include the relative importance of access security versus trade-gain objectives for regional trade agreements, tactical considerations between regional and multilateral trade agreements, and sequencing issues as to who one negotiates with first, and other considerations.

This model has primarily been used to analyze the implications of recent regional arrangements between small and large countries, and principally the Canada-U.S. agreement, using an enlarged version of the Nash retaliatory tariff and trade structure first used by Johnson (1953–54), and Gorman (1957), and subsequently expanded on in Hamilton and Whalley (1983), Markusen and Wigle (1989), Kennan and Riezman (1990), and elsewhere. In the process, Perroni and I have been able to compute Nash equilibria in tariff rates in higher dimensional space than previous literature, with a more complex analytical structure and without the restriction to constant-elasticity, excess-demand forms used in some of the earlier literature.

The Perroni-Whalley model incorporates seven regions (United States, Canada, Mexico, Japan, the EC, other Western Europe [OWE], and a residual rest-of-the-world [ROW]) allowing it to capture some of the key regional trading arrangements currently operating in the global economy. It is calibrated to 1986 regional production, consumption, and interregion trade-flow data, and to literature-based trade elasticity estimates. Because of the large dimensionalities involved in computing Nash equilibria in the presence of multiple goods and regions, it is restricted to one produced good for each region—with importables in each region treated as qualitatively different across sources of supply (by exporting country). Preferences in each region are defined over the own good, and a composite of importables; with substitution among the import sources entering as part of the definition of the composite. This specification, in effect, amounts to a pure exchange economy, where trade offer curves are fully determined by endowments and preferences.

The model incorporates regional trade arrangements not only as barrier reductions, but also as mutually agreed constraints on retaliation. In the event that retaliation breaks out between regions in the model, regional trade agreements are assumed to hold. Using the model, if no retaliation is considered, incremental gains or losses to regions from any given agreement can be computed in the conventional way using the status quo as the reference point, assessing the incremental effects of regional barrier reductions. But relative to an unconstrained trade war, the introduction of such constraints produces a different set of gains and losses for the countries involved.[5] Smaller countries gain substantially, while larger countries suffer from the restraints on their retaliatory power.

Indeed, compensation in the form of other nontrade concessions by smaller to larger regions may be required for an agreement to proceed. Perroni and Whalley estimate the side payments involved using a two-stage game structure as described in Riezman (1985). In the first stage of this game, countries form coalitions; in the second stage of the game, Nash tariffs are determined. Riezman's framework, however, is extended by allowing for side payments within coalitions, and by introducing uncertainty in the first-stage bargaining game.

Nash tariff equilibria, whether constrained or unconstrained, are computed in the model by sequentially determining optimal tariff rates for each region, holding the other region's tariff rates constant. Each calculation in the sequence involves the computation of a global competitive equilibrium, with a search across the relevant equilibria for that which gives maximum regional utility. A lengthy computational procedure is thus involved.[6]

In this, all regions are assumed to play strategically in their tariff setting, with the exception of the ROW, which offers no strategic response. This assumption reflects the observation that trade policies in a large number of countries belonging to the ROW bloc are, in reality, not coordinated in any meaningful way, implying that the strategic power of each individual country in the ROW is negligible.[7] In the central-case version of the model, the objective of the tariff-setting authority in each region is welfare maximization for its representative consumer. For CUs, the tariff-setting authority is assumed to maximize a linear combination of the welfare levels of the representative consumers of its member countries, where the weights are proportional to benchmark GNP levels.[8]

5. The risk to smaller countries, in reality, is that their largest trading partner (the United States for Canada) may turn protectionist, more than the outbreak of a full global trade war.

6. The GAMS/MINOS (General Algebraic Modeling System) numerical optimization software (Brooke, Kendrick, and Meeraus 1988) is used.

7. This assumption is clearly a little strong, as the ROW includes a number of larger countries such as China, India, and Brazil, although their individual shares in total world trade are small.

8. Gatsios and Karp (1991) show that it may be optimal for smaller countries to fully delegate tariff setting to larger countries in a CU.

In those cases where two or more regions form an FTA or a CU, model computation of Nash equilibria takes place in the presence of additional constraints on each region's optimization problem. Regions within an FTA have tariffs on bilateral trade frozen at zero. For CUs, external barriers are identical for all members of the union, in addition to freezing bilateral tariffs. For simplicity, Perroni and Whalley also require that import duties set by all other regions against members of the union are uniform across exports originating from all members of the union.[9]

Model parameters are calibrated to 1986 output, trade flows, and protection data by region using the procedures described in Mansur and Whalley (1984). On the basis of surveyed elasticity studies supplemented by information on relative country size, a central case configuration of price and income elasticities is adopted. Perroni and Whalley perform sensitivity analyses around these by varying elasticities values, limited by the number of potential combinations of elasticity configurations that can be considered.[10]

The model described above has been used by Perroni and Whalley to compute a number of counterfactual equilibria to analyze the impact of regional trade agreements. These include Nash (postretaliation) equilibria where trade wars are unconstrained; cases where countries entering into an FTA or CU agree not to retaliate against each other; cases where trade wars occur with differing regional groupings; and, for the sake of comparison, cases where no trade wars occur, but regional agreements are implemented. As noted above, in all cases, the assumption is made that the ROW uses no retaliatory tariffs. This implies that retaliation is limited to six of the seven regions in the model.

Table 3.5 reports welfare results for a variety of regional trade agreements that constrain retaliation, with results for an unconstrained Nash tariff war reported in the first column. In the presence of a CUSTA, in which Canadian and U.S. tariffs remain bilaterally at zero, even in a trade war, large benefits accrue to Canada. This is because of both continued and preferential access to U.S. markets, which is ever more valuable as U.S. tariffs against other regions rise. Relative to an unconstrained trade war, shown in the first column of table 3.5, gains to the United States are converted to a loss, and the previous large loss to Canada is now converted to a small gain. This small gain reflects not only continued access to the U.S. market, but also the added feature that this access is preferential. As barriers rise progressively in the U.S. markets against other

9. They also assume that the ROW, which does not set its tariffs strategically, also conforms to this rule.

10. In model results, postretaliation Nash tariffs are directly related to import demand elasticities (hence, to export supply elasticities), with tariff levels increasing sharply as import demand elasticities approach unity (in absolute value). With the Armington treatment in preferences, two levels of substitution are involved: one between imports as a composite and domestically produced goods (which in the model is determined by import demand elasticities) and the other between imports of different origin (which in the model is determined by export demand elasticities). These two separate elasticities jointly determine import demand elasticities by import type with region and, at the same time, export supply elasticities in all regions.

Table 3.5 Perroni and Whalley's Calculations of Postretaliation Trade-War Equilibria under Retaliation-Constraining Regional Trade Arrangements (comparison to 1986 benchmark)

Region	Unconstrained Trade War[a]	Canada-U.S. FTA[b]	Canada-U.S. CU[c]	North American FTA[b]	North American CU[c]	Simultaneous[d] North American and European FTA[b]	Simultaneous[d] North American and European CU
	Hicksian Equivalent Variations (billions of U.S. dollars)						
U.S.	+52.5	−9.5	+22.1	−15.3	+18.6	−4.5	+19.6
Canada	−100.2	+5.1	+3.4	+1.2	+1.5	+13.6	−2.9
Mexico	−32.1	−19.9	−32.2	−0.3	+0.5	+4.6	−1.2
Japan	−73.9	−33.8	−73.7	−28.7	−73.6	−17.4	−76.7
EC	+128.4	+142.0	+119.4	+145.3	+116.6	+38.7	+87.3
OWE	−131.7	−119.7	−135.5	−118.1	−137.0	+42.3	+41.5
ROW	−1051.0	−879.1	−1082.5	−857.9	−1101.9	−461.7	−1330.0
World	−1208.1	−914.8	−1179.0	−873.9	−1175.2	−384.4	−1262.3
	Hicksian Equivalent Variations as a Percent of National Income						
U.S.	+1.2	−0.2	+0.5	+0.4	−0.4	−0.1	+0.5
Canada	−25.5	+1.3	+0.9	+0.3	+0.4	+3.5	−0.7
Mexico	−8.5	−5.2	−8.5	−0.07	+0.1	+1.2	−0.3
Japan	−5.2	−2.4	−5.2	−2.0	−5.2	−1.2	−5.4
EC	+3.7	+4.1	+3.4	+4.2	+3.4	+1.1	+2.5
OWE	−32.2	−29.2	−33.1	−28.9	−33.5	+10.3	+10.1
ROW	−10.6	−8.8	−10.9	−8.6	−11.1	−4.6	−13.4
World	−6.0	−4.5	−5.8	−4.3	−5.8	−1.9	−6.2

Source: Perroni and Whalley 1994.

[a]Unconstrained trade war involves all regions except ROW adopting optimal bilateral tariffs against each and all trading partners.

[b]In an FTA, tariffs are bilaterally zero among member countries, and remain so throughout any retaliatory trade war.

[c]In a CU, tariffs are bilaterally zero among member countries, remaining so throughout any retaliatory trade war, and a common external tariff is set strategically by the union against third countries.

[d]North America is United States, Canada, and Mexico; European implies EC plus OWE.

suppliers from Japan, the EC, and elsewhere, the value of trade preferences to Canada become progressively larger. Gains to the EC are higher in the event of a Canada-U.S. FTA than in the unconstrained trade war case, because a free trade agreement constrains retaliation by the United States, owing to the significantly lowered tariff that Canada applies to third-country markets in the event of a global trade war between Canada and the United States. This result is reversed if the United States and Canada form a CU rather than an FTA, since their retaliatory power against the EC is now enhanced (third column of table 3.5). In the CU case, bilateral tariffs are zero as in an FTA, but a common external tariff applies against third countries. A surprisingly large difference occurs in results for the United States with this change. There are significant benefits to the United States and reduced benefits to Canada. Positive benefits for the United States reflect the feature that, with a common external tariff, the United States can now induce Canada to follow a higher tariff, against third countries along with the United States. As a result, and as results in table 3.5 indicate, gains to the EC in a trade war are reduced. These results clearly suggest that a bilateral trade agreement between Canada and the United States would not occur were it not also accompanied by side payments, since it would represent a losing proposition for the United States compared to a full Nash equilibrium, while it would be a strongly gaining proposition for Canada. The form of Canada-U.S. regional agreement that has emerged as essentially safe-haven driven with side payments is thus consistent with these country objectives.

North American trilateral arrangements have similar effects to those of the bilateral Canadian and Mexican agreements, except that now the benefits of access are shared by Canada and Mexico, and benefits to the United States are lowered. Under a trade war in the presence of a North American FTA, the United States loses rather than gains as it would with a CU. Also, the United States gains less with a three-way CU than it would in a two-way union with either Canada or Mexico.

Welfare effects of simultaneous bloc enlargements occurring in Europe and in North America are reported in the final two columns of table 3.5.[11] The gains to the EC and the United States are significantly lower than in a full unconstrained trade war, the more so with FTAs than with regional CUs. The biggest loser is the ROW bloc, which loses even more than in the unconstrained case. Also, a trade war with the simultaneous formation of a North American and a European CU produces a larger negative aggregate welfare effect than an unconstrained trade war.[12]

Perroni and Whalley also report the welfare effects of alternative regional

---

11. The European trade arrangements considered here are more comprehensive than the current EC EFTA agreement, since the OWE bloc includes countries that do not belong to EFTA.

12. Kennan and Riezman (1990) also show that the formation of a CU in a strategic tariff setting has ambiguous welfare effects, whereas the formation of an FTA unambiguously improves world welfare.

arrangements in the absence of any strategic tariff setting. Generally speaking, the effects are small relative to a trade war. In most cases, participants in the regional arrangements all benefit, the more so with CUs than with FTAs. In a few cases where regional participants lose, this is a reflection of elasticity parameters and asymmetric initial protection levels. For the purpose of the discussion here, however, the small size of these welfare effects from regional agreements emphasizes the dominance of access guarantee objectives for these agreements from a smaller-country point of view over conventional barrier reduction.

Perroni and Whalley also provide details as to the model outcome of a Nash tariff war with no prior regional agreement constraining retaliation. Postretaliation Nash tariffs are extremely high, and the more so the larger the country. These results correspond with the widespread intuition that an all-out global trade war would be extremely destructive of trade, and yield large shocks to individual economies. Thus, in the case of the EC, tariffs in the range of 900 to 1000 percent are generated by the model, with rates around 500 percent in the case of the United States,[13] the difference between these two reflecting the relative importance of trade to GDP in these countries. Smaller estimates are obtained for Mexico and Canada, which have less retaliatory power than the EC, and the United States, and Japan. These high postretaliation tariffs are in part a reflection of the elasticity values used in the central case specification of the model,[14] which, while literature-based, are still on the low side. Associated impacts on trade flows in the Nash tariff equilibrium show large reductions in particular bilateral trade linkages, such as between Canada, and the United States, where high retaliatory tariffs occur in the larger country.

Results also suggest that large countries benefit substantially from unconstrained retaliation. Large countries thus have more strategic leverage than small countries in regional trade negotiations, and small countries experience sharp reductions in bilateral trade flows with their largest trading partners (Canada, Mexico with the United States, and OWE with the EC). Thus, smaller countries lose from an all-out trade war, and in the case of Canada and OWE, these losses are large, in the region of 25 percent of national income.

These results thus underscore the proposition that it is the threat of global trade war in which small countries are excluded from access to large-country markets that propels the smaller countries into regional trade negotiations with the larger countries. In other words, on quantitative grounds it is sensible that a key objective of smaller countries in regional negotiations should be the qual-

---

13. In some cases such high tariff rates effectively amount to prohibitive import barriers, resulting in reductions in trade flows of almost 100 percent, although, with internationally differentiated products in the model trade, flows never becomes zero.

14. The U.S.-Canada Nash tariffs computed by Markusen and Wigle (1989) are much smaller then the ones here. This model, however, is calibrated to demand and supply elasticities, and not directly to literature estimates of trade elasticities.

Table 3.6   **Perroni and Whalley's Estimates of the Welfare Effects of Sequential Entry into North American Regional Trade Agreement, Central Case Elasticity Model ($\pi_w = 0.5$, $\rho = 1.3$)**

Sequence	Expected Utilities		
	U.S.	Canada	Mexico
Free trade area			
U.S.-Canada, U.S.-Canada-Mexico	1.015	0.883	0.977
U.S.-Mexico, U.S.-Canada-Mexico	1.013	0.889	0.987
U.S.-Canada-Mexico	1.014	0.873	0.994
Customs unions			
U.S.-Canada, U.S.-Canada-Mexico	1.018	0.917	0.971
U.S.-Mexico, U.S.-Canada-Mexico	1.017	0.872	1.018
U.S.-Canada-Mexico	1.016	0.894	1.009

Source: Perroni and Whalley 1994.

Notes: π_w = subjective probability of a trade war occurring. ρ = coefficient of relative risk aversion.

ity and reliability of access rather than primarily improvement in amounts of access.

Results reported in table 3.6 relate to a different set of country objectives: tactical issues involving sequential formation of regional agreements. Here, model results evaluate the desirability, or otherwise, of first negotiating with a large country, or allowing the others to negotiate, and then joining the regional agreement later, the issue of interplay between localized and wider trade negotiations.[15] For the CU case, model results suggest that there are substantial gains for both Canada and Mexico in being first in entering into an agreement with the United States. This is because the exclusion from the initial regional grouping increases the bargaining power of the larger group, and thus makes it more costly to enter later.

For the FTA case, there are benefits to Canada from following Mexico in the arrangement. This is because, as the results in table 3.6 show, the first entry of Canada into an FTA with the United States would entail a substantial loss for the United States; the side payment requested by the United States for a first entry by Canada would be accordingly large. By delaying entry, Canada can thus lower the cost of its admission into a North American FTA.

This result is opposite to that which is now frequently ascribed to NAFTA, which is thought to have detrimental effects on sequential entrants because of their limited ability to obtain new benefits, since their entry merely reapportions gains that have already accrued to other trading partners. The opposite

15. Perroni and Whalley (1994) first compute the Nash bargaining solution for the first-stage bilateral arrangement (assuming myopic behavior in the first-stage bargaining game) and use this outcome to define the disagreement point for the second-stage trilateral bargaining game.

result for Mexico in this case is a reflection of the relative sizes of Canada and Mexico, and of the consequent reduced impact of a Mexico-U.S. free trade agreement in the retaliatory power of the United States.

In both the FTA and CU cases, the United States is better off by negotiating sequentially with its smaller partners than by engaging in a single three-country trade negotiation. This result also serves to emphasize the dynamic instability of a regime in which large countries turn away from multilateralism, raising the risk of trade wars, increasing the size of the side payments they can extract, and further raising the incentives for a weakened commitment to multilateralism.

Like all analytical structures, this has limits in its application to the issues at hand. It gives no guide to the importance of strategic objectives in regional trade agreements, nor is it able to analyze the security offered to domestic policy reform. Nonetheless, its results do emphasize how particular country objectives in particular cases can be dominant (access guarantees for Canada in the Canada-U.S. agreement); and how, if the main objectives set for individual agreements are not kept firmly in mind, analyses of the impacts of agreements can be misleading.

3.5   Concluding Remarks

This paper stresses the need to recognize the varied objectives countries set for their involvement in regional trade agreements when evaluating the impacts of any particular agreement. It emphasizes how different regional trade arrangements are around the globe, reflecting the range of objectives that take countries into negotiations on these arrangements. Among those identified are the use of regional trade agreements to underpin domestic policy reforms (Mexico in NAFTA); the desire to achieve firmer market access with large trading partners (Canada in CUSTA); the link between trade agreements and strengthened security arrangements (EU); the use of agreements to strengthen collective bargaining power in multilateral trade negotiations (EU); the use of regional negotiations as a threat to driving multilateral negotiations forward (the United States in CUSTA, NAFTA). The paper closes by reporting previous model-based results that suggest that some objectives seem to quantitatively dominate others for particular agreements.

References

Anderson, K., and R. Blackhurst, eds. 1993. *Regional Integration and the Global Trading System.* Hemel Hempstead, England: Harvester Wheatsheaf.
Brooke, A., D. Kendrick, and A. Meeraus. 1988. *GAMS: A User's Guide.* Danvers, MA: Scientific Press.

De La Torre, A., and M. R. Kelley. 1992. Regional Trade Agreements. Occasional Paper no. 93. Washington, DC: International Monetary Fund.

de Melo, J., and A. Panagariya, eds. 1993. *The New Regionalism in Trade Policy.* Washington, DC: World Bank.

Gatsios, K., and I. Karp. 1991. Delegation Games in Customs Unions. *Review of Economic Studies* 58:391–97.

Gorman, W. M. 1957. Tariffs, Retaliation, and the Elasticity of Demand for Imports. *Review of Economic Studies* 25:133–62.

Hamilton, B., and J. Whalley. 1983. Optimal Tariff Calculations in Alternative Trade Models and Some Possible Implications for Current World Trading Arrangements. *Journal of International Economics* 15:323–48.

Hamilton, C., and J. Whalley. 1996. *The World Trading System after the Uruguay Round.* Washington, DC: Institute for International Economics.

Haveman, J. D. 1992. Some Welfare Effects of Dynamic Customs Union Formation. Mimeo.

Johnson, H. G. 1953–54. Optimum Tariffs and Retaliation. *Review of Economic Studies* 21:142–63.

Kennan, J., and R. Riezman. 1990. Optimal Tariff Equilibria with Customs Unions. *Canadian Journal of Economics* 23:70–83.

Krugman, P. R. 1991. Is Bilateralism Bad? In E. Helpman and A. Razin, eds., *International Trade and Trade Policy.* Cambridge: MIT Press.

———. 1993. Regionalism versus Multilateralism: Analytical Notes. In J. de Melo and A. Panagariya, eds., *New Dimensions in Regional Integration.* Cambridge: Cambridge University Press.

Mansur, A. H., and J. Whalley. 1984. Numerical Specifications of Applied General Equilibrium Models: Estimation, Calibration, and Data. In H. E. Scarf and J. B. Shoven, eds., *Applied General Equilibrium Analysis.* Cambridge: Cambridge University Press.

Markusen, J. R., and R. M. Wigle. 1989. Nash Equilibrium for the United States and Canada: The Roles of Country Size, Scale Economics, and Capital Mobility. *Journal of Political Economy* 97:368–86.

Perroni, Carlo, and John Whalley. 1994. The New Regionalism: Trade Liberalization or Insurance? NBER Working Paper no. 4626. Cambridge, MA: National Bureau of Economic Research, January.

Riezman, R. 1985. Customs Unions and the Core. *Journal of International Economics* 19:355–65.

Schott, J. J. 1989. *Free Trade Areas and the U.S. Trade Policy.* Washington, DC: Institute for International Economics.

Stoeckel, A., D. Pearce, and G. Banks. 1990. *Western Trade Blocs: Game, Set, or Match for Asia-Pacific and the World Economy.* Canberra: Centre for International Economics.

UN Conference on Trade and Development (UNCTAD). 1987. *Guidebook for the GSTP: The Global System of Trade Preferences among Developing Countries: Origins, Dimensions, Negotiations, and Prospects.* New York: UN Conference on Trade and Development.

Viner, J. 1950. *The Customs Union Issue.* Lancaster, PA: Carnegie Endowment for International Peace.

Whalley, J. 1993. Regional Trade Arrangements in North America: CUSTA and NAFTA. In J. de Melo and A. Panagariya, eds., *New Dimensions in Regional Integration,* 352–82. Washington, DC: World Bank.

World Trade Organization. Secretariat. 1995. *Regionalism and the World Trading System.* Geneva: World Trade Organization.

Comment   Eric W. Bond

John Whalley's paper provides a very nice survey of the different reasons why countries enter regional trading arrangements. These include the traditional welfare gains from preferential tariff reductions, the market-power benefits of forming a larger unit for tariff setting and bargaining, and strategic/political benefits from integrating markets and committing to preferential arrangements. Some of these reasons, such as the static welfare gains, have been extensively studied theoretically and empirically. Other reasons, such as the political and strategic benefits, are exceedingly difficult to quantify. Whalley points out that these differences in objectives are reflected in the heterogeneity in coverage of existing regional arrangements.

The novel aspect of the paper is his emphasis on the attempt by small countries to use a regional trade agreement to ensure market access to a large-country market, and his attempt to quantify the magnitude of these gains. The Canada-U.S. Free Trade Agreement is the prototype for this type of regional arrangement, because one of Canada's primary negotiating objectives was to obtain exemption from U.S. anti-dumping and countervailing duty actions. Since these types of administrative actions account for a major portion of trade barriers in industrialized countries currently, the benefits from this type of market assurance may in many cases dominate any benefits obtained from reductions in tariff rates.

Whalley then uses a computable general equilibrium model to argue that the benefits from this form of market assurance may in fact be quite large. These gains stand in stark contrast to the static welfare effects of preferential arrangements, which typically yield very small numbers. The benefits that he calculates are based on the use of a regional trade arrangement as insurance against a global trade war. The simulation model assumes that there are two states of the world: normal trade relations in which GATT-negotiated tariffs apply and a trade war in which each country sets its optimal tariff. The simulations suggest that the small countries experience fairly significant losses during the trade war, because of their lack of market power, while some of the large countries actually gain. The formation of a regional trade agreement is assumed to commit the members to zero tariffs on intraunion trade in the event of a trade war. The small country obtains a higher payoff in the trade war when it is part of a regional agreement, because it obtains better terms of trade in dealing with the large country. Whalley's argument is that the small country should be willing to make transfers to the large country to receive this "insurance" against a trade war, and that the apparent willingness of small countries to make concessions to obtain regional agreements is evidence of the payment of this insurance premium.[1] Perroni and Whalley (1994) report explicit calculations of the side payments for this model, where the formation of a regional trading ar-

Eric W. Bond is professor of economics at Pennsylvania State University.

1. Of course, the existence of transfers could merely reflect the superior threat point of the large country due to its market power. If the large country is better off in a trade war with the small

rangement is derived from a two-stage game in which countries negotiate side payments in the first stage.

I have two reservations about this approach to capturing the benefits of market assurance. First, I don't think that the reason that Canada is worried about administered protection in the U.S. market is because of the possibility of a global trade war. A global trade war would result from a complete breakdown of multilateral trade agreements. Once these agreements break down, I see no reason why countries would limit themselves to "safeguards" type of protection. I would expect the trade war to be carried on through raising of tariff rates generally, so that insurance against the use of anti-dumping duties and safeguard actions per se would be of limited value. I find it more plausible to think of administered protection as arising from political pressure from special interests in the large-country market, with new protectionist measures coming from sector-specific shocks that lead to an increase in pressure for protection.

Ideally a trade agreement between countries would be a complete contract that would specify the tariff rates and/or transfers between countries for all possible realization of these shocks.[2] Of course, such a contract would be costly to write because of the extremely large number of potential states. Here some of the insights from the literature on long-term contracting may be useful. In practice, parties to long-term contractual relationships do not fully specify all the terms of a contract, but instead include a negotiation process that will deal with circumstances that arise in the future. This introduces some flexibility into the process, while trying to minimize opportunism by the parties (Williamson 1979). I think that the dispute settlement procedures that were finally incorporated in the Canada-U.S. Free Trade Agreement can be interpreted as being part of a negotiation process in a long-term contractual relationship. This contractual approach to the bilateral trade agreement is similar in spirit to the Whalley argument, in the sense that it results from an attempt to complete a missing market or missing elements in global trade agreements. However, an attempt to quantify the gains from this type of approach would proceed quite differently.

The second point concerns the way in which the "insurance" benefits of regional arrangements are calculated in the computable general equilibrium model. In the event of a trade war, table 3.5 indicates that the United States has a gain of US$52.5 billion and Canada has a loss of US$100.2 billion, yielding a net loss of $47.7 billion to the two countries in the trade-war state. An optimal insurance contract between the two (risk-averse) countries would involve a net transfer from the United States to Canada in the trade war, whose magnitude would depend on the countries' respective income levels and risk aversion. This could then be used to derive the benefits of this insurance agreement for

---

country than under free trade with that country, the small country must make transfers to the large country to induce it to sign a free trade agreement. Kowalczyk and Sjöström (1994) illustrate how side payments can be used to facilitate international negotiations.

2. For example, Feenstra and Lewis (1991) model such a contract when the realization of the shocks is private information of one of the countries.

each country. One problem with this calculation is that the Nash equilibrium tariffs calculated for the trade war strike me as implausibly large—the Smoot-Hawley tariffs look tiny compared with Nash equilibrium tariffs of 400–500 percent calculated for the United States. I suspect that the low elasticity assumptions that generate these tariffs bias upward the benefits from the calculation of the benefits of an optimal insurance contract. A second problem is that the calculation of the benefits from the formation of a preferential trading arrangement qua insurance contract will involve both insurance and market-power effects. A customs union between the United States and Canada results in the two countries' obtaining a net gain of US$25.5 billion in the trade-war state. The additional market power obtained by the two countries when they are setting external tariffs jointly results in a net gain to the two countries in the trade-war state, so that the customs union would clearly be desirable for the two countries even if the two countries were risk neutral (or had an optimal insurance contract in place). A free trade agreement provides similar, although smaller, net gains to the two countries in the trade-war state.

Another question that is of importance to the trade war/insurance argument is why the trade war results in a breakdown of multilateral trade agreements, but not of regional agreements. Implicit in this argument is a greater degree of commitment power on the part of countries in regional trade agreements, which allows them to write binding contracts to free intraregional trade.[3] This seems a reasonable assumption for the European Union and the Canada-U.S. agreement. Given the number of examples of unsuccessful regional agreements, however, I would argue that GATT has had a more successful and enduring impact on trade relations than the median regional agreement. Thus, the potential for new regional agreements with the ability to commit to insure against trade wars may be relatively limited. The source of this ability to commit, which may be related to some of the strategic and political reasons cited by Whalley, is an area worthy of further analysis.

In summary, the variety of motives that lead countries to form regional agreements suggests that evaluation of whether the move toward more regionalism is a good thing requires a greater understanding of the implications of these various explanations. Perroni and Whalley's market assurance idea is an intriguing explanation of the role of regional agreements, and I think that this paper makes a useful first step in developing a formal model of this notion.

---

3. This asymmetry between commitment power is emphasized in Bagwell and Staiger (1997), Bond and Syropoulos (1995), and Bond, Syropoulos, and Winters (1995). In these papers, countries are assumed to be able to write binding agreements with regional trading partners, but not with nonmember countries. Multilateral trade agreements are treated as a repeated game, in which the threat of a global trade war is used to support trade policies that are more liberal than those in the trade-war equilibrium. There is no insurance element to agreements in these models, because trade wars never occur. However, these models are capable of addressing how the formation of regional agreements affects the multilateral agreement. This issue is not addressed in the Perroni and Whalley approach, where the normal tariff rates and the probability of a trade war are taken as exogenously given.

References

Bagwell, Kyle, and Robert Staiger. 1997. Multilateral Tariff Cooperation during the Formation of Regional Free Trade Areas. *International Economic Review* 38:291–319.

Bond, Eric, and Costas Syropoulos. 1996. Trading Blocs and the Sustainability of Inter-Regional Cooperation. In M. Canzoneri, W. J. Ethier, and V. Grilli, eds., *The New Transatlantic Economy.* London: Cambridge University Press.

Bond, Eric, Costas Syropoulos, and Alan Winters. 1995. Deepening of Regional Integration and Multilateral Trade Agreements. Pennsylvania State University working paper.

Feenstra, Robert, and Tracy Lewis. 1991. Negotiated Trade Restrictions with Private Political Pressure. *Quarterly Journal of Economics* 106:1287–1307.

Kowalczyk, Carsten, and Tomas Sjöström. 1994. Bringing GATT into the Core. *Economica* 61:301–17.

Perroni, Carlo, and John Whalley. 1994. The New Regionalism: Trade Liberalization or Insurance? NBER Working Paper no. 4626. Cambridge, MA: National Bureau of Economic Research, January.

Williamson, Oliver. 1979. Transaction-Cost Economics: The Governance of Contractual Relations. *Journal of Law and Economics* 22:233–62.

Comment   Dani Rodrik

This is essentially two papers, one of which is a useful discussion and categorization of *reasons* countries choose to enter regional arrangements, and the other a summary of the author's earlier work with Perroni on a CGE model that focuses on one of these motives (insurance). I found the first paper to be extremely well done, and I have nothing to add to it. I will focus my comments on the second paper.

The insurance idea that forms the core of the analytics in this paper is quite appealing and plausible. The message is that countries want regional arrangements in no small part because they would like to buy insurance against *future* protection. The implication is that evaluating the gains from regional integration by taking as the relevant counterfactual the *current* situation will yield a serious underestimate. This is an important point.

How do we think about the insurance motive? Whalley proceeds as follows. First, he constructs a world CGE model of trade. Second, he simulates the Nash equilibrium tariffs under various assumptions about who enters into regional arrangements with whom. A key assumption here is that trade wars (i.e., a Nash equilibrium) occur only among blocs, not within groups of countries that have entered into a regional arrangement with each other. Countries within a bloc are assumed to always maintain zero tariffs vis-à-vis each other. Third,

Dani Rodrik is the Rafiq Hariri Professor of International Political Economy at Harvard University and a research associate of the National Bureau of Economic Research.

These comments refer to the version of the paper that was presented at the conference.

he compares the benchmark (1986) situation to these various outcomes, focusing on gains to being inside a regional arrangement during a global trade war.

One can list here the usual quibbles about CGE models. Since these are well known, I'd rather skip the quibbles and move on to my main reactions. My main methodological quarrel with the paper is that the setup cannot adequately deal with the question that motivates it. Since the theme is "insurance," one expects the framework to be about risk and uncertainty. But in fact, the model does not have uncertainty explicitly built into it, and therefore cannot address issues of risk and insurance. And for that reason, the model does not allow for a direct quantitative assessment of the importance of the insurance motive. My main substantive reaction is that, partly as a consequence, the paper probably overstates the quantitative significance of the insurance motive. Let me list here my three reasons for believing so, as these will also highlight the methodological issues.

First, the model generates Nash-equilibrium tariffs that are implausibly high: around 500 percent for the United States and 900 percent for the EU. These result in huge welfare losses for small countries that remain outside blocs. Canada, for example, loses a quarter of its GNP, and other Western Europe loses a third. What drives these results are two things: (1) the trade elasticities used in the model are low; and (2) governments are assumed to be driven only by the terms-of-trade motive when playing Nash. The latter assumption is commonplace in models of this sort, but is probably unrealistic. (Think, for example, of how governments often play the game of competitive devaluation, despite the associated terms-of-trade losses.) This is not to say that a global trade war of such proportions should be regarded as a zero-probability event. But surely it is a low-probability event, and the associated "insurance" gains have to be scaled down according to this low probability of occurrence.

Second, and leaving aside the question of what global trade war would entail, it is implausible to think that countries like Canada and Mexico really thought they were buying insurance against a truly global trade war. It is likely that they had a much more limited insurance motive: to prevent localized, product-specific surges in protectionism through safeguard or anti-dumping (AD) action in the United States. Indeed, the initial discussion in the paper on what type of insurance these countries were really after seems more accurate (and considerably more limited). Incidentally, one wonders whether there is any evidence that the insurance policy is paying back. For example, has U.S. trade action against Canada been reduced after 1992? In any case, the anticipated gains from this kind of insurance would be considerably smaller.

Third, the discussion does not take into account that the formation of regional arrangements may itself increase the likelihood of "trade wars." In other words, what is being insured against may well be a situation that becomes more likely as more countries buy insurance. For example, when Canada and Mexico insure themselves against AD action in the U.S. market, this probably increases the protectionist pressures felt by other exporting countries. It is because of this kind of spillover that the incentive to join a regional arrangement increases with the number of countries already in. This would suggest that there is a wedge between what may be individually rational for a country (go and buy insurance) and what is globally rational. Correspondingly, in equilibrium the value of insurance is likely to be lower (than anticipated) for all concerned.

Let me end with two facts that this paper made me aware of, which need further thought. First, with the exception of the Israel-U.S. Free Trade Agreement, all regional arrangements are indeed *regional,* that is, they involve geographically contiguous countries. That's why we use the term "regional integration" in the first place. But going back to Whalley's discussion of the reasons why countries join such arrangements, very few of the things that we normally focus on have any geographical content at all. I am not sure what the implication of this is, but it does suggest to me that our discussions often leave an important dimension out. Second, it appears that most GATT/WTO members are now members of at least one regional arrangement also. This is a striking fact. It suggests to me that governments clearly regard regional and multilateral approaches as complementary. So we should stop thinking of these as mutually exclusive choices.

4   Continental Trading Blocs: Are They Natural or Supernatural?

Jeffrey A. Frankel, Ernesto Stein, and Shang-Jin Wei

4.1 Introduction

The world trading system seems to be moving, not just to a system of regional free trade areas (FTAs) but to a system of large continental groupings. In Europe, the European Union (formerly the European Community) removed internal barriers in 1992 and admitted three new members in 1994, bringing the total to fifteen. In December 1994, the leaders of Western Hemisphere countries met in Miami and agreed to form an FTA for the Americas. In East Asia, despite a relative paucity of explicit preferential trading arrangements, one also hears of the emergence of an implicit Japan-centered trade bloc.

This paper seeks to investigate three questions. According to bilateral trade data, is the world indeed breaking up into a small number of continental trade blocs? In theory, is a small number of continental blocs good or bad for world welfare? The answer to the second question is that it depends on parameter values. Thus we also make an attempt to examine the following question:

Jeffrey A. Frankel is professor of economics at the University of California, Berkeley, and a research associate of the National Bureau of Economic Research, where he is also director of the program in International Finance and Macroeconomics. After this project was completed, he took leave to serve on the Council of Economic Advisers. Ernesto Stein is a research economist at the Inter-American Development Bank. Shang-Jin Wei is associate professor of public policy at the Kennedy School of Government, Harvard University, a faculty research fellow of the National Bureau of Economic Research, a research associate of the Center for Pacific Basin Monetary and Economic Studies of the Federal Reserve Bank of San Francisco, and a Davidson Institute Research Fellow at the University of Michigan Business School.

The authors thank Benjamin Chui and Jungshik Kim for research assistance, and Warwick McKibbin, Gary Saxonhouse, and Alan Winters for supplying data. They would also like to thank for support the Center for International and Development Economics Research, funded at University of California, Berkeley, by the Ford Foundation; the Japan–United States Friendship Commission, a U.S. government agency; and the Institute for International Economics. This paper was written while Frankel was a professor at Berkeley and research associate of the NBER; it does not represent the views of the U.S. government.

for actual parameter values, is the current pattern of regionalization welfare-promoting or welfare-reducing?

Paul Krugman has helped to focus the recent debate on the welfare implications of regional trade blocs. He has, however, supplied equally clever arguments on both sides. In his first contribution (Krugman 1991a), he argued that a small number of trade blocs tends to be welfare-reducing, relative to the case when every country charges a common tariff against all other countries. In the latter case, the distortions introduced relative to global free trade are relatively small. For plausible parameter values, three regional blocs turned out to be the worst outcome for the world. This is a worrisome conclusion since this is precisely the direction toward which many observers think the world is moving.

Krugman's second contribution (1991b) included a simple argument for a diametrically opposite conclusion. If transportation costs are very high between continents, then regional trade blocs, if they are formed along continental lines, must be welfare-improving. The intuition is simple. With prohibitively high intercontinental transport costs, trade takes place mainly among countries on the same continents even in the absence of trade blocs. Therefore, the case for regional blocs that eliminate tariffs among countries in the same continents ("natural blocs" in Krugman's terminology) is the same as the standard case for global free trade. Such natural blocs are contrasted with "unnatural blocs," free trade agreements between individual countries in different continents, which are less likely to be welfare-improving.[1]

Each of these two arguments is valid within its own assumptions. The first argument assumes zero transport cost. The second argument relies on a prohibitively high intercontinental transport cost. The world is somewhere between these two extremes. In order to investigate the welfare implication of the current pattern of trade regionalization, we develop a more general model that can handle intermediate cases. We identify conditions under which trade blocs are welfare-reducing, even when formed along continental lines.

With the more general model, we also investigate whether a particular aspect of article XXIV of General Agreement on Tariffs and Trade (GATT) is sensible. Under this rule, countries that want to form a regional trade bloc must eliminate all barriers among themselves. (There are other restrictions as well: the members must not raise barriers against nonmembers.) In our model, however, we find that partial liberalization within a regional bloc is generally better than 100 percent liberalization, in contrast to the article XXIV provision.

The welfare implication of continental blocs depends on the values of some crucial parameters. In the final part of the paper, we make an attempt—perhaps best described as illustrative—to extract estimates of the real-world counterparts of these key parameters, particularly the magnitude of transport costs.

---

1. It should be noted that the idea of proximity as a desideratum for successful FTAs, on the grounds that it would minimize the amount of trade diversion, was not entirely new with Krugman. (See Balassa 1987, 44; and Wonnacott and Lutz 1989). The leading opponent to the idea is Bhagwati (1993).

The resulting estimates suggest that the current pattern of trade blocs features a degree of regional preferences that is likely to exceed what can be justified on "natural" geographic grounds. We propose the term "supernatural" for blocs that reduce economic welfare in this way.

Most of our conclusions regarding economic welfare presume worldwide symmetry. We look at the consequences of a worldwide regime that allows continental FTAs to form everywhere, not at the consequences of forming a single FTA with trade policies in the rest of the world taken as given. Many other possible considerations, in addition to asymmetry, are omitted from the analysis as well. For example, we focus only on the static economic effects.

4.2   Are Continental Trade Blocs Forming?

It may appear obvious that world trade is increasingly regionalized. A popular statistic to look at is intraregional trade as a percentage of the region's total trade. Table 4.1 shows that intraregional trade shares increased during the 1980s in each of three major parts of the world: from 54 percent to 60 percent in Europe, from 23 percent to 29 percent in East Asia, and (less strikingly) from 27 percent to 29 percent in the Western Hemisphere.

Such statistics are ill-suited, however, for the purpose of examining the degree of regional bias in trade policy. There are many factors that may contribute to the spatial distribution of trade. First, neighboring countries tend to trade more with each other. Second, large countries tend to trade more, and faster-growing economies tend to increase their mutual trade volume at a faster pace. Hence, the observed increasing share of intra-Asia trade, for example, could be entirely due to the region's above-average growth rate, with no explicit or implicit trade bloc in formation. A more useful way to detect the effectiveness of an existing trade bloc is to see whether trade among a given group of countries is unusually high after controlling for factors that naturally contribute to the volume of trade.

4.2.1   The Gravity Model of Bilateral Trade

The natural empirical framework for studying bilateral trade is the gravity model, which offers a systematic way to measure what patterns of bilateral trade are normal around the world. The simplest specification says that trade between two countries is proportionate to the product of their GDPs and inversely related to the distance between them, by analogy to the formula for

Table 4.1   **Intraregional Trade Shares (%)**

	1965	1970	1975	1980	1985	1987	1990
East Asia	.199	.198	.212	.229	.256	.263	.293
Western Hemisphere	.315	.311	.309	.272	.310	.279	.286
Western Europe	.502	.532	.524	.538	.548	.601	.602

gravitational attraction between two bodies. A dummy variable can be added to represent when both countries in a given pair belong to the same regional grouping. We can then see how much of the trade within each region can be attributed to a special regional effect.

The gravity model has a fairly long history and fits the data remarkably well empirically, though its theoretical foundations have hitherto been considered limited.[2] Earlier work by Anderson (1979) and other papers surveyed by Deardorff (1984, 503–6) have provided a partial foundation for the approach. Specifically, the idea that bilateral trade depends on the product of GDPs can be justified by the modern theory of trade under imperfect competition, as shown in recent work by Helpman (1987) and Helpman and Krugman (1985, section 1.5).[3]

Some recent papers that apply the gravity model to trade-bloc issues (e.g., Frankel 1993 and Frankel and Wei 1994, which focus on East Asia, among others) are incapable of distinguishing between regional biases reflecting discriminatory trade policies, and those that might derive from historical, political, cultural, and linguistic ties. In this paper, we include terms representing pairs of countries that speak a common language or have other historical ties.

The dependent variable is trade (exports plus imports), in log form, between pairs of countries in a given year. Our data source is the United Nations trade matrix, which covers sixty-three countries in our data set, so that there are 1,953 data points ($= 63 \times 62/2$) for a given year. In the regressions reported here, we use data for 1970, 1980, and 1990.

A large part of the apparent bias toward intraregional trade is certainly due to simple geographical proximity. Krugman (1991b) and Summers (1991) opine that *most* of it may be due to proximity. (At the other extreme, Bhagwati [1993] and Panagariya [1995, 9–10] assert that very little of the apparent bias is due to proximity, emphasizing rather regional trade arrangements that are already in place.) Surprisingly, empirical studies often neglect to measure this factor. Our measure is the log of distance between the two major cities (usually the capitals) of the respective countries. We also add a dummy *ADJACENT* variable to indicate when two countries share a common land border.

The other of the most important factors in explaining bilateral trade flows is one that we have already identified as the essence of the gravity model: the

---

2. The results of one extensive early project along these lines were reported in Tinbergen (1962, appendix 6, pp. 262–93) and Linnemann (1966). Recent empirical studies include Bergstrand (1989), Wang and Winters (1991), and Hamilton and Winters (1992).

3. It has long been considered that the classical Heckscher-Ohlin theory of comparative advantage does not have this property. Deardorff (chap. 1 in this volume), however, now argues that the gravity relationship can also be derived from the Heckscher-Ohlin model as well as the imperfect substitutes model. The proportionality between trade and the product of GDPs is also a property of our theoretical model introduced in section 4.3. Frankel, Stein, and Wei (1995) includes a more detailed exposition of how our model offers improved foundations for the gravity model, in that the effects of both size and distance are derived.

economic size of the two countries. In addition to the well-established effect of size on trade, there is reason to believe that GDP per capita has a positive effect on trade, for a given size: as countries become more developed, they tend to specialize more and to trade more. Finally, *LANG* is the dummy variable reflecting a common language.

The equation to be estimated is thus

$$\log (Trade_{ij}) = \alpha + \beta_1 \log (GNP_i GNP_j) + \beta_2 \log (GNP/pop_i GNP/pop_j)$$
$$(1) \qquad + \beta_3 \log (DIST_{ij}) + \beta_4 (ADJACENT_{ij}) + \beta_5 (LANG_{ij})$$
$$+ \gamma_1 (EC_{ij}) + \gamma_2 (WH_{ij}) + \gamma_3 (EA_{ij}) + u_{ij}.$$

The last five explanatory factors are dummy variables. *EC*, *WH*, and *EA* are three of the dummy variables we use when testing the effects of membership in a common regional grouping, standing for European Community, Western Hemisphere, and East Asia, respectively. We will estimate average intraregional biases over 1970–90, and possible trend increases in the biases.

Table 4.2 reports pooled time-series-cross-section estimates of equation (1) that extend from 1970 to 1990. All gravity variables are highly significant statistically (>99 percent level). The coefficient on the log of distance is about −0.5, when the *ADJACENT* variable (which is also highly significant statistically) is included at the same time. This means that when the distance between two nonadjacent countries is higher by 1 percent, the trade between them falls by about 0.5 percent. We checked for possible nonlinearity in the log-distance term, as it could conceivably be the cause of any apparent bias toward intraregional trade that is left after controlling linearly for distance, but this did not seem to be an issue.[4] We should note that physical shipping costs may not be the most important component of costs associated with distance. What we call transport costs would better be understood as transactions costs, encompassing not just each physical transportation of goods, but also costs of communications and the idea that each country tends to have a better understanding of its close neighbors and their institutions.

The estimated coefficient on GNP per capita is 0.23, indicating that richer countries do trade more.[5] The estimated coefficient for the log of the product of the two countries' GNPs is about 0.7, indicating that, although trade increases with size, it increases less than proportionately (holding GNP per cap-

---

4. The log of distance appears to be sufficient; the level and square of distance add little. We have also tried distance measures that take into account the greater distances involved in sea voyages around obstacles like the Cape of Good Hope and Cape Horn (the data generously supplied by Wang and Winters), with little effect on the results.

5. We have also tried an estimate for 1991 using GNPs adjusted by purchasing power parity, in place of using exchange rates to translate GNPs. The coefficient on GNP/capita is 0.35, with little qualitative change in the estimates otherwise. (The sum of the coefficients on GNP and GNP/capita is about 1. Thus there is another, approximate way to describe the results: openness [as measured by trade/GNP] falls by 0.23 percent for every 1 percent increase in size [as measured by population].)

Table 4.2   **Gravity Estimation of Continental Trade Blocs (total trade 1970–90)**

Dependent Variable: log ($Trade_{ij}$)		
Intercept	−9.70*	−9.78*
	(0.27)	(0.27)
1980 dummy	−1.01*	−1.06*
	(0.05)	(0.05)
1990 dummy	−1.29*	−1.37*
	(0.06)	(0.06)
GNP	0.72*	0.73*
	(0.01)	(0.01)
Per capita GNP	0.23*	0.23*
	(0.01)	(0.01)
Distance	−0.51*	−0.51*
	(0.02)	(0.02)
Adjacency	0.72*	0.72*
	(0.10)	(0.09)
Common language	0.47*	0.47*
	(0.05)	(0.05)
EC bloc	0.31*	0.24*
	(0.06)	(0.09)
East Asia bloc	2.12*	2.26
	(0.09)	(0.18)
Western Hemisphere bloc	0.31*	−0.32*
	(0.08)	(0.10)
EC*Trend		0.006
		(0.006)
East Asia*Trend		−0.013
		(0.012)
Western Hemisphere*Trend		0.063*
		(0.009)
Observations	4555	4555
Standard error of regression	1.15	1.14
Adjusted R^2	0.76	0.76

Notes: Standard errors are in parentheses. All variables except the intercepts and dummy variables are in logs. Trend = Year − 1970.

*Significant at the 1% level.

ita constant). This presumably reflects the widely known pattern that small economies tend to be more open to international trade than larger, more diversified economies.

The linguistic dummy, *LANG,* represents pairs of countries that share a common language or had colonial links earlier in the century. We allowed for English, Spanish, Chinese, Arabic, French, German, Japanese, Dutch, and Portuguese. Two countries sharing linguistic/colonial links tend to trade roughly 60 percent more than they would otherwise (exp (0.47) = 1.60). We tested whether some of the major languages were more important than the others, and found little in the way of significant differences.

4.2.2 Estimation of Trade-Bloc Effects

If there were nothing to the notion of trading blocs, then the five basic variables in table 4.2 might soak up most of the explanatory power. There would be little left to attribute to a dummy variable representing whether two trading partners are both located in the same region. In this case the level and trend in intraregional trade would be due solely to the proximity of the countries, and to their rates of overall economic growth.

We found, however, that all three regional dummies are statistically significant. The coefficient for the EC dummy is 0.31. This means that over the period 1970–90, two EC countries traded 36 percent (exp (0.31) = 1.36) more than two otherwise similar countries. As is indicated by the EC–time-trend interactive term in the second column, the within-EC bias increases at the rate of about 0.6 percent a year, although this trend is not statistically significant. Averaged over time, the intra–Western Hemisphere trade bias is of the same order of magnitude as the EC. But it started out low in 1970 (in fact, negative), and increased over time at the rate of 6 percent a year. This relatively rapid trend increase is statistically significant. By 1990, two Western Hemisphere countries traded 150 percent more than two otherwise-similar countries (exp $[-0.323 + (20 \times 0.063)] = 2.55$). The East Asian grouping exhibits the highest intraregional bias. Intra–East Asian trade, however, once we have controlled for the gravity variables, shows no significant increase in bias over the period. If anything, this bias diminished over time, rather than rising, as often assumed.[6]

In table 4.3, we employ a dummy for all of Western Europe, instead of considering the EC bloc alone. The motivation is to treat the European continent on a par with the other two.[7] The intraregional bias for Western Europe is slightly smaller than that for the EC. The coefficients for other variables in the specification are essentially unchanged.

We have conducted more robustness checks in addition to those that have been mentioned earlier. Chapter 7 of this volume tests the effect of bilateral exchange rate variability on trade, and the effect of the degree of openness (more trade with all countries, as distinct from more trade just with other members of the grouping). Other extensions that we tried include allowing a role for differences in factor endowments as additional regressors, a correction for

6. In other words, the rapid growth of East Asian economies is in itself sufficient to explain the increase in the intraregional trade share evident in table 4.1. This finding, that intraregional trade bias in Asia did not rise in the 1980s as often assumed, confirms Frankel (1993), Petri (1993), Saxonhouse (1993), and Anderson and Norheim (1993).

7. Some readers are less interested in the effects of three continental blocs than of explicit FTAs, like the EC and NAFTA. The effects of such subregional blocs are estimated in Frankel, Stein, and Wei (1995). (The results suggest that regionalization in the Western Hemisphere during 1980–90 is concentrated in the Andean Pact and Mercosur groupings. The NAFTA grouping is not statistically significant in this sample period.)

Table 4.3   **Gravity Estimation, Western Europe instead of European Community (total trade 1970–90)**

Dependent Variable: log ($Trade_{ij}$)		
Intercept	−9.77*	−9.89*
	(0.28)	(0.28)
1980 dummy	−1.00*	−1.04*
	(0.05)	(0.05)
1990 dummy	−1.28*	−1.33*
	(0.06)	(0.06)
GNP	0.73*	0.73*
	(0.01)	(0.01)
Per capita GNP	0.22*	0.23*
	(0.01)	(0.01)
Distance	−0.50*	−0.50*
	(0.02)	(0.02)
Adjacency	0.72*	0.72*
	(0.10)	(0.09)
Common language	0.47*	0.48*
	(0.05)	(0.05)
Western Europe bloc	0.21*	0.35*
	(0.06)	(0.08)
East Asia bloc	2.12*	2.29*
	(0.09)	(0.19)
Western Hemisphere bloc	0.32*	−0.29*
	(0.09)	(0.10)
Western Europe*Trend		−0.015*
		(0.004)
East Asia*Trend		−0.015
		(0.012)
Western Hemisphere*Trend		0.061*
		(0.009)
Observations	4555	4555
Standard error of regression	1.15	1.14
Adjusted R^2	0.76	0.76

Notes: Standard errors are in parentheses. All variables except intercepts and dummy variables are in logs. Trend = Year − 1970.
*Significant at the 1% level.

heteroscedasticity related to the size of the countries (weighted least squares), and the inclusion of country pairs recorded with zero trade. The answers to the question of interest here, the estimates of the intraregional biases, are fairly robust to these variations.

The gravity model results thus show that, on average over 1970–90, the three regions did exhibit inward trade bias. The next question is whether these biases constitute an undesirable threat to the world trading system.

4.3   The Theory of Bilateral Trade with Imperfect Substitutes and Transport Costs

We now attempt to settle the Krugman versus Krugman controversy regarding the desirability of trading blocs. We construct in this section a more general model that can handle the intermediate realistic case where transport costs between continents are less than infinite, while greater than zero. Section 4.4 derives the implications of this model for trading blocs. Section 4.5 aims to match up the theory of sections 4.3 and 4.4 with section 4.2's empirical estimates of the effects of transport costs and regional trading arrangements on the volume of bilateral trade, in order to evaluate the welfare implications of regionalization of the world economy.

4.3.1   The Differentiated Products Model

We employ a monopolistic competition model similar to Krugman (1980), who in turn followed Dixit-Stiglitz. A representative consumer has the utility function

$$(2) \qquad\qquad U = \sum_i c_i^\theta; \qquad 0 < \theta < 1,$$

where c_i is the consumption of the ith variety. This utility function results in preference for variety by consumers. The higher the parameter θ, the lower the love for variety. In the limit of perfect substitutability, $\theta = 1$. In the limit of complete love for variety, consumers care only about the number of varieties consumed, and not at all about the quantity: $\theta = 0$.

Labor is the only factor of production. The total national supply of labor is L. Increasing returns are introduced by assuming a fixed cost and a constant marginal cost in the production of each of the varieties. We assume that individual firms maximize profits, and free entry assures a zero-profit equilibrium. Under these simple assumptions, the scale of output of each variety does not depend on the size of the economy. Rather, it is the number of varieties n that increases when the size of the economy (L) increases:

$$(3) \qquad\qquad n = \frac{L(1 - \theta)}{\alpha},$$

where α is the parameter representing the fixed costs of production of a new variety. Notice that in the case of very low substitutability (as θ tends to 0), the number of varieties produced approaches L/α, and an infinitely small amount of each of them is produced, since consumers care only about the number of varieties available.[8]

To see the gains from international trade, which arise here from the opportu-

---

8. Details of derivations are given in Stein and Frankel (1994).

nity to consume a greater variety of goods, we assume that countries have similar tastes and technologies. If we have two countries of equal size, allowing for unfettered trade will double the number of available varieties in each country and thus raise utility. The gains from trade have nothing to do with differences in factor endowments or technology.

Deardorff and Stern (1994) question the realism of this setup. In their view, the Krugman result that a few large blocs are worse than many small ones can be attributed to excessive emphasis on the utility of consuming a large variety of goods that may differ only in the location of production (i.e., brand name). In a model based on comparative advantage, they show how FTAs formed by a few dissimilar countries can yield welfare levels that are very close to those under free trade. They suggest that the emphasis on love for variety in the monopolistic competition model overstates the trade-diversion effect, leading to an overly pessimistic view of FTAs. An unfortunate limitation of their model is the assumption of prohibitive tariffs between countries that do not belong to the same bloc. As Haveman (1992) shows, the addition of optimal tariffs to a comparative-advantage-type model results in welfare effects similar to those of Krugman's product-variety model.

We believe that the product-variety approach is relevant, since it helps explain an important and increasing portion of world trade, in particular in manufactures. This is reflected in the increase in intraindustry trade as a proportion of total trade. Ideally, one would like to come up with a model where gains from trade are explained both by comparative advantage and by increase in variety. (This avenue of research is explored by Spilimbergo and Stein in chap. 5 of this volume.) In the meantime, we think both the comparative advantage and the product variety models help to illustrate some of the effects of the formation of trading blocs, and are useful in their own right.

4.3.2   Introduction of Transport Costs and Tariffs

We will think of the world as being divided into a number of continents (C), each of them equidistant from one another. Each of these continents is composed of a number of countries (N). The transportation system we assume within each continent is a hub-and-spoke network. In each continent there is a hub, through which all trade involving that continent must pass. Each hub has N spokes, all assumed of equal length, connecting it to the N countries in the continent.

Transport costs will be assumed to be of Samuelson's iceberg type, which means that only a fraction of the shipped good arrives; the rest is lost along the way. The cost of transport through two spokes will be represented as a, while that of transport from hub to hub (across the ocean) is given by b, where $0 \leq a, b \leq 1$. Trade involving two countries on the same continent will have to be transported from the exporting country to the hub, and from the hub to the importing country. This involves two spokes, and so the fraction of a good shipped that arrives at the market is $1 - a$. Similarly, the fraction of a good that arrives in the case of trade between countries in different continents, which involves two spokes and a hub-to-hub section, is $(1 - a)(1 - b)$.

When a consumer buys a foreign good, the government levies an ad valorem tariff t. We assume that the tariff is levied on the c.i.f. price.[9] The level of tariffs is exogenous and assumed to be uniform across countries, representing the most-favored-nation (MFN) principle, until we are ready to examine FTAs. Tariff receipts are returned to the consumer as a lump-sum transfer.

For simplicity, we will assume that the countries are equal in size. The symmetry of the model now assures that producers' prices are the same in every country. The same is true of the number of varieties and the quantity of each variety produced in every country.

Prices of home and foreign goods faced by home consumers are different due to transport costs and tariffs. If the producer prices in every country are p, then the price the domestic consumer will have to pay for every unit of foreign good consumed would be

$$(4) \qquad p_c = \frac{p(1 + t_c)}{1 - a}, \qquad p_{nc} = \frac{p(1 + t_{nc})}{(1 - a)(1 - b)},$$

where the subscript c refers to goods imported from within the continent, and nc otherwise (across continents). The corresponding tariffs imposed on the two types of foreign goods are t_c and t_{nc}.

It is useful to fix some more notation here. The situation in which there are no continental trade blocs and every country charges the same positive tariff on goods from all other countries (MFN) can be represented by $t_c = t_{nc} = t > 0$. Global free trade is described by $t_c = t_{nc} = 0$. Finally, the case of every continent forming an FTA is characterized by $t_c = 0$ but $t_{nc} = t > 0$.

The next step is to derive from the utility function the consumption of each foreign variety (both from neighbor countries and from countries in other continents), relative to the consumption of each home variety. We begin with the MFN case $t_c = t_{nc} = t > 0$.

For ease of exposition, we will index goods in such a way that the home country produces varieties $1, \ldots, n$; neighbors produce varieties $n + 1, \ldots, n + n^c$; and countries across the ocean produce varieties $n + n^c + 1, \ldots, n + n^c + n^{nc}$. The home consumer maximizes

$$(5) \qquad U = \sum_{i=1}^{n+n^c+n^{nc}} c_i^\theta$$

subject to the budget constraint

9. I.e., tariffs are a proportion of the value of the good including transport costs, in terms of the iceberg model. This assumption is simpler, and probably more realistic as well, than letting tariffs be levied on the f.o.b. price.

(6)
$$\sum_{i=1}^{n} c_i p + \sum_{n+1}^{n+n^c} c_i p_{c,t} + \sum_{n+n^c+1}^{n+n^c+n^{nc}} c_i p_{nc,t} \leq w + T,$$

where w is the wage and T is the lump-sum transfer received by each consumer, which they regard as being fixed.

From the maximization problem of the consumers it is possible to derive the elasticity of demand for exports faced by the producers, which turns out to be $\varepsilon_x = 1/(1 - \theta)$, the same as the elasticity of domestic demand. The equality of these elasticities guarantees that the price resulting from the firm's profit maximization is the same as in the case of the closed economy. So are the quantity produced of each variety and the number of varieties n produced in each country. Transport costs and tariffs thus introduce no changes in these variables. But the key point is the effect on consumption patterns.

The first-order conditions for the consumer's problem yield the relative consumption of each variety:

(7)
$$\frac{c_i^c}{c_i^h} = \left(\frac{p}{p_{c,t}}\right)^{1/(1 - \theta)}$$

and

(8)
$$\frac{c_i^{nc}}{c_i^h} = \left(\frac{p}{p_{nc,t}}\right)^{1/(1 - \theta)},$$

where c_i^c and c_i^{nc} are the domestic consumer's consumption of foreign varieties, from countries within the continent and across the ocean, and c_i^h is the domestic consumer's consumption of the home varieties.

4.3.3 Welfare Implications of Trade Agreements

To evaluate world welfare, we derive the utility of a representative individual in any country. To determine the utility of the consumer, we need to know how much he or she consumes of each good, and introduce these values into the utility function. Equations (7) and (8) above give us the consumption of foreign relative to home varieties, so we need only to determine the consumption of each home variety, c_i^h. We do this by expressing the budget constraint in terms of c_i^h, and taking into account the redistribution of the tariff revenue to consumers.

If we normalize p to be 1, we can obtain, after some algebra,

(9) $\quad c_i^h =$

$$\frac{w/n}{1 + (N - 1)\left(\dfrac{1}{p_c}\right)^{\varepsilon}\left(p_c - \dfrac{t}{1 - a}\right) + (C - 1)N\left(\dfrac{1}{p_{nc}}\right)^{\varepsilon}\left(p_{nc} - \dfrac{t}{(1 - a)(1 - b)}\right)}$$

where $\varepsilon = 1/(1 - \theta)$, and $w/n = \theta\alpha/L\beta(1 - \theta)$.[10] Once we have the consumption of domestic varieties, the consumption of foreign varieties can be obtained from the relative consumption equations (7) and (8). Replacing these in the utility function, we obtain the value of the utility of the representative individual:

$$(10) \quad U = c_i^{h\theta} \left[1 + (N - 1) \left(\frac{1}{p_{c,t}} \right)^{\theta/(1 - \theta)} + (C - 1) N \left(\frac{1}{p_{nc,t}} \right)^{\theta/(1 - \theta)} \right].$$

Given values for the parameters a, b, t, θ, N, and C, we can first obtain the value of c_i^h by plugging the price equations (4) into (9), substitute into (7), (8), and (10), and thus find the value of the utility of the representative individual, which is our measure of world welfare.

Equation (10) is the expression for utility in the absence of free trade agreements. It is straightforward to calculate utility under other arrangements in the same manner. When trading blocs are formed, we just introduce the new set of relative prices faced by the home consumers into their maximization problem, and we can obtain new values for utility in a similar way.

4.4   Welfare Effects of Continental Trade Blocs

We have presented a model that allows us to analyze the desirability of different trade arrangements from a world welfare perspective, as well as the changes associated with these different arrangements in terms of the bilateral volume of trade between countries. In the absence of transport costs, our model is reduced to Krugman's model (1991a). That is, we obtain a U-shaped welfare curve as a function of the number of trade blocs. For plausible values of parameters, a system of three or so trade blocs is the worst outcome. We now use the model *with* transport costs, to examine the desirability of trade blocs formed along continental lines.

In our first exercise, we explore the desirability of forming natural and unnatural trading blocs as a function of transport costs. In particular, in this application we look at FTAs, where the intrabloc tariffs are completely eliminated.

In our second exercise, we analyze the implications of what could be considered an intermediate degree of regionalization, a partial movement toward the creation of (natural) FTAs, and compare it to the outcome associated with a full movement in that direction. We allow for the formation of preferential trade agreements (PTAs) that differ from the FTAs in that the tariff level is reduced among partners, but not necessarily eliminated. Even though it is technically prohibited by article XXIV, many existing regional arrangements are in fact partial. We will show that a partial movement toward regional integration, as in the case of PTAs with preference below 100 percent, is usually superior

---

10. This last equality can be derived from equation (3) together with the profit maximization condition.

to a complete one, associated with FTAs.[11] At the same time, this application illustrates the need for a more complete characterization of trading blocs, one that goes beyond the natural/unnatural distinction.

Throughout, we consider only exercises involving symmetric formation of equal-sized blocs around the world. Deardorff and Stern (1994) and Srinivasan (1993) have taken exception to the symmetric logic of Krugman's bloc question. We, like Krugman, do not address here the asymmetric partial equilibrium exercise of examining the effects of forming a single bloc in one part of the world, particularly the effects on countries unfortunate enough to be left out of any bloc.[12] The motivation, as we see it, is to address the desirability of the international regime with respect to blocs worldwide, that is, article XXIV. It is of course true, however, that variation in GNPs across countries, if nothing else, renders the real world an inherently asymmetric place.

4.4.1   Transport Costs and Free Trade Agreements' Welfare Effects

In this application, we study how the effect of the formation of continental free trade agreements on welfare depends on intercontinental transport costs. Thus we are able to fill in the realistic intermediate case between Krugman's polar cases of zero and infinite intercontinental transport costs. We start with the simple case where the world consists of three continents comprising two countries each. Transport costs *within* continents, a, are for simplicity assumed to be zero in the simulations reported here.

Figure 4.1 shows the percentage change in welfare associated with the formation of trading blocs, both of the natural and unnatural type, for $\theta = 0.75$ and $t = 0.3$.[13] We can see that there is a critical level of intercontinental transport costs b, which governs the welfare effects. For the case of natural trading blocs, where each country forms a bloc with its neighbor, the critical value of b is 0.186: for values of b higher than this, the formation of continental FTAs will result in improvements in welfare. (Remember, in the limiting Krugman's case where $b = 1$, natural blocs are necessarily welfare-improving.) For lower values of b, continental FTAs would reduce welfare. (Remember the limit case where $b = 0$.) As noted in the introduction, we label such welfare-reducing arrangements "supernatural blocs," to indicate that intercontinental transport costs are not high enough to justify the formation of FTAs even along the lines of geographical proximity.[14]

---

11. Admittedly, the usual pattern in practice is not to reduce tariffs partway on all goods. Rather, agreements tend to exempt certain "sensitive" sectors from liberalization, which raises extra problems of distortions and rent-seeking behavior that are not considered here, but that constitute valid arguments in favor of article XXIV. (Less worrisome is the tendency for agreements to phase in tariff cuts gradually over time.)

12. This question is considered, however, by Stein (1994).

13. Some sensitivity analysis with respect to these and other parameters is reported in Frankel, Stein, and Wei (1995).

14. When tariffs are assumed to be levied on f.o.b. instead of c.i.f. values, the critical value of b is approximately 0.15.

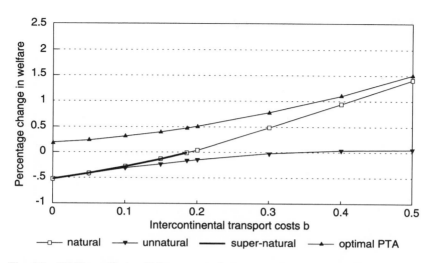

Fig. 4.1   Welfare effects of blocs: natural, unnatural, and supernatural
Notes: $\theta = 0.75$; $t = 0.3$; $a = 0$; $N = 2$; $C = 3$.

Unnatural trading blocs, where each country forms a bloc with one other country outside the continent, result in distinctly lower welfare for small values of b. Krugman's idea (1991a) that natural trade arrangements have a better chance of improving welfare than arrangements between unnatural partners is thus confirmed.

4.4.2   Allowing for Preferential Trade Agreements

In this application, we take another look at trading blocs of the "natural" kind (among neighbors), but we will allow for the formation of PTAs, that is, partial liberalization. To do this, we need to modify our model slightly. The tariff level between partners, instead of zero, will now be $(1 - k)t$, where $0 \leq k \leq 1$, and k is the degree of preference for intrabloc trade or the degree of intrabloc liberalization. The price of partner varieties faced by domestic consumers becomes

$$p_c = \frac{p\,[1 + (1 - k)t]}{1 - a}.$$

Until now we were considering only the two special cases of $k = 0$ (MFN, or the absence of trading blocs) and $k = 1$ (FTAs). Now we consider the whole range of possible levels of intrabloc preference. We will begin as in the previous application, with a world that consists of three continents, each formed by two countries.

What level of intrabloc preference maximizes welfare? Figure 4.2 shows the welfare level as a function of k, for $t = 0.3$, $\theta = 0.75$, $a = 0$, and several values

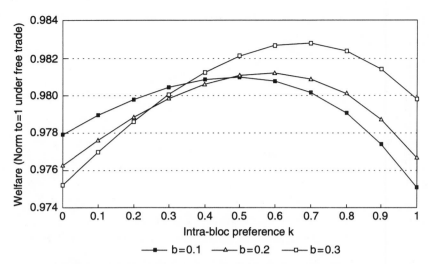

Fig. 4.2   Effects of preferential trade arrangements
Notes: $\theta = 0.75$; $t = 0.3$; $a = 0$; $C = 3$; $N = 2$.

of b.[15] This figure is closely related to figure 4.1. There we were comparing the welfare levels associated with the two extremes of $k = 0$ and $k = 1$ for every possible level of intercontinental transport cost b. For $b < 0.186$, figure 4.1 indicates that the formation of FTAs along natural regional lines is welfare-reducing (supernatural). In figure 4.2, this translates into a higher welfare level for the MFN or no-preference extreme ($k = 0$) relative to the opposite endpoint of full continental FTAs ($k = 1$) for $b = 0.1$.

The important thing to notice in figure 4.2 is that, for every level of intercontinental transport costs, the degree of intrabloc preference associated with maximum welfare is between 0 and 1. In general, PTAs with less than 100 percent preferences are superior to FTAs. This confirms a conjecture by Meade (1955). The key to this result is the diminishing marginal utility for the consumption of each variety. The intuition is easier to understand under zero transport costs, where trade policy does not affect total consumption. Under MFN, households will consume the same amount of every foreign variety, but a larger amount of the home varieties. Imagine that the formation of FTAs entails successive small reductions of intrabloc tariffs. With the first reduction, trade diversion has a small welfare effect, since there is a shift between varieties that were consumed in similar quantities. But trade creation effects are large, since home varieties (with smaller marginal utility) are replaced by member varieties (with larger marginal utility). Thus, a small reduction in intrabloc tariffs starting from MFN will improve welfare. The opposite is true for the last reduction of intrabloc tariffs. Under FTAs, the consumption of member and home varie-

15. For each set of parameter values in the figure (transport cost and θ), welfare is normalized to be 1 under free trade.

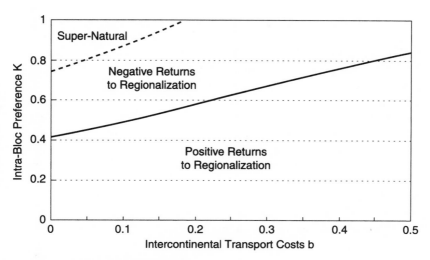

Fig. 4.3   Returns to regionalization
Notes: $\theta = 0.75$; $t = 0.3$; $a = 0$; $N = 2$; $C = 3$.

ties is the same (in the absence of transport costs), while the consumption of other foreign varieties is lower. In this case, the welfare effects of trade creation are negligible, while trade diversion has a larger effect, since varieties with larger marginal utility (those from other foreign countries) are replaced by varieties from member countries, which have smaller marginal utility.

Figure 4.3 provides another way of looking at this issue. For the set of parameters chosen, it represents all possible combinations of intercontinental transport cost b and intrabloc preference k. (As in the other graphs, we only show b up to 0.5 here, under the reasoning that transport costs higher than 50 percent are not plausible.) The solid line represents the level of intrabloc preference that maximizes welfare at each level of transport cost b. Below this line, there are positive returns to regionalization, that is, in this range increasing the degree of preference will result in higher welfare. Above this line, increases in the preference are welfare-reducing. We call this the area of negative returns to regionalization, *NRR*.

Within the NRR area, the dotted line represents, for every level of intercontinental transport cost, the intrabloc preference level that yields the same welfare as $k = 0$ (i.e., MFN). The trade arrangements that lie above this dotted boundary are the ones we call "supernatural" trading blocs. The term "natural" does not seem appropriate to describe trade arrangements that, even when formed along the lines of geographical proximity, represent a movement so deep toward regionalization that welfare is reduced compared to the no-bloc situation.[16]

16. The supernatural bloc area does not always exist. For certain values of the parameters—for example, the combination ($\theta = 0.85$, $t = 0.35$) in the stylized world of three two-country conti-

For $b = 0.10$, our base-case parameter values, and a world consisting of three continents of two countries each, NRR set in when preferences are 49.5 percent. Any greater degree of regional preference moves into the zone of NRR (figures 4.2 and 4.3). For this world, 87.6 percent preferences put the economy into the supernatural zone.

In reality, the status quo that should be compared to continental blocs is a world that contains more than two countries (or FTAs) per continent. We have repeated the experiment for the more realistic, if still stylized, case where the world consists of four continents of sixteen countries each. This sixty-four country setup has the virtue of corresponding roughly to our gravity-model data set examined in section 4.2. (We could get to four continents by adding the Mideast/Africa group of countries to the other three.) NRR set in sooner than before. If intercontinental transport costs are 0.2, then the world attains the welfare optimum as soon as intrabloc preferences reach 10.4 percent, and enters the supernatural zone when they reach 20.4 percent.[17] If intercontinental transport costs are only 0.1, then NRR set in even sooner. For a world consisting of four sixteen-country continents, the optimum degree of continental preferences is 7.6 percent, and the supernatural zone begins at 14.8 percent.

We now return to figure 4.1, to look at the welfare effects of trade agreements, this time not only allowing for less than 100 percent preferences, but also assuming the world trade system chooses the preference level optimally.[18] (We return, for the moment, to a hypothetical world of three continents consisting of two countries each.) The "optimal PTA" curve shows up as welfare-improving no matter what the intercontinental transport costs are. It makes a big difference if the preferences are set at the optimal level, rather than the 100 percent level that is called for in a true FTA.

This application, together with the last one, has provided some answers, within the limitations imposed by the structure of our model, to what Bhagwati (1993) calls the static-impact-effect question regarding the creation of trading blocs. Starting from the absence of trading blocs, a small movement in the direction of increased regionalization (by increasing intrabloc preference) is always a good thing. We can say that there are positive returns to regionalization up to the point of maximum welfare, and NRR thereafter. If intrabloc preferences are set at the optimal level, regionalism will have an immediate

---

nents—welfare under FTAs is higher than welfare under the MFN rule for every value of transport cost b. This eliminates the possibility of "supernatural" blocs. (An earlier footnote noted some sensitivity analysis with respect to the parameters. In general, the higher θ and t, the less likely blocs will be "supernatural." In addition, the higher θ and t, the higher the optimal preference level k for every level of transport cost b, which translates into a smaller area corresponding to negative returns to regionalization.)

17. If tariffs are levied on the f.o.b. value, the welfare optimum occurs when intrabloc preferences are as low as 27.0 percent, and enters the supernatural zone when they are 51.5 percent.

18. This "optimal" level is not the result of a Nash noncooperative equilibrium, where each bloc chooses the optimal preference level given the preference level chosen by the rest of the blocs (and given the tariff level t). It is just the preference level that maximizes welfare in a symmetric world, and can be interpreted as the cooperative solution (again, given the tariff level t).

positive effect on world welfare. If trade blocs are constrained to have 100 percent preferences (as in article XXIV in GATT), then world welfare could be made lower, assuming transport costs are relatively low and there is sufficient preference for variety.

From the purely static viewpoint of our model, 100 percent preference within a trade bloc is not optimal. Does this mean that GATT should eliminate article XXIV's requirement that FTAs stipulate complete liberalization? Not necessarily. We think that article XXIV can probably be rationalized in a dynamic political-economy framework. The ultimate goal is the achievement of global free trade. The requirement of article XXIV may be the best "dynamic time-path" (Bhagwati 1993) to achieve this goal. An explicit political-economy model that would be helpful for this issue is beyond the scope of this paper.[19]

4.5   Some Estimates of Intercontinental Costs to Evaluate the Extent of Regionalization

Where does the current pattern of trade regionalization lie in the welfare spaces mapped out above? To answer this question, it would be useful to obtain estimates of the key parameters, especially that of intercontinental transport costs, b. In this section, we make an audacious attempt to do this. We cannot claim any precision to the estimates, but hope that the exercise is instructive.

Perhaps the most natural place to look for an estimate of b is the difference between the c.i.f. value of a country's trade and its f.o.b. value as a percentage of its total trade. One disadvantage here is that the data are not comprehensively available on a bilateral basis. Another disadvantage of using aggregate c.i.f./f.o.b. numbers is that they depend on the composition of trade (which is in turn influenced by the true transport costs).

If we were willing to leave aside these deficiencies, we could proceed as follows. The ratio of total worldwide import values, including insurance and freight costs, to export values in 1990 was about 1.06.[20] Assume that 6 percent is a weighted average of intracontinental costs and intercontinental costs: $0.06 = ICS\,a + (1 - ICS)(a + b - ab)$, where ICS is the fraction of the world trade that is between countries on the same continents. In our sample, the ratio of intracontinental to total trade, ICS, is roughly 0.4. Without knowing the value of parameter a, we cannot get an exact estimate of b. But we can infer a rough upper bound: $b = (0.06 - ICSa)/[(1 - ICS)(1 - a)] - a/[1 - a] \le 0.06/(1 - ICS) = 0.06/(1 - 0.4) = 0.10$. Even if the intercontinental transport cost takes this upper bound, we observe from figures 4.1 and 4.3 that supernatural trading blocs are a real danger.

However, there is reason to think that the 10 percent estimate could in fact

---

19. A country that joins an FTA may then experience an increase in political support for further steps toward liberalization. See the second half of Frankel and Wei (chap. 7 in this volume).

20. In 1980 it was 1.066 and in 1989, 1.053 (UNCTAD 1991, table 36).

be too low. Although the parameter b is labeled as "intercontinental transport cost" in the model, we noted earlier that it should represent all transaction costs pertaining to intercontinental trade (other than trade barriers imposed by governments). Certain costs such as those associated with personal contact between buyers and sellers are not captured well by the c.i.f./f.o.b. ratio. Recent literature on spillovers and geographic concentration suggests that the effects of proximity on stimulating production are much greater than mere transport costs. In the classic gravity model of world trade, Linnemann (1966) concluded that the effect of distance on trade comes from three channels rather than one: (1) transport costs, (2) the time element (involving concerns of perishability, adaptability to market conditions, irregularities in supply, and interest costs), and (3) "psychic" distance (which includes familiarity with laws, institutions, and habits).

If we were willing to assume that the observed tendency for countries to trade with neighbors was the result solely of these proximity-related aspects that we wish to measure, and not of preferential trading policies, the parameter b could be estimated in a simple way from the data on intraregional trade shares, within the confines of our theoretical model.[21] Such an estimate of b is, however, almost certainly *overstated*. We know from our gravity estimation that statistically significant tendencies toward regional trade preferences already exist, and thus explain part of the proclivity toward intraregional trade that shows up in table 4.1.

For this reason, our preferred approach is to infer the value of b based on estimates of elasticities in our gravity regression. This approach holds constant for the effects of regional trading arrangements already in existence, as well as the effect of per capita GNPs, common languages, and so forth.

We combine several pieces of information. First, in the algebra in section 4.3, the elasticity of demand, $\varepsilon_x = d\log\,(Trade)/d\log\,(P)$, is given by $1/(1 - \theta)$. Second, in our sample, the mean distance between countries on the same continent is 2,896 kilometers, and on different continents is 11,776 kilometers—four times as great. If transport costs show up fully in the price facing the consumer, the percentage change in price associated with being located on a different continent is given by $(p_{nc}/p_c) - 1 = b/(1 - b)$. This follows from equation (4). Third, this price effect, or $b/(1 - b)$, should be approximately equal to

$$\frac{d\log\,(P)}{d\log\,(DIST)}\log\,(11{,}776/2{,}896) = \frac{d\log\,(Trade)/d\log\,(DIST)}{d\log\,(Trade)/d\log\,(P)}1.403$$
$$= [0.50(1-\theta)]\,1.403.$$

---

21. Krugman (1991b) and Summers (1991), for example, use simple calculations to infer roughly the importance of distance in determining trading patterns, without explicitly allowing for the effect of existing trade preferences.

Choosing again our baseline value $\theta = 0.75$, our sample calculation suggests that intercontinental transport costs are roughly on the order of 15 percent ($= 0.175/1.175$). It is interesting to note that this estimate is indeed greater than 10 percent, the rough estimate implied by the c.i.f./f.o.b. data.[22] The estimate for b, together with our simulations, suggests that continental FTAs would put us firmly over the line into the supernatural zone.

What about PTAs? If taken at face value, the estimate of $b = 0.15$ together with figure 4.3 suggests that the optimal degree of preferences within a continental grouping, k^*, is roughly 55 percent in a stylized six-country world. In other words, intraregional trade barriers should be lowered to 45 percent of the level of worldwide barriers. When intrabloc preference proceeds past that point, it enters into the zone of negative returns to liberalization. For the more realistic sixty-four-country world, NRR set in as early as at 9 percent preferences and the supernatural zone at around 18 percent preferences.

The last step is to try to extract from our gravity estimates of section 4.2 a measure of k, the degree of preferences prevailing in existing regional trading blocs. If we take our point estimates in column 2 of table 4.2 at face value, they suggest that the EC in 1990 operated to increase trade among its members by roughly 43 percent ($\exp (0.245 + (20 \times 0.0057)) = 1.43$). Other parts of the world have varying intraregional biases. Let us ask the hypothetical question, what would the effect be on world economic welfare if the trading system settled down to an array of continental blocs that each had the same level of preferences as the EC?

Let the percentage effect on trade of bloc formation be represented by γ. Using our model in section 4.2, a bit of algebra reveals that the formation of a bloc with preferences of k lowers the prices of goods in intrabloc trade by $-tk/(1 + t)$. The ratio of the change in quantity to the change in price is equal to the elasticity of demand:

$$\frac{\gamma}{tk/(1 + t)} = \varepsilon_x = 1/(1 - \theta).$$

Solving for the parameter we wish to estimate,

$$k = \gamma(1 + t)(1 - \theta)/t.$$

Taking $\gamma = 0.43$ from the EC estimate, $\theta = 0.75$, and $t = 0.30$, the implied estimate of k is 0.47. In other words, in this illustrative calculation, EC preferences operate to reduce trade barriers by 47 percent for intrabloc trade. This parameter value is not far from the optimum for our three-continent six-country world, but lies in the supernatural zone for our more realistic four-continent sixty-four-country world. It follows, within the assumptions of our model, that if all continents followed the EC example, the regionalization of

22. It is also, as expected, lower than the estimate following the Krugman-Summers approach.

world trade would be excessive, in the sense that world economic welfare would be reduced relative to the MFN norm.

The tentative conclusion of this study is that some degree of preferences along natural continental lines, such as a Western Hemisphere PTA or enlargement of the EC into a European economic area, would be a good thing, but that the formation of FTAs where the preferences approach 100 percent would represent an excessive degree of regionalization of world trade, within the confines of our static economic model. The overall conclusion is that the world trading system is currently in danger of entering the zone of excessive regionalization.

The optimal path to liberalization apparently features a sharp departure from article XXIV. It entails reducing intracontinental barriers partway, for example by only an estimated 10 percent or so. The strategy of concentrating on reducing trade barriers at the multilateral level *before* (or at the same time as) liberalizing completely within any one continental trading arrangement appears under our assumptions to be preferable.

References

Anderson, James. 1979. A Theoretical Foundation for the Gravity Equation. *American Economic Review* 69 (March): 106–16.
Anderson, Kym, and Hege Norheim. 1993. History, Geography, and Regional Economic Integration. In Kym Anderson and Richard Blackhurst, eds., *Regionalism and the Global Trading System.* London: Harvester Wheatsheaf.
Balassa, Bela. 1987. Economic Integration. In *The New Palgrave Dictionary of Economics,* 43–47. London: Macmillan.
Bergstrand, Jeffrey. 1989. The Generalized Gravity Equation, Monopolistic Competition, and the Factor-Proportions Theory in International Trade. *Review of Economics and Statistics* 71 (February): 143–53.
———. 1993. Regionalism and Multilateralism: An Overview. In J. de Melo and A. Panagariya, eds., *New Dimensions in Regional Integration.* New York: Cambridge University Press.
Deardorff, Alan. 1984. Testing Trade Theories and Predicting Trade Flows. In R. Jones and P. Kenen, eds., *Handbook of International Economics,* 1:467–517. Amsterdam: Elsevier.
Deardorff, Alan, and Robert Stern. 1994. Multilateral Trade Negotiations and Preferential Trading Arrangements. In Alan Deardorff and Robert Stern, eds., *Analytical and Negotiating Issues in the Global Trading System.* Ann Arbor: University of Michigan Press.
Frankel, Jeffrey. 1993. Is Japan Creating a Yen Bloc in East Asia and the Pacific? In Jeffrey Frankel and Miles Kahler, eds., *Regionalism and Rivalry: Japan and the U.S. in Pacific Asia.* Chicago: University of Chicago Press.
Frankel, Jeffrey, Ernesto Stein, and Shang-Jin Wei. 1995. Trading Blocs and the Americas: The Natural, the Unnatural, and the Super-Natural. Abridged version, *Journal of Development Economics* 47:61–96.
Frankel, Jeffrey, and Shang-Jin Wei. 1994. Yen Bloc or Dollar Bloc: Exchange Rate

Policies of the East Asian Economies. In T. Ito and A. Krueger, eds., *Macroeconomic Linkage,* 295–329. Chicago: University of Chicago Press.

Hamilton, Carl, and L. Alan Winters. 1992. Opening Up International Trade in Eastern Europe. *Economic Policy* 14:77–117.

Haveman, Jon. 1992. On the Consequences of Recent Changes in the Global Trading Environment. Ph.D. diss., University of Michigan.

Helpman, Elhanan. 1987. Imperfect Competition and International Trade: Evidence from Fourteen Industrial Countries. *Journal of the Japanese and International Economies* 1:62–81.

Helpman, Elhanan, and Paul Krugman. 1985. *Market Structure and Foreign Trade.* Cambridge: MIT Press.

Krugman, Paul. 1980. Scale Economies, Product Differentiation, and the Pattern of Trade. *American Economic Review* 70:950–59.

———. 1991a. Is Bilateralism Bad? In E. Helpman and A. Razin, eds., *International Trade and Trade Policy.* Cambridge: MIT Press.

———. 1991b. The Move toward Free Trade Zones. In Federal Reserve Bank of Kansas City, *Policy Implications of Trade and Currency Zones,* 7–42. Kansas City: Federal Reserve Bank.

Linnemann, Hans. 1966. *An Econometric Study of International Trade Flows.* Amsterdam: North-Holland.

Meade, James. 1955. *The Theory of Customs Unions.* Amsterdam: North-Holland.

Panagariya, Arvind. 1995. The Free Trade Area of the Americas: Good for Latin America? Center for International Economics Working Paper no. 12. College Park: University of Maryland.

Petri, Peter. 1993. The East Asian Trading Bloc: An Analytical History. In J. Frankel and M. Kahler, eds., *Regionalism and Rivalry: Japan and the U.S. in Pacific Asia.* Chicago: University of Chicago Press.

Saxonhouse, Gary. 1993. Pricing Strategies and Trading Blocks in East Asia. In Jeffrey Frankel and Miles Kahler, eds., *Regionalism and Rivalry: Japan and the U.S. in Pacific Asia,* 89–119. Chicago: University of Chicago Press.

Srinivasan, T. N. 1993. Comment. In J. de Melo and A. Panagariya, eds., *New Dimensions in Regional Integration.* New York: Cambridge University Press.

Stein, Ernesto. 1994. The Welfare Implications of Asymmetric Trading Blocs. In Essays on the Welfare Implications of Trading Blocs with Transportation Costs and Political Cycles of Inflation, Ph.D. diss., University of California, Berkeley.

Stein, Ernesto, and Jeffrey Frankel. 1994. The Welfare Implications of Trading Blocs in a Model with Transport Costs. Pacific Basin Working Paper no. PB94–03. San Francisco: Federal Reserve Bank, May.

Summers, Lawrence. 1991. Regionalism and the World Trading System. In Federal Reserve Bank of Kansas City, *Policy Implications of Trade and Currency Zones,* 295–302. Kansas City: Federal Reserve Bank.

Tinbergen, Jan. 1962. *Shaping the World Economy.* New York: Twentieth Century Fund.

UN Conference on Trade and Development (UNCTAD). 1991. *Review of Maritime Transport 1990.* New York: UNCTAD.

Wang, Zhen Kun, and L. Alan Winters. 1991. The Trading Potential of Eastern Europe. CEPR Discussion Paper no. 610. London: Centre for Economic Policy Research, November.

Wonnacott, Paul, and Mark Lutz. 1989. Is There a Case for Free Trade Areas? In Jeffrey Schott, ed., *Free Trade Areas and U.S. Trade Policy,* 59–84. Washington, DC: Institute for International Economics.

Comment   Paul Krugman

A warning to any economist who works in applied theory: your models may have real consequences. You may find yourself at the head of a large movement. You may say to yourself, "This is not my movement"; you may say to yourself, "My God, what have I done?" But there it is.

When I wrote down a stylized model of the consequences of regional trading blocs a number of years ago—a model that was intended to provide a language for discussing the competing hopes and fears regarding such blocs, rather than to be a basis for serious policy analysis—I did not expect to launch a subliterature. But in a way it should not be surprising that papers that take off from that original, almost tongue-in-cheek effort (either building on the original model or, with considerable justification, calling the whole approach into question) should have become a minor academic industry, and even have begun to have some influence on actual policy discussions. After all, a model—even a crude, small, somewhat silly model—often offers a far more sophisticated, insightful framework for discussion than scores of judicious, fact-laden, but model-free pontifications. But while worrying too much about realism can be a very bad thing—there is nothing worse than the would-be wise man who knows all the facts but has no sense of how they might fit together—it is also always a bit worrying when very simple models are made to bear too much weight. One always wants to stand back and ask whether the simplicity of the model is missing too much.

Now I found this paper by Frankel, Stein, and Wei completely admirable. Not only does it develop a very clever way to take account of the role of geography in influencing the impact of trade blocs; it makes ingenious use of econometric results to make the model, if not exactly empirical, at least constrained by statistical evidence. I would never have thought one could get so far with this general approach. Moreover, this paper is part of a very important wider project by the authors, which has turned the classic gravity approach to trade modeling into a tool of policy-oriented research in a way nobody had thought of before.

So I have no criticisms. I do, however, have two observations.

The first, minor concern is one of practical relevance. When I first wrote about trading blocs, it was an item of faith among many commentators that regional trade liberalization was the wave of the future—that the political success of the European Single Market and the Canada-U.S. Free Trade Agreement would soon be matched by a series of regional integrations. Meanwhile the multilateral system was regarded as being in desperate straits—those were the days when Lester Thurow's pronouncement that "the GATT is dead"

Paul Krugman is professor of economics at the Massachusetts Institute of Technology and a research associate of the National Bureau of Economic Research.

was taken very seriously by world leaders. But that was a long time ago. Since then, the Uruguay Round has been successfully passed, albeit in more modest form than originally hoped. And meanwhile, regional trade liberalization, while it has continued, has proved to be far more difficult politically than people had imagined. Maybe I can summarize this briefly by saying that a ninth GATT round these days seems more plausible to me than an extension of NAFTA to include Brazil or an extension of the European Economic Area to include Ukraine. If there is to be a world of regional trading blocs, it seems likely at this point that it will at the very least involve some distinction between the advanced-country cores and developing-country peripheries within each bloc. This, too, could be modeled; a crucial question would then be the division of gains within each bloc between core and periphery.

My second, more analytical concern is with the way Frankel, Stein, and Wei map the theoretical model onto the real world. In their conclusion that actual regionalization may well be "supernatural," they make use of stylized worlds in which there are several continents consisting of a number of countries—for example, a world of four continents of sixteen countries each. At first this seems more or less right—if one counts North and South America as a single unit, there are indeed four major inhabited continents, with close to a hundred national units among them. But there is a crucial assumption in the model that is not nearly true of the real world: that countries themselves are of equal economic size. In reality, of course, the size distribution of GDPs is highly unequal, and this surely makes a major difference when we try to model the effects of integration.

How should this be accommodated within the model? One answer would be to put the real size distribution of countries into the analysis. In a way, however, the whole point of this style of model is to assume away asymmetries among countries, so as to avoid the mind-numbing taxonomies of customs-union theory. This suggests that we might instead try to loosely deal with the unequal size of nations by using, not actual numbers, but some index of the number of "country-equivalents"—say the inverse of a Herfindahl index.

If we do this, the picture of the world is strikingly different. I recently made an estimate of the number of country-equivalents, using the inverse of the sum of squares of world GDP; while this index has risen over time, with the erosion of U.S. dominance, there are still fewer than ten country-equivalents in the world economy as a whole. Exactly how this observation should be mapped into the model is arguable, but I would suggest that a world of three continents with three "countries" each is in some sense closer to the truth than the version the authors actually use.

In the end, of course, one cannot avoid the asymmetries. Regional trade liberalization will not have the same effects on the United States and Mexico, on Germany and Estonia. It was always a distorting assumption to imagine that we could suppose otherwise; but this paper shows that the assumption has proved far more productive than I had any right to expect.

Comment   T. N. Srinivasan

The revival of interest in regional preferential trading arrangements (RPTAs) in the late eighties after the failure of many such arrangements (except the European Community [EC] and the European Free Trade Association) in the past was in part triggered by the fear that the ongoing Uruguay Round of multilateral trade negotiations would fail and the global trading system would end up in a few trading blocs. Surprisingly, even after the successful conclusion of the Uruguay Round with the signing of its Final Act by countries in April 1994 and the establishing of the World Trade Organization in January 1995, the interest in RPTAs has not only not disappeared but has gathered further momentum. Countries in the Western Hemisphere, members of the Asia-Pacific Economic Cooperation (APEC) forum, the Association of Southeast Asian Nations (ASEAN), and others have agreed to remove all barriers to trade among themselves in the next two decades. Whether RPTAs are stepping stones or stumbling blocks in the path toward a liberal global trading system continues to be debated. It is being suggested that the proposed RPTAs differ from those in the past in that they go far beyond border measures and cover ostensibly trade-related but domestic policies as well. Nonetheless, a convincing case has yet to be made as to why removal of such policy distortions is feasible only through regional approaches.

The implication of the formation of a customs union (CU), free trade area (FTA), or more generally an RPTA for the welfare of the residents of member and nonmember nations has been a central analytical issue for economists, starting with Jacob Viner. A concern for the welfare of nonmembers can be seen in article XXIV of the General Agreement on Tariffs and Trade (GATT), 1947, on CUs and FTAs. It requires in part that barriers to trade of nonmembers should not go up whenever a CU or FTA is to be formed with a waiver from GATT's most-favored-nation (MFN) principle. One of the central propositions of the analytical literature is that associated with Kemp and Wan (1976), who showed (using a standard neoclassical general-equilibrium setup) that there exists a common tariff structure for a CU consisting of any arbitrary number of countries, which ensures that no consumer outside the union is made worse off and at least one consumer within the union is better off compared to the preunion global equilibrium, as long as lump-sum transfers among consumers *within* the union are feasible. Thus a path ending in global free trade consisting of successive enlargements of CUs, each enlargement being Pareto noninferior to the preceding one, exists in the Kemp-Wan world. Of course, whether a CU in the real world satisfies the Kemp-Wan condition is another question. Two more recent propositions established by Krugman (1991a, 1991b) for a world

T. N. Srinivasan is the Samuel C. Park, Jr., Professor of Economics at Yale University.

The author thanks Edward Leamer and Philip Levy for their valuable comments on an earlier draft.

of many identical countries are that, in the absence of transport costs, the number of trading blocs that *minimizes* global welfare is two or three; however, in a world of identical countries located in continents separated by almost prohibitive transport costs, continental trading blocs are welfare-improving because such blocs create trade among members without diverting trade away from nonmembers.

The paper of Frankel, Stein, and Wei is in two, in effect *unrelated,* parts, the first consisting of a simple econometric analysis of actual bilateral trade flows, and the second of numerical analysis from a stylized model that is a generalization of the Krugman setup. In the first part, bilateral *total* trade flows among sixty-three countries for 1970, 1980, and 1990 are put through the well-known gravity model but with a few additional explanatory variables (apart from dummies for the years 1980 and 1990) such as dummies for adjacency of the countries, membership in regional country groupings (EC or Western Europe, East Asia, and Western Hemisphere) and, in one version, separate time trends for each country group as well. The authors find that all three regional dummies are positive and statistically significant, so that any two countries within any one of the groups traded significantly more with each other than with two otherwise similar countries that are not within the same region. The authors view this as indicating a pronounced "regional bias" in trade. Since distance, adjacency, and so forth have been controlled for and, except for the EC, *the other two regions were not formally a trading bloc* during the period covered by the data set, I would argue that the coefficient of regional dummies, like that of any other dummy (or should I say "dumb") variable, merely assigns a quantitative magnitude for ignorance! In other words, for reasons that are not known and hence not captured in the explanatory variables, such as GNP, distance, and so forth, two countries within a region trade more with each other by a percentage indicated by the magnitude of the coefficient of the dummy.[1] The effect of the formation of a trade bloc is not the coefficient of the regional dummy, but the change in it in separate regressions *before* and *after* the region formally becomes a trade bloc.[2]

Interestingly, a time trend interacting with the regional dummy is significantly positive in the case of Western Hemisphere and significantly negative in the case of Western Europe. In the Western Hemisphere, however, the positive trend is so strong that it offsets the *negative coefficient* of the regional dummy (i.e., a *bias* away from trade within the region) in about five years, whereas in

---

1. The authors conclude from the fact that EC dummy is 0.31, for example, that any two EC countries trade 36 percent (exp $(0.31) = 1.36$) more than two otherwise similar countries. Strictly speaking, since the estimated coefficient for large samples is normally distributed, its exponential is log-normally distributed. Now, if X is log-normally distributed, i.e., if log X is normally distributed with mean μ and variance σ^2, then $EX = E[\exp \log X] = e^{\mu + (1/2)\sigma^2}$. Frankel, Stein, and Wei have ignored the $\frac{1}{2}\sigma^2$ term and as such underestimate the "regional bias"! I should also add that, since measured GNP, GNP per capita, and distance contain errors relative to their true values, the estimated regression coefficients are biased. The authors do not recognize this.

2. I owe this observation to Edward Leamer.

the case of Western Europe, a positive coefficient of regional dummy (i.e., a bias in favor of regional trade) is almost eliminated by the negative trend. The authors do not comment on this. Be that as it may, the short empirical section based on gravity model does not help in understanding the reasons for regional bias, if any, or its welfare implications for each region or those outside the region. As such, it does not have much to contribute to explaining the current enthusiasm for RPTAs and to the debate about its consequences for multilateralism.

Let me turn to the stylized model and numerical analysis based on it. I cannot emphasize enough that the model is *extremely special:* countries are *identical,* an *identical* number (*N*) of them are located in each of a number (*C*) of continents. The transport cost (measured in terms of the Samuelson iceberg-melting coefficient) between *any* two countries within any continent is the *same* and that between *any* country in *any* continent and any country in *any other* continent is also the same. All countries produce varieties (with costless product differentiation) from a continuum of possible varieties using the *same* technology that requires a fixed cost in terms of labor (the only factor of production) as well as a constant marginal cost, again in terms of labor. Labor is identical in productivity everywhere and is inelastically supplied. Consumers anywhere have the same utility function that is the *sum* of the utility from consuming each variety, which is assumed to be a constant elasticity function of consumption. Market structure is of monopolistic competition of the large group with free entry.[3] Of course, almost by definition all models are stylized representations of a complex reality. But a robust model is one that simplifies inessential details of the real world. As I argue below, the Krugman model, while robust for analyzing some aspects of trade, is not so far the case that Frankel, Stein, and Wei make of it.

Initially all countries have the same tariffs on all imported varieties, whether from a country within or outside their continent. In all experiments, the authors consider only symmetric formation of equal-sized blocs around the world. In the first experiment, there are three continents with two countries each, with no transport cost within continents. "Natural" blocs are continental blocs, while "unnatural" ones involve countries in two different continents. The welfare effects depend on the level of intercontinental transport costs. If they are sufficiently low, FTAs along "natural" blocs are welfare-reducing. For even lower level of transport costs, unnatural blocs are welfare-reducing. This is consistent with Krugman's first proposition.

3. Presumably this model due to Krugman is by now so familiar that the authors do not state all its technology, taste, and market-structure assumptions! Because of this, one is likely to miss the facts that their normalization of number of varieties, price of each variety, and the wage rate to be unity implies relationships between technology and taste parameters and the labor endowment and is dependent on the extreme symmetry of the model. I am not sure that this normalization is innocuous, except, possibly, in the "symmetry" case: after all, in a model with scale economies, the size of the economy (here, the size of the labor endowment) matters. For example, if countries differ in size, normalizing all three variables to unity is not feasible.

In the second experiment, within each bloc there is only partial liberalization in the sense that the tariff applicable to imports from a country within the bloc is a proportion of the tariff applicable to imports from outside. Unsurprisingly it turns out that, given any level of intercontinental transport cost, the optimal margin of preference for imports within a "natural" bloc is strictly above zero so that a *preferential trading* arrangement is welfare superior to a *free trade* arrangement within a bloc. The authors view this finding as implying that the requirement of GATT article XXIV that *all* trade within a CU or FTA be free is inappropriate, though they recognize there are other political-economy considerations for the requirement. The "optimal" margin of preference is shown to be an increasing function of the intercontinental transport costs, so that welfare increases (respectively falls) as regional preference increases from any level below (respectively above) the optimal level. If the regional preference margin is increased sufficiently above the optimal level, welfare falls below its no-trading-bloc (i.e., regional preference margin of zero) level.

The authors make what they appropriately term an "audacious attempt" to obtain estimates of their key parameters in order to find out whether the current pattern of regionalization has gone beyond the welfare-improving range. Quite rightly they do not claim any precision to their analysis, while concluding that "within the assumptions of our model . . . if all continents followed the EC example, the regionalization of world trade would be excessive, in the sense that world welfare would be reduced relative to the MFN norm."

It should be obvious that the authors' model is extreme not only in its symmetry but also in the assumption that *all* trade is based on preference for variety, market structure is of the Chamberlinian monopolistic competition of the large group with free entry, and transport costs are of the iceberg-melting variety. Indeed, the last assumption (and the assumption that tariffs are ad valorem) ensures that the price *gross* of costs of transport and tariffs is proportional to the price *net* of such costs, so that the relevant demand price elasticities (as perceived by each producer) are unaffected. Because of unchanging price elasticities, producer decisions, in particular production-level producer prices and number of varieties produced, are *unaffected* by tariffs or transport costs. Certainly the extreme symmetry and other assumptions make it easy to derive analytically the global equilibrium and numerically simulate the comparative statics. However, whether the simulations are more than illustrative of the possibilities is arguable. I am not convinced that the simulations are enough to conclude, even tentatively, that "some degree of preferences along natural continental lines, such as a Western Hemisphere PTA or enlargement of the EC into a European economic area, would be a good thing, but that the formation of FTAs where the preferences approach 100 percent would represent an excessive degree of regionalization of world trade." To be fair, the authors refer to other works in which the symmetry assumption is relaxed to a limited extent and comparative advantage considerations are introduced, with some significant differences in their conclusion. But robust policy conclusions have to await less stylized and more realistic and empirically grounded analyses.

References

Kemp, M. C., and H. Y. Wan, Jr. 1976. An Elementary Proposition concerning the Formation of Customs Unions. *Journal of International Economics* 6, no. 1: 95–97.

Krugman, Paul. 1991a. Is Bilateralism Bad? In E. Helpman and A. Razin, eds., *International Trade and Trade Policy*. Cambridge: MIT Press.

———. 1991b. The Move toward Free Trade Zones. In Federal Reserve Bank of Kansas City, *Policy Implications of Trade and Currency Zones*, 7–42. Kansas City: Federal Reserve Bank.

5   The Welfare Implications of Trading Blocs among Countries with Different Endowments

Antonio Spilimbergo and Ernesto Stein

5.1   Introduction

Over the last decade, a large number of bilateral trading arrangements have been created, strengthened, or proposed in nearly every region of the world. The North American Free Trade Agreement (NAFTA), the European Union, Asia-Pacific Economic Cooperation (APEC), and Mercosur are just a few examples of this trend. Furthermore, empirical evidence on bilateral trade flows shows that this phenomenon has been accompanied by increased trade regionalization, at least in some regions (Frankel, Stein, and Wei, chap. 4 in this volume). Therefore, the study of the welfare implications of trading blocs has become very relevant.

One important contributor to the debate has been Krugman (1991a, 1991b). He uses a model of trade under monopolistic competition to study how welfare of the world depends on the number of blocs into which the world is divided. In Krugman's model, the world is completely symmetrical, so all blocs are exactly the same size. He finds that the number of blocs associated with the lowest possible welfare is three. The fact that welfare declines starting from one bloc (free trade) requires no explanation. The reason for the increase in welfare beyond three blocs, however, is more subtle: the distortions associated with a given tariff level become smaller as the number of blocs becomes larger and consumers buy a larger proportion of the varieties they consume from outside the bloc. This happens because a smaller portion of the relative prices

Antonio Spilimbergo is a research economist at the Inter-American Development Bank. Ernesto Stein is a research economist at the Inter-American Development Bank.

The authors thank Deborah Davis, Jeffrey Frankel, Luis Jorge Garay, Jon Haveman, Arvind Panagariya, Roberto Rigobón, participants in the NBER conference, and participants at the seminar at the Federal Reserve Board for useful comments. The authors take responsibility for any errors. The opinions expressed in the paper are the authors' and do not necessarily reflect those of the Inter-American Development Bank.

are affected by the tariff.[1] The conclusion is that a potential consolidation of the world into three trading blocs would have a negative effect on welfare.

Krugman's model has been criticized by Deardorff and Stern (1992) and by Haveman (1992) on the grounds that it relies too heavily on the Armington assumption: goods that differ in their country of origin are imperfect substitutes. This means that each country will be importing goods from every other country in the world. The critics claim that this feature of the model increases the likelihood of trade diversion when trading blocs are formed, and therefore results in an overly pessimistic view of the prospects for regionalization.

Deardorff and Stern reach a very different conclusion, using a model in which there are more countries than goods and trade is explained by comparative advantage. In their model, trading with a few countries is enough to realize most of the benefits that trade has to offer. Expected world welfare increases monotonically as the world consolidates into trading blocs, reaching a maximum for the case of a single bloc, or free trade. However, in order to obtain this result, the authors go to the other extreme. This happens because they assume that tariffs between countries that are not members of the same bloc are infinite! In effect, they eliminate any possibility of trade diversion altogether.

By adding optimal tariffs to the basic Deardorff and Stern model, Haveman obtains results that are rather similar to Krugman's: expected world welfare will be reduced with the expansion of blocs except at the last stage when the last barrier falls, resulting in worldwide free trade. However, for the case of exogenous tariffs, his results become consistent with those of Deardorff and Stern: expected world welfare increases monotonically as the number of blocs becomes smaller.[2]

There are a number of reasons why studying the effects of regionalization under the assumption of exogenous tariffs is important. One is that article XXIV in GATT does not allow increases in tariffs to outside countries when preferential trade agreements (PTAs) are formed. Moreover, the optimal tariff argument does not seem to be what drives governments to impose tariffs. In addition, the optimal tariffs calculated by Krugman and Haveman seem to be too large in comparison to those we see in the real world (even when tariffs are used as shorthand for all protection). We are left, then, with one model that is pessimistic regarding the prospects of regionalization, partly due to its overstating the extent of trade diversion (product-variety model), and with another model that is optimistic and probably understates the extent of trade diversion (comparative advantage).

By adding transport costs to the differentiated-products model, Stein and Frankel (1994) have produced a model that allows the study of how the welfare

1. The fact that Krugman assumes that tariffs are set optimally contributes to the increase in welfare beyond three blocs, but is not crucial for this result.

2. Haveman actually restricts the tariff level in the bloc to be smaller or equal to that of the least protectionist member. Since these restrictions are binding, for our purposes they are equivalent to exogenous tariffs.

effects depend on such costs, as well as on the geographical character of trading blocs (natural versus unnatural). In addition, including transport costs makes the model more realistic regarding the extent of trade diversion, since now natural barriers appear that restrict trade between countries that are far apart, therefore reducing the amount of trade diversion when blocs are formed.

In this paper, we go a step further in the direction of resolving the issue of the likely welfare effects of world regionalization in trade, by using a two-factor model where trade is explained both by product variety and by comparative advantage. In fact, by appropriately setting the values of some parameters, the model can be transformed into either a pure product differentiation model (as in Krugman or Stein and Frankel) or a comparative advantage model.

In addition, introducing two factors of production will enable us to study the welfare implications of the formation of trading blocs among countries at different stages of development (north-south integration), as well as those formed among similar countries (north-north and south-south integration).[3] Our framework allows us to evaluate the case of PTAs as well as that of free trade areas (FTAs), the effects of transport costs, and the effects of different countries having different tariff levels.

After setting up the model for the closed economy in the next section, we allow for trade in section 5.3. In section 5.4 we study the welfare implications of different types of trade arrangements. Section 5.5 offers our conclusions.

5.2   The Model for the Closed Economy

We will work with a model where there are three sectors: agriculture (a), intermediate inputs (v), and manufactures (m); and two factors of production: capital (K) and labor (L).[4] On the demand side, consumers share a Cobb-Douglas utility function given by

$$(1) \qquad\qquad U = M^\alpha c_a^{1-\alpha},$$

where $0 < \alpha \leq 1$, and M and c_a are the consumptions of manufactures and agriculture. The Cobb-Douglas specification results in consumers spending a fixed proportion of their income on each type of good.

On the production side, we make the assumption that each factor of production is specific to the production of one good. Agriculture is a homogeneous good produced under constant returns to scale, and labor is the only factor used in its production. The production function is given by $q_a = L$, which means

3. Another model that incorporates both product variety and comparative advantage can be found in Bond and Syropoulos (1993). In their work, however, countries are completely symmetric except that each of them is particularly adept at producing a different variety. Therefore, the problem of blocs when there are differently endowed countries cannot be tackled with their model. Levy (1993) has a two-factor model that combines comparative advantage and product variety with a specification that is different from the one used here. He assumes, as do Deardorff and Stern, that tariffs are either prohibitive or zero.

4. The basic structure of our model is in the tradition of Dixit and Norman (1980).

that each unit of labor is transformed into one unit of agriculture. Therefore, given perfect competition, $p_a = w$, where p_a is the price of the agriculture good and w is the wage.

There is a very large number of potential varieties of intermediate inputs, which are produced under monopolistic competition and use only capital as a factor of production. Increasing returns to scale are introduced by assuming a fixed cost (γ) and a constant marginal cost (β):

$$(2) \qquad x_i = \frac{K_i - \gamma}{\beta},$$

where x_i is the production of the ith variety, and K_i the amount of capital used in its production. Each intermediate input enters symmetrically into the production of the final manufactured good, produced under a Dixit-Stiglitz technology with constant returns to scale:

$$(3) \qquad M = \left(\sum x_i^\theta \right)^{1/\theta},$$

where $0 < \theta < 1$. This production function results in preference for variety, which becomes stronger as the parameter θ becomes closer to 0. Note that we use M to denote both consumption and production per capita of the manufactured good, since in this model they are always equal.[5]

We assume that each individual is endowed with one unit of labor and k units of capital. In this way, L represents population size as well as labor, and k is the capital-to-labor ratio. The total capital in the economy is, therefore, $K = kL$. Since every individual is equally endowed, we can set aside distributive considerations and work with a representative agent. Equilibrium in the intermediate input market is given by

$$(4) \qquad x_i = Lc_i.$$

Equilibrium in the capital market is given by

$$(5) \qquad K = \sum_{i=1}^{n} K_i = \sum_{i=1}^{n} (\beta x_i + \gamma).$$

As consumers, the individual maximization problem is

$$(6) \qquad \max M^\alpha c_a^{1-\alpha} \quad \text{subject to} \quad M p_m + c_a p_a = I,$$

where $I = rk + w$ is the per capita income. From the first-order conditions we can obtain the inverse demand function:

$$(7) \qquad p_m = \frac{\alpha}{1 - \alpha} p_a \frac{c_a}{M}.$$

---

5. In fact, M could alternatively be interpreted as the utility derived from the consumption of the heterogeneous product in a two-good model. In that case, we would have a utility function that is Cobb-Douglas between goods, and Dixit-Stiglitz between varieties. Both specifications are equivalent.

As producers of the final manufactured good, individuals take p_m as given (since manufactures are produced competitively), and solve the following problem:

$$(8) \qquad \max \left(\sum_{i=1}^{n} c^{\theta i} \right)^{1/\theta} \quad \text{subject to} \quad \sum_{i=1}^{n} p_i c_i = M p_m.$$

The elasticity of demand for each variety of intermediate inputs can be derived from the inverse demand function, which in turn follows from the first-order conditions. For a sufficiently large n, it can be approximated by

$$(9) \qquad \varepsilon_i \equiv - \frac{\partial c_i}{\partial p_i} \frac{p_i}{c_i} \simeq \frac{1}{1 - \theta}.$$

Note that the elasticity does not depend on the quantity demanded, but only on the parameter θ. The firms in the intermediate inputs sector are monopolistically competitive and set the price to maximize profits:

$$(10) \qquad \pi_i = p_i x_i - (\gamma + \beta x_i) r.$$

Using equation (9) and the first-order condition for profit maximization, we obtain the profit-maximizing price:

$$(11) \qquad p_i = \frac{\beta r}{\theta}.$$

Since β is the same for all the intermediate inputs, the price of each variety will be the same. Note that the price in equilibrium does not depend on output.

Free entry condition combined with equation (11) yields the output per variety:

$$(12) \qquad x_i = \frac{\theta \gamma}{\beta (1 - \theta)}.$$

Introducing equation (12) into the capital market equilibrium condition (5), we get the number of varieties:

$$(13) \qquad n = \frac{K(1 - \theta)}{\gamma}.$$

Note that the production of each variety in equilibrium depends only on the cost parameters and on the substitution parameter θ. On the other hand, the number of varieties depends on the capital endowment of the economy. The fact that production of each variety in equilibrium is fixed is the result of the assumptions made about the production and utility functions, and will be used later when solving for the effects of trading blocs.

Using the zero-profit condition in the final manufactured good sector, and plugging in the equations for n, p_i, and x_i, we obtain the price of the final manufactured good as a function of r:

$$(14) \qquad p_m = \frac{\sum_{i=1}^{n} p_i c_i}{M} = \frac{n p_i c_i}{(n c_i^\theta)^{1/\theta}} = \left(\frac{K(1-\theta)}{\gamma}\right)^{1-1/\theta} \frac{\beta r}{\theta}.$$

Plugging equation (14) into the inverse demand function (7), substituting for M and p_m, and using $w = p_a$ and $c_a = L$, we obtain the relative returns to the factors of production:

$$(15) \qquad \frac{r}{w} = \frac{\alpha}{1-\alpha} \frac{L}{K}.$$

Note that the relative price of the factors of production depends only on the relative endowments (L and K), while the relative price (p_m/p_a) has a scale effect that depends on the capital endowment of the economy: the bigger K is, the lower p_m is, as can be verified by dividing the left-hand side of equation (14) by p_a, and the right-hand side by w.

5.3 Allowing for Trade

We assume that countries have similar tastes, technologies, and population size.[6] We will proceed in steps. First, we allow for tariffs in a world formed by N countries, assuming for the moment that they have the same factor proportions. In this first step, gains from trade arise only due to increased variety. Next, we introduce capital-rich and capital-poor countries. In this case, there are gains due to both comparative advantage and product variety. Note that if the parameter α in the utility function (1) were equal to 1, all gains would come from increase in variety, as in Stein and Frankel (1994). On the other hand, if the parameter θ were equal to 1, there would be no preference for variety, and all gains would arise from comparative advantage. Finally, we will allow, in turn, for the formation of trading blocs, and for transport costs.

5.3.1   Allowing for Tariffs in a World with N Identical Countries

We introduce ad valorem tariffs, uniform across countries, and for the moment nondiscriminatory. The tariff revenue is redistributed equally to all consumers as a lump-sum transfer.[7] Now, the producer of the manufactured good faces different prices for different varieties of the intermediate inputs, depending on whether they are produced at home or abroad. The price of a foreign variety in terms of a domestic one is

$$(16) \qquad p_f = p_h(1 + t).$$

The producer of the final good now faces the following problem:

---

6. A recent model that addresses the consequences of trade between north and south when preferences are different is Spilimbergo (1994).

7. We assume that the number of consumers is sufficiently large that they view this transfer as exogenous.

(17) $\max M = \left(\sum c_i^\theta\right)^{1/\theta}$ subject to $\sum c_h p_h + \sum c_f p_f \leq M p_m$.

The first-order conditions yield

(18) $$c_f = c_h \left(\frac{p_h}{p_f}\right)^{1/(1-\theta)} = c_h \left(\frac{1}{1+t}\right)^{1/(1-\theta)}.$$

In equilibrium, the per capita production of the manufactured good will be

(19) $$M = c_h n^{1/\theta} \left[1 + (N-1)\left(\frac{1}{1+t}\right)^{1/(1-\theta)}\right]^{1/\theta} = c_h n^{1/\theta} \Psi^{1/\theta},$$

where

(20) $$\Psi = 1 + (N-1)\left(\frac{1}{1+t}\right)^{\theta/(1-\theta)}.$$

The zero-profit condition in the production of manufactures yields the price of final manufactured goods in terms of the intermediate home variety:

(21) $$p_m = p_h n^{(\theta-1)/\theta}\left(\frac{1}{\Psi}\right)^{(1-\theta)/\theta} = \underbrace{\frac{\beta r}{\theta}}_{p_h}\left[\underbrace{\frac{K(1-\theta)}{\gamma}}_{n}\right]^{(\theta-1)/\theta}\left(\frac{1}{\Psi}\right)^{(1-\theta)/\theta}.$$

We can interpret $(1/\Psi)^{(1-\theta)/\theta}$ as the price index of the intermediate inputs in terms of the price of the domestic variety. We can see that the price of manufactures is proportional to the price of the home varieties. As expected, it depends negatively on n, the number of varieties produced in each country, due to preference for variety in the production function.

We have solved the problem of the manufacturer of final goods, who takes p_m as given. Now we need to solve the problem of the consumer. We can express this problem as

(22) $\max M^\alpha c_a^{1-\alpha}$ subject to $p_m M + p_a c_a \leq rk + w + T$,

where T is the per capita tariff receipts that are handed back to consumers as a lump-sum transfer:

(23) $$T = t p_h \underbrace{n(N-1)}_{\text{\# of foreign varieties}} \underbrace{c_h \left(\frac{1}{1+t}\right)^{1/(1-\theta)}}_{\text{consume per variety}}.$$

The first-order conditions yield

(24) $$\frac{c_a}{M} = \frac{(1-\alpha)}{\alpha}\frac{p_m}{p_a}.$$

Substituting p_m, p_a, c_a, and M in equation (24), we can obtain the consumption of the home variety in terms of exogenous parameters:

$$(25) \qquad c_h = \frac{\theta k}{\beta n} \frac{1}{\left[1 + (N - 1) \left(\dfrac{1}{1 + t} \right)^{1/(1 - \theta)} \right]}.$$

Plugging c_h in expression (19), we can find the production of manufactures in terms of exogenous variables. Plugging c_m and c_a into (18), we obtain

$$(26) \qquad \frac{r}{w} = \frac{\alpha}{(1 - \alpha)} \left(\frac{1 + (N - 1)\left(\dfrac{1}{1 + t} \right)^{1/(1 - \theta)}}{1 + (N - 1) \left(\dfrac{1}{1 + t} \right)^{\theta/(1 - \theta)}} \right) \frac{1}{k}.$$

A comparison with expression (15) shows that, in the absence of tariffs, the relative return to the factors of production are the same as in the case of the closed economy. As the tariff rate increases, the relative return to capital falls. Note that this effect disappears in the case where the intermediate inputs are perfect substitutes ($\theta = 1$).

5.3.2   Trade When Countries Have Different Factor Proportions

We now introduce two types of countries, which differ only in their capital endowment. In poor countries, each individual is endowed with one unit of capital, as well as one unit of labor ($k_p = 1$). In rich countries, each individual owns one unit of labor and k_r units of capital (where $k_r > 1$). Since the capital-to-labor ratio in the poor country is 1, we will drop the subscript for the case of the rich country, and denote its capital-to-labor ratio simply as k. From equation (13), the number of varieties produced in rich countries will be larger than that in poor countries by a factor of k. We make the assumption that k is sufficiently large relative to the tariff rate to ensure that there is trade in agriculture.[8]

The solution of the model involves solving for the prices of the factors of production (w_r, w_p, r_r, r_p); the equilibrium conditions in trade in an intermediate input and agriculture, together with a normalization and the law of one price for agriculture, give us the conditions to solve the system.

We first find the demand for intermediate inputs. The relative price of capital in rich and poor countries will be denoted as ρ. Given that the cost and substitution parameters β and θ are assumed to be the same across countries, it follows from equation (11) that ρ is also equal to the price of the home varieties in a rich country (p_{hr}) relative to that of the home varieties in a poor country (p_{hp}):

$$(27) \qquad \frac{r_r}{r_p} = \frac{p_{hr}}{p_{hp}} = \rho.$$

8. The condition for trade in agriculture to occur is $((1 - \alpha)I_r(k))/(w_r(k)) > 1$, where $I_r(k)$ and $w_r(k)$ are the income and wage in the rich country.

We can now write the prices of intermediate inputs faced by producers of manufactures in a rich country, in terms of the ones produced at home:

$$\frac{P_{fr}}{P_{hr}} = 1 + t;$$

(28)

$$\frac{P_{fp}}{P_{hr}} = \frac{1 + t}{\rho},$$

where the subscript f denotes foreign variety. Likewise, in a poor country, the prices are

$$\frac{P_{fp}}{P_{hp}} = 1 + t;$$

(29)

$$\frac{P_{fr}}{P_{hr}} = (1 + t)\,\rho.$$

The producers of manufactures facing these relative prices will demand the following relative quantities of intermediate inputs. In rich countries,

$$\frac{c_{fr}}{c_{hr}} = \left(\frac{P_{hr}}{P_{fr}}\right)^{1/(1-\theta)} = \left(\frac{1}{1+t}\right)^{1/(1-\theta)};$$

(30)

$$\frac{c_{fp}}{c_{hr}} = \left(\frac{P_{hr}}{P_{fp}}\right)^{1/(1-\theta)} = \left(\frac{\rho}{1+t}\right)^{1/(1-\theta)}.$$

In poor countries,

$$\frac{c_{fp}}{c_{hp}} = \left(\frac{P_{hp}}{P_{fp}}\right)^{1/(1-\theta)} = \left(\frac{1}{1+t}\right)^{1/(1-\theta)};$$

(31)

$$\frac{c_{fr}}{c_{hp}} = \left(\frac{P_{hp}}{P_{fr}}\right)^{1/(1-\theta)} = \left(\frac{1}{(1+t)\rho}\right)^{1/(1-\theta)}.$$

We use these relative consumptions to write the equation for equilibrium in the market for a variety produced in a rich country:

(32) $\underbrace{\dfrac{\theta\gamma}{\beta(1-\theta)}}_{\text{supply}} =$

$$L\left[\underbrace{c_{hr}}_{\substack{\text{demand} \\ \text{from home}}} + \underbrace{(N_r - 1)c_{hr}\left(\frac{1}{1+t}\right)^{1/(1-\theta)}}_{\text{demand from other rich countries}} + \underbrace{N_p c_{hp}\left(\frac{1}{(1+t)\rho}\right)^{1/(1-\theta)}}_{\text{demand from poor countries}}\right],$$

where N_r and N_p are the number of rich and poor countries, respectively. Notice that the supply for each variety is constant, as given by equation (12); c_{hr} and

c_{hp}, on the other hand, depend on the respective prices of factors in rich and poor countries.[9]

Now we find the equilibrium condition in agriculture. Since agriculture is a homogeneous good, the law of one price requires that the price at home be the same whether the good is imported or produced domestically. Therefore, we can write $p_{ar} = p_{ap}(1 + t)$. The relative wage in rich and poor countries, then, is

$$(33) \qquad \frac{w_r}{w_p} = 1 + t.$$

The equilibrium in the agriculture sector is given by

$$(34) \qquad NL = N_r \frac{(1 - \alpha)}{p_{ar}} I_r + N_p \frac{(1 - \alpha)}{p_{ap}} I_p.$$

The system formed by equations (32), (34), and (33), together with the normalization $w_p = 1$, determines the prices of factors of production (r_p, w_p, r_r, w_r). Since the equations in the system above are nonlinear, an analytical solution is not possible, so the model will be solved through simulations.

5.3.3   Introducing Trade Arrangements

The framework outlined in the previous section can be used to examine the welfare implications of different types of trading blocs. Their formation simply introduces changes in the set of relative prices faced in each type of country. For the case of a rich country, the set of relative prices faced by the producers of manufactures will now be

$$(35) \qquad \begin{aligned} \frac{p_{frb}}{p_{hr}} &= 1, \\[2mm] \frac{p_{fr}}{p_{hr}} &= 1 + t, \\[2mm] \frac{p_{pb}}{p_{hr}} &= \frac{1}{\rho}, \\[2mm] \frac{p_{fp}}{p_{hr}} &= \frac{1 + t}{\rho}, \end{aligned}$$

---

9. The results are derived following the same procedure of the previous section. c_{hr} is equal to

$$\frac{\theta a}{\beta n} \frac{\frac{w_r}{r_r} L + k(t + 1)}{\Psi_r + \alpha t k},$$

where

$$\Psi_r = k + k(N_r - 1) \left(\frac{p_{hr}}{p_{fr}}\right)^{\theta/(1-\theta)} + N_p \left(\frac{p_{hr}}{p_{fp}}\right)^{\theta/(1-\theta)}$$

is analogous to equation (20). The detailed derivations are available upon request.

where the subscript b denotes members of the bloc. Likewise, in the poor country,

$$\frac{p_{fpb}}{p_{hp}} = 1,$$

$$\frac{p_{fp}}{p_{hp}} = 1 + t,$$

(36)

$$\frac{p_{frb}}{p_{hp}} = \rho,$$

$$\frac{p_{fr}}{p_{hp}} = (1 + t)\rho.$$

In addition, whenever rich and poor countries are joined in a bloc, the price of agriculture in both countries becomes equal, except in the case of transport costs, which will be introduced below. With this new set of relative prices, it is possible to solve for the utility in both types of countries following the same procedure used in section 5.3.2.

5.3.4   Introducing Transport Costs

We will think of the world as being divided into C continents, each of them equidistant from one another. Each of these continents is formed by an equal number of rich and poor countries (Nr, Np). The transportation system within each continent is assumed to be a hub-and-spoke network.[10] In each continent there is a hub, through which all trade involving that continent must pass. Each hub has N spokes (where $N = Nr + Np$), all assumed to be of equal length, connecting it to the N countries on the continent. Note that this is a completely symmetric world, except that some countries are rich and some are poor. Transport costs will be assumed, following Krugman (1980), to be of Samuelson's iceberg type, which means that only a fraction of the good shipped arrives; the rest is lost along the way. The cost of transport from spoke to hub to spoke will be represented as a, while that of transport from hub to hub (across the ocean) is given by b, where $0 \leq a, b \leq 1$. Trade involving two countries belonging to the same continent will have to be transported from the exporting country to the hub, and from the hub to the importing country. This involves two spokes, and therefore the transport cost within a continent is a, so the fraction of a good shipped that arrives at the market is $1 - a$. Similarly, the fraction of a good that arrives in the case of trade between countries in different continents, which involves two spokes and a hub-to-hub section, is $(1 - a)(1 - b)$.

We assume that tariffs are levied on the total price paid for the good in the country of origin, which includes what is lost in transportation. An important thing to keep in mind is that once transport costs are allowed, there is a gap between consumption and quantity demanded. For example, in the case of a

10. In this, we follow Stein and Frankel (1994).

poor country, the relative price of a variety produced in a rich extracontinental country in the absence of blocs will be

$$(37) \qquad \frac{p_{frx}}{p_{hp}} = \frac{(1 + t)\rho}{(1 - a)(1 - b)},$$

where the subscript x stands for extracontinental. The relative consumption will be

$$(38) \qquad \frac{c_{frz}}{c_{hp}} = \left(\frac{(1 - a)(1 - b)}{(1 + t)\rho} \right)^{1/(1-\theta)},$$

and the relative demand will be

$$(39) \qquad \frac{d_{frx}}{d_{hp}} = \left(\frac{(1 - a)(1 - b)}{(1 + t)\rho} \right)^{1/(1-\theta)} \frac{1}{(1 - a)(1 - b)}.$$

The rest of the relative prices, consumptions, and demands are determined accordingly. In particular, the relative wage between the rich and poor country will be $1/[(1 - a)(1 - b)]$, if they belong to the same bloc, and $(1 + t)/[(1 - a)(1 - b)]$ otherwise.

5.4 Welfare Implications of Trade Agreements

In this section, we use our model to analyze the welfare implications of different types of trade arrangements. First, we come back to the question of the welfare effects of the consolidation of the world trading system into a few trading blocs. By changing the substitution parameters in the model, we will be able to see how these effects change as we move from the case where trade is explained mostly by product-variety considerations to one where comparative advantages play a large role in explaining trade. Second, in a simple world of four countries (two rich and two poor), we ask what is the optimal type of arrangement for each type of country, and how the answer changes for different values of the parameters. Finally, we introduce the possibility of PTAs (rather than just FTAs), and study the optimal level of intrabloc tariffs when continental trading blocs are formed.

5.4.1 Does Welfare Increase as the World Consolidates into Blocs?

We now address the Krugman versus Deardorff and Stern debate. As discussed in the introduction, Krugman's product-variety model finds that, in the absence of transport costs, a world of a few large blocs results in the lowest level of welfare. In contrast, Deardorff and Stern suggest, using a comparative-advantage model, that welfare increases monotonically as the number of blocs becomes smaller, reaching maximum welfare under free trade. In figure 5.1, we present the results of simulations using our model, which incorporates both product variety and comparative advantages as motives for trade.

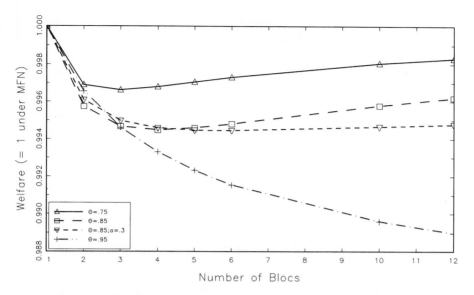

Fig. 5.1   Product variety versus comparative advantages

Notes: $\alpha = 0.5$; $t = 0.3$; $k = 3$; $a = b = 0$ (except $a = 0.3$ where noted in key); $C = 1$, $N = 60$.

Each curve represents the welfare of the world under different parameter values, as a function of the number of symmetrical blocs into which the world is divided. We work with a world of sixty countries, thirty rich and thirty poor. World welfare is obtained simply by averaging the welfare in rich and poor countries. All countries are assumed to levy the same tariff level on imports from outside the bloc (we use 30 percent in our simulations). Tariffs within the bloc are completely eliminated, as in FTAs.[11] We use a value of $\alpha = 0.5$, which means that half of the consumer's income is spent in agriculture and the other half in manufactures, and a value of $k = 3$, meaning that each individual in the rich country is endowed with three units of capital. The highest curve corresponds to a value of $\theta = 0.75$. In this case, the elasticity of substitution among varieties is 4. The rest of the curves correspond to higher values of θ. As θ increases in value, preference for variety decreases, increasing the relative importance of comparative advantage as a source of gains from trade. As θ approaches 1, preference for variety disappears, and only differences in factor proportions explain trade. Intraindustry trade is eliminated, and only interindustry trade remains.

For $\theta = 0.75$, the number of blocs associated with minimum welfare is three. This suggests that adding different factor proportions to a model with product variety does not change the implications in any significant way. It is

---

11. Since the tariff for the case of trade with countries outside the bloc is uniform, we do not distinguish here between FTAs and customs unions.

only for extremely low preference for variety (high θ) that the model yields results similar to those in Haveman and in Deardorff and Stern.[12] Krugman's conclusion, then, is more robust to the inclusion of comparative advantage in his model than Deardorff and Stern's is to the introduction of preference for variety in one of the goods. The reason for this result is that the elasticity of substitution among varieties (given in our model by $1/(1 - \theta)$) is much higher than that between goods (which is 1 under our Cobb-Douglas specification).[13] Thus, the elimination of tariffs when blocs are formed has a substantial effect on trade due to preference for variety (intraindustry trade), but a much smaller effect on trade due to comparative advantage.

There is a sense, however, in which Krugman's critics were right to suggest that he overestimated the extent of trade diversion. If one introduces transport costs into the picture, the factor-proportions motive for trade becomes relatively more important, since transport costs have a larger effect on intraindustry trade than on interindustry trade, precisely because of the different elasticities of substitution discussed above. Lower intraindustry trade means that there is less trade to be diverted once trading blocs are formed. Therefore, the effect of increasing transport costs a is not very different from that of increasing the value of θ, as is shown in figure 5.1, where the dotted line with triangles represents welfare as a function of the number of blocs for the case of $\theta = 0.85$ and $a = 0.3$. We also tried different values of k and α, but the results did not change in any significant way.

5.4.2   What Type of Bloc Maximizes Welfare for Rich and Poor Countries?

In this section, we work with a simple single-continent world that consists of four countries, two of them rich and two poor. Our model provides an ideal framework for the analysis of the welfare effects of different trade arrangements. For example, what is the effect of north-north integration, on both rich countries and poor ones? Are the rich countries better off by forming blocs with poor countries or among themselves?

We provide a framework to think about these questions. Figures 5.2 through 5.5 show how the welfare of the rich (figures 5.2 and 5.3) and the poor (figures 5.4 and 5.5) depends on the type of trading arrangements that exist in the world, for different combinations of the parameters α and θ. For each set of parameter values, the welfare is normalized to be 1 for the case of nondiscriminatory tariffs, as under the most-favored-nation (MFN) clause.

Note that an increase in θ results in a higher elasticity of substitution between varieties, and thus in greater changes in the consumption bundles in response to given changes in relative prices. For this reason, the welfare effects

12. The values of θ for which Krugman's result goes away correspond to elasticities of substitution that seem unreasonably high.

13. This follows from the requirement that θ be a positive number. It is a natural assumption to make, since one would expect the different varieties of intermediate inputs to be closer substitutes than the different goods.

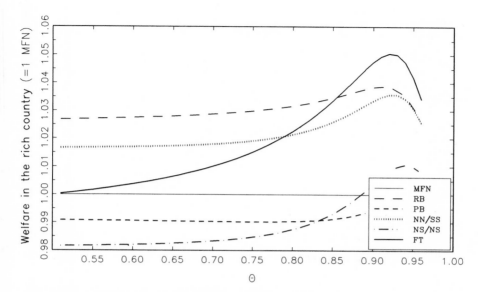

Fig. 5.2   Which arrangement should the rich country seek?
Notes: $\alpha = 0.9$; $t = 0.3$; $k = 3$; $a = b = 0$; $C = 1$; $N = 4$.

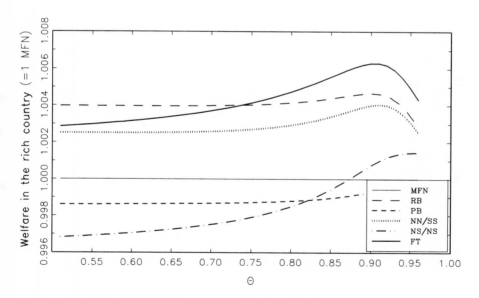

Fig. 5.3   Which arrangement should the rich country seek?
Notes: $\alpha = 0.1$; $t = 0.3$; $k = 3$; $a = b = 0$; $C = 1$; $N = 4$.

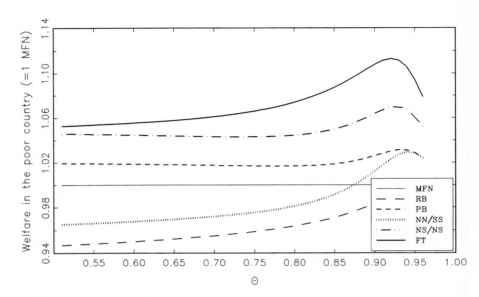

Fig. 5.4   Which arrangement should the poor country seek?
Notes: $\alpha = 0.9$; $t = 0.3$; $k = 3$; $a = b = 0$; $C = 1$; $N = 4$.

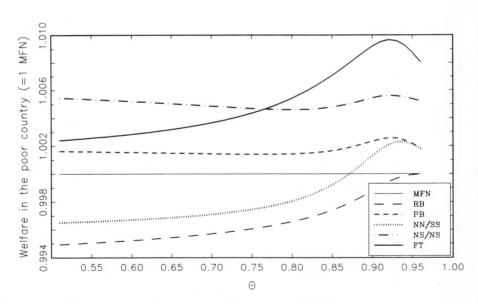

Fig. 5.5   Which arrangement should the poor country seek?
Notes: $\alpha = 0.1$; $t = 0.3$; $k = 3$; $a = b = 0$; $C = 1$; $N = 4$.

of trading blocs generally become more important for higher values of θ. As θ approaches 1, however, the taste for variety disappears, and so does the intraindustry trade, thus reducing the effects of trading blocs. This is the explanation for the shape of the curves in figures 5.2 through 5.5.

As can be seen in figures 5.2 and 5.3, it is always the case that a bloc among the rich countries (RB in the figure) makes the rich better off than MFN, while a bloc among the poor (PB) always hurts them. For parameter values that increase the relative importance of product variety as a source of gains from trade (high values of α and low values of θ), welfare in the case of a bloc among the rich is even higher than under free trade (FT). In the case of the poor countries, a similar pattern can be observed in figures 5.4 and 5.5: their own bloc improves their welfare, while a bloc among the rich countries lowers it. This confirms the results obtained in Stein (1994) and Goto and Hamada (1994) for the case of blocs among similar countries: those countries that are left behind when blocs are formed are always worse off. This happens because those that form the bloc experience an improvement in their terms of trade, as each member of the bloc diverts demand from nonmembers toward fellow members. As expected, the effect of a rich bloc on the poor is larger than that of a poor bloc on the rich.

In the case of north-south integration (represented by NS/NS), we did not allow for the formation of a single bloc between two countries.[14] For this reason, we compare each country's welfare under the north-south blocs with that under the north-north/south-south blocs (NN/SS). Figures 5.2 through 5.5 suggest that poor countries will always prefer north-south integration. This is true for both comparative-advantage and product-variety considerations. The rich country, however, would prefer to join another rich rather than a poor when product variety plays a large role. This preference becomes weaker for high values of θ and low values of α, when trade occurs mainly due to comparative advantage. Under comparative advantage, the rich country would obviously prefer to join a poor. This, however, is not reflected in the figure, due to the considerations discussed in footnote 14.

So far, we have worked under the assumption that tariffs are the same in rich and poor countries. However, developed countries typically have lower rates of protection than developing countries. For this reason, in what follows we will allow the tariff in the rich country (t_r) to differ from that in the poor country (t_p).[15] In figures 5.6 and 5.7, t_p is set at 30 percent, while t_r varies between 0 and 40 percent. For high levels of t_r, the results are qualitatively similar to the ones presented above. For low tariff levels in the rich country, however, the implications are very different: a rich country would rather join a poor than

14. The reason is that doing so would force us to consider four types of countries: rich in the bloc and outside the bloc, and poor in the bloc and outside the bloc. One does not gain too much insight by doing so, and the model would get much more complicated.

15. The idea of allowing for different tariffs in rich and poor countries was suggested to us by Arvind Panagariya.

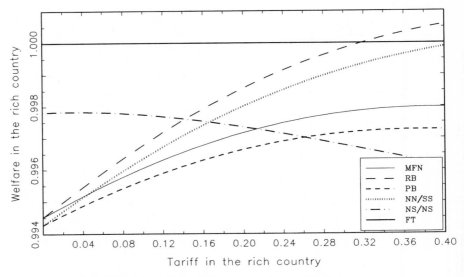

Fig. 5.6   Differentiated tariffs: the effects on the rich countries
Notes: $\alpha = 0.5$; $\theta = 0.75$; $t_p = 0.3$; $k = 3$; $a = b = 0$; $C = 1$; $N = 4$.

another rich country (figure 5.6); and, as figure 5.7 shows, the poor would rather integrate among themselves than join the rich![16] The key to these results is the effect of the formation of blocs on the terms of trade. These effects are very different when the countries start from different tariff levels. We will present a simple example to provide the intuition for this result.

Take a world of three symmetric countries, A, B, and C, where tariffs are nondiscriminatory, and uniform across countries. What are the effects on the terms of trade of the formation of an FTA between A and B? As explained above, both countries deviate trade away from C, and in favor of their partners. As a result, relative world demand for goods produced in C declines, and so do its terms of trade, while those in A and B improve. In addition to the trade-diversion effect, there is a trade-creation effect: both A and B will demand more goods from each other, at the expense of the demand for home goods. In this symmetric setting, this trade creation effect has no consequences for the terms of trade of A and B, since the effects in both countries cancel out, leaving demand unchanged. However, this changes when tariffs in A and B are not the same.

Take now the extreme example where tariffs in A are zero, while those in B are positive. The following effects will take place if A forms an FTA with B: country B will deviate trade away from C in favor of A; B will also shift demand from itself to A (trade-creation effect). However, A will neither create nor deviate trade, since its tariff structure has not changed at all. The resulting

16. We performed simulations for different values of t_p. The results are qualitatively similar.

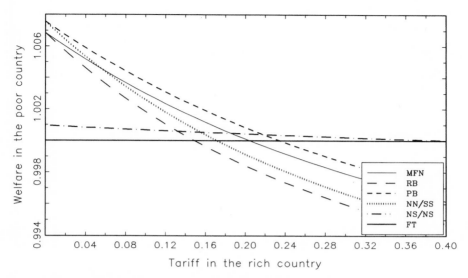

Fig. 5.7   Differentiated tariffs: the effects on the poor countries
Notes: $\alpha = 0.5$; $\theta = 0.75$; $t_p = 0.3$; $k = 3$; $a = b = 0$; $C = 1$; $N = 4$.

effect is a fall in the demand for the goods produced in country B. Therefore, the terms of trade of country B may actually fall when it enters into a bloc with A. In contrast, the improvement in country A's terms of trade is even larger than in the case where the tariff levels in A and B are similar. We chose a tariff level in A of zero for simplicity, but the result goes through for any tariff in A sufficiently low.

In the case where tariffs in the rich countries are sufficiently lower than those in the poor countries, this example helps us understand why both rich and poor countries might prefer to integrate with the poor.[17]

This type of analysis helps us understand some of the issues involved when a country like Chile has to decide whether to join NAFTA or Mercosur. We use this only as an illustrative example since our framework leaves out a number of other important considerations in making this decision.

Under which conditions, then, will Chile prefer to join Mercosur rather than NAFTA?[18] The passage above suggests that the larger the tariff in the rich country (NAFTA) relative to the poor (Mercosur and Chile), the more inclined Chile will be to join Mercosur.

17. The results of our simulations involving different tariff rates are consistent with the conclusions reached by Panagariya (1995) using a three-country example. In his example, countries lose by granting preferential treatment to their partners, and gain when preferential treatment is extended to them. In this sense, Panagariya claims that the mercantilist approach is valid for analyzing PTAs.

18. In what follows we treat Mercosur as a single poor country, and NAFTA as a single rich country.

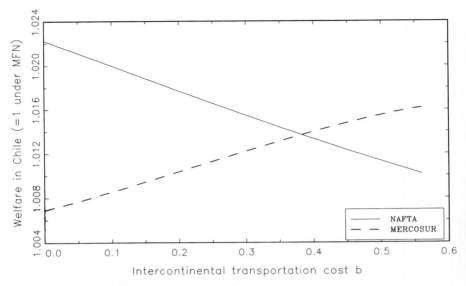

Fig. 5.8   Should Chile join NAFTA or Mercosur?
Notes: $\alpha = 0.9$; $t_r = 0.3$; $t_p = 0.3$; $k = 3$; $a = 0$; $C = 2$; $N = 4$; $\theta = 0.75$.

Another factor that plays a role in such a decision is the importance of inter-continental transport costs. To address this question, we use a simulation in which the world consists of two continents with four countries each, and compare the poor country's welfare under two different arrangements: one where each poor country joins the other poor on their continent, and another where each poor country joins a rich country on a different continent.

The results for the case of $t_r = t_p$ are shown in figure 5.8. Under these parameter values, only for very high transport costs across continents would Chile choose Mercosur instead of NAFTA.

Figure 5.9 shows how much things can change when tariffs in rich and poor countries are different. In this case, $t_r = 0.1$. The effects of joining Mercosur are qualitatively similar to those in figure 5.8. But now the effects of joining NAFTA are completely different. Notice that for $b = 0$, joining NAFTA reduces welfare with respect to MFN, as it does in figure 5.7 for the case of low tariffs in the rich countries. The reason is the same: when a high-tariff country joins a low-tariff country, its terms of trade will fall, provided the tariff differential is sufficiently high. What figure 5.9 clearly illustrates is that transport costs can have surprising effects. In this case, the negative effect on Chile's terms of trade becomes smaller as trade with NAFTA decreases due to the increase in transport costs. When transport costs are sufficiently high, Chile prefers NAFTA to Mercosur.

In fact, this analysis suggests a reason why NAFTA itself might result in welfare losses for Mexico: it represents a trading bloc with a large proximate country (so terms-of-trade effects are large), which has much lower tariffs than

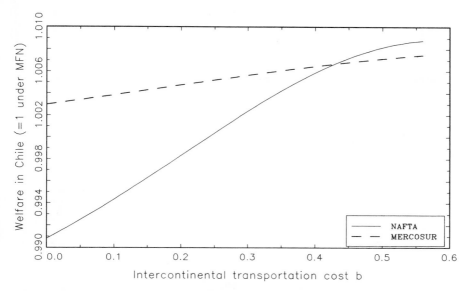

Fig. 5.9   Should Chile join NAFTA or Mercosur?
Notes: $\alpha = 0.5$; $t_r = 0.1$; $t_p = 0.3$; $k = 3$; $a = 0$; $C = 2$; $N = 4$; $\theta = 0.75$.

they did (so terms-of-trade effects can be negative). This suggests that the association between "natural" (meaning proximate) blocs and increases in welfare is valid only when the countries involved have tariff levels of the same order of magnitude.

5.4.3   Product Variety, Comparative Advantage, and Supernatural Blocs

Several authors, among them Krugman (1991b) and Summers (1991), have argued that if trading blocs are formed along "natural" lines of geographical proximity, they are likely to be good. Stein and Frankel (1994) and Frankel, Stein, and Wei (chap. 4 in this volume) have shown, in a model based on product variety, that it is possible for regionalization to go too far, even when blocs are formed along natural geographical lines.

To reach this conclusion, they allowed for continental PTAs, where tariffs within the bloc are reduced but not necessarily eliminated, as in the case of FTAs. Starting from a nondiscrimination situation as under MFN, a small reduction in intrabloc tariffs always improves welfare: there are positive returns to regionalization. As intrabloc tariffs continue to fall, however, welfare reaches a maximum level and starts to decline. Beyond the preference margin that maximizes welfare, there are negative returns to further regionalization. If the intrabloc tariff level continues to decline, welfare might become even lower than at the starting point, under MFN. In this case, the authors suggested that blocs were supernatural: regionalization is much deeper than what would be warranted by "natural" geographical considerations.

In this section, we verify whether the conclusion that continental blocs could

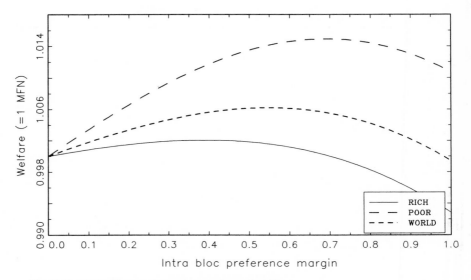

Fig. 5.10   Intrabloc preference margin and welfare
Notes: $\alpha = 0.5$; $\theta = 0.85$; $t = 0.3$; $k = 3$; $a = 0$; $b = 0.35$; $C = 4$; $Nr = Np = 4$.

become supernatural is robust to the inclusion of comparative advantages in the model. To allow for PTAs, the model has to be modified slightly. The intrabloc tariff level, instead of zero, will now be $(1 - \pi) \times t$, where π represents the preference margin within the bloc. We considered a world of four continents of eight countries each, four of them poor and four rich. Since the capital endowment in the rich countries was set at $k = 3$, this setting closely matches that in Stein and Frankel, where a world of four continents with sixteen countries each was considered.

Figure 5.10 shows the effects of increasing the preference margin π on the welfare of the world, both the rich and the poor countries, for a value of intercontinental transport costs $b = 0.35$. In the figure, the welfare of each type is normalized to be 1 under MFN. We can see that the inclusion of comparative advantage does not change the pattern reported by Stein and Frankel. For this set of parameter values used in the simulation ($\theta = 0.75$; $\alpha = 0.5$; $t = 0.3$), the optimal preference margin is 43 percent, which corresponds to a level of intrabloc tariffs of around 17 percent. Blocs become supernatural for $\pi = 0.82$ or when intrabloc tariffs are reduced below 6 percent.[19]

Keep in mind that, throughout this exercise, we ask about the welfare effects of symmetrical trading blocs. As shown in Stein (1994) for the case of similar countries, in a noncooperative game each bloc would in fact benefit from completely eliminating intrabloc tariffs, since doing so improves their terms of

19. Our results are consistent with the implication in Meade (1955) that PTAs are in general better than FTAs.

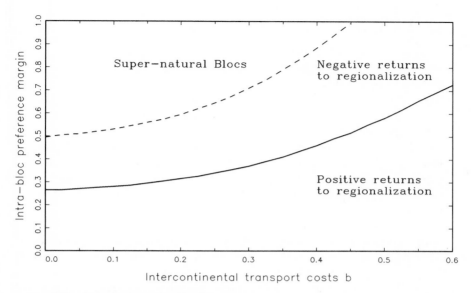

Fig. 5.11   Returns to regionalization
Notes: $\alpha = 0.5$; $\theta = 0.75$; $t = 0.3$; $k = 3$; $a = 0$; $C = 4$; $Nr = Np = 4$.

trade. However, this would result in lower welfare in each country as a result of a coordination failure in determining the margin of preference.

In contrast, here we are focusing on the perspective of an organization such as the World Trade Organization (WTO), asking what would be the preference margin that, if adopted in every continent, would lead to the highest possible world welfare, assuming that free trade is not attainable and that tariff levels outside the bloc cannot be lowered rapidly. Figure 5.10 highlights an interesting issue that was not captured before: the margin of preference that maximizes the welfare of the world does not maximize the welfare of either the rich or the poor. In general, the poor will benefit from a greater preference margin. If WTO ever abandons article XXIV of GATT, which allows for FTAs but not for PTAs as exceptions to the MFN rule, and instead imposes the level of intrabloc preference margin allowed, the determination of this preference margin would depend on the relative political power of rich and poor countries in the WTO.

Figure 5.11 shows how the optimal preference margin depends on intercontinental transport costs. As they become larger, welfare maximization requires a greater degree of continental integration. This result is similar to that obtained in Stein and Frankel (1994) and in Frankel, Stein, and Wei (chap. 4 in this volume). In the limit, if transport costs are prohibitive across continents, welfare will be maximized under continental FTAs, which in this case would represent the ideal of free trade in each relevant world.[20]

---

20. This extreme of prohibitive transport costs across continents was used by Krugman (1991b) as an example of how natural trading blocs would be beneficial.

5.5   Conclusions

Previous models that analyzed the welfare effects of trading arrangements were based either on product variety or on comparative advantage. The use of these models provided contradictory answers to some important questions. In this paper, we have presented a framework that encompasses both types of models. We used our framework to address a number of important questions, and reached the following conclusions:

1. In the absence of transport costs, the consolidation of the world into a few trading blocs reduces welfare, as predicted by Krugman's product-variety model. When transport costs are considered, a move toward free trade zones is more likely to improve welfare, as suggested by the models based on pure comparative advantage.

2. As long as all countries have similar tariff levels, poor countries will always prefer to integrate with rich countries, due to both product-variety and comparative-advantage considerations. The rich country maximizes welfare by joining other rich, except in the cases where product variety does not play a large role. A poor country would consider joining another poor rather than a rich only if the two poor countries are proximate and transport costs are sufficiently high.

3. However, differentiated tariff levels between rich and poor countries have important consequences for the welfare effects of trading arrangements. In the case of FTAs, joining a high-tariff country will enhance welfare more than joining a low-tariff country, other things being equal. Therefore, if rich countries have lower tariffs, the poor might choose to integrate among themselves.

4. The association between "natural" (meaning proximate) blocs and increases in welfare is valid only when the countries involved have tariff levels of the same order of magnitude.

5. The result that integration can be too deep, even if drawn along natural geographical lines, is not affected by the inclusion of comparative advantages into a model where there is preference for variety. The level of intrabloc preference margin that maximizes welfare is different for the rich and for the poor. In general, poor countries would prefer deeper integration.

References

Bond, E., and C. Syropoulos. 1993. Optimality and Stability of Regional Trading Blocs. University of Birmingham, Department of Economics Discussion Paper 93-11, May.

Deardorff, A., and R. Stern. 1992. Multilateral Trade Negotiations and Preferential Trading Arrangements. RFIE Discussion Paper no. 307. University of Michigan, July.

Dixit, A., and V. Norman. 1980. *Theory of International Trade.* Cambridge: Cambridge University Press.

Goto J., and K. Hamada. 1994. Economic Integration and the Welfare of Those Who Are Left Behind: An Asian Perspective. December. Mimeo.

Haveman, J. 1992. Some Welfare Effects of Dynamic Customs Union Formations. In On the Consequences of the Recent Changes in the Global Trading Environment, Ph.D. diss., University of Michigan.

Krugman, P. 1980. Scale Economies, Product Differentiation, and the Pattern of Trade. *American Economic Review* 70:950–59.

———. 1991a. Is Bilateralism Bad? In E. Helpman and A. Razin, eds., *International Trade and Trade Policy.* Cambridge: MIT Press.

———. 1991b. The Move toward Free Trade Zones. In Federal Reserve Bank of Kansas City, *Policy Implications of Trade and Currency Zones.* Kansas City: Federal Reserve Bank.

Levy, P. 1993. A Political Economy Analysis of Free Trade Arrangements. CEPR Publication no. 347. Stanford University. Center for Economic Policy Research, January.

Meade, J. 1955. *The Theory of Customs Unions.* Amsterdam: North-Holland.

Panagariya, A. 1995. The Free Trade Area of the Americas: Good for Latin America? Center for International Economics Working Paper no. 12. College Park: University of Maryland.

Spilimbergo, A. 1994. Growth and Trade: The North Can Lose. In Three Essays on Trade, Growth, and Labor Mobility, Ph.D. diss., MIT, Cambridge, MA.

Stein, E. 1994. The Welfare Implications of Asymmetric Trading Blocs. In Essays on the Welfare Implications of Trading Blocs with Transportation Costs and Political Cycles of Inflation. Ph.D. diss., University of California, Berkeley.

Stein, E., and J. Frankel. 1994. The Welfare Implications of Trading Blocs in a Model with Transport Costs. Pacific Basic Working Paper Series no. PB94-03. San Francisco: Federal Reserve Bank, May.

Summers, L. 1991. Regionalism and the World Trading System. In Federal Reserve Bank of Kansas City, *Policy Implications of the Trade and Currency Zones.* Kansas City: Federal Reserve Bank.

Comment   Jon Haveman

This paper provides a nice contribution to a young and growing literature. When I first sat down to think about this paper, I spent a little time, for my own benefit, putting the paper in its place within this literature. As my thoughts progressed, so did a convenient graphic depiction of the relevant work; this depiction is figure 5C.1.

The literature was really initiated by Krugman (1991a). In this piece, Krugman developed a trade model with differentiated products and optimal tariffs. He proceeded to analyze, in the context of this regime, the effect on world welfare of a sequential process of customs union formation. His original finding was that world welfare would decline until we reached a world configuration of three countries. Shortly thereafter, this work was supplemented by Deardorff and Stern (1994) and Haveman (1996). Both of these papers provided results similar in spirit if not nature to those of Krugman. Instead of a

Jon Haveman is professor of economics at Purdue University.

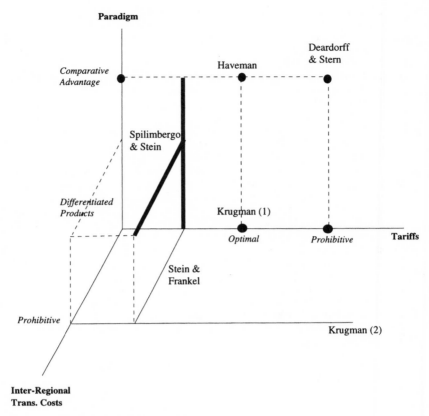

Fig. 5C.1   Mapping out the literature

world with differentiated products, trade in their world is determined by more traditional comparative advantage. The results provided by Deardorff and Stern run counter to the Krugman result, but this is due to the inclusion of prohibitive tariffs. Having isolated trade diversion (Krugman 1) and trade creation (Deardorff and Stern), the results in Haveman stem from an approach that incorporates equal parts of each. The results largely reinforce the negative Krugman result and establish its robustness across different trade paradigms (the vertical axis in figure 5C.1). He goes on, however, to note that the decline in welfare can be eliminated if the blocs are restricted in their ability to raise their ex post external tariffs.

Not to be outdone, Krugman also extended the literature and overturned his own result in Krugman (1991b) by incorporating prohibitive interregional transport costs. With this modification, welfare is seen to be an increasing function of bloc formation. In a similar vein, Stein and Frankel (1994) provide a bridge between these extremes by allowing interregional transport costs to vary between zero and infinity. What they find is that bloc formation will increase world welfare if it is undertaken by natural trading partners, those with sufficiently low transport costs.

Having set this background, it is now clear where the current paper fits into the literature. The Spilimbergo and Stein paper is in the same spirit as the Stein and Frankel paper. That is, it is general enough to allow for a continuum of options along two separate dimensions. Spilimbergo and Stein allow for a continuum of possible interregional transport costs and all manner of trading regimes between comparative advantage and differentiated products. Their contribution, then, is the bold lines in the figure. On its face, their contribution appears to be more substantial than that of any other author. Other aspects of their model include countries of different sizes and varied degrees of bloc preference; that is, countries need not totally eliminate the barriers between them when forming a bloc.

Having filled in the literature map, we can now turn to more specific issues associated with this paper. Having contributed to the literature myself, I was predisposed to appreciate this work. Whenever one sees a simulation analysis, however, one has to ask if this is an appropriate place for it. Simulation analysis does have a place in economic analysis, and my take is that the current model is sufficiently complex that this is as good a place as any for it. That notwithstanding, I do have a number of concerns.

First, I admire Spilimbergo and Stein's effort to incorporate production into the analysis. This was notably absent from the Krugman and Haveman work. On the other hand, it is not clear that production is present in other than its name. That is, in the absence of the ability to substitute capital for labor and vice versa, and a differentiated products model with the number of varieties given exogenously, is production really incorporated into the model in any meaningful way? I would contend that in fact it is not; what we have is really a world full of endowment economies. While stealth can work for warfare, it can be rather misleading in a paper such as this; that is, it makes it very difficult for the reader to discern the true source of the results.

A second concern stems from the choice of tariffs in the model. Without some notion as to where the tariffs lie relative to some benchmark, perhaps optimal tariffs, one is unsure how to go about the interpretation of their effects. In particular, in figure 5.3, as we increase the degree of product differentiation, the extent to which the tariffs influence matters changes. The greater the degree of product differentiation, the higher will be optimal tariffs, and the less relevant will be any fixed tariff. So, while I admit that we seldom witness optimal tariffs in practice, I will put them forward as a useful theoretical tool. When analyzing phenomenon that we do not understand, it is best to make use of tools that we understand. I argue that we understand the impact of optimal tariffs to a greater extent than we understand the influence of any arbitrary tariff.

Third, the model introduces an asymmetry of country size. While I applaud this addition, it is not clear what it contributes to our understanding. Asymmetry for its own sake is not terribly meaningful unless you think about the motivation for its introduction. There are any variety of motivations to which one might appeal to justify its inclusion, none of which seem to apply here. In particular, the motivation for small countries to join into blocs with large countries is to obtain an enhanced number of varieties of goods. I would argue that this motivation is not well represented in reality. Poor countries are more often striving to secure a source of supply for their limited needs than they are trying to vary their day-to-day diet. My fear is that without a firm grounding in reality, the asymmetry assumption and its corresponding result on the preference margins are rendered vacuous.

Finally, I would like to address the presentation of the results. The difference between standard theory and simulations is somewhat akin to the difference between a Ferrari and a Jeep Cherokee. The Ferrari is a wonderful tool, and it will do many special things for you. If, however, your goal is to climb the Himalayas, one would do better driving the Cherokee. Granted the Cherokee will not take you to the top, but it will smooth out many rough spots. What these authors have done is to abandon their Ferrari, an act with which I have no problem, jumped into the Cherokee, driven up to the end of the foothills of the Himalayas, stepped out of the Cherokee, and examined the view from there. All of this rather than pushing the Cherokee to its limits.

All of this is by way of saying that they are using a powerful tool but are not making use of all that it has to offer. As an example, in each of the graphs, a small number of observations is presented. The computer is capable, and is tireless in this endeavor, of producing a nice smooth continuum of observations for each of the figures provided. In addition, with respect to my remarks on the chosen tariff level, there is no reason not to produce results for many different choices of tariffs and then publish an average, with perhaps a high-low element built into the figure. There are powerful tools that might be brought to bear on this project, and the results would be strengthened tremendously by using them.

Having said my piece, I would like to finish by saying that I like the direction in which this paper is heading. It will be an important contribution to an important literature. As trading blocs become the call of the day, understanding their influence on the world as a whole is very important.

References

Deardorff, A. V., and R. M. Stern. 1994. Multilateral Trade Negotiations and Preferential Trading Agreements. In A. V. Deardorff and R. M. Stern, eds., *Analytical and Negotiating Issues in the Global Trading System*. Ann Arbor: University of Michigan Press.

Haveman, J. D. 1996. Some Welfare Effects of Sequential Customs Union Formation. *Canadian Journal of Economics* 29:941–58.

Krugman, P. R. 1991a. Is Bilateralism Bad? In E. Helpman and A. Razin, eds., *International Trade and Trade Policy*. Cambridge: MIT Press.

————. 1991b. The Move to Free Trade Zones. In Federal Reserve Bank of Kansas City, *Policy Implications of Trade and Currency Zones.* Kansas City: Federal Reserve Bank.

Stein, E., and J. Frankel. 1993. Transport Costs and the Welfare Implications of Free Trade Agreements. Manuscript.

Comment   Edward E. Leamer

Spilimbergo and Stein have tackled a very difficult and extremely important problem: Are we in a Heckscher-Ohlin world or a Chamberlinian world? Is it factor supplies that drive trade, or is it economies of scale, product differentiation, and strategic interactions?

As NAFTA was under consideration, workers earning $10 an hour in the United States looked south with Heckscher-Ohlin glasses and saw a huge Mexican low-skilled low-wage workforce that was prepared to do the same work for less than a $1 an hour. A sharp fall in U.S. wages for low-skilled workers seemed an inevitable consequence of economic integration with Mexico.

Many Mexicans looked north with Chamberlinian glasses. They saw the technological leadership of the United States and the skilled U.S. workforce and the large, highly efficient operations of U.S. businesses, and they worried that in an economic partnership with such a country Mexicans would be stuck with the "bad" jobs in the "bad" sectors, namely those that offered no economies of scale and very low levels of learning by doing. Mexicans in the twenty-first century would be sewing shirts in sweatshops and assembling electronics while U.S. workers would be writing software in fancy office buildings.

Which are the "right" kind of glasses? How much of the consequences of NAFTA will be driven by Heckscher-Ohlin comparative-costs considerations and how much by economies of scale, externalities, and hysteresis?

Answers to these important questions can be sought using four different methodologies: theory, calibration, indirect estimation, and direct observation.

By *theory* I mean writing down a fairly simple model that includes both Heckscher-Ohlin (HO) and Chamberlinian possibilities and then deriving qualitative results about the conditions under which one effect dominates. For example, a familiar result in an HO framework is that an abundant factor benefits from economic integration and a scarce factor suffers. Maybe one could write down a structure that would lead to a new result: in countries abundant in human capital, both skilled and unskilled workers benefit from economic integration; but in countries that are scarce in human capital, unskilled workers benefit but skilled workers suffer. Or something like this.

Edward E. Leamer is the Chauncey J. Medberry Professor of Management and professor of economics at University of California, Los Angeles, and a research associate of the National Bureau of Economic Research.

By *calibration* I mean writing down a relatively complex model into which are inserted "plausible" numerical values for the parameters, and then using the system to simulate an intervention such as NAFTA. The system has to be too complex to solve analytically because it includes features that are intended to capture all the relevant aspects of the problem. By *indirect estimation* I mean writing down a not too complex model and estimating it with appropriate econometric techniques. By *direct observation* I mean finding equivalent historical events such as the entrance of Portugal and Spain into the European Common Market, or waiting to see what happens as a result of NAFTA.

Which of these approaches is fruitful? Which is best? What do we mean by best?

I take it as given that the goal should be to change our minds. With that as the goal, each of these four approaches can be fruitful. Any of them can change the mind of the analyst and if he or she is lucky can also change the mind of the analyst's audience. But each can turn out disappointing. And if we don't keep our eyes firmly focused on the goal, sometimes an approach is bound to be disappointing.

This paper that I am discussing falls somewhere between the first two approaches, theory and computable general equilibrium modeling. The model that is used is too complex to allow qualitative theorems. But it is not as complex as most CGE models, which attempt more completely to include all relevant factors. It looks to me to be equivalent to a model with taste for variety driven by a Cobb-Douglas utility function written in terms of agricultural goods and the services of manufactures, the latter being a Dixit-Stiglitz index of product variety in manufactures. Each variety is produced subject to a fixed cost. The model also includes transport costs that separate countries. Using this structure, the authors provide what might be called numerical theorems. As such, the approach will make neither the theorists nor the CGE modelers very happy. Theorists will not be happy because numerical theorems by their very nature are extremely special cases. Theorems derive their value from being both mathematically fragile and substantively sturdy. A theorem is mathematically fragile if no assumption can be relaxed without altering the validity of the theorem. A theorem is substantively sturdy if substantively "minor" changes in the assumptions do not alter the "content" of the theorem. The problem with a numerical theorem is that it is very hard to tell if it is mathematically fragile and substantively sturdy. Spilimbergo and Stein do attempt to address the question of fragility. Here is a quotation: "It is only for extremely low preference for variety (high θ) that the model yields results similar to those in Haveman and in Deardorff and Stern. Krugman's conclusion, then, is more robust to the inclusion of comparative advantage in his model than Deardorff and Stern's is to the introduction of preference for variety in one of the goods." I wonder what they would say if I used their model with $\gamma = \theta^{1/100}$, and claimed that for wide ranges of γ the model is similar to Haveman and Deardorff and

Stern? In other words, the words "extremely low preference for variety" have no real meaning.

A useful theorem makes us look at the world in a new way. Either it lays out the issues with increased clarity or it suggests some surprising implications. This paper is very good in terms of laying out the issues: comparative costs, fixed costs, and distance. But I don't think that the results are both sturdy and surprising. If one mixes together distance, comparative costs, and economies of scale/product differentiation, what are the possibilities? A country should look for a faraway partner? Probably not. Not much to be gained there. A poor country should look for a rich neighbor or a poor one? A rich country should look for a rich partner or a poor one? This could go either way. If you tell me there is a definite answer, I think that I could produce an equally plausible model with the reverse answer. Should a country look for a partner with high tariff walls or low ones? If you are planning to sell into the partner's market, better that it is a protected market with a high tariff.

Theorists won't find these numerical theorems much to their liking. CGE modelers will also be unhappy with the model presented here because it is far too simple. There are no Mexican oil exports, no migration from southern Mexico to the north or to the United States, no Mexican apparel exports, no Chinese apparel exports, no maquiladoras, no capital flows, no Japanese direct investment, no Mexican land policy, no Pacto, no . . .

As for myself, I like methods 3 and 4: Give me data, or give me death.

6   Regional Patterns in the Law of One Price: The Roles of Geography versus Currencies

Charles Engel and John H. Rogers

6.1 Introduction

The failure of the law of one price has been a puzzle for economists at least since Isard's classic 1977 study. There has been renewed interest in this problem recently. A significant motivation for this resurgence of interest has been the apparently large misalignment of prices between the United States and other countries, most notably Japan. For example, in April 1995, according to the *Economist,* a Big Mac cost $2.32 in the United States but the dollar price of a Big Mac in Japan was $4.65. In June 1995, the cover price of an issue of the *Economist* was $3.50 in the United States, but the equivalent dollar price in Japan was $10.24.

A related question in international trade has concerned the degree to which markets have become regionalized. That is, are goods markets more integrated within regions than across regions? That is the question Frankel, Stein, and Wei (1994) address by examining the flow of goods between countries intraregionally and interregionally. They found that the claims that regional trading blocs are emerging are greatly exaggerated. We address this issue by examining whether price variability is smaller within regions than between regions.

A region might consist, for example, of the nations of the European Union, or the states of the United States. There are several reasons why there may be

Charles Engel is professor of economics at the University of Washington and a research associate of the National Bureau of Economic Research. John H. Rogers is an economist at the Board of Governors of the Federal Reserve System.

The authors thank Anthony Creane, Jeffrey Frankel, Kenneth Froot, and Michael Knetter for useful comments and discussions. Part of the work on this project was completed while Engel was a visiting scholar at the Federal Reserve Bank of Kansas City and at the International Monetary Fund. The views expressed in this paper are not necessarily shared by the Federal Reserve System or the IMF. Engel also acknowledges assistance from the National Science Foundation, NSF grant SBR-932078.

smaller price disparities intraregionally than interregionally. Most obviously, two locations within a region are usually closer than two locations in different regions. The pricing-to-market literature (see, for example, Dornbusch 1987; Krugman 1987; Froot and Klemperer 1989; and Knetter 1989) has generally assumed that locations are completely separated, so that price discrimination is feasible, without any possibility of consumers arbitraging differences in final goods prices. Engel and Rogers (1995) have noted that, while little arbitrage is used to take advantage of differences in prices of consumer goods, at the intermediate goods level some constraints on the degree of price discrimination are possible. The closer two locations are, the less dispersion is likely in these intermediate goods prices. This in turn will reflect on the amount of cohesion in final goods prices. We would expect the amount of price dispersion to be positively related to the distance between the locations.

Another reason why there may be less price variability intraregionally is that the nominal exchange rate between locations within a region is often fixed, or at least not very variable. Cities within the United States share a common currency; the exchange rate between Germany and the Netherlands has been virtually fixed for a number of years; and the French franc has floated against the German mark within a narrow band under the exchange rate mechanism of the European Monetary System. If nominal prices are sticky in the currency of the country in which the final good is sold, then when the nominal exchange rate between two countries is highly volatile, the relative prices of similar goods across the two countries will be similarly volatile. On the other hand, when the exchange rate is quiescent, there is not much variance in relative prices.

A third possible explanation for the importance of regions is that frequently countries in a region form free trade areas, customs unions, or common markets. The absence of barriers to trade clearly could help to explain why the law of one price holds more nearly within regions.

Price dispersion may be smaller for countries within a region because price-discriminating monopolists may charge similar markups. The pricing-to-market literature has placed emphasis on how these markups respond to changes in the exchange rate. We note that variation in markups could account for fluctuations in prices of similar goods between locations. Within a region there may be smaller differences in demand elasticities across locations, so there may be little variation in markups intraregionally.

The pricing-to-market literature focuses on the prices of exports. Our work examines consumer prices. One channel for price variation that would be important in retail prices, but not reflected in export prices, arises from the costs associated with distribution and marketing. If these costs vary from location to location, they can contribute to price dispersion. We shall argue that a distinguishing feature of locations within a region is that they share a unified distribution system for final goods. For example, if a nationwide department-store chain in the United States sells some product, many of the costs of bringing that good to market are not specific to the location in which the good is sold. Advertising, packaging, and services undertaken at the corporate headquarters are reflected in the final goods price, but are not a function of conditions in the retailing location. So prices of goods distributed under a unified system share a significant common cost component.

Recent studies have amassed important new evidence on the nature of failures of the law of one price. The large empirical literature on pricing-to-market—which examines export and import prices of very homogeneous products—has recently been augmented by Knetter's study (1994) of pricing to market of German exports. Knetter concludes that German firms charge much higher prices to Japanese importers than to other markets, and thus pricing to market accounts in large part for the high Japanese retail prices. Engel (1993) examines the extent to which failures of the law of one price can explain real exchange rate movements. He finds that the relative prices of similar goods across countries have much greater variance than relative prices of different goods within a country. Rogers and Jenkins (1995) reach similar conclusions regarding the degree of persistence of shocks to relative prices. Engel and Rogers (1995) find that the dispersion of prices of similar goods between cities in Canada and the United States is greater the farther apart the cities are. This evidence favors the notion that price discrimination can account for price differences between locations. But they find that the variance is much greater for cities that lie in different countries compared to equidistant cities in the same country. This indicates that marketing costs or price stickiness is important.

Ghosh and Wolf (1994), examining the cover price of the *Economist,* find evidence in favor of the sticky-price story as opposed to pricing to market. They find that the time pattern of price adjustment is consistent with a menu-cost explanation of price adjustment. Froot, Kim, and Rogoff (1995) examine several decades of data on individual goods prices of commodities in England and Holland. They find that the degree of persistence of deviations from the law of one price has not changed much over the centuries, suggesting that nominal exchange rate volatility cannot account for all of the failure. Cumby (1993) finds that in fact there is fairly rapid convergence to the law of one price for Big Macs during the floating rate period: 70 percent of the price gap across countries disappears within a year.

Here we explore further the notions that pricing to market and nominal price stickiness matter for the failures of the law of one price. The basic notion of this paper is that the degree of failure of the law of one price for goods sold in two different locations will depend on the distance between those locations if price discrimination is significant. To the degree that nominal price stickiness is important, however, prices of similar goods will exhibit more variance between countries the greater is the variation in the nominal exchange rate of those two countries' currency. So, using price data on individual goods from dozens of countries, we relate the variation in prices of similar goods across countries to the distance between those countries, and the variance of their nominal exchange rates.[1]

But, as we have noted, we pay special attention to the variability of prices within regions. If the markups are more similar within regions, or if the distribution system is more homogenized, then we expect that price dispersion will be lower for pairs of countries located within regions.

In section 6.2, we review some of the standard explanations for the failure of the law of one price. We discuss how market segmentation and price discrimination can lead to failures, and the role of sticky nominal prices. Our story about unified distribution systems within a region is less familiar, so we lay out a simple model and explore its implications.

Then we proceed to examination of the data. First, we describe the data on goods prices and provide some summary statistics. The remainder of the paper is concerned with the regressions relating price dispersion to distance and other geographic factors, exchange rate variability, measures of trade barriers, and regional variables.

6.2 Failure of the Law of One Price and Regionalization

When the law of one price fails between two locations, there is evidence that the markets are not completely integrated. One of the most direct implications of rational behavior is that two identical goods selling in the same market should have the same price.

Clearly one reason that prices may not be equalized is that there is some cost to shipping goods between locations. Even prices of such homogeneous and durable goods as copper, for which international commodity markets are well-established, have some price variation across locations. When goods are costly to transport, then arbitrage may not fully equalize prices.

If transport costs are sufficiently high, then no arbitrage takes place. That is the assumption implicit in much of the "pricing-to-market," or exchange rate "pass-through," literature. In fact, there seems to be very little evidence of arbitrage in final goods beyond a few well-known anecdotes. For example, we know that shopping malls appeared on the northern border of the United States at a time when many prices of consumer goods were lower in the United States than they were in Canada (when prices were expressed in a common currency). More recently, before the peso devaluation in late 1994, similar outlets opened on the U.S. side of its southern border. At times it has been relatively easy for consumers to import luxury German cars directly from Germany, rather than buying them from a U.S. dealer. And there is the famous puzzle that, for some consumer products, Japanese find it cheaper to fly to the United States and buy

1. Wei and Parsley (1995), in a work done simultaneously and independently, address many of the issues we do. However, their main focus is on the convergence to PPP.

the goods from American retailers than to buy them at Japanese outlets. However, all of these practices are small relative to the total volume of trade.

But the dearth of opportunities for arbitrage in final goods undoubtedly masks the constraints that international trade places on final goods prices. As Engel and Rogers (1995) note, the final good purchased by consumers is really a joint product—the actual good itself, and the retailing services that bring the good to market. We can think of the physical good as an intermediate good, with price q, that is an input into the final consumer good. Suppose there were iceberg transport costs, so that only a fraction of the good, δ, remained after the good was shipped to a foreign country. Arbitrage insures that $q \leq q^*/\delta$, where q^* is the price of the intermediate good in the foreign country. If this relationship did not hold, arbitrageurs would export the good from the home to the foreign country, which would tend to drive up prices domestically and down abroad. Similarly, we must have $\delta q^* \leq q$, lest arbitrageurs export goods from the foreign country to the home. So fluctuations in the relative price of the intermediate good in the two locations are constrained within bands: $\delta \leq q/q^* \leq 1/\delta$.

Tariffs or other barriers to trade act much like transport costs in creating wedges between prices of traded goods in different locations. Suppose that the foreign country puts an ad valorem tariff of τ^* on imports from the domestic country. Then, arbitrage guarantees only $q^* \leq (1 + \tau^*)q$. Likewise, if τ is the tariff rate imposed by the domestic country, $q \leq (1 + \tau)q^*$. So the relative price q/q^* can fluctuate in the range from $1/(1 + \tau^*)$ to $1 + \tau$.

The distribution and marketing services contribute to the cost of the final good. If the good were sold in competitive markets, the price of the good would be greater than q by an amount equal to the value of the marginal product of the factors providing the distribution and marketing services. Even if the intermediate product were to have the same price in the two locations, the retail price could differ because nontraded inputs go into marketing. Sanyal and Jones (1982) present a general equilibrium model that has this structure—no final goods are traded, but all consumer goods contain an intermediate traded component, which they call a "middle product." As returns to the nontraded inputs into marketing vary over time, the final goods prices will vary between locations.

If final goods could be traded costlessly, then taxes (other than trade taxes) should not contribute to differences in prices between locations. Gasoline sells for the same price on either side of State Line Road, which separates Kansas City, Kansas, from Kansas City, Missouri, although gasoline taxes are different in the two states. But, if the final product is not traded, then both taxes levied on producers and consumers may cause prices to differ between locations. These would cause differences in prices in exactly the same way as returns to nontraded factors used in marketing and distribution: variation over time in taxes can lead to variation over time in relative final goods prices.

It is probably not accurate to describe most consumer goods markets as competitive. If there is some monopoly in the final goods market, then the price may exceed marginal cost. In most models of imperfect competition, the size of the markup is inversely related to the elasticity of demand for the product. The elasticity of demand may be different in different locations, and may vary over time, both because tastes are different (and changing) and because the elasticity of demand may change as we move along a given demand curve.

We note that our empirical work detects movement in the prices of similar goods in different locations. If prices were not equalized, but the discrepancy were constant, it would not show up in our data. We can conclude that deviations from the law of one price of the type we detect can be attributed to (1) the wedge in the price of traded intermediate goods that arises from transport costs or from trade taxes; or (2) variation in the prices of nontraded inputs into distribution, in consumer and producer taxes, and in the markup over marginal costs. Constant ad valorem tariffs or iceberg transport costs allow variation in the relative prices between locations. However, the differences in prices of nontraded inputs, consumer or producer taxes, or markups across locations need to change over time to account for variation in relative prices.

One other explanation for failures of the law of one price that vary over time arises when final goods prices are set in the currency of the location where the good is sold. If these prices are preset, and thus do not respond rapidly to shocks, then the prices between locations will change if they are expressed in a common currency and the nominal exchange rate varies. Floating exchange rates have been very volatile—much more volatile than aggregate price levels at the least (see Mussa 1986), so the sticky-price theory seems a natural path to explore. A complete theory of sticky nominal prices would take into account some of the factors we have already noted.

For example, consider a menu-cost model of the type proposed by Mankiw (1985). When there is an infinitesimal shock to demand, the loss in profits from not adjusting prices in that model is second-order. For a small but finite shock to demand, there is a loss in profits if the price is not adjusted optimally. However, if there is a small menu cost, then nonadjustment may be optimal. The size of menu costs needed to make sticky prices optimal depends on the elasticity of demand. If demand were perfectly elastic, as in competitive markets, then the firm would lose all of its sales if it did not adjust prices. The more inelastic is demand, the smaller the loss from nonadjustment.

In the international context, distance between locations could contribute to price stickiness. The more isolated a country is, the fewer foreign competitors it will have. U.S. car manufacturers are less vulnerable to imports of German cars than are French producers, because of transport costs. When a firm faces fewer competitors, the elasticity of demand for its product will be lower, thus increasing the likelihood of nominal price stickiness.

In the introductory remarks, we noted that two countries within a region may have a higher correlation of prices of similar goods for a number of reasons. Distance is smaller, trade barriers are lower, demand elasticities (and hence markups) may be more similar, and their nominal exchange rate may be less variable. These effects are familiar. In section 6.3, we advance a theory based on distribution costs. Locations in a region may share a common distribution system.

6.3 Distribution Costs and Regions

6.3.1 Prices within a Region

A model in which intermediate goods are traded but final goods are sold only to domestic consumers by a monopolistic distributor captures the essential features described in section 6.2. Prices differ between locations because of location-specific costs of marketing, and because of differences across locations in the markup by the monopolist.

Not all marketing costs are local. Corporations often set up distribution networks to many locations. The distribution entails fixed costs that are not specific to the point where the good is sold. For example, advertising campaigns generally entail significant up-front costs that are large relative to the local costs. The services performed at corporate headquarters—accounting, legal, management, and so forth—are not location specific. Packaging and assembly often occurs at a single plant, with the final product distributed to many locations.

Our definition of "region" is a group of locations that share a distribution system. This region may consist of cities in one country or a part of a country, or a group of countries. Indeed, a set of locations may be a region for some goods while for other goods it is not.

Our definition of region stems in part from our earlier work (Engel and Rogers 1995). There we investigated the dispersion of prices of similar goods among twenty-three cities in Canada and the United States. We found that distance between locations was important in explaining the range of fluctuations of prices between city pairs. However, taking distance into account, there was much more dispersion between city pairs that lay on opposite sides of the international border than for city pairs within either country. One explanation for this finding is that prices are sticky in terms of the currency of the country that the good is sold in. Because the exchange rate was floating between these two countries, the relative prices between cross-border city pairs fluctuated as the exchange rate changed.

However, we found that the sticky-price story cannot account for more than half of the border effect. We can measure relative prices between locations without taking the exchange rate into account. For example, we can take the price of food in Toronto relative to the overall consumer price index (CPI) in Toronto, and compare that to the price of food in Chicago relative to the overall CPI in Chicago. There is a significant border effect even when using these relative-relative prices. That is, relative-relative prices among cross-border city pairs are still much more variable than relative-relative prices for intranational city pairs, taking into account distance effects. One cannot attribute this finding to sticky prices and floating exchange rates, since the exchange rate is not used in the calculation of prices. Although we do not pinpoint the source of this border effect, a plausible explanation is that there is more integration of the distribution and marketing systems for cities within each country than there is across countries.

Our model consists of two small countries in general equilibrium. We consider two cases. When intermediate goods are traded, but not final goods which require marketing inputs, then the two countries are not members of a region. When the two countries share a marketing system so that all final goods can be traded between themselves, but not with the rest of the world, they are in a region. To keep matters simple, we eliminate all of the complications discussed in section 6.2—transport costs, tariffs and taxes, sticky prices, and so forth. Furthermore, when we consider two countries within a region, we assume an exporter bears no marketing costs that are local in the importing country.

We first consider the model with no "region."

There are four goods. A unit of good z, which is the numeraire, is produced with one unit of labor in all countries—at home, abroad, and in the world economy. This good is consumed by individuals, and does not require any marketing. It can be thought of as a simple, homogeneous product such as fuel oil. Engel (1993) finds that, even for consumer prices, the failure of the law of one price is not too large for such products.

Good x also requires a fixed labor input. Its price in the world economy is p_x. The required labor input for good x may differ in the home country and the foreign country, and in each country this may differ from p_x. There is a fixed supply of labor at home and abroad. In each country that labor force is devoted entirely to the production of good x or good z, depending on the pattern of comparative advantage.[2] Each country acquires the good it does not produce through international trade, either with the other small country or with the rest of the world.

So, let L be the labor supply in the domestic country. If the country produces good z, then $L - z$ is the amount of exports of good z, and we have

$$L - z = p_x x.$$

If the country produces good x, its exports are $L - p_x x$ and its imports are z.

There are also two final goods that require marketing. For concreteness, think of the two goods as McDonald's hamburgers (good 1) and Wimpy's hamburgers (good 2). Consumers in each of the domestic and foreign countries get utility from consumption of both goods. However, both goods are not necessarily marketed in each country.

---

2. Except, of course, in the knife-edge case in which the required labor input for good x equals p_x.

Both goods use x as an intermediate input. For now, we concentrate on the home country. Output of goods 1 and 2 is determined by the production functions

$$y_1 = \gamma x_1 - a,$$

and

$$y_2 = \eta x_2 - b.$$

The marginal costs in units of good x of marketing goods 1 and 2 respectively are $1/\gamma$ and $1/\eta$. These costs may be different in the foreign country. The fixed costs of marketing—a and b—may also be different in the foreign country.

When the two small countries are not in a region, goods 1 and 2 are not traded. Consumers must buy these goods from local producers.

The representative consumer maximizes

$$U = \frac{\alpha}{1 - \phi} c_1^{1-\phi} + \frac{\beta}{1-\phi} c_2^{1-\phi} + c_z, \qquad 0 < \phi < 1,$$

subject to the constraint

$$\Pi + L = p_1 c_1 + p_2 c_2 + c_z.$$

The representative consumer owns shares in the firms that produce goods 1 and 2. It takes the profits from these firms as given. The sum of the profits the consumer receives from these firms is Π.

Demand for each good is given by

$$c_1 = (p_1/\alpha)^{-1/\phi},$$

$$c_2 = (p_2/\beta)^{-1/\phi},$$

and

$$c_z = \Pi + L - c_1 - c_2.$$

We assume that L is so large that consumption of z is always positive. Note that the elasticity of substitution between c_1 and c_2, as well as the elasticity of demand for c_1 and c_2 with respect to p_1 and p_2 respectively, are given by $1/\phi$. If, in equilibrium, either good 1 or good 2 is not produced, then its demand is zero, but the demand for the other goods is as given.

The monopolists that produce goods 1 and 2 set prices to maximize profits given by

$$\Pi_1 = p_1 y_1 - p_x x_1, \qquad \text{subject to } y_1 = c_1,$$

and

$$\Pi_2 = p_2 y_2 - p_x x_2, \qquad \text{subject to } y_2 = c_2.$$

The optimal prices are markups over marginal costs:

$$p_1 = \frac{p_x}{\gamma(1 - \phi)},$$

and

$$p_2 = \frac{p_x}{\eta(1 - \phi)}.$$

If, at these prices, one or both firms' profits are negative, the firm chooses not to produce at all. (The fixed costs—a and b—are not sunk costs.)

The equilibrium condition for the economy,

$$p_x x + z = p_x(x_1 + x_2) + c_z,$$

is equivalent to the representative consumer's budget constraint, with $\Pi = \Pi_1 + \Pi_2$.

If both Wimpy's and McDonald's hamburgers are sold in the home country, the exact price index for hamburgers, p, is given by

$$p = \left(\omega p_1^{(\phi-1)/\phi} + (1 - \omega)p_2^{(\phi-1)/\phi} \right)^{\phi/(\phi-1)}$$

$$= \frac{p_x}{1 - \phi} \left(\omega\gamma^{(\phi-1)/\phi} + (1 - \omega)\eta^{(\phi-1)/\phi} \right)^{\phi/(\phi-1)},$$

where the weight that good 1 receives in the index, ω, is given by

$$\omega = \frac{\alpha^{1/\phi}}{\alpha^{1/\phi} + \beta^{1/\phi}}.$$

Of course, if only one of the burgers is sold in the home country, the burger price index is simply the price of that burger.

The setup is the same in the foreign country, but any of the taste or technology parameters may be different than in the home country. We have

$$p_1^* = \frac{p_x}{\gamma^*(1 - \phi^*)},$$

and

$$p_2^* = \frac{p_x}{\eta^*(1 - \phi^*)},$$

if both goods are produced.

There are a large number of cases to consider when the countries are not part of a region, but we will focus on one in which only McDonald's burgers are sold in the home country and only Wimpy's burgers are sold in the foreign country. In other words, in the home country, the fixed cost a is low enough so that good 1 is profitable, but b, the fixed cost for good 2, is too high for that firm to make profits. The situation is reversed in the foreign country. So, $p = p_1$ and $p^* = p_2^*$.

In this case, there are two reasons why hamburger prices could be different at home and abroad—the marginal cost of distribution could be different ($1/\gamma$ versus $1/\eta^*$), and the markup could differ ($1/(1 - \phi)$ versus $1/(1 - \phi^*)$).

Now, compare this to the case in which the two countries are in a region. For simplicity, we consider a world in which McDonald's in the home country is licensed to sell McDonald's hamburgers in both countries (so that the foreign producer of McDonald's is ruled out of the market) and the foreign Wimpy's is licensed to sell Wimpy's burgers in both countries. Alternatively, we could think of this as being the case in which the fixed costs b and a^* are so high that firm 2 at home and firm 1 abroad would never find it profitable to sell burgers.

Each producer can price discriminate, since it is the only one with the distribution facilities to sell its burgers in both countries. So McDonald's will set prices as

$$p_1 = \frac{p_x}{\gamma(1 - \phi)},$$

and

$$p_1^* = \frac{p_x}{\gamma(1 - \phi^*)}.$$

Wimpy's prices will be

$$p_2 = \frac{p_x}{\eta^*(1 - \phi)},$$

and

$$p_2^* = \frac{p_x}{\eta^*(1 - \phi^*)}.$$

Note that, if $\phi = \phi^*$, then prices of both burgers are the same at home and abroad.

Even if $\phi = \phi^*$, the burger price indexes need not be identical. Home-country residents, for example, might have a preference for McDonald's hamburgers, so $\omega > \omega^*$. Under these assumptions, however, it is easy to show that $(p/p^*)_R$, the ratio of the price indexes if these two countries were in a region, is closer to unity than p_1/p_2^*, which would be the ratio of the price indexes if the two countries were not in a region.[3] This means that the range of fluctuation of the relative burger price indexes would be smaller for two countries that are in the same region.

However, if the elasticities of demand in the two countries are sufficiently

---

3. This proposition and the one discussed in the next paragraph are demonstrated in appendix B.

different, so that the difference in the markups is large, it is possible that the burger price index could fluctuate even more for two countries that are in the same region than for countries that are not in the same region. This theoretical possibility seems unlikely to occur in practice, however, because it requires large differences in tastes between residents in the two locations.

The utility function in this section is separable in consumption of goods 1 and 2. This results in a demand curve for good 1 that does not depend on p_2, and likewise for good 2. This rules out an important case that section 6.3.2 discusses: that McDonald's could drive out Wimpy's (or vice versa) if the two countries are in a region. In the model of this section, regionalization might cause the burger price indexes in the two locations to be more nearly equal because it leads to a diffusion of products across the regions. Wimpy's and McDonald's are consumed in both regions after regionalization, so the burger price indexes are weighted averages of both burger prices in both locations. In the model of section 6.3.2, regionalization leads to harmonization of burger prices simply because one burger firm becomes dominant and drives out the other. Everybody in both locations ends up eating only McDonald's burgers.

Before turning to that model, we close out the model of a country within a region by noting the equilibrium conditions for the home country, which produces good 1. Profits for industry 1 are given by

$$\Pi_1 = p_1 y_1 - p_x x_1.$$

The budget constraint for individuals is given by

$$\Pi_1 + L = p_1 c_1 + p_2 c_2 + z.$$

Combining these two yields the trade balance condition, with exports on the left-hand side (assuming the country exports good x as well as good 1):

$$p_1(y_1 - c_1) + L - p_x x_1 = z + p_2 c_2.$$

6.3.2   Can Regionalization Reduce Variety?

In this section, we consider a world in which consumers might switch from Wimpy's burgers to McDonald's burgers if the price of McDonald's burgers were low enough. When the two countries are isolated, Wimpy's could exist in one and McDonald's in the other. But, if firms are able to extend their distribution system across both countries, we may find that the firm that is most efficient at marketing drives out its competitor, even when the goods are not identical. What we are describing, of course, is the homogenization of consumer products across countries that any world traveler will have noticed.

The model presented here is highly parameterized, because what we wish to show is that, for some parameter values, McDonald's might drive Wimpy's out. We will first consider the equilibrium when the two countries are in a region so that final goods can be marketed in both countries, and show how only McDonald's might sell burgers. Then we show that, if the two countries were not members of a region, Wimpy's might be sold in one of the countries.

Consumers in both countries have the same preferences. In the home country, they maximize

$$U = \ln\left(2c_1^{1/2} + 2c_2^{1/2}\right) + z.$$

If both goods 1 and 2 are sold in the market, the demand by a typical consumer is

$$c_1 = \frac{p_2}{2p_1(p_1 + p_2)},$$

and

$$c_2 = \frac{p_1}{2p_2(p_1 + p_2)}.$$

We assume that world population is 2, so, letting a tilde represent world demand, we have $\tilde{c}_1 = 2c_1$ and $\tilde{c}_2 = 2c_2$.

Suppose one of the goods, good 2, is not sold. Then demand for good 1 is given by

$$c_1 = \frac{1}{2p_1},$$

and $\tilde{c}_1 = 1/p_1$.

Firm 1 in the home country can produce McDonald's burgers according to

$$y_1 = x_1 - a.$$

Firm 2 in the foreign country can produce Wimpy's burgers with the production function

$$y_2^* = x_2^* - b^*.$$

We will assume that b and a^* are so high that there are no competitors to these two monopolists that sell the same type of burger. Of course, they compete with each other, since the demand for one's burger depends on the price of the other's.

For notational convenience, we will drop the * when denoting firm 2's price and output.

Firms 1 and 2 are nearly symmetric. They face symmetric demand curves, and they have the same marginal cost of production. The only difference is that their fixed costs could differ. We will assume that McDonald's has the lower fixed costs, so $a < b^*$.

The fixed costs are not sunk costs, so if the firm decides not to produce, it does not bear any costs. Still, it is helpful first to calculate the equilibrium prices and profits if the costs were sunk, as a step toward finding the full equilibrium. So we will use the superscript SC (for sunk costs) to denote prices and profits from this Bertrand equilibrium.

We shall see that in this equilibrium both firms choose to produce if they ignore fixed costs. Hence, each firm faces the demand curve derived under the assumption that both goods are produced.

From the first-order condition for firm 1, taking firm 2's prices as given, we have

$$p_1^{SC} = p_x + \left(p_x^2 + p_x p_2 \right)^{1/2}.$$

For firm 2, we have

$$p_2^{SC} = p_x + \left(p_x^2 + p_x p_1 \right)^{1/2}.$$

Solving these two equations, we get

$$p_1^{SC} = p_2^{SC} = 3p_x.$$

Profits for firm 1 are given by

$$\Pi_1^{SC} = p_1^{SC} \tilde{c}_1 - p_x x_1 = 3p_x \tilde{c}_1 - p_x(\tilde{c}_1 + a) = 2p_x \tilde{c}_1 - p_x a.$$

We see that firm 1 chooses to produce at this price if it is ignoring fixed costs, since its profits exceed $-p_x a$. Using the fact that $p_1^{SC} = p_2^{SC} = 3p_x$, we can solve for c_1 and calculate

$$\Pi_1^{SC} = \frac{1}{3} - p_x a.$$

Parallel computations show

$$\Pi_2^{SC} = \frac{1}{3} - p_x b^*,$$

so, ignoring fixed costs, firm 2 also decides to produce.

Firm 1 might want to set its price lower than p_1^{SC}, however. If it set its price low enough, demand for firm 2's product might fall so low that firm 2 would not make a profit if it took into account its fixed costs. If firm 2 decided not to compete, then firm 1 has captured the entire market. Its demand will be higher and its profits may be higher than when it sets its price at p_1^{SC}.

Specifically, if firm 1 has captured the entire market, then its revenues are unity irrespective of the price it charges, since $p_1 c_1 = 1$ in that case. If firm 1 had the whole market to itself with no threat of entry by firm 2, it would produce arbitrarily close to zero and charge an arbitrarily high price. Because firm 2 is a potential entrant, however, it would set a price just low enough so that firm 2's profits would be zero. If its profits in that case were greater than Π_1^{SC}, then that is the equilibrium.

We will use the superscript *LP* (for limit pricing) to denote equilibrium prices and profits in this case. Three conditions must hold for an *LP* equilibrium. First, firm 1's profits must be greater than under the *SC* equilibrium. We have

$$\Pi_1^{LP} = p_1^{LP}\tilde{c}_1 - p_x x_1 = 1 - p_x(\tilde{c}_1 + a) = 1 - \frac{p_x}{p_1} - p_x a.$$

So, for $\Pi_1^{LP} > \Pi_1^{SC}$, we need

$$p_1^{LP} > \frac{3}{2}p_x.$$

The second condition is that at p_1^{LP}, firm 2's profits are just zero. Note that the best that firm 2 can do is set its price as above, according to

$$p_2 = p_x + \left(p_x^2 + p_x p_1\right)^{1/2}.$$

Firm 2 cannot price firm 1 out of the market since its fixed costs are higher than firm 1's. So, firm 1 sets p_1 so that

$$(p_2 - p_x)\frac{p_1}{p_2(p_1 + p_2)} - p_x b^* = 0.$$

If $p_x b^*$ is sufficiently high (greater than 0.2251),[4] then a value for p_1^{LP} exists that satisfies the first two conditions.

For $p_x b^* = 0.2251$, $p_1^{LP} = 3/2p_x$, and firm 1 is indifferent between setting p_1 at $3/2p_x$ and setting it at $3p_x$.

For $p_x b^* < 0.2251$, firm 1 and firm 2 set prices at $3p_x$. Both firms produce, and they both make profits in this case, since $p_x a < p_x b^* < 1/3$.

The third condition for an *LP* equilibrium is simply that, at the value of p_1^{LP} that satisfies the first two conditions, Π_1^{LP} be positive. If the fixed cost, a, is sufficiently low, this condition is satisfied. (For example, it is always satisfied if $a = 0$.)

So, if $p_x b^* > 0.2251$ and a is sufficiently low, McDonald's will price Wimpy's out of the market if the two countries are in the same region.

Regionalization means that Wimpy's may not produce. Regionalization might mean the number of brand declines, if in fact Wimpy's would have produced were it just serving the foreign market. It is easy to produce an equilibrium under which $p_x b^* > 0.2251$, but Wimpy's would sell burgers in the foreign country if it were isolated from the home country. For example, if fixed costs for the potential firm 1 in the foreign country were very high, so that $p_x a^*$ were large, then firm 2 in the foreign country would set its price just low enough to keep firm 1 from entering. If firm 1 were kept out of the market, then, when country 2 is in isolation and has a population of one, $p_1^* c_2^* = 1/2$, so that firm 2's revenue would not depend on its output. With $p_x a^*$ sufficiently

---

4. Or, more exactly, $3\sqrt{5}/[10\sqrt{2} + 7\sqrt{5}]$.

large, p_2^* could be so high and c_2^* so low, that $\Pi_2^* = p_2^* c_2^* - p_x x_2^* = 1/2 - p_x$ $(c_2^* + b^*)$ would be positive.

The implications of this example for hamburger prices are straightforward. If the two countries are not in the same region, their burger prices are different. Indeed, they do not even sell the same type of burger. But, if the countries become regionalized, only one type of burger is marketed in the region—in this example, at the same price in both countries.

6.4 Empirical Findings

We investigate the behavior of final goods prices for eight goods (plus the aggregate CPIs) measured in as many as twenty-three countries and eight North American cities. We investigate the determinants of failures of the law of one price between the locations.

Our data are monthly price indexes for the overall CPI and subcategories of the CPI such as food, fuel, and so forth. The data are described in detail in appendix A. For each good i, and for each pair of locations jk, we construct a relative price, q_{jk}^i. Naturally, when the prices are from different countries, we use the nominal exchange rate to express prices in a common currency in constructing q_{jk}^i. Because our data are indexes and not actual prices, the level of q_{jk}^i does not reveal anything about whether the law of one price holds or not. If the law of one price holds closely, however, then q_{jk}^i would not vary much over time. Our measure of the magnitude of failures of the law of one price is a measure of the volatility of q_{jk}^i: the standard deviation of the first difference of this series.

The coverage of our price data varies from good to good. We have sufficiently long time series for the aggregate CPI for twenty-nine locations. For the individual goods, our country coverage ranges from twenty-nine locations for food prices down to fourteen locations for health and recreation prices. If N is the number of locations, then we have $N(N-1)/2$ location pairs.

While our data is both time-series and cross-section, the only use we make of the time series is to calculate the measure of volatility for q_{jk}^i. Once we have those measures in hand, we proceed to a cross-sectional analysis that attempts to explain differences in the volatility of q_{jk}^i between locations according to characteristics of the location pair jk.

We focus on four explanatory variables: distance, the volatility of the nominal exchange rate, trade barriers, and regional groupings. Our basic empirical work regresses the standard deviation of changes in q_{jk}^i on measures of these four variables.

Table 6.1 contains some summary statistics. The top two lines of the table present the average standard deviation of q_{jk}^i for pairs of locations that are in selected regions. Note that not all location pairs in our sample would be included in one of these regions because many pairs lie in different regions.

These first two lines reveal a fairly strong correlation between the standard

Table 6.1   **Selected Summary Statistics**

Standard deviation (%)	North America	U.S.-Canada	Europe	EC	Asia
Aggregate CPI	2.05	1.80	1.40	1.75	2.33
Nominal exchange rate	1.72	0.55	1.23	1.51	2.01
Food	2.20	1.02	1.66	2.14	2.92
Housing	2.41	1.22	1.56	2.19	2.21
Fuel and electricity	2.91	2.91	2.41	2.63	N/A
Clothing	2.97	2.55	3.63	1.85	3.35
Transportation	2.25	1.85	4.83	10.3	2.82
Household equipment	3.09	1.34	2.03	2.42	2.86
Health	2.85	1.15	1.80	N/A	3.12
Recreation	1.21	1.21	1.99	N/A	3.39
Food/CPI	0.82	0.76	0.87	1.14	1.37
Housing/CPI	1.04	0.85	1.08	1.55	1.08
Fuel and electricity/CPI	2.69	2.69	1.84	2.08	N/A
Clothing/CPI	2.01	2.40	3.11	1.56	2.76
Transportation/CPI	1.73	1.68	1.97	3.19	1.22
Household equipment/CPI	1.61	1.14	0.94	1.20	0.40
Health/CPI	1.46	1.04	1.15	N/A	1.19
Recreation/CPI	1.08	1.08	1.08	N/A	1.58
Average distance between locations (mi.)	1,389	1,210	651	733	1,738

Notes: Column entries give the standard deviation of the relative price (the average standard deviation across all combinations) within the stated region. Each of the relative prices used is in terms of log first differences. The average distance between locations is given in the final row. *N/A* indicates that there is no more than one pair of locations in the grouping.

   The following locations are included (by region): North America: Chicago, Los Angeles, New York, Philadelphia, Ottawa, Toronto, Vancouver, Winnipeg, and Mexico. Asia: Hong Kong, Japan, Singapore, and Taiwan. Europe: Austria, Belgium, Denmark, Finland, France, Germany, Greece, Italy, the Netherlands, Norway, Portugal, Spain, Sweden, Switzerland, and the United Kingdom. EC: Belgium, Denmark, France, Germany, Greece, Italy, the Netherlands, Portugal, Spain, and the United Kingdom.

deviation of nominal exchange rates and the standard deviation of q_{jk}^i. Both series have low volatility for country pairings within the European Community, or within Europe more broadly defined, as well as for city pairs in the United States and Canada. On the other hand, Asian country pairs and location pairs in North America when Mexico is included have relatively high nominal exchange rate and relative price variability.

   The next eight rows in table 6.1 report the average volatility for each of our eight goods for regional location pairs. We note that there are some large differences in the degree of volatility across the goods, but there still seems to be an overall correlation with the volatility of the nominal exchange rate.

   The next set of numbers in table 6.1 calculate the volatility of "relative-relative" prices. We will discuss the significance of these numbers below.

The final row of table 6.1 reports the average distance for location pairs within a region. Two things are worth noting here. First, while the European country pairs tend to have the lowest relative price volatility, they also are quite close—an average of only 651 miles apart. Second, the average distance between all of our location pairs is 3,887 miles. Note that location pairs within regions tend to be much closer on average than this.

In table 6.2, we investigate the hypothesis that the law of one price holds more nearly within regional groupings. Here we simply regress the measure of volatility of relative prices against regional dummy variables.[5] For example, when the dependent variable is the standard deviation of q_{jk}^i, the North American dummy variable takes on a value of one if both locations j and k are within North America, and a zero otherwise. In the first column of table 6.2, we report the result of regressing the standard deviation of the relative aggregate CPIs between locations (adjusted for the exchange rate) on dummy variables for North America, Europe, and Asia. We find that the volatility is significantly lower for location pairs that are within North America or within Europe compared to the typical location pair. That conclusion is indicated by the significantly negative coefficients on the North American and European regional dummies. We note that the coefficient on the Asian dummy variable, however, is positive, though not significantly different from zero. It seems as though the law of one price holds no better between two Asian countries than between a typical pair of countries that are not within a regional grouping. But, because our Asian grouping consists of only four countries, we need to be very cautious in our interpretation.

Table 6.2, in fact, shows that across almost all of our individual goods, the law of one price holds more nearly for locations that are within North America or within Europe. The only case in which the coefficient on the North American or European dummies is not significantly less than zero is for the recreation goods category for Europe. The last column of table 6.2 pools all of our goods together (not including the aggregate CPI) and constrains the coefficients on the dummy variables to be the same for all goods. We find the coefficient on the North American and European dummy variables is strongly significantly negative, while the Asian dummy variable has a coefficient that, while negative, is not significantly different from zero.

While table 6.2 shows that the law of one price holds better among locations that are within North America or Europe, because the standard deviation of relative prices is lower for location pairs within those regions, it offers no clue as to why this might be true. We hypothesize three explanations for this finding: that nominal exchange rate variability is lower for these intraregional pairs; that they are closer in distance to each other; and that their mutual trade barriers are lower.

So we specify that the volatility of q_{jk}^i is related to the natural log of the

---

5. We include a dummy variable for each individual location, as well.

Table 6.2   **Regressions Relating Price Volatility to Regional Dummies**

	CPI	Food	Housing	Clothing	Fuel and Electricity	Health	Household Equipment	Recreation	Transport	Combined
North America	-1.34 -02	-1.35 -02	-1.01 -02	-1.16 -02	-1.64 -02	-7.63 -03	-1.20 -02	-3.04 -01	-5.86 -03	-1.08 -02
	(-12.7)	(-14.4)	(-9.20)	(-5.96)	(-9.39)	(-1.14)	(-5.66)	(-11.1)	(-1.94)	(-14.7)
Europe	-1.83 -02	-1.59 -02	-1.90 -02	-1.21 -02	-8.34 -03	-1.73 -02	-1.22 -02	-4.52 -04	-1.16 -02	-1.54 -02
	(-20.3)	(-19.9)	(-19.2)	(-4.77)	(-4.95)	(-1.09)	(-4.20)	(-0.10)	(-2.75)	(-19.8)
Asia	2.95 -03	2.37 -03	3.89 -03	-3.14 -03	N/A[a]	-2.86 -02	5.00 -03	8.70 -03	-4.87 -03	-1.88 -04
	(1.60)	(1.45)	(2.18)	(-1.05)		(-1.37)	(0.89)	(1.04)	(-1.04)	(-0.13)

Notes: All regressions contain as explanatory variables a dummy for each individual location, in addition to the variables listed in the cell. Individual goods dummies are contained in the combined regression. Heteroscedasticity-consistent t-statistics (White 1980) are reported in parentheses. The dependent variable is the standard deviation of the first difference in the relative price.

[a]Japan is the only Asian country for which data is available for this good.

distance between locations j and k. We choose the natural log function because it has been used in the empirical literature on distance and the volume of trade, and because it has the appealing property of being very concave. A priori, we doubt very much that if two countries are 7,000 miles apart that adding another 500 miles makes much difference in their degree of integration, but there is a substantial difference between two countries that are 200 miles apart and two that are 700 miles apart.

Next, if nominal prices exhibit a particular kind of stickiness, then volatility of q_{jk}^i should be closely related to variability of the nominal exchange rate between locations j and k. Specifically, if goods prices are set in the currency where the good is sold, the q_{jk}^i should fluctuate one for one with the exchange rate.

One problem with including the volatility of the nominal exchange rate as a right-hand-side variable in the regression is that it may be endogenous. That is, there may be a relation between the volatility of the exchange rate and the volatility of q_{jk}^i that is not causal. Exogenous shocks may influence both the exchange rate and q_{jk}^i. One way of dealing with this potential problem is by using instrumental variables. However, it is difficult to conceive of a valid instrument in this case. We estimate our basic equation using ordinary least squares, but we will return to this problem later.

We also consider measures of trade barriers: average tariff rates and the fraction of industries affected by nontariff barriers.

If our marketing and distribution costs story has any merit, then the law of one price should hold more nearly for intraregional pairs even when distance, exchange rate volatility, and trade barriers are taken into account. So we include the regional dummy variables in some of our specifications along with the other explanatory variables.

Finally, all of our regressions contain dummy variables for each location. That is, for the relative price q_{jk}^i, both the dummy variables for location j and location k receive a value of one. These variables are included as a way of dealing with different measurement practices in our various countries. Some countries may record prices in such a way as to increase (or decrease) their volatility compared to other countries. This will be reflected in a larger (smaller) than average coefficient on that country's dummy. Because we include a dummy for each location, there is no need to include a constant term in the regressions.

Table 6.3 reports regressions that include the log distance and the standard deviation of the nominal exchange rate as explanatory variables. Both variables do well in accounting for relative price variability. The coefficient on the distance variable has the correct sign for seven of the nine goods, and is significant in all of these cases. Only for health and transport does distance take on the wrong sign, but it is not statistically significant in either case.

The standard deviation of the nominal exchange rate is significant (and has the correct sign) in all of the regressions. In fact, this variable has exceptionally

Table 6.3   Relative Price Volatility, Distance, and Nominal Exchange Rate Volatility

	CPI	Food	Housing	Clothing	Fuel and Electricity	Health	Household Equipment	Recreation	Transport	Combined
Log (distance)	9.55 −04	1.25 −03	6.39 −04	2.23 −03	9.49 −04	−4.45 −04	1.13 −03	8.57 −04	−8.77 −04	7.89 −04
	(3.71)	(5.41)	(2.24)	(3.29)	(2.46)	(−1.52)	(1.53)	(5.72)	(−1.26)	(3.15)
Standard deviation of nominal exchange rate	0.85	0.74	0.77	0.53	0.57	1.06	0.66	0.76	1.02	0.72
	(31.6)	(30.7)	(26.0)	(6.12)	(15.0)	(27.5)	(7.41)	(25.4)	(12.1)	(26.3)
Numbers of pairs in sample	406	406	325	171	190	91	120	91	153	1,547

Notes: The regression contains a dummy for each individual location, in addition to the variables listed in the cell. Individual goods dummies are contained in the combined regression. Heteroscedasticity-consistent *t*-statistics (White 1980) are reported in parentheses. The dependent variable is the standard deviation of the first difference in the relative price.

For each good, the sample includes the following locations: CPI and Food: all countries in table 6.1 plus South Africa. Housing: all North America and Asia, all Europe except Portugal and Sweden. Clothing: all North America and Asia, plus Italy, the Netherlands, Norway, Sweden, the United Kingdom, and South Africa. Fuel and electricity: all North America except Mexico, plus Japan, and all Europe except Greece, Portugal, Spain, and Sweden. Health: all North America, Japan, Taiwan, the Netherlands, Norway, and Switzerland. Household equipment: all North America, Japan, Hong Kong, Denmark, Norway, Sweden, the United Kingdom, and South Africa. Recreation: all North America except Mexico, plus Japan, Taiwan, Norway, Sweden, and Switzerland. Transportation: all North America and Asia, Denmark, the Netherlands, Norway, Sweden, and Switzerland.

great power in explaining the standard deviation of relative prices. The *t*-statistics are all very large, even when the sample size is small. Moreover, the coefficients are large—ranging from 0.53 to 1.06. An increase in the standard deviation of nominal exchange rates of one unit translates into nearly a one-unit increase in the standard deviation of relative prices. That is the type of response one would expect if nominal price stickiness were important. If nominal prices were completely fixed in the country where the good is sold, then nominal exchange rate variability would translate one for one into relative price variability. We do not see a one-to-one relation in our data, but it is close.

The last column of table 6.3 reports regression results when the data for the eight goods (but not the aggregate CPI) are pooled. There we see that the effect of distance on price variability is positive and significant at the 5 percent level. The border dummy variable receives a coefficient of 0.72 and is highly significant.

In panel 1 of table 6.4, we include dummy variables for whether location pairs lie in North America, Europe, or Asia. We note that these dummy variables are highly collinear with distance. We saw in table 6.1 that location pairs within these regions tend to be much closer than nonregional pairs. As a result of this collinearity, the individual significance of the distance coefficients and the regional dummies is diminished. But, across the regressions, patterns emerge that are worth noting.

First, nominal exchange rate variability is still significant and important quantitatively in these regressions.

Second, distance still is positive in seven of the nine regressions, but it is significant in only four.

Finally, the following patterns emerge for the regional dummies: the North American dummies and European dummies tend to be negative. For several of the individual goods regressions, these dummy variables have negative coefficients and are significant. For the regression using the aggregate CPI, both coefficients are negative and significant. For the regression that pools the individual goods data, the North American dummy is negative and significant at the 5 percent level, and the European dummy is negative and significant at the 10 percent level (in a one-sided test). This indicates that price dispersion is lower among locations within these regions than average.

The results for the Asian dummy are more mixed. Most of the coefficients tend to be positive but insignificant. The coefficient in the regression using the pooled data, however, is negative and significant at the 10 percent level. We note that the weak findings for the Asia region parallel the findings of Frankel, Stein, and Wei (1995), who found weaker evidence that the Asian nations have formed a trading bloc than for North America or Europe.

In panel 2 of table 6.4, we drop the distance variable, so that we use only the regional dummy variables and nominal exchange rate variability as explanatory variables. The statistical significance of the North American and European dummy variables jumps up for many of the individual goods. This is a

Table 6.4   Regressions Relating Price Volatility to Nominal Exchange Rate Volatility, Distance, and Regional Dummies

	CPI	Food	Housing	Clothing	Fuel and Electricity	Health	Household Equipment	Recreation	Transport	Combined
					Panel 1					
Log (distance)	3.33 −04	6.81 −04	−7.57 −05	2.68 −04	1.51 −03	4.06 −04	7.30 −05	9.24 −04	−2.53 −04	−1.73 −04
	(0.94)	(2.18)	(−0.18)	(0.23)	(3.33)	(0.98)	(0.07)	(5.80)	(−0.23)	(−0.47)
Standard deviation of nominal exchange rate	0.78	0.68	0.68	0.47	0.67	1.00	0.57	0.76	1.05	0.68
	(22.4)	(22.2)	(17.2)	(4.19)	(11.9)	(24.7)	(5.43)	(19.1)	(12.0)	(20.0)
North America	−3.55 −03	−4.21 −03	−3.18 −03	−5.92 −03	3.97 −03	6.70 −03	−3.61 −03	7.32 −04	1.76 −03	−3.73 −03
	(−3.84)	(−5.17)	(−3.06)	(−2.02)	(2.03)	(2.87)	(−1.24)	(0.63)	(0.65)	(−4.07)
Europe	−2.42 −03	−1.39 −03	−3.46 −03	−3.65 −03	2.68 −03	−8.13 −03	−4.61 −03	−9.61 −04	3.50 −03	−1.76 −03
	(−2.52)	(−1.64)	(−2.82)	(−1.03)	(1.71)	(−2.21)	(−1.32)	(−0.90)	(0.88)	(−1.55)
Asia	8.84 −04	1.29 −03	6.19 −04	−4.51 −03	N/A[a]	−5.31 −03	1.20 −02	2.29 −03	−1.48 −03	−2.15 −03
	(0.65)	(1.07)	(0.41)	(−1.27)		(−1.10)	(0.23)	(1.04)	(−0.41)	(−1.55)
					Panel 2					
Standard deviation of nominal exchange rate	0.78	0.69	0.68	0.47	0.71	1.03	0.57	0.93	1.04	0.68
	(23.4)	(23.4)	(17.7)	(4.23)	(12.5)	(36.5)	(5.50)	(27.7)	(12.3)	(20.1)
North America	−4.00 −03	−5.15 −03	−3.07 −03	−6.36 −03	2.65 −03	5.01 −03	−3.72 −03	1.01 −03	2.14 −03	−3.48 −03
	(−5.11)	(−7.40)	(−3.58)	(−2.87)	(1.34)	(3.19)	(−1.56)	(0.72)	(0.99)	(−4.64)
Europe	−2.78 −03	−2.13 −03	−3.37 −03	−4.06 −03	−6.20 −06	−7.56 −03	−4.74 −03	−4.06 −04	4.06 −03	−1.48 −03
	(−3.16)	(−2.73)	(−3.01)	(−1.32)	(−0.004)	(−2.09)	(−1.64)	(−0.32)	(1.28)	(−1.52)
Asia	2.42 −04	−2.73 −05	7.68 −04	−5.00 −03	N/A[a]	−5.45 −03	1.09 −03	−1.77 −03	−1.11 −03	−1.86 −03
	(0.20)	(−0.03)	(0.61)	(−1.74)		(−1.13)	(0.22)	(−0.70)	(−0.35)	(−1.49)

Notes: All regressions contain as explanatory variables a dummy for each individual location, in addition to the variables listed in the cell. Individual goods dummies are contained in the combined regression. Heteroscedasticity-consistent *t*-statistics (White 1980) are reported in parentheses. The dependent variable is the standard deviation of the first difference in the relative price.

[a]Japan is the only Asian country for which data is available for this good.

result of the high collinearity between the regional dummy variables and distance. The Asian regional dummy variable is still insignificant in almost all of the regressions.

We tried various other dummy variables for regional groupings of location pairs: just the cities in Canada and the United States, the countries of the European Community, and the countries of the European Free Trade Association. These dummy variables generally are not significant.

We next ask whether formal trade barriers contribute to price dispersion. In table 6.5, we add two measures of trade barriers between pairs of countries to our regression that includes the log of distance and the standard deviation of the nominal exchange rate. The first measure is based on the trade-weighted average tariff rate in 1988. The tariff measure between location j and location k is taken to be $(1 + \tau_j)(1 + \tau_k)$, where τ_i is the average tariff rate in location i $(i = j, k)$. We adopt this measure since, following the discussion in section 6.2, it gives a rough measure of the range of fluctuation in relative prices allowed for by constant tariff rates. When locations j and k are both cities within either Canada or the United States, or if both are in Europe, we set the tariff measure equal to one. This measure of trade barriers is clearly very crude. It cannot distinguish any sort of discriminatory tariffs between two locations, except for the U.S. and Canadian cities and the European countries. Additionally, the barriers are only measured during one year, and are not distinguished by good.

The second measure is based on a calculation of the fraction of traded goods industries affected by nontariff barriers on imports for each country in 1988. To get the relevant observation for location jk, we add the nontariff-barrier index for locations j and k. For pairs of cities within the United States or Canada, and country pairs within Europe, this measure is set to zero.

There is a great deal of collinearity in the two measures of trade barriers, so we run regressions separately for the tariff measure and the nontariff-barrier measure. There is also high collinearity between the degree of openness and the regional dummies. We note that, when all of these variables are included in the regression, essentially no individual coefficient is statistically significant.

In panel 1 of table 6.5, we report results for regressions that include tariffs, distance, and the standard deviation of the nominal exchange rate. We expect the coefficient on the tariff variable to be positive—when there are higher tariff barriers, there should be more relative price volatility. However, there is only one instance where the coefficient is positive and significant in these regressions—in the regression for clothing.

The regression with nontariff barriers included, along with distance and exchange rate volatility, is reported in the second panel of table 6.5. These results are puzzling. Generally we find that pairs of countries that have high nontariff barriers actually have lower relative price dispersion. The coefficient on the nontariff barriers is negative and significant in most regressions.

In general, however, we should probably not put too much stock in the regressions in table 6.5, since our measures of trade barriers are so crude. In

Table 6.5   Regressions Relating Price Volatility to Distance and Trade Barriers

	CPI	Food	Housing	Clothing	Fuel and Electricity	Health	Household Equipment	Recreation	Transport	Combined
				Panel 1						
Log (distance)	1.03 −03	1.31 −03	7.24 −04	2.12 −03	9.17 −04	1.56 −04	1.15 −03	7.81 −04	−8.65 −04	8.26 −04
	(3.74)	(5.33)	(2.46)	(3.13)	(2.38)	(0.24)	(1.45)	(2.70)	(−1.20)	(3.26)
Standard deviation of nominal exchange rate	0.89	0.78	0.81	0.35	0.53	1.07	0.66	0.76	1.03	0.73
	(22.9)	(22.4)	(19.5)	(2.74)	(10.5)	(26.4)	(4.37)	(25.2)	(10.5)	(19.0)
Tariff	−8.66 −03	−8.52 −03	−9.03 −02	3.62 −02	9.14 −03	−6.70 −03	−1.53 −03	7.17 −04	−8.21 −04	−1.96 −03
	(−1.34)	(−1.47)	(−1.24)	(1.96)	(1.21)	(−1.03)	(−0.08)	(0.31)	(−0.07)	(−0.32)
				Panel 2						
Log (distance)	1.09 −03	1.33 −03	8.49 −04	2.29 −03	9.46 −04	−3.22 −04	9.17 −04	7.90 −04	−6.81 −04	8.63 −04
	(4.05)	(5.51)	(3.02)	(3.35)	(2.45)	(−1.09)	(1.27)	(5.73)	(−1.05)	(3.44)
Standard deviation of nominal exchange rate	0.92	0.79	0.85	0.58	0.55	1.06	0.92	0.81	1.18	0.80
	(27.8)	(26.5)	(25.1)	(5.67)	(12.4)	(28.0)	(8.38)	(26.9)	(13.8)	(24.7)
Nontariff barrier	−5.88 −05	−4.12 −05	−7.62 −05	−3.34 −05	1.25 −05	−4.99 −05	−1.53 −04	−4.47 −05	−1.99 −04	−6.76 −05
	(−3.62)	(−2.81)	(−4.46)	(−0.83)	(0.69)	(−1.96)	(−4.12)	(−3.98)	(−4.70)	(−4.83)

Notes: All regressions contain as explanatory variables a dummy for each individual location, in addition to the variables listed in the cell. Individual goods dummies are contained in the combined regression. Heteroscedasticity-consistent t-statistics (White 1980) are reported in parentheses. The dependent variable is the standard deviation of the first difference in the relative price. The sample includes the locations listed in table 6.1.

Table 6.6   **Correlation Matrix of Right-Hand-Side Variables**

	Log (distance)	Standard deviation of nominal exchange rate	Tariff	Nontariff barrier	Region dummy
Log (distance)	1.00				
Standard deviation of nominal exchange rate	0.49	1.00			
Tariff	0.67	0.58	1.00		
Nontariff barrier	0.54	0.25	0.73	1.00	
Region dummy	−0.87	−0.46	−0.71	−0.57	1.00

Notes: Entries give the correlation between each pair of series. Region dummy is unity when each country in a pair is in *the same* region, and is zero otherwise. The other series are as defined in the text.

addition, the measures of trade barriers are highly correlated with the other explanatory variables. Table 6.6 displays the correlation matrix for our five right-hand-side variables: the log of distance, the standard deviation of the nominal exchange rate, tariffs, nontariff barriers, and regional dummies. The regional dummy variable in this table has the form that location pair jk receives a value of one if both locations are within one of the three regions (North America, Europe, Asia), and a zero otherwise. The degree of correlation among these variables is striking. Location pairs within regions tend to be close together, have a stable exchange rate, and have low trade barriers. So it is difficult to separate out these effects on the law of one price.

Finally, in table 6.7, we return to the issue of endogeneity of the nominal exchange rate. We have seen that in all of our regressions, the standard deviation of the exchange rate is highly significant. Our preferred explanation for this is that as s_{jk}, the nominal exchange rate between locations j and k, varies, then q_{jk}^i varies because of nominal price stickiness. We calculate q_{jk}^i as $p_j^i / s_{jk} p_k^i$, where p_j^i is the nominal price level in location j, expressed in location j's currency, and similarly for p_k^i. If p_j^i and p_k^i are fixed (the most extreme form of nominal price stickiness), then q_{jk}^i moves one for one with s_{jk}.

However, an alternative explanation for the correlation of s_{jk} and q_{jk}^i is that both variables are influenced by some sort of real shocks. For example, shocks to productivity in the nontraded sectors in countries j and k might cause q_{jk}^i to change. Monetary policy might be conducted in such a way that the nominal exchange rate tends to be influenced by the same real shocks.

If this type of explanation were true, the real shocks should also be reflected in p_j^i / p_j and p_k^i / p_k, where p_j and p_k represent the aggregate CPIs in locations j and k. That is, real shocks that affect relative prices will cause the price of good i to vary relative to the overall price level in each location. So we consider an alternative measure of the relative price variability between locations j and k: $\tilde{q}_{jk}^i \equiv (p_j^i / p_j)/(p_k^i / p_k)$.

Summary statistics for these "relative-relative" prices are presented in the

Table 6.7   Relative-Relative Price Volatility, Distance, and Nominal Exchange Rate Volatility

	Food	Housing	Clothing	Fuel and Electricity	Health	Household Equipment	Recreation	Transport	Combined
Log (distance)	3.89 −04	−8.57 −04	1.28 −03	2.45 −04	1.87 −04	2.83 −05	6.19 −04	−5.51 −04	1.76 −05
	(5.54)	(−0.77)	(2.29)	(0.61)	(1.21)	(0.23)	(4.02)	(−2.10)	(0.07)
Standard deviation of nominal exchange rate	−9.85 −03	2.49 −02	0.15	0.11	0.13	4.09 −02	6.90 −02	0.33	6.77 −02
	(−1.30)	(2.15)	(2.11)	(2.82)	(6.24)	(2.74)	(2.23)	(10.2)	(2.56)

Notes: The regression contains a dummy for each individual location, in addition to the variables listed in the cell. Individual goods dummies are contained in the combined regression. Heteroscedasticity-consistent *t*-statistics (White 1980) are reported in parentheses. The dependent variable is the standard deviation of the first-differenced goods price divided by the CPI.

bottom half of table 6.1. There we report the average standard deviation of $\tilde{q}^i_{jk}$ for location pairs in various regions.

In table 6.7, we regress the standard deviation of $\tilde{q}^i_{jk}$ on log of distance and the standard deviation of the nominal exchange rate. With the exception of the regression for food (and the pooled regression), the coefficients on the nominal exchange rate variable are still positive and significant in all of the regressions. This correlation cannot be a result of fluctuating nominal exchange rates and sticky nominal prices, since the nominal exchange rate does not appear in the calculation of $\tilde{q}^i_{jk}$. This indicates some simultaneity in the determination of nominal exchange rate variation and relative price variation. Both may be responding to real shocks.

Of course, the ideal way to deal with this problem statistically is to use an instrumental variable for the nominal exchange rate variable, but we were unable to find a satisfactory instrument. We note that, in the regressions reported in table 6.7, the explanatory power for nominal exchange rate variability is much lower than in our other regressions, while still statistically significant in most cases. This probably means that, while the mutual response of relative prices and the nominal exchange rate to real shocks accounts for some of the correlation we find between the standard deviation of q^i_{jk} and s_{jk}, it does not account for most of it. It is likely that nominal price stickiness accounts for much of this relation.

6.5   Conclusions

Our empirical analysis indicates that nominal exchange rate variability and distance between locations account for much of the failure of the law of one price between locations. We also find some evidence that locations within regions lower relative price dispersion even taking into account these factors.

Nominal price stickiness accounts for large divergences in prices between locations. As the nominal exchange rate varies, relative prices swing widely. However, we also note that to some extent the nominal exchange rate and relative prices respond to common shocks. The significance of sticky prices for allocation of resources is an open question. It could be that these failures of the law of one price represent significant distortions. The relative price of a good should respond to its relative scarcity. But, when we look at prices of similar goods between locations, prices do not seem to be responding to those types of signals. It is not clear to what extent resources are misallocated as a result. It is possible that nonprice mechanisms have developed that circumvent the problem. This is certainly an important area for future research.

When we include only distance along with nominal exchange rate variability in our regressions, we find that locations that are more distant are less integrated. This result is not surprising, and is consistent with the findings of the gravity model of trade. We note, however, that distance may matter for reasons other than simply transport costs. Engel and Rogers (1995) find evidence that labor markets are more closely integrated for nearby locations. In that study, price dispersion was found to be significantly influenced by wage dispersion. This is interesting, because if distance matters for regionalization because of transport costs, then there is little that policymakers can hope to achieve to increase market integration. But there may be some room for increased integration if factor markets can be made more open. We note, however, that the significance of distance as an explanatory variable drops when regional dummy variables are added to the regressions, although its significance does not entirely disappear.

Our crude measures of trade barriers find little evidence to confirm the hypothesis that greater protection leads to greater failures in the law of one price. We hesitate to conclude from this that trade barriers have little effect on final goods prices, however. First, as we explain, our measures of trade barriers are aggregate measures undifferentiated by good, by country of origin of the import, or by time. Second, there is a high degree of collinearity between our measure of openness and our other explanatory variables, so it is difficult to separate out their individual effects.

Finally, we find that relative price dispersion is affected by whether or not the location pair are within a region. For European and North American locations, relative price variability is significantly smaller than for other location pairs. We have offered a potential explanation for why regions matter: distribution and marketing are more integrated for locations within regions. We can offer, however, no direct evidence on this hypothesis. We note that price dispersion is not reduced for country pairs within the Asian region.

The question of whether markets have become more regionalized is an interesting one. It is sparked by the observation that regional trade arrangements have increased in number and perhaps importance in recent years. But our findings suggest that further study of regionalization can be greatly enhanced by taking a broader view of the determinants of market integration.

Appendix A
Data

Our data set contains monthly consumer prices from January 1980 to December 1994. The data is from Datastream, and consists of eight disaggregated components of the CPI: food; fuel and electricity; housing; clothing; health; transportation; recreation and education; and household equipment, durables, and furniture. We also use data on the overall CPI.

In addition, comparable CPI data for four Canadian cities—Ottawa, Toronto, Winnipeg, and Vancouver—were obtained from Statistics Canada. Data for four U.S. cities—New York, Los Angeles, Chicago, and Philadelphia—are from the Bureau of Labor Statistics.

All of the price data is seasonally unadjusted.

Nominal exchange rates are monthly averages from the International Monetary Fund's International Financial Statistics.

Distances are calculated as great circle distances between locations, obtained from PCGLOBE. They are measured from a country's capital when country data is used.

The data on average tariff rates and nontariff barriers is from Lee and Swagel (1994), who in turn obtained the data from the UN Conference on Trade and Development Micro TCM System. The tariff data is the trade-weighted average tariff rate. The nontariff barrier numbers are the fraction of Customs Cooperation Council Nomenclature four- or five-digit categories in each country for which any nontariff barriers are in place. Both series were measured in 1988.

Appendix B
Proofs of Propositions in Section 6.3.1

We prove the two propositions at the end of section 6.3.1.

First, take the case of $\phi = \phi^*$. Suppose that $1/\eta^* < 1/\gamma$, so that

$$p_2 = p_2^* < p_1 = p_1^*.$$

Now, note that

$$p^{(\phi-1)/\phi} = \omega p_1^{(\phi-1)/\phi} + (1 - \omega)p_2^{(\phi-1)/\phi} < p_1^{(\phi-1)/\phi},$$

so $p < p_1$. Likewise, $p_2^* < p^*$. If $\omega > \omega^*$, then $p^* < p$. So

$$p_2^* < p^* < p < p_1.$$

Thus we have $1 < p/p^* < p_1/p_2^*$. Analogously, if $1/\gamma < 1/\eta^*$, we have $p_1/p_2^* < p/p^* < 1$. So, p/p^* is closer to unity than p_1/p_2^* is.

If $\phi \neq \phi^*$, p/p^* may be farther from unity than p_1/p_2^*. Suppose, for example, that $1/\eta^* < 1/\gamma$. Then, from above, $p < p_1$ and $p_2^* < p^*$. It is possible, if the markups are sufficiently different, that $p_1 < p_2^*$, even with $1/\eta^* < 1/\gamma$. In that case, we have

$$p < p_1 < p_2^* < p^*,$$

so $1 < p_1/p_2^* < p/p^*$. In this case, p/p^* is farther from unity than p_1/p_2^* is.

References

Cumby, Robert. 1993. Forecasting exchange rates on the hamburger standard: What you see is what you get with McParity. Georgetown University. Manuscript.

Dornbusch, Rudiger. 1987. Exchange rates and prices. *American Economic Review* 77:93–106.

Engel, Charles. 1993. Real exchange rates and relative prices: An empirical investigation. *Journal of Monetary Economics* 32:35–50.

Engel, Charles, and John H. Rogers. 1995. How wide is the border? University of Washington. Manuscript.

Frankel, Jeffrey, Ernesto Stein, and Shang-Jin Wei. 1995. Trading blocs and the Americas: The natural, the unnatural, and the super-natural. *Journal of Development Economics* 47:61–95.

Froot, Kenneth A., Michael Kim, and Kenneth Rogoff. 1995. The law of one price over 700 years. NBER Working Paper no. 5132. Cambridge, MA: National Bureau of Economic Research.

Froot, Kenneth A., and Paul D. Klemperer. 1989. Exchange rate pass-through when market share matters. *American Economic Review* 79:637–54.

Ghosh, Atish R., and Holger C. Wolf. 1994. Pricing in international markets: Lessons from the *Economist*. NBER Working Paper no. 4806. Cambridge, MA: National Bureau of Economic Research.

Isard, Peter. 1977. How far can we push the law of one price? *American Economic Review* 67:942–48.

Knetter, Michael N. 1989. Price discrimination by U.S. and German exporters. *American Economic Review* 79:198–210.

———. 1994. Why are retail prices in Japan so high? Evidence from German export prices. NBER Working Paper no. 4894. Cambridge, MA: National Bureau of Economic Research.

Krugman, Paul. 1987. Pricing to market when the exchange rate changes. In Sven W. Arndt and J. David Richardson, eds., *Real-financial linkages among open economies*. Cambridge: MIT Press.

Lee, Jong-Wha, and Phillip Swagel. 1994. Trade barriers and trade flows across countries and industries. Board of Governors of the Federal Reserve System. International Finance Discussion Papers no. 476.

Mankiw, N. Gregory. 1985. Small menu costs and large business cycles: A macroeconomic model of monopoly. *Quarterly Journal of Economics* 100:529–39.

Mussa, Michael. 1986. Nominal exchange rate regimes and the behavior of real exchange rates: Evidence and implications. In K. Brunner and A. Meltzer, eds., *Carnegie-Rochester Conference Series on Public Policy* 25:117–214.

Rogers, John H., and Michael Jenkins. 1995. Haircuts or hysteresis? Sources of movements in real exchange rates. *Journal of International Economics* 38:339–60.

Sanyal, Kalyan, and Ronald Jones. 1982. The theory of trade in middle products. *American Economic Review* 72:16–31.

Wei, Shang-Jin, and David C. Parsley. 1995. Purchasing power disparity during the floating rate period: Exchange rate volatility, trade barriers, and other culprits. NBER Working Paper no. 5032. Cambridge, MA: National Bureau of Economic Research.

White, Halbert. 1980. A heteroskedasticity-consistent covariance matrix estimator and a direct test for heteroskedasticity. *Econometrica* 48:817–38.

Comment   Kenneth A. Froot

Charles Engel and John Rogers have written a stimulating paper, one that is apropos of the topics in this conference. Some of the papers we have discussed thus far have focused on trade flows and the predictive ability of gravity models. As several people have remarked, the standard neoclassical equilibrium does not predict gravity trade patterns. Indeed, in a neoclassical world of perfect competition and complete integration, bilateral trade patterns are not defined. In such a world, there are always perfect substitutes available for any good (since every producer is by definition "small"). Thus, volumes of trade do not tell us much; moreover, no observed pattern of trade can rule out perfect integration and competition in traded goods markets.

In this context, it is nice to have Engel and Rogers's paper, which focuses on prices rather than volumes. Under the hypothesis that complete integration and perfect competition prevail, bilateral trade volumes may not be defined, but relative prices are—the law of one price should hold. With this as a well-defined null hypothesis, Engel and Rogers ask whether gravity-type factors are important for deviations from the law of one price. Thus, we have tests of a well-specified null against a well-specified alternative hypothesis. This cannot be said of the gravity models, which try to explain trade flows.

In spite of this clear advantage to examining prices, there is, unfortunately, also a dark side to these data. Engel and Rogers use final consumption prices in their regressions. This has real disadvantages if one wants to understand the composition of trade and the integration of traded goods markets. All traded goods contain nontraded components by the time they are consumed—distribution and delivery services, advertising services, name-brand value, and so forth. These components differ markedly, even when the underlying "good" is exactly the same. Thus, it is not clear that one should interpret all deviations from the law of one price as a deviation from the law of one price.

As an example of this, I checked the price of a pint of Vermont-state pure maple syrup on my drive up to this conference in Woodstock, Vermont. The price of syrup at a tourist store was more than 40 percent higher than an identical pint at a large grocery store. This differential persists, in spite of the lack of a border or real distance between the stores. The differential might represent a rent to the tourist store; it might represent the tourist store's less efficient distribution system; or it might represent the value and cost of the service of providing a collection of Vermont gifts to the tourist. If it is the first, then a deviation from the law of one price has legitimately occurred, but if it is some combination of the latter two, then the pints of syrup are different goods when sold in the different stores. No strict comparison of price is, in that case, totally appropriate.

Kenneth A. Froot is the Industrial Bank of Japan Professor of Finance and director of research at Harvard Business School and a research associate of the National Bureau of Economic Research.

With this as a caveat, I applaud the emphasis on distribution systems in the theoretical portion of Engel and Rogers paper. They have traded intermediate products being sold by a monopolistic "distributor." Two products sold in the same country (or in two countries within a "region") have the same distribution system. As a result, their price can differ only if the underlying traded good differs.

I have no doubt that differences in distribution systems are an important aspect of deviations from the law of one price. Unfortunately, Engel and Rogers have no means to identify the component of the deviation attributable to the distribution system, as opposed to, say, sticky prices. Thus, while their theory section is interesting and somewhat original, it does little to inform the tests that follow.

These tests demonstrate that the volatility of deviations from the law of one price is sensitive to the volatility of exchange rates, as well as, to a lesser extent, distance and regional grouping. When Engel and Rogers use as the dependent variable the "relative-relative price," they get similar answers. This relative-relative price is the ratio of a particular good relative to the CPI compared to the same ratio for another country. The idea of using this price is that the nominal exchange rate never enters in its computation, so that if sticky prices are driving the results, there should be little correlation of nominal exchange rate volatility with the volatility of relative-relative prices.

In fact, Engel and Rogers note that there is still a strong positive association between the volatility of relative-relative prices and that of nominal exchange rates. However, I wonder about this association. It is noteworthy that, in the regression estimates, the magnitudes of the coefficients are very different, yet the measured standard errors for each are small. This is unlikely to be an unbiased representation of what is going on. It suggests that the true standard errors are larger, thereby understating the importance of sticky prices in the results.

Two other points. First, it seems that the results, which rely on volatilities measured from monthly price changes, pick up mostly high frequency fluctuations. An alternative approach would measure the volatility of levels of relative prices (perhaps even around the theoretical mean dictated by the law of one price). This would provide lower-frequency information on the relationship between relative price volatility and exchange rate volatility.

Second, the ambiguous results on trade barriers do not seem surprising to me. Ceteris paribus, trade restrictions may enlarge deviations from the law of one price. In practice, however, trade policy is endogenous, and may respond to misaligned exchange rates. Thus, it is possible that highly restrictive trade policies will tend to kick in during periods when there are large misalignments, thereby tending to diminish deviations from the law of one price.

Overall, I found this paper an interesting and useful extension of work that both Engel and Rogers have pursued. This work is beginning to get at the difficult question of what explains intercountry price differentials. In this paper Engel and Rogers show that region and gravity have only a modest effect on prices in comparison to exchange rate volatility. This tells us that the lack of integration is not really spatial, and that, if anything, it depends strongly on exchange rate arrangements that explain nominal exchange rate volatility.

Comment   Michael Knetter

In general, I am a very big fan of Engel and Rogers—especially the recent paper entitled "How Wide Is the Border?" Rather than flatter you with the details of what I like about your work, I will focus mainly on how I think you might improve this paper, which appears to be a sequel.

First, some general comments about the dependent variable, the relative price volatility measure. It is likely that market baskets are different in different countries. Consequently, there is a source of measurement error that will exaggerate the volatility of the relative price index. Furthermore, this measurement error will be correlated with many of the right-hand-side variables— distance between markets and exchange rate volatility in particular. This is because many of the city pairs will have identical market baskets and neighboring countries probably have more similar consumption patterns. I am also bothered by the use of monthly volatility measures to study sources of failure in the law of one price. One month is not sufficient time for the forces of arbitrage to operate in goods markets. In general, it might be more helpful to study deviations in price levels rather than their volatilities. Although that is not possible with your data, there are some problems of interpretation that arise when you focus on volatilities. In a sense you've stacked the deck in favor of your nominal-price-stickiness story.

The mapping from regression coefficients to underlying trade frictions could benefit from more discussion. The underlying trade frictions that you seek to compare are transportation costs, trade barriers, and "nominal price stickiness." I consider the latter to be a manifestation of frictions, while the former are true frictions themselves. Furthermore, the proxies for transport costs and trade barriers at least in principle are good measures of these frictions (distance and average tariff rates or coverage ratios). The exchange rate volatility variable is in some sense a measure of a "friction," but I don't see a direct mapping to nominal price stickiness in the way your other right-hand-side variables map to the frictions they are intended to measure. Therefore, I don't really know how to interpret the regression results. You are regressing a measure of a real exchange rate volatility on a nominal exchange rate volatility and two measures of friction. I am not surprised that the nominal exchange rate volatility and the

Michael Knetter is associate professor of economics and business administration at the Amos Tuck School, Dartmouth College, and a faculty research fellow of the National Bureau of Economic Research.

real exchange rate volatility are highly correlated—this has been a big issue in international finance for years. To say that you have found that violations in the law of one price are due to nominal price stickiness because real and nominal exchange rate volatilities are highly correlated begs the question. What are the frictions that make nominal prices sticky?

Another reason that nominal volatilities are the dominant variable in your work is that you measure deviations from the law of one price as volatilities rather than absolute deviations between prices. Transport costs and trade barriers will help to explain differences in the level of prices, but may not increase volatility very much. Exchange rate volatility will directly increase relative price volatility, especially at the monthly frequency. Just as theory models can be "rigged" to find particular results, I feel this empirical paper is "rigged." I'd be more interested, for example, in regression results without the exchange rate volatility measure. I'd also like to see a simple correlation matrix so I have a better sense of what is driving the partial correlations. Because of the above issues, I think you need to be very careful about interpretations and conclusions. In particular, you should not claim too much about the relative importance of distance and trade barriers in explaining deviations from the law of one price. Indeed, the fact that trade barriers are uncorrelated or negatively correlated with your measure of relative price volatility suggests to me there is a fundamental problem with the empirical framework. No one could seriously believe that increased trade barriers have no effect or positive effects on price integration.

Part of the problem could be in the measurement of trade barriers. Sometimes average tariff rates or coverage ratios will understate the degree of trade frictions. Furthermore, much of the unmeasured forms of protection are probably the main tools used to keep export competitors from fully passing through exchange rate changes to gain market share. For example, the threat of antidumping suits and countervailing duties may well increase when exchange rate fluctuations grant temporary competitive advantage to foreign producers in an industry. In this sense, the tools of unmeasured protection might well be correlated with nominal exchange rate volatilities.

In the end, I don't think this paper teaches me much beyond what I learned from "How Wide Is the Border?" Looking at the simple correlations between the variables used in this paper as well as a regression without the nominal exchange rate volatility measure might help me better interpret the data in this paper. Although data on price levels for specific products are hard to obtain across countries, they may be essential to understanding the sources of violations in the law of one price.

7

Regionalization of World Trade and Currencies: Economics and Politics

Jeffrey A. Frankel and Shang-Jin Wei

7.1 Introduction

A modern Pandora's box has been opened. Coming out are such creatures as free trade areas (FTAs), regional trading arrangements, and currency blocs. Regional blocs are an age-old phenomenon, but in their vibrant new incarnation they have spread to the corners of the world with unusual speed. Some believe that the box was opened by the Western Europeans when they consolidated their European Economic Community by the Single Market Initiative that took effect in 1992 and by the Maastricht Treaty. Others blame (or credit) the United States for the final lift when it signed a free trade agreement with Canada in 1988 and thereby abandoned its forty years of opposition in principle to regional initiatives.

Regardless of who is responsible, the important point is that the box is open. Three new members joined the European Community (EC), now the European Union (EU) in 1994, bringing the total to fifteen. After the North American Free Trade Agreement (NAFTA) expanded the U.S.-Canada FTA to include Mexico, Chile began negotiations to join as well. Four South American countries have formed their own customs union (Mercosur). Other countries in the region, rather than sitting idle, have dusted off their existing treaty to form an

Jeffrey A. Frankel is professor of economics at the University of California, Berkeley, and a research associate of the National Bureau of Economic Research, where he is also director of the program in International Finance and Macroeconomics. After this project was completed, he took leave to serve on the Council of Economic Advisers. Shang-Jin Wei is associate professor of public policy at the Kennedy School of Government, Harvard University, a faculty research fellow of the National Bureau of Economic Research, a research associate of the Center for Pacific Basin Monetary and Economic Studies of the Federal Reserve Bank of San Francisco, and a Davidson Institute Research Fellow at the University of Michigan Business School.

The authors thank Jungshik Kim and Greg Dorchak for excellent research and editorial assistance. This paper was written while Frankel was a professor at Berkeley and a research associate of the NBER; it does not represent the views of the U.S. government.

Andean FTA. The Association of Southeast Asian Nations (ASEAN) countries in the Pacific also have decided to get serious about their FTA.

Opening the box created a controversy. There is no lack of economists and politicians who are excited about the new wave of regionalization and opportunities it has brought upon the world. Others, however, fear it may corrupt the fragile efforts of the General Agreement on Tariffs and Trade (GATT) or the World Trade Organization (WTO) to make progress toward global free trade.

Worries about regional blocs date back to the early 1950s, when Viner (1950) called economists' attention to the distinction between trade-creation and trade-diversion effects of regional FTAs. Specifically, trade diversion occurs when members of a grouping reorient their trade away from low-cost nonmember countries toward higher-cost member countries. Regional blocs may reduce world welfare if the trade-diversion effect dominates the trade-creation effect.

More recently, Krugman (1991a) derived a model in which every regional bloc pursues an optimal tariff. He showed via simulation that three regional blocs may minimize world welfare. In a generalized version of Krugman's model that includes transport costs, Frankel, Stein, and Wei (chap. 4 in this volume) show that even after one takes into account the geographic pattern of trading blocs, which can be seen to justify a certain degree of regional preferences as "natural," the current degree of regionalization is likely to be excessive, that is, welfare-reducing.

In this paper, we have several objectives. In the first half, we extend earlier econometric results to gauge the effects that regional economic arrangements have had on bilateral trading patterns. We map out the current pattern of regionalization using an updated data set covering 1970–92. We then present some estimates of the role that currency links within some major groupings might have played in promoting intragroup trade. In the second half of the paper, we consider welfare effects of regional arrangements. However, we go beyond the analysis in Frankel, Stein, and Wei (chap. 4 in this volume), by relaxing the assumption that tariffs maintained by FTA members against outsiders are exogenously set. We review various political-economy arguments that others have made regarding how regional initiatives might either undermine movement toward more general liberalization, or help build political support for it. In other words, trade blocs might be stumbling blocks or they might be building blocks. We present a simple model of our own that illustrates one possible beneficial effect of trade blocs as a political building block to further trade liberalization. We return to the gravity-model estimates to make a tentative assessment on which of the contrasting political-economy effects of regionalism, favorable or unfavorable, are likely to dominate. Our tentative verdict is favorable: those groupings, such as the EC and East Asia, that have increased trade disproportionately with each other, have at the same time increased trade with nonmembers.

7.2 Our Latest Estimates of the Regionalization of Trade with a Modified Gravity Model

Economists often say that inferences should be based on what people do rather than what people say. In terms of regionalization of trade blocs and currency blocs, there can be discrepancies between regional blocs on paper and trade and financial integration in reality. In history, there have been many formal proclamations of FTAs that have not been followed by full implementation. In the 1960s and 1970s, announced groupings that did not turn out to live up to their advanced billing included ASEAN, the Latin American Free Trade Area (LAFTA) and the Economic Community of West African States (ECOWAS, launched in 1975), among many others. There is often a failure to translate generalities into specifics, to keep to timetables, and to enforce agreements.

On the flip side of the coin, there are reasons to suspect that important de facto trade blocs can arise even in the absence of de jure trading arrangements. For example, it is often claimed that an implicit trade bloc (sometimes called a "yen bloc") is forming in Asia and the Pacific, although the countries in the region have very few explicit preferential trade agreements.

7.2.1 A Modified Gravity Model

To estimate the effect of regional blocs on trade pattern, it is useful to have a framework that defines a "norm" of bilateral trade volume based on economic, geographic, and cultural factors. The gravity model is the framework that is most often used. Once the norm has been established, dummy variables can be used to check for biases, that is, for policies that member countries of a bloc may use to concentrate trade among themselves and away from the rest of the world.

In this paper, we estimate a modified version of the gravity model. To explain bilateral trade between a country and a specific trading partner, it incorporates the distance of each country from its average trading partner (which we call remoteness), in addition to the direct bilateral distance. This extension of the basic gravity formulation is based in part on a new formulation in Deardorff (chap. 1 in this volume). To our knowledge, this has not been done in the empirical literature. For an illustration of conventional gravity-model specification, readers are referred to the earlier papers.

Some other features distinguish the empirical estimation here from those in our earlier papers. First, the dependent variable here is country i's exports to country j, rather than their total trade (exports plus imports). This allows one to estimate different income elasticities for exports and imports. Second, we examine groups that have (eventually) agreed to a formal regional trading arrangement, such as the EC or Mercosur, rather than continent-based groupings that may not have had an explicit preferential agreement. Third, we update the data to cover 1970–92.

A representative specification is

$$
\begin{aligned}
\log (Export_{ij}) = {} & \alpha + \beta_1 \log (GNP_i) + \beta_2 \log (GNP_j) \\
& + \beta_3 \log (GNP/pop_i) + \beta_4 \log (GNP/pop_j) \\
& + \beta_5 \log (Distance_{ij}) \\
& + \beta_6 \log (Overall\ Distance_i) \\
& + \beta_7 \log (Overall\ Distance_j) \\
& + \beta_8 (ADJACENCY) + \beta_9 (LANGUAGE) \\
& + \gamma_1 (EC\_I_{ij}) + \gamma_2 (MERCOSUR\_I_{ij}) \\
& + \gamma_3 (ASEAN\_I_{ij}) + u_{ij}.
\end{aligned}
$$

(1)

The *GNP*s and bilateral distance are standard gravity variables. Per capita GNPs, an *ADJACENCY* dummy for country pairs sharing a common land border, and a *LANGUAGE* dummy for countries with linguistic or colonial ties have been found to be useful in previous work.

The remoteness, or "overall distance," variable measures how far an exporting (or importing) country is from all other countries. It is a measure of remoteness. An exporter's remoteness is its average distance from its trading partners, using partners' GNPs as the weights. An importer's remoteness is defined analogously. The hypothesis is that the remoteness of an exporter from the rest of the world has a *positive* effect on trade volume. An example will illustrate the intuition. Assume that the distance between Australia and New Zealand is the same as the distance between Spain and Sweden. Spain and Sweden have lots of other natural trading partners close at hand, but Australia and New Zealand do not. One might thus expect the antipodean pair, who have less in the way of alternatives, to trade more with each other, holding other influences constant, than the European pair. The idea is that it is not just the absolute level of bilateral distance that matters, but also bilateral distance expressed *relative* to the distances of each of the pair from their *other* partners.

The last three explanatory factors are regional dummies. *EC* (European Community), *MERCOSUR* (customs union of the Southern Cone countries in South America), and *ASEAN* (Association of Southeast Asian Nations) are examples of the dummy variables we use when testing the effects of membership in a common regional grouping.

7.2.2 Data and Definition of the Regional Bloc Dummies

Our data set covers sixty-three countries (or, in principle, 3,906 exporter-importer pairs) for 1970, 1980, 1990, and 1992. The source is the United Nations trade matrix for 1970 and 1980, and the International Monetary Fund's *Direction of Trade Statistics* for 1990 and 1992.

In this paper, we focus on six regional groupings that by the end of the sample have set up a preferential arrangement among member countries. They are the EC, European Free Trade Area (EFTA), Canada-U.S. FTA, Mercosur,

Andean Group, and ASEAN. Some blocs went into effect only toward the end of our sample. For example, the Andean Group was formally revived during 1989–90. Mercosur was established in spring 1991. In order to track the evolution of the trade pattern of these blocs, and to maintain comparability of coefficient estimates, we include the same set of regional dummies in every year. Hence, Mercosur dummy appears in regressions for 1970, 1980, and 1990, even though it had not yet come into existence. Similarly, we define the EC bloc as comprising twelve countries throughout our sample, even though the membership of the EC expanded three times during the sample (from six to nine in 1973, adding Greece in 1981, and adding Portugal and Spain in 1986).

Again for comparability of coefficient estimates, we restrict regressions on the subsample of the data for which observations for the same country pairs are available in each of the four years. As a result, we have 2,699 observations every year.

For every regional bloc, we define two dummies. For example, *ASEAN_I* takes the value of one for exports from one ASEAN member to another, and zero otherwise. *ASEAN_N* assumes the value of one for imports by any ASEAN member from any non-ASEAN member, and zero otherwise. The coefficient on *ASEAN_I* describes the degree to which ASEAN countries concentrate their trade among themselves beyond what can be expected from their economic and geographic characteristics. We call this "intra-ASEAN bias" for short. The coefficient on *ASEAN_N* reveals the extent to which ASEAN members may underimport or overimport from the rest of the world relative to the prediction of the gravity model. We call this "ASEAN's extrabloc openness."

7.2.3   Intrabloc Bias and Extrabloc Openness

The basic results are reported in table 7.1. We first note that the conventional gravity variables behave very much the same way as the model predicts and as in our previous studies. The coefficients on exporters' and importers' GNPs are about 0.9 and statistically significant, indicating that larger economies trade more, but trade increases less than proportionally as GNP expands. Per capita GNP also has a positive and statistically significant coefficient: richer economies trade more. Bilateral distance has an economically and statistically large effect on trade: as distance increases by 1 percent, trade declines by 0.9 percent. The coefficient for *ADJACENCY* dummy shows that two countries with a common land border have a larger amount of trade than two otherwise identical countries, although the difference was not significant in 1970 and 1980. A common language or past colonial connection facilitates trade. In our estimates, this brings in 30 to 60 percent more trade than otherwise.

Of particular interest are the coefficient estimates on the remoteness variables. The coefficient on the exporter's remoteness is always positive and, three out of four times, statistically significant. Other things equal, if country Z is farther from the rest of the world than country S by 1 percent, then Z's exports to a common third country, say A, will be higher than that of S by 0.3–0.6

Table 7.1   **Trade Blocs and Openness: Gravity Estimation with GNP-Weighted Relative Distance Measures**

	1970	1980	1990	1992
	Dependent Variable: log (Exports from i to j)			
GNP$_i$	.87*	.90*	.84*	.96*
	(.03)	(.02)	(.02)	(.02)
GNP$_j$	.87*	.91*	.87*	.89*
	(.03)	(.03)	(.02)	(.02)
Per capita GNP$_i$	.40*	.41*	.17*	.21*
	(.04)	(.03)	(.02)	(.02)
Per capita GNP$_j$	.28*	.27*	.04	.06*
	(.04)	(.03)	(.03)	(.03)
Bilateral distance$_{ij}$	−.89*	−.82*	−.86*	−.93*
	(.06)	(.05)	(.05)	(.05)
Remoteness of i	.40	.28*	.64*	.33*
	(.13)	(.12)	(.10)	(.10)
Remoteness of j	−.45*	−.83*	−.65*	−.52*
	(.16)	(.14)	(.12)	(.13)
Adjacency	.13	.04	.54*	.42*
	(.21)	(.19)	(.16)	(.16)
Language linkage	.34*	.53*	.35*	.59*
	(.10)	(.09)	(.08)	(.08)
EC_N	.40*	.26*	.02	.10
	(.13)	(.11)	(.10)	(.10)
EC_I	−.43*	−.35**	−.25	−.29**
	(.21)	(.19)	(.17)	(.16)
EFTA_N	−.18	−.44*	−.86*	−.75*
	(.16)	(.14)	(.13)	(.12)
EFTA_I	.21	−.21	−.36	−.37
	(.42)	(.37)	(.33)	(.32)
US-Canada_N	−.46*	−.15*	−.08	−.17
	(.22)	(.18)	(.16)	(.16)
US-Canada_I	−.77	−.28	−.44	−.73
	(1.28)	(1.14)	(1.00)	(.98)
MERCOSUR_N	−.12	.27	.18	−.21**
	(.15)	(.14)	(.13)	(.12)
MERCOSUR_I	.86	1.72*	2.09*	.78**
	(.54)	(.49)	(.43)	(.42)
Andean_N	.14	.21	−.02	.25*
	(.15)	(.14)	(.12)	(.12)
Andean_I	.31	1.56*	1.33*	1.38*
	(.44)	(.39)	(.35)	(.34)
ASEAN_N	.64*	.77*	1.02*	.82*
	(.15)	(.13)	(.11)	(.11)
ASEAN_I	2.21*	2.85*	1.76*	1.80*
	(.43)	(.38)	(.33)	(.33)
Observations	2,699	2,699	2,699	2,699
Adjusted R^2	0.61	0.68	0.72	0.75

Notes: Standard errors are in parentheses. Intercept estimates are not reported. All variables except the dummies are in logarithmic form.
*Significant at the 5% level.
**Significant at the 10% level.

percent. Another way of stating this result is to break down the coefficient on bilateral distance (0.9), into an effect of bilateral distance *relative* to the average distance of the exporter (0.3 to 0.6) plus an effect an *absolute* distance effect (0.6 to 0.3).

The coefficient on the importer's remoteness is consistently negative, surprisingly, and statistically significant at the 5 percent level. Apparently, if Z's average distance from the world is greater than S by 1 percent, then Z's imports from M, other things equal, is less than S by 0.4–0.8 percent. We have not yet figured out why this might be.

Our central focus is estimates of intrabloc bias and extrabloc openness. We discuss them bloc by bloc. Notice that for a regional bloc with a small number of members, intrabloc bias is estimated imprecisely (i.e., with a large standard error), while extrabloc openness can be estimated more accurately. For example, the Mercosur group has four members. The dummy for intrabloc bias, *MERCOSUR_I*, takes the value of one only for 6 exporter-importer pairs and zero for the remaining 3,900 pairs. On the other hand, the dummy describing the bloc's openness with respect to imports from nonmember countries, *MERCOSUR_N*, assumes the value of one 236 times. We have to bear in mind the relative preciseness of the estimates in the subsequent discussions.

The coefficients on *EC_N* are positive in every single year, suggesting that EC countries on average have low trade barriers so that their imports from the rest of the world are higher than the prediction of the modified gravity model. In terms of time trend, however, EC's extrabloc openness appears to have declined over the sample. The EC's imports from the rest of the world used to be higher than the gravity-model prediction by 40 percent. But that shrank to 26 percent in 1980 and eventually to zero by the early 1990s.

Similarly, the year-by-year point estimates of the EC bloc effect and their dynamics tell an interesting story. In terms of levels, within-EC trade has always been below the prediction of the gravity model. In terms of trend, however, the degree of within-EC bias has clearly risen. This suggests that while the European countries were more open to trade than many countries, for historical or other reasons, their trade pattern exhibits evidence of increasing bias among members and increasing trade diversion away from member countries.

EFTA countries, in contrast to the members of the EC, appear to import less from the rest of the world than the gravity-model prediction in every single year. Trade among these countries seems below what one would have expected based on their economic, geographic, and linguistic linkages, although the difference is not statistically significant. EFTA's extrabloc openness appears to diminish over time (from −18 percent in 1970, to −44 percent in 1980, and to −75 percent in 1992).

The United States and Canada imported less from the rest of the world in 1970 than the model's prediction. However, there has been a general trend increase in the degree of openness of these two economies to imports from other countries, as the extrabloc openness parameter changes from a statistically significant −46 percent in 1970, to a statistically insignificant −17 percent in 1992. Judging from the point estimates, there was a slight reduction in openness from 1990 to 1992, possibly reflecting the effect of the U.S.-Canada free trade agreement implemented in 1989, although both estimates are not different from zero at the 10 percent level.

The four South American countries that constitute Mercosur traded more intensely among themselves than the gravity-model prediction, as judged from the estimates for the *MERCOSUR_1* variable. There appears to have been an increase in the intragroup trade intensity in the 1970s and 1980s. On the other hand, during the same two-decade period, there also seems to have been an increase in the group's general openness to other countries' products. Hence, at least some modest across-the-board liberalization may have been undertaken at the same time as these countries expanded their trade to each other.

The Andean Group, the other major set of South American countries, also appears to show a certain degree of intragroup trade bias. On the other hand, their imports from the rest of the world were roughly in accordance with the gravity-model prediction. It is worth noting the jump in the extrabloc openness coefficient from essentially zero in 1990 to 25 percent in 1992. This suggests that these countries had an effective trade liberalization program during the period when they started to revive the slumbering regional association.

As a check for robustness, we have computed overall distance for exporters and importers as equally weighted distance from their trade partners. Gravity estimations with these measures are reported in table 7.2. As far as extrabloc openness and intrabloc bias are concerned, the qualitative features of the new estimates are similar to those in table 7.1. Thus, we omit detailed discussion.

Finally, we come to ASEAN, the only explicit regional trading arrangement among Asian countries in the sample. We note first that the intra-ASEAN trade bias is positive and significant in every year. However, the bias appears to be diminishing in the last decade, from 2.85 in 1980 to 1.80 in 1992. Second, ASEAN countries are far more open to the world than an average country, based on their economic, geographic, and cultural linkages. For example, in 1980, the imports by the ASEAN countries from the rest of the world were 116 percent ($= \exp(.77) - 1$) higher than the prediction of the gravity model. The 1991 decision to form an ASEAN FTA could conceivably be related to a slight (insignificant) drop in openness from 1990 to 1992. But ASEAN countries were still more open in 1992 than they were in 1980.

To summarize this section, a large number of regional blocs in the sample show positive openness to trade with outsiders. When countries choose to liberalize their trade with their neighbors, it may also facilitate multilateral liberalization. This is particularly possible for regional blocs in Asia and South America. But the results are mixed. For example, there are significant trade-diversion effects for EFTA. Thus regionalism may in some cases not lead to more general liberalization. We will examine the arguments in more detail in a later section.

Table 7.2　　　**Trade Blocs and Openness: Gravity Estimation with Equally Weighted Relative Distance Measures**

	1970	1980	1990	1992
	Dependent variable: log (Exports from i to j)			
GNP$_i$	.87*	.90*	.83*	.96*
	(.03)	(.02)	(.02)	(.02)
GNP$_j$	.86*	.91*	.88*	.90*
	(.03)	(.03)	(.02)	(.02)
Per capita GNP$_i$	.41*	.40*	.16*	.20*
	(.04)	(.03)	(.02)	(.02)
Per capita GNP$_j$	.28*	.28*	.06*	.07*
	(.04)	(.03)	(.03)	(.03)
Bilateral distance$_{ij}$	−.89*	−.79*	−.87*	−.89*
	(.07)	(.06)	(.05)	(.05)
Remoteness of i	.01	.17	.75*	.26*
	(.16)	(.12)	(.11)	(.10)
Remoteness of j	.30	−.82*	−.77*	−.62*
	(.22)	(.14)	(.12)	(.12)
Adjacency	.17	.08	.54*	.46*
	(.21)	(.19)	(.16)	(.16)
Language linkage	.32*	.54*	.34*	.61*
	(.10)	(.09)	(.08)	(.08)
EC_N	.67*	.33*	−.43	.08
	(.13)	(.11)	(.10)	(.10)
EC_I	−.19	−.27	−.25	−.28**
	(.21)	(.19)	(.17)	(.16)
EFTA_N	.08	−.33*	−.84*	−.74*
	(.16)	(.14)	(.12)	(.12)
EFTA_I	.47	−.11	−.37	−.36
	(.42)	(.37)	(.33)	(.32)
US-Canada_N	−.33	.02	.04	−.10
	(.21)	(.19)	(.16)	(.15)
US-Canada_I	−.70	−.22	−.51	−.71
	(1.27)	(1.14)	(.99)	(.98)
MERCOSUR_N	−.31**	−.61	.19	−.21**
	(.16)	(.14)	(.13)	(.12)
MERCOSUR_I	.67	1.75*	2.11*	.86*
	(.55)	(.49)	(.43)	(.42)
Andean_N	.04	.30*	.08	.34*
	(.16)	(.14)	(.13)	(.12)
Andean_I	.19	1.63*	1.34*	1.45*
	(.45)	(.40)	(.35)	(.34)
ASEAN_N	.42*	.75*	1.07*	.84*
	(.15)	(.13)	(.11)	(.11)
ASEAN_I	2.00*	2.91*	1.77*	1.89*
	(.44)	(.38)	(.33)	(.33)
Observations	2,699	2,699	2,699	2,699
Adjusted R^2	.62	.68	.73	.75

Notes: Standard errors are in parentheses. Intercept estimates are not reported. All variables except the dummies are in logarithmic form.
*Significant at the 5% level.
**Significant at the 10% level.

7.3   The Regionalization of Currencies and Its Effect on Trade

In this section, we consider the possibility that currency links contribute to bilateral trade patterns. We show that bilateral exchange rates have been partially stabilized within the two major blocs, but that the effects on trade have been fairly small. Thus little of the intrabloc trade links estimated in the preceding section can be attributed to the intrabloc currency links.

7.3.1   Stabilization of Exchange Rates within the Blocs

It is instructive to look at statistics on the variability of exchange rates among various groupings of countries. Worldwide, monthly real exchange rate variability rose in the 1980s, from a standard deviation of 3.22 percent in 1980 to 6.98 percent in 1990. The latter figure suggests that, for a typical pair of countries, approximately 95 percent of monthly exchange rate changes are smaller than 14 percent (under the simplifying assumption of a log-normal distribution).

There is a tendency for nominal exchange rate variability to be lower within most of the groups than across groups, supporting the idea of currency blocs. These statistics are reported in table 7.3. The lowest variability occurs within Europe. The 1980 statistic is a monthly standard deviation of 2 percent, and it falls by half during the course of the decade. Even though the members of the EC correspond roughly to the members of the European Monetary System (EMS),[1] non-EC members in Europe show as much stability in exchange rates (both vis-à-vis themselves and vis-à-vis other European countries) as EC members. These results no doubt in part reflect that the United Kingdom and the Mediterranean countries have not been consistent members of the Exchange Rate Mechanism, especially not within the narrow margins that the others observed until 1993. But it also reflects that such countries as Austria are loyal members of the currency club de facto, even though they are not yet in that club de jure.

One way that countries in a given area could achieve the observed lower levels of intraregional bilateral exchange rate variability is to link their currencies to the single most important currency in the region. In a simple version of the currency-bloc hypothesis, one would expect that the dollar has dominant influence in the Western Hemisphere, the yen in East Asia, and the mark in Europe. In Frankel and Wei (1994b), we examine the influences that the most important international currencies have on the determination of the values of currencies of smaller countries, by estimating implicit weights in a currency basket benchmark. Unsurprisingly, the mark has the overwhelmingly dominant weight in determining the value of most European currencies. In the Western Hemisphere, most of the countries tested give dominant weight to the dollar.

---

1. Of the EC members, only Greece had not joined the Exchange Rate Mechanism by early 1992 (though Italy and England dropped out soon thereafter).

Table 7.3   Mean Volatility of Monthly Real and Nominal Exchange Rates

Entire World (63 countries)

	Real Rate	Nominal Rate
Observations	1,081	1,770
1965	0.042075	0.028132
1970	0.029120	0.019186
1975	0.044608	0.036175
1980	0.032227	0.031364
1985	0.080961	0.072245
1990	0.069847	0.077298

Western Hemisphere

	Among Members		With the Rest of the World	
	Real Rate	Nominal Rate	Real Rate	Nominal Rate
Observations	78	78	442	611
1965	0.087273	0.079522	0.056805	0.047818
1970	0.056393	0.048040	0.037712	0.029744
1975	0.064088	0.056925	0.053026	0.046059
1980	0.030026	0.021343	0.033670	0.030500
1985	0.16410	0.17915	0.11148	0.11540
1990	0.13824	0.19515	0.094498	0.12487

European Economic Community (predecessor of the European Union)

	Among Members		With the Rest of the World	
	Real Rate	Nominal Rate	Real Rate	Nominal Rate
Observations	45	55	370	539
1965	0.017975	0.0013808	0.033617	0.018203
1970	0.013521	0.0077273	0.023547	0.014857
1975	0.023947	0.018182	0.039339	0.032903
1980	0.020350	0.017834	0.032199	0.031967
1985	0.019171	0.016586	0.064494	0.058641
1990	0.012036	0.0097418	0.055230	0.059050

East Asia (EAEC)

	Among Members		With the Rest of the World	
	Real Rate	Nominal Rate	Real Rate	Nominal Rate
Observations	3	21	172	416
1965	0.016960	0.041700	0.029392	0.031197
1970	0.058080	0.026516	0.035399	0.020715
1975	0.025727	0.026994	0.035500	0.032326
1980	0.030570	0.026914	0.029284	0.028659
1985	0.047970	0.034891	0.064616	0.057851
1990	0.033250	0.019260	0.060240	0.058726

(*continued*)

Table 7.3   (continued)

| | Asia Pacific Economic Cooperation Forum (APEC) | | | |
| | Among Members | | With the Rest of the World | |
	Real Rate	Nominal Rate	Real Rate	Nominal Rate
Observations	28	66	312	576
1965	0.008594	0.024897	0.029889	0.026718
1970	0.025547	0.017227	0.027609	0.018375
1975	0.029604	0.028851	0.038648	0.033309
1980	0.019988	0.021441	0.028438	0.027949
1985	0.045946	0.038942	0.067632	0.060800
1990	0.035360	0.026978	0.058762	0.060894

Notes: Volatility is defined as the standard deviation of the first difference of the logs of the monthly exchange rate over the current and preceding years (24 months). To ensure comparability over time, all computations are performed over country pairs that have nonmissing values throughout 1965–90.

The pattern of linking to the major currency of the region is broken in East Asia, however. The weight on the dollar is very high in most East Asian countries, with no special role for the yen. The Japanese currency is statistically significant in Singapore, and occasionally in some of the other countries in the region, but the coefficient is low. Each of the Asian countries is more properly classed in a dollar bloc than in a yen bloc. It thus appears that there are not three currency blocs in the world, but two: a mark bloc in Europe and a dollar bloc in the Pacific.

7.3.2   An Attempt to Estimate the Effect of Exchange Rate Variability on Trade

One rationale for a country to assign weight to a particular currency in determining its exchange rate is the assumption that a more stable bilateral exchange rate will help promote bilateral trade with the partner in question. This is a major motivation for exchange rate stabilization in Europe. There have been quite a few time-series studies of the effect of exchange rate uncertainty on trade overall,[2] but fewer cross-section studies of bilateral trade.

Three exceptions are Thursby and Thursby (1988) and De Grauwe (1988), which look only at a group of industrialized countries, and Brada and Mendez (1988). We will reexamine the question here using a data set that is broader, covering sixty-three countries. We return to a version of the gravity model of bilateral trade as in Frankel, Stein, and Wei (chap. 4 in this volume), but add an additional variable to capture the effect of exchange rate variability alongside the other variables. A problem of simultaneous causality should be noted at the outset: if exchange rate variability shows up with an apparent negative effect on the volume of bilateral trade, the correlation could be due to the gov-

2. The literature is reviewed in Edison and Melvin (1990).

Table 7.4   **Effect of Exchange Rate Volatility: Nominal Rates (total trade, 1965–90)**

	1965	1970	1975	1980	1985	1990
GNP	0.63*	0.64*	0.72*	0.76*	0.76*	0.76*
	(0.02)	(0.02)	(0.02)	(0.02)	(0.02)	(0.02)
GNP per capita	0.27*	0.36*	0.27*	0.27*	0.25*	0.12*
	(0.02)	(0.02)	(0.02)	(0.02)	(0.02)	(0.02)
Bilateral distance	−0.40*	−0.51*	−0.68*	−0.62*	−0.71*	−0.60*
	(0.04)	(0.04)	(0.05)	(0.04)	(0.04)	(0.04)
Adjacency	0.78*	0.69*	0.53*	0.64*	0.73*	0.68*
	(0.17)	(0.17)	(0.18)	(0.18)	(0.18)	(0.16)
WH2	0.05	0.01	0.26***	0.44*	0.34**	0.71*
	(0.16)	(0.14)	(0.15)	(0.15)	(0.16)	(0.14)
EAEC2	1.59*	1.60*	0.87*	0.81*	0.60**	0.67*
	(0.31)	(0.29)	(0.33)	(0.26)	(0.28)	(0.25)
APEC2	0.60*	0.70*	0.87*	1.35*	1.21*	1.39*
	(0.22)	(0.17)	(0.23)	(0.18)	(0.19)	(0.17)
EE2	0.20	0.08	−0.10	0.01	0.45**	0.51*
	(0.16)	(0.21)	(0.18)	(0.18)	(0.18)	(0.16)
Nominal exchange rate variability	−3.81*	−2.47*	−1.49**	−7.65*	0.13	2.24*
	(0.60)	(0.09)	(0.74)	(0.08)	(0.34)	(0.27)
Observations	1,115	1,231	1,401	1,653	1,589	1,519
Adjusted R^2	0.70	0.72	0.72	0.72	0.74	0.78
Standard error of estimation	1.04	1.06	1.18	1.18	1.17	1.05

Notes: Standard errors are in parentheses. All variables except the dummies are in logarithms. *WH2, EAEC2, APEC2,* and *EE2* are dummy variables for both countries belonging to the same bloc. For example, *WH2* = 1 if both countries are in the Western Hemisphere, and 0 otherwise.
*Significant at the 1% level ($t \geq 2.576$).
**Significant at the 5% level ($t \geq 1.96$).
***Significant at the 10% level ($t \geq 1.645$).

ernment's deliberate efforts to stabilize the currency vis-à-vis a valued trading partner, as easily as to the effects of stabilization on trade.

Volatility is defined to be the standard deviation of the first difference of the logarithmic exchange rate. We start with the volatility of nominal exchange rates and embed this term in our gravity equation. The results are reported in table 7.4. Table 7.5 does the same for the volatility of real exchange rates. Most coefficients are similar to those reported in the earlier paper (chap. 4 in this volume) without exchange rate variability: the Western Hemisphere, East Asia, Asia-Pacific Economic Cooperation (APEC), and the EC all show statistically significant bloc effects.

The ordinary least squares (OLS) show a negative effect of exchange rate volatility (whether nominal or real) on bilateral trade that is highly significant in 1965, 1970, 1975, and 1980. Only in 1985 and 1990 does the negative effect disappear (indeed, turn positive). Henceforth we concentrate our discussions on the regressions involving real exchange rate variability.

Table 7.5 Effect of Exchange Rate Volatility: Real Rates (total trade, 1965–90)

	1965	1970	1975	1980	1985	1990
GNP	0.72*	0.65*	0.72*	0.74*	0.76*	0.76*
	(0.02)	(0.02)	(0.02)	(0.02)	(0.02)	(0.02)
GNP per capita	0.24*	0.36*	0.27*	0.26*	0.25*	0.12*
	(0.03)	(0.02)	(0.02)	(0.02)	(0.02)	(0.02)
Bilateral distance	−0.53*	−0.50*	−0.67*	−0.62*	−0.71*	−0.57*
	(0.05)	(0.04)	(0.05)	(0.04)	(0.04)	(0.04)
Adjacency	0.59*	0.77*	0.58*	0.73*	0.73*	0.80*
	(0.18)	(0.16)	(0.18)	(0.18)	(0.18)	(0.16)
WH2	0.02	0.02	0.27***	0.42*	0.30***	0.74*
	(0.15)	(0.13)	(0.15)	(0.15)	(0.15)	(0.14)
EAEC2	0.99**	1.80*	0.85*	0.76*	0.60**	0.71*
	(0.50)	(0.32)	(0.32)	(0.26)	(0.27)	(0.25)
APEC2	0.44***	0.67*	0.90*	1.35*	1.16*	1.38*
	(0.26)	(0.21)	(0.22)	(0.18)	(0.18)	(0.17)
EE2	0.04	0.08	−0.06	0.02	0.40**	0.57*
	(0.17)	(0.16)	(0.18)	(0.18)	(0.17)	(0.16)
Real exchange	−3.02*	−2.72*	−1.57**	−6.97*	0.12	3.19*
rate variability	(0.67)	(0.83)	(0.82)	(0.08)	(0.37)	(0.27)
Observations	773	1,053	1,316	1,503	1,500	1,494
Adjusted R^2	0.76	0.76	0.74	0.75	0.75	0.78
Standard error	0.94	0.99	2.21	1.13	1.14	1.04
of estimation						

Notes: Standard errors are in parentheses. All variables except the dummies are in logarithms. *WH2, EAEC2, APEC2,* and *EE2* are dummy variables for both countries belonging to the same bloc. For example, *WH2* = 1 if both countries are in the Western Hemisphere, and 0 otherwise.
*Significant at the 1% level ($t \geq 2.576$).
**Significant at the 5% level ($t \geq 1.96$).
***Significant at the 10% level ($t \geq 1.645$).

By way of illustration, these point estimates can be used for some sample calculations. They suggest that if the level of EC real exchange rate variability that prevailed in 1980, a standard deviation of 2 percent, had been eliminated altogether, the volume of intra-EC trade would have increased by 14.18 percent ($= 6.97 \times 2.04$). This OLS estimate should be regarded very much as an upper bound. For one thing, the 1980 point estimate of the effect of exchange rate volatility is the largest of all the years. In the earlier observations, the magnitude of the estimated effect is one-fifth to one-half the size.

Worldwide, the average level of exchange rate variability in 1980 was 3.22 percent. The OLS-estimated effect on trade of adopting fixed exchange rates worldwide was thus 22.44 percent ($= 6.97 \times 3.22$).

The exchange rate disruptions of September 1992 and August 1993 may herald a return to the level of variability among the EMS countries that prevailed in 1980. Table 7.3 shows that this would represent an approximate doubling of the standard deviation of exchange rates, relative to the stability that had been achieved by 1990. What would be the predicted effects on trade? The

Table 7.6   **Sample Calculation of the Effects of Exchange Rate Stabilization by the European Union on Trade during 1980–90 (upper-bound estimate)**

Changes in Volatility from 1980 to 1990	Elasticity of Trade with Respect to Volatility (1980 estimate)	Estimated Change in Trade due to Bilateral Currency Stabilization (%)
Nominal exchange rate volatility		
(OLS) 0.0097 − 0.0178 = −0.0081	−7.65	+6.2
Real exchange rate volatility		
(OLS) 0.0120 − 0.0204 = −0.0084	−6.97	+5.9
Real exchange rate volatility		
(instrumental-variables method)		
0.0120 − 0.0204 = −0.0084	−0.28	+2.4

OLS estimate in table 7.5 suggests that trade would fall by 5.85 percent (= 6.97 × (2.04 − 1.20)). Table 7.6 reports this calculation, and the corresponding calculations for some other possible estimates.

Interpretations of the estimates in tables 7.4 and 7.5 are complicated by the likelihood of simultaneity bias in the above regressions. Governments may choose deliberately to stabilize bilateral exchange rates with their major trading partners. This has certainly been the case in Europe. Hence, there could be a strong observed correlation between trade patterns and currency linkages even if exchange rate volatility does not depress trade.

To address this problem, we use the method of instrumental variable estimation, with the standard deviation of relative money supply as our instrument for the volatility of exchange rates. The argument in favor of this choice of instrument is that relative money supplies and bilateral exchange rates are highly correlated in theory (they are directly linked under the monetary theory of exchange rate determination), and in our data as well, but monetary policies are less likely than exchange rate policies to be set in response to bilateral trade patterns. The instrumental variables results, reported in table 7.7, show the same sign pattern across the years as the OLS estimates, but the negative effect is statistically significant only in 1965. The coefficient for 1980 is (a completely insignificant) 0.28; even if the point estimate is taken at face value, it would imply that the elimination of exchange rate variability worldwide would increase trade by only 0.9 percent (= 0.28 × 3.22).

These results, while less robust than most of the other gravity equation findings, are generally consistent with the hypothesis that real exchange rate volatility has depressed bilateral trade a bit in the 1960s and 1970s. But the evidence for a negative trade effect, which starts out relatively strong in 1965, diminishes steadily in the 1970s and 1980s, especially if one takes due account of the simultaneity. The proliferation of currency options, forward contracts, and other hedging instruments over this period may explain why the effect that appears once to have been there, has more recently disappeared.

Table 7.7   **Effect of Real Exchange Rate Volatility: Using Volatility of Relative Money Supply as Instrument (total trade, 1965–90)**

	1965	1970	1975	1980	1985	1990
GNP	0.82*	0.66*	0.72*	0.74*	0.78*	0.77*
	(0.05)	(0.02)	(0.02)	(0.02)	(0.02)	(0.02)
GNP per capita	−0.07	0.33*	0.25*	0.26*	0.21*	0.11*
	(0.12)	(0.04)	(0.02)	(0.03)	(0.02)	(0.02)
Bilateral distance	−0.50*	−0.51*	−0.69*	−0.67*	−0.74*	−0.61*
	(0.12)	(0.08)	(0.05)	(0.05)	(0.05)	(0.04)
Adjacency	1.09*	0.69*	0.51*	0.62*	0.66*	0.70*
	(0.47)	(0.18)	(0.20)	(0.19)	(0.20)	(0.17)
WH2	1.10***	0.16	0.42**	0.49*	0.33***	0.55*
	(0.60)	(0.43)	(0.17)	(0.15)	(0.17)	(0.17)
EAEC2	1.28	1.71*	0.90**	0.79**	0.70***	0.52***
	(0.92)	(0.43)	(0.35)	(0.32)	(0.36)	(0.27)
APEC2	0.26	0.74*	1.09*	1.49*	1.22*	1.39*
	(0.46)	(0.23)	(0.24)	(0.20)	(0.21)	(0.17)
EE2	−0.17	0.00	−0.12	0.00	0.39***	0.59*
	(0.35)	(0.18)	(0.24)	(0.22)	(0.20)	(0.16)
Real exchange	−38.03**	−4.54	−2.05	−0.28	0.18	3.89*
rate variability	(0.28)	(11.73)	(1.54)	(3.22)	(0.46)	(0.59)
Observations	393	921	1,076	1,187	1,163	1,319
Adjusted R^2	0.51	0.76	0.73	0.74	0.76	0.79
Standard error of estimation	1.40	0.97	1.14	1.13	1.12	1.03

Notes: Standard errors are in parentheses. All variables except the dummies are in logarithms. *WH2, EAEC2, APEC2,* and *EE2* are dummy variables for both countries belonging to the same bloc. For example, *WH2* = 1 if both countries are in the Western Hemisphere, and 0 otherwise.
*Significant at the 1% level ($t \geq 2.576$).
**Significant at the 5% level ($t \geq 1.96$).
***Significant at the 10% level ($t \geq 1.645$).

7.4   Stumbling Blocks or Building Blocks? The Political Economy of Regional Blocs

Although the multilateral system has made large strides toward freer trade, most recently in the form of the successful conclusion of the Uruguay Round negotiations in December 1993, political constraints inevitably prevent the immediate attainment of the economist's nirvana. Since some influential producer interest groups in each country typically stand to lose from free trade, full unilateral liberalization rarely occurs, and the world must instead await the outcome of step-by-step multilateral negotiations. In these negotiations, countries trade concessions with each other in such a way that at each step the percentage of the population that stands to gain is sufficiently high to overcome the political opposition.

In this light, the case in favor of regional trading arrangements is a second-best argument that takes as given the impossibility of further most-favored-nation (MFN) liberalization. The uninitiated might assume that free trade economists would under these circumstances necessarily support FTAs. But from the standpoint of static economic welfare, trade economists are ambivalent about the desirability of FTAs. So long as tariffs and other barriers against third countries remain in place, the elimination of barriers between two FTA members can as easily intensify distortions as eliminate them.[3]

The classical distinction is between the harmful trade-diverting effects of FTAs and their beneficial trade-creating effects. Although modern theories of trade have gone beyond the diversion/creation distinction, it is still a useful intuitive guide to likely welfare effects.[4] Grossman and Helpman (1995), for example, find in a lobbying model that an FTA is most likely to be adopted when trade diversion outweighs trade creation, which unfortunately is also when it is most likely to reduce aggregate welfare.

7.4.1   Negative Political Implications for Multilateral Trade Liberalization

There are a variety of arguments as to how the adoption of a regional trading area might undermine movement toward unilateral or multilateral liberalization for political reasons: these fall under the headings "incentive to protect" or market power, scarce negotiator resources, political deadend, and manipulation of the process by special interests. We consider these antiregionalization arguments first, before considering some arguments that go the other way.

Blocs' Market Power and Incentive to Protect

The standard experiment presumes that the level of trade barriers against outsiders remains unchanged when a customs union is established. However, Krugman (1991a) shows that, in a world consisting of a few large blocs, each unit will have more monopoly power and thus will be more tempted to seek to shift the terms of trade in its favor by raising tariffs against the other blocs. This is the "incentive to protect." This temptation will be minimized in a world of many small trading blocs (or in a world of MFN, i.e., each country its own bloc). A world of a few large blocs is thus one in which the noncooperative equilibrium features a higher level of interbloc tariffs and a lower level of economic welfare. In Krugman's simulation, three turns out to be the worst number of blocs to have. Haveman (1992) gets essentially the same result, with expected world welfare minimized in a world of only two customs unions, using a model where trade arises from comparative advantage rather than from product differentiation (following the Deardorff-Stern critique of Krugman).

---

3. On the grounds of such trade-diversion effects, and other considerations discussed below, Bhagwati, Krueger, and Panagariya generally oppose regional trading arrangements. Bhagwati (1995, 11) and Panagariya (1995, 20, n. 8) have confessed that they were prepared to oppose the NAFTA publicly, if asked. They are now skeptical of other ongoing initiatives, including APEC.

4. Stein and Frankel (1994) show in a model of imperfect competition that a simulation comparison of the magnitudes of trade creation and trade diversion provides the right answer to the question whether FTAs raise the welfare of the representative consumer, under many plausible parameter values, though not all.

The Krugman model assumes that members of a trade bloc set their external tariffs together, that is, that the arrangement is a customs union. The "incentive to protect" story would be different for a standard FTA, in which each country is able to set its tariffs independently with respect to nonmembers. Sinclair and Vines (1994) argue that in the FTA case there is actually an incentive for each country to *reduce* its external tariffs, just the opposite of the customs union case. Richardson (1993a) derives the result, that is, the superiority of an FTA to a customs union, in a model where tariffs are set endogenously, by a government that seeks to maximize a function of the profits of protected industries, in addition to consumer welfare. The FTA member with a comparative disadvantage in a particular good will experience a decline in the political influence of that industry as competition within the FTA diminishes the industry's economic size. Thus the country will tend to reduce protection for that industry, in a way that would not be possible if bound by the common external tariff of a customs union. Panagariya and Findlay (1994) assume that protection is the endogenous outcome of lobbying, and derive the opposite results regarding the FTA/customs union comparison from Richardson and Sinclair and Vines: the lobby chooses a lower external tariff under a customs union than under an FTA. The customs union is more effective at diluting the power of interest groups.

In reality, governments in one sense are less capable of national economic optimization than the Krugman model presupposes, and in another sense they are more capable. In both respects, large trading blocs are less vulnerable to the incentive to raise tariffs against each other than under Krugman's assumptions. Governments are less capable of optimization, in that maximum exploitation of the terms of trade (through imposition of the "optimum tariff") is in practice one of the *less* prevalent determinants of trade policy. More commonly seen are arguments regarding infant industries, protecting the scarce factor of production, increasing employment, and adjustment costs. Governments are *more* capable of optimization in that they have already instituted the cooperative international regime of GATT, as Bergsten (1991) pointed out in his comment on Krugman (1991b). Article XXIV of GATT explicitly rules out Krugman's concern. This provision allows deviations from the MFN principle only for FTAs or customs unions that do not raise the average level of their tariffs against nonmembers.

There are several reasons to worry that blocs' "incentive to protect" survives despite the existence of article XXIV. First, and most obviously, article XXIV is often disregarded, as Bhagwati (1992) reminds us. Second, as Bagwell and Staiger (1993, n. 25) point out, exacerbation of the incentive to protect in customs unions can take the form of "gray-area" measures when explicit tariff increases are ruled out. Third, one hopes that the multilateral process is on a path whereby worldwide tariff rates are gradually reduced through negotiation, and that this path is the relevant benchmark, not unchanging tariffs. Bond and Syropoulos (1996) show that arriving at the cooperative equilibrium of an agreement for interbloc liberalization in a repeated game, which is seen as GATT's role to facilitate, becomes more difficult as the size of the blocs, and therefore their monopoly power, rises.

Scarce Negotiator Resources

The scarce-negotiator-resources argument points out that negotiations are not costless. If they were, then the world would have achieved free trade by now. If the U.S. special trade representative is spending all his or her time—and spending all the White House's political capital with Congress—on a regional agreement (e.g., NAFTA), there is presumably less time or capital left over to spend on multilateral negotiations (e.g., the Uruguay Round). As with the incentive-to-protect argument, regional trading arrangements may set back the process of negotiating worldwide trade liberalization under GATT.

Some authors—for example, Summers (1991) and Krugman (1993)—have argued that the costs of negotiation go up with the number of countries involved, so that it is easier to negotiate customs unions first, and then proceed to multilateral liberalization among the smaller number of larger units. Others question the practicality of the small numbers claim—Bhagwati (1993b), Winters (1996), and Panagariya (1994, 830–31).

Political Deadend

Some have suggested political models in which regional initiatives can prevent multilateral initiatives because the sequence of decisions matters. The forces in favor of liberalization might win out over protectionists if the only choice is between the status quo and multilateral liberalization; but when offered the option of a regional FTA, the political process might then take the regional route to the exclusion of the multilateral route. Bhagwati (1993b, 28–29) worries that businessmen and bureaucrats, after having achieved regional integration, might then find the effort involved in multilateral negotiation too difficult. "Lobbying support and political energies can readily be diverted to preferential trading arrangements such as FTAs. . . . That deprives the multilateral system of the support it needs to survive, let alone be conducive to further trade liberalization" (Bhagwati 1993a, 162).

Levy (1993) offers what might be called a median-voter deadend model, in which a bilateral free trade agreement can undermine support for multilateral liberalization because it is a deadend in the political process. It is assumed that trade policy is determined by the median voter. Trade itself is determined in some sectors by differences in factor endowments, and in others by considerations of imperfect substitutes. As others have argued, the intraindustry sort of trade that is generated in imperfect substitutes is easier to accept politically than the factor-endowment kind of trade. The reason is that adjustment to import competition requires workers only to move from the assembly line for one product variety to the assembly line for another variety of the same product. Trade based on differences in factor endowments is much more difficult to accept politically, because it requires workers in previously protected industries to move to different industries (and at lower wages, in the case of capital-intensive industrialized countries).

Levy argues that policy toward trade is thus always a trade-off between the gains afforded by increased varieties and the losses inflicted by a fall in the relative price of the product that is intensive in the scarce factor (labor, in the case of industrialized countries). If liberalization is not attainable, it is because the losses from factor-endowment trade dominate. If a vote is held first on whether to join a bilateral FTA, the proposition is more likely to pass when the potential partner has similar factor endowments. (It is easier politically to achieve an EU than a NAFTA or APEC.) The reason is that the gains from increased trade in imperfect substitutes will be large, while the losses from a fall in the relative price of labor-intensive products will be small. But if a vote is then held on multilateral liberalization, it will fail: those key sectors that stand to profit from trade in imperfect substitutes will already have reaped those gains, and there will be fewer political forces to countervail the sectors that lose from the additional factor-endowment trade. In this way regional free trade agreements undermine political support for multilateral liberalization in this model.

Manipulation by Special Interests

The special-interests argument points out that the process of instituting a regional trading arrangement features abundant opportunities for trade-sensitive industries to manipulate the process, particularly those sectors that might be adversely affected. Examples abound. First, Wonnacott and Lutz (1989, 65–66) emphasize that negotiators frequently seek to exclude from regional FTAs precisely those of their sectors that would be most threatened by welfare-enhancing trade creation. The members of ASEAN, for example, have until now exempted almost all the important sectors from the system of preferences that they are supposed to grant each other (Panagariya 1994, 828–29). Grossman and Helpman (1995, 680–87) have used their lobbying model to understand how the possibility of such industry exclusions increases the chances of FTAs being adopted. This was the primary reason for another restriction that GATT article XXIV places on FTAs, that "substantially all" barriers within the region be removed. In practice, FTAs have tended to comply less than completely with this provision. Examples include the European Economic Community's exclusion of agriculture and, in practice, steel and many other goods.

Second, Anne Krueger (in press, 1995) emphasizes the exploitation of rules of origin. An FTA, unlike a customs union, does not involve the setting of common external tariffs. Rules of origin are a mechanism by which a country can prevent imports from nonmembers, transshipped via the FTA partner, in those sectors where the partner has lower tariffs. Richardson (1993b), Krueger (in press), and Krishna and Krueger (1995) show how individual industries in the FTA negotiation can enhance the extent of protection they receive when their governments use rules of origin to enable them to capture their FTA partner's market in addition to their own, thus diverting trade from foreign suppliers. Richardson (1993b) emphasizes that prices at which producers can sell are equalized within an FTA, even when rules of origin are successful in keeping the consumer price higher in the higher-tariff country.[5] Krueger (1995), on the other hand, argues that customs unions are always Pareto superior to FTAs, because they have no rules of origin that can be exploited in this way.

Bhagwati (1993b, 30–31; 1995, 22) and Panagariya (1995, 16–21) point out that large countries like the United States may use their overwhelming bargaining power within regional groupings to obtain from small countries distorting concessions that they might not obtain in more balanced multilateral negotiations. Perroni and Whalley (1994) and Whalley (chap. 3 in this volume) point out that small countries have been the supplicants in recent regional agreements, and show how large countries have all the bargaining power on their side.

7.4.2   Positive Political Implications for Multilateral Trade Liberalization

Other arguments go the other way. They offer the hope that the adoption of a regional trading area might undermine protectionism and reinforce movement toward liberalization more generally. The arguments concern locking in unilateral liberalization, the efficiency of negotiating with larger units, mobilization of regional solidarity, building export constituencies to create domestic political momentum, and competitive liberalization.

Lock-in and Mobilizing Regional Solidarity

In the late 1980s, Mexican president Salinas reversed a half century of Mexican protectionism and imposed sweeping unilateral liberalization measures. Future presidents of Mexico might seek to reverse this liberalization. Thus, a good argument for NAFTA was that it locked in the Salinas reforms in a manner that would be difficult to reverse in the future (e.g., Lawrence 1991).

Elsewhere, such as in Andean Pact countries, leaders have used popular support for regional solidarity to achieve liberalization that would be politically impossible if pursued unilaterally. De Melo, Panagariya, and Rodrik (1993, section 3) model the process whereby governments can adopt rules or institutions in a regional grouping to insulate themselves from pressure by private-sector lobbies for intervention on their behalf.

Efficiency of Negotiating with Larger Units

Within the context of multilateral negotiations, it is awkward to negotiate separately with over a hundred small countries. It has been argued that if small

---

5. Competition for tariff revenue among the FTA members may then result in an equilibrium where external tariffs are reduced to zero.

countries form themselves into larger groupings, which presumably have to be customs unions with common external trade policies, then they can negotiate as a group.[6] This is thought to increase the efficiency of the negotiations, and to make a satisfactory worldwide agreement more likely. The EU is certainly the most important example of this. Other groupings, such as ASEAN and South Asian Association for Regional Cooperation (SAARC), have also been urged to integrate regionally, so as to be able to talk with the larger powers.

Competitive Liberalization

In an important analysis of the political economy of regional blocs, Oye (1992) argues that the expected costs of exclusion from groupings change the political dynamics, by strengthening the antiprotectionist constituencies domestically, so as to draw countries into multilateral negotiations. Whereas many authors might read the recent experience as regionalism helping build support for multilateral liberalization, Oye finds that this was also true of the 1930s experience.

"Competitive liberalization" refers to building political momentum for liberalization among countries, rather than domestically (Bergsten 1995). An illustration is President Clinton's "triple play" of late 1993 (Bergsten 1994, 18–20; Kahler 1994, 19, 25). By upgrading the Seattle meeting of APEC ministers that had been scheduled for November 1993 into a high-profile leaders' meeting, he signaled to the Europeans that if they continued to allow French farmers to hold up the Uruguay Round, other countries might proceed without them. This message carried credibility because of its fortunate timing, coming as it did on the heels of the hard-fought approval of NAFTA in the U.S. Congress. Thus, the NAFTA outcome demonstrated the political will necessary for meaningful agreements, while the APEC meeting demonstrated the possibility that agreements would cover a fraction of the world economy that was sufficiently large and dynamic to give the Europeans cause for worry at the prospect of being left out. German policymakers have reportedly confirmed that this was part of their motive for concluding the Uruguay Round in December. In this episode at least, it appears that regional initiatives helped bring about multilateral agreement.

Of course, the game need not always come out so well. The trouble with making credible threats is that sometimes they must be carried out. The process that is traditionally feared is *competitive regionalization,* where the formation of one regional grouping puts pressure on other countries to form a bloc of their own, rather than to liberalize unilaterally or multilaterally. The worst situation for a country is to be one of the few that do not belong to any bloc, because the terms of trade then turn against it. For this reason, there is a danger

---

6. E.g., Deardorff and Stern (1994), Krugman (1993), and Summers (1991). Kahler (1994) suggests that plurilateral negotiations among a small number of regional neighbors may allow more efficient treatment of new individual issue areas than do global negotiations.

that the world will become stuck in a Nash noncooperative equilibrium of several continental FTAs: each continent forms an FTA because, given that the next continent is doing so, it will be hurt if it does not respond in kind. In the resulting equilibrium, all are worse off than they were under the status quo of MFN. (Hence the argument for discouraging FTAs in GATT in the first place, as under article XXIV.) Furthermore, even if continents are allowed to choose the level of intrabloc preference to maximize their individual welfares, rather than being constrained to go all the way to FTAs, in equilibrium they will still choose a level of preference that is so high as to leave everyone worse off. This is the "incentive to protect" argument we have already seen. These points are shown in a model with intercontinental transport costs by Stein (1994, 83–93).[7]

On the other hand, since the ultimate goal is worldwide free trade, it is not clear that the ultimate political-economy dynamic is bad. Worldwide economic welfare is so reduced by a noncooperative equilibrium of four continental FTAs that it may then become politically possible for them to agree multilaterally to remove the barriers that remain between them and go to worldwide free trade. This would seem to follow if the obstacle to a move from MFN to worldwide free trade is a moderate fixed resource cost to negotiations (say 1 percent of GDP, to buy off producers that stand to lose). The leap to free trade would be all the more likely to follow if the resource cost to negotiation increases with the number of distinct entities involved.

What happens if the first bloc allows other countries to join? (This is one possible interpretation of the phrase "open regionalism.") A number of authors have shown that nonmember countries will, one by one, find it in their interest to join a given FTA.[8] While the bloc expands, its members gain progressively, as the terms of trade are shifted further and further in their favor. Those that continue to be left out lose progressively. In the model of Deardorff and Stern (1994), the bloc continues to grow until it encompasses the whole world, the happy outcome of global free trade. Their model, however, assumes that the bloc at each stage places prohibitive tariffs on outsiders, a rather extreme assumption.

Saxonhouse (1993) and Stein (1994) consider the same problem, while allowing trade with nonmembers. They find that when the bloc reaches a certain size (20 out of 30 members in Saxonhouse, and 16 out of 30 in Stein), it will choose not to accept any new members, because its own welfare starts to decline after that. What makes this story especially alarming from the viewpoint of ultimate multilateral liberalization is that the single bloc is truly a

---

7. In a simulation, the status quo of MFN features worldwide welfare that falls short of free trade by only about 0.5 percent of GNP (which may not be enough to overcome negotiating costs). Each continent in sequence has an incentive to form an FTA, raising its welfare but lowering that of all the other continents, until all four have done so. In that noncooperative equilibrium, the loss relative to global free trade is about 2.5 percent.

8. Bond and Syropoulos (1996), Deardorff and Stern (1994), Saxonhouse (1993), and Stein (1994), each with somewhat different specifications of the model.

deadend: welfare of the bloc members is higher than it would be under worldwide free trade, so that they have an incentive to reject multilateral liberalization that they did not have when the alternative was MFN. At this unhappy deadend point, worldwide welfare is close to its minimum, the very low welfare of the nonmembers outweighing the high welfare of the members.

At some point, the nonmembers will presumably wise up and form a bloc of their own. But given two competing blocs, the incentive for individual countries will be to join the larger of the two to share in its monopoly power. A world of two equal-sized blocs is unstable (Bond and Syropoulos 1996). A simulation in Stein (1994, 99–102) shows that the stable equilibrium has twenty-six out of thirty countries in one large bloc, and four in the other. Again, the large bloc has no incentive to take mercy on those excluded.

Stein (1994, 103–5) has a proposed solution to this difficulty: that article XXIV be amended to state that preferences within a bloc cannot go beyond a specified low level (22 percent is the magic limit, in his simulation). We have already seen (in the Frankel-Stein-Wei model) that such a restriction—the opposite of the current article XXIV requirement for 100 percent preferences— would be welfare-improving in a world of equal-sized continental blocs. The same is true when there are no intercontinental transport costs and there is a temptation for countries to join the larger of two blocs. The equilibrium still features one large bloc (twenty-four countries) and one small (six countries). But with the limit on the margin of preferences in place, the large bloc has nothing to lose by moving to worldwide free trade, so that the happy outcome is still ultimately attainable. Of course the members of the large bloc would vote against such a rule in GATT. However, if the issue is decided before any single incipient grouping is large enough to know that it will be the dominant bloc, then everything will work out for free trade.

7.5 A Simple Political-Economy Model

In this section, we sketch a simple political-economy model of our own that illustrates another potentially beneficial role that regional blocs can play to promote further trade liberalization. A fuller version can be found in Wei and Frankel (1996). We set up the model using the structure in Fernandez and Rodrik (1991). By construction, global free trade is not obtainable directly in a political process. We then show how a regional initiative may break this impasse. The essential argument is isomorphic to that of Wei (forthcoming), which illustrates some political-economy benefits of gradualist reforms over big bang in transition economies.

Consider a two-period world. Countries A and B are two small open economies. The rest of the world is labeled country C. There are three goods, x, y, and z. All can be produced by a constant-returns-to-scale (CRTS) technology with labor being the only input. Specifically, for country k, the technology to produce good j is

$$j^k = \frac{L_j^k}{\theta_j^k},$$

where k = A, B, and C, and j = x, y, and z.

To minimize notational complication while still preserving enough richness for our discussion, we will assume that the technology parameter Θ takes one of two values.

$$\tau_j^k = \alpha, \qquad \text{if } (k, j) = (A, x), (B, y), \text{ or } (C, z);$$

$$= \beta \qquad \text{otherwise,}$$

where $\alpha < \beta$ and the index (k, j) represents the value of unit labor requirement for good k in country j.

Trade policy decisions are made by majority vote. The labor distribution in countries A and B has the feature that no single sector has a majority, and the sum of any two sectors constitutes a majority. For example, the labor force can be evenly divided among the three sectors. On the other hand, in country C (i.e., the aggregation of all the other countries in the world), workers in sector z constitute a majority. Hence, country C always wants global free trade if it can get it. This assumption on country C allows us to focus our discussion on countries A and B.

7.5.1   Global Free Trade Is Infeasible

With this configuration, each country has an unambiguous winner (e.g., sector x for A). Suppose that in countries A and B the two less efficient sectors receive tariff protection at the ad valorem rate r. Because of the symmetry between the two countries, we restrict our attention to one, say A. Trusting it will not lead to confusion, we omit the country superscript for all variables.

Assume perfect competition in each sector. The constant returns to scale technology ties down the wage rates to the cum-tariff goods prices. That is,

$$w_j = p_j / \Theta_j.$$

By appropriately choosing the values of Θ, we can let the wages be the same in the three sectors in the absence of any change in the status quo. From the viewpoint of country A, global free trade means removal of tariffs on goods y and z. With the removal of the two tariffs, w_y and w_z fall.

The crucial assumption of the model is that job relocation is costly. The cost is individual-specific. But individuals do not know their own switching costs before the trade liberalization takes place. All they know is the probability distribution of the costs. We use c_i to denote the cost for individual i of switching from one sector to another.

With this setup, it is easy to demonstrate the following possibility using the Fernandez-Rodrik (1991) argument. On the one hand, global free trade will benefit a majority in countries A and B if it has a chance to be implemented.

On the other hand, a (different) majority will oppose it ex ante. Those who oppose it do it rationally, as the expected loss from free trade may outweigh the expected gain. (See Wei and Frankel 1996 for a more detailed exposition.)

7.5.2   Regional Bloc Is Feasible

Consider a proposal to form an FTA between A and B. Ex post, as a result of tariff removal, the price of good y in country A (and that of good x in country B) will decline. Not surprisingly, people in sector x in country A unambiguously benefit from this and will support the regional bloc. Interestingly, people in sector z also benefit from a lower price on good y. Hence, if they base their action on this period's utility, they will also support the move, which makes the number of supporters in country A a majority.

7.5.3   Global Free Trade Reconsidered

Once a free trade bloc with country B is in place, we can reconsider the political feasibility of a proposal for global free trade. Those people who remain in sector y, although suffering a real income loss from the regional bloc, realize that further liberalization, as under a global free trade agreement, will not cause another drop in their wage; rather it will lead to a drop in the price of good z. Therefore, people in sector y together with those in sector x will now collectively support a move to global free trade.

Note, to be completely correct, that this analysis assumes voters are myopic in the sense that, when voting on the regional bloc, they ignore the prospect of a future vote on global free trade. However, the behavior can be rational, if the voters have a high discount rate or there is uncertainty about the future (for example, about whether there is going to be a second vote at all), so that the expected future loss would be sufficiently small relative to the current gain from the regional deal.

The behavior can also be rational in an alternative setting. Assume, instead of having a forever-young population, we have successive generations in each country. Assume further that each period (appropriately defined) is dominated by a different generation, and there is little intergenerational altruism. Then, the referenda on the regional bloc and global free trade take place in different generations. Each will succeed politically exactly in the way as delineated above.

7.5.4   Regional Blocs as a Divide-and-Conquer Device

In our above story, a regional bloc works as a stepping stone toward global free trade under several scenarios, including a high discount rate and independent generations. Does the result hold without these assumptions? In particular, if people in sector z realize that free trade with B will lead to free trade with C, or the tariff on z will eventually be removed, would they still support the regional trade arrangement?

We would like to argue that the result still holds in a two-period model. To do this, we need to assume that the government is able to set an agenda and commit to it. The agenda is simply a two-stage plan: in period 1, the government will hold a referendum on forming a free trade bloc with country B; and in period 2, regardless of the outcome of the first referendum, the government will hold another referendum on forming a free trade bloc with country C (the rest of the world).

Notice that when $t = 2$, it is the people in sector y together with those in x that push the country toward further trade liberalization. Therefore, in order to block the regional trade arrangement, which by itself is in the interest of people in sector z, people in sector y have to promise and convince people in sector z that they will not agree to free trade with country C at $t = 2$. But such a promise is not time-consistent. That is, when $t = 2$, it is in the interest of people in sector y to vote for free trade with C. Given that free trade with C will likely be the outcome at $t = 2$, the best strategy for people in sector z at $t = 1$ is to vote for free trade with country B. In this way, they at least get the benefit of a lower price on good y. Hence, by using a regional bloc as an intermediate step, the government can pursue global free trade as an end result of a two-step process.

The logic of the above argument derives from the inability of one group of people to precommit their future actions to another group. Hence, using backward induction, we can show that the same argument holds in a multiple but finite-period world. The prospect of collusion cannot be ruled out ex ante in an infinite-period model. However, the large number of people in each sector in the real world and the uncertainty about the future make collusion difficult.

7.5.5   Regionalism as a Possible Deadend

The discussion so far has centered on how regional trade blocs may change the dynamics of domestic political forces so as eventually to render global free trade feasible. It is important to make clear that regionalism is not a panacea for political opposition to multilateral free trade. Indeed, it is just as easy to construct models such that regional trade blocs may develop into a deadend, so that the countries involved may never be able to move toward global free trade.

7.6   Concluding Discussion

Using a modified gravity model that incorporates relative remoteness of exporters and importers from the world and an updated data set covering 1970–92, we have mapped out the current pattern of regionalization in trade. Bloc effects are apparent in many parts of the world. We also presented some estimates of the role that currency links within some major groupings might have played in promoting intragroup trade. We find that the world is better described as falling into two currency blocs, rather than three: a dollar bloc in the Pacific and a mark bloc in Europe. The tendency to stabilize bilateral exchange rates within these blocs apparently gave a statistically significant boost to bilateral trade in the 1970s, but this effect vanished in the 1980s.

Next, we reviewed various political economy arguments that others have made regarding regionalism, either to the effect that it can help build political momentum for multilateral liberalization (building blocs) or to the effect that it can undermine more general liberalization (stumbling blocs). We review a simple model of our own that is in the first category: it illustrates one possible beneficial effect of trade blocs as a political building block to further trade liberalization.

Are regional blocs building blocks or stumbling blocks to multilateral liberalization? Given that political-economy forces could go either direction, it would be useful to know which effect dominates in practice. The gravity-model estimates offer us a tentative assessment on this question. A majority of FTAs, such as ASEAN and the Andean Pact, have increased trade with nonmembers, even as the members may have increased trade to an even greater extent with each other. In these cases, regionalism has apparently been consistent with more general liberalization. The pattern is mixed, however. Other FTAs, such as EFTA, show evidence of trade diversion. Apparently regionalism can, depending on the circumstances, be associated with either more or less general liberalization.

References

Anderson, Kym. 1993. European Integration in the 1990s: Implications for World Trade and for Australia. In D. G. Mayes, ed., *External Implications of European Integration*. London: Harvester Wheatsheaf.

Arase, David. 1991. U.S. and ASEAN Perceptions of Japan's Role in the Asian-Pacific Region. In Harry Kendall and Clara Joewono, eds., *Japan, ASEAN, and the United States*. Berkeley: University of California, Institute for East Asian Studies.

Bagwell, Kyle, and Robert Staiger. 1993. Multilateral Tariff Cooperation during the Formation of Customs Unions. NBER Working Paper no. 4543. Cambridge, MA: National Bureau of Economic Research, November.

Bergsten, C. Fred. 1991. Commentary: The Move toward Free Trade Zones. In Federal Reserve Bank of Kansas City, *Policy Implications of Trade and Currency Zones*, 43–57. Kansas City: Federal Reserve Bank.

———. 1994. Sunrise in Seattle. *International Economic Insights* 5 (January/February).

———. 1995. *Competitive Liberalization*. Washington, DC: Institute for International Economics.

Bhagwati, Jagdish. 1992. Regionalism vs. Multilateralism. *World Economy* 15 (September): 535–56.

———. 1993a. Beyond NAFTA: Clinton's Trading Choices. *Foreign Policy* 15 (summer): 155–62.

———. 1993b. Regionalism and Multilateralism: An Overview. In Jaime de Melo and Arvind Panagariya, eds., *New Dimensions in Regional Integration*. New York: Cambridge University Press.

———. 1995. President Clinton's Trade Policy: Is It Really a Triumph? Presented at American Economics Association meetings, Washington, DC, January.

Bond, Eric, and Costas Syropoulos. 1996. Trading Blocs and the Sustainability of Inter-

Regional Cooperation. In M. Canzoneri, W. J. Ethier, and V. Grilli, eds., *The New Transatlantic Economy.* London: Cambridge University Press.

Brada, Josef, and Jose Mendez. 1988. Exchange Rate Risk, Exchange Rate Regimes, and the Level of International Trade. *Kyklos* 41, no. 2:198.

Deardorff, Alan, and Robert Stern. 1994. Multilateral Trade Negotiations and Preferential Trading Arrangements. In Alan Deardorff and Robert Stern, eds., *Analytical and Negotiating Issues in the Global Trading System.* Ann Arbor: University of Michigan Press.

De Grauwe, Paul. 1988. Exchange Rate Variability and the Slowdown in Growth of International Trade. *IMF Staff Papers* 35:63–84.

de Melo, Jaime, Arvind Panagariya, and Dani Rodrik. 1993. Regional Integration: An Analytical and Empirical Overview. In Jaime de Melo and Arvind Panagariya, eds., *New Dimensions in Regional Integration.* New York: Cambridge University Press.

Dhar, Sumana, and Arvind Panagariya. 1995. *Is East Asia Less Open Than North America and the EEC? No.* Policy Research Working Paper Series No. 1370. Washington, DC: World Bank, January.

Dornbusch, Rudiger. 1989. The Dollar in the 1990s: Competitiveness and the Challenges of New Economic Blocs. In *Monetary Policy Issues in the 1990s.* Kansas City: Federal Reserve Bank of Kansas City.

Edison, Hali, and Michael Melvin. 1990. The Determinants and Implications of the Choice of an Exchange Rate System. In William Haraf and Thomas Willett, eds., *Monetary Policy for a Volatile Global Economy.* Washington, D.C.: AEI Press.

Encarnation, Dennis. 1992. *Rivals beyond Trade: America versus Japan in Global Competition.* Ithaca: Cornell University Press.

Fernandez, Raquel, and Dani Rodrik. 1991. Resistance to Reform: Status Quo Bias in the Presence of Individual-Specific Uncertainty. *American Economic Review* 81 (December): 1146–55.

Frankel, Jeffrey. 1991. Is a Yen Bloc Forming in Pacific Asia? In Richard O'Brien, ed., *Finance and the International Economy,* AMEX Bank Review Prize Essays. Oxford: Oxford University Press.

———. 1993. Is Japan Creating a Yen Bloc in East Asia and the Pacific? In Jeffrey Frankel and Miles Kahler, eds., *Regionalism and Rivalry: Japan and the U.S. in Pacific Asia,* 53–85.

Frankel, Jeffrey, and Shang-Jin Wei, 1994a. A "Greater China" Trade Bloc? *China Economic Review* 5 (fall): 179–90.

———. 1994b. Yen Bloc or Dollar Bloc? Exchange Rate Policies of the East Asian Economies. In Takatoshi Ito and Anne Krueger, eds., *Macroeconomic Linkage: Savings, Exchange Rates, and Capital Flows,* 295–329. Chicago: University of Chicago Press.

———. 1995. Is a Yen Bloc Emerging? In Robert Rich, ed., *Economic Cooperation and Challenges in the Pacific,* vol. 5. Washington, DC: Korea Economic Institute of America.

Frankel, Jeffrey, Shang-Jin Wei, and Ernesto Stein. 1995. APEC and Regional Trading Arrangements in the Pacific. In Wendy Dobson and Frank Flatters, eds., *Pacific Trade and Investment: Options for the 90s,* 289–312. John Deutsch Institute, Queen's University.

Grossman, Gene, and Elhanan Helpman. 1995. The Politics of Free Trade Agreements. *American Economic Review* 85 (September): 667–90.

Hamilton, Carl, and L. Alan Winters. 1992. Opening Up International Trade in Eastern Europe. *Economic Policy* 14 (April): 77–117.

Haveman, Jon. 1992. Some Welfare Effects of Dynamic Customs Union Formation. In On the Consequences of Recent Changes in the Global Trading Environment, Ph.D. diss., University of Michigan.

Kahler, Miles. 1994. Regional Futures and Transatlantic Economic Relations. Council on Foreign Relations, New York, December. Manuscript.

Krishna, Kala, and Anne Krueger. 1995. Implementing Free Trade Areas: Rules of Origin and Hidden Protection. In Jim Levinsohn, Alan Deardorff, and Robert Stern, eds., *New Directions in Trade Theory*. Ann Arbor: University of Michigan Press.

Krueger, Anne. In press. Rules of Origin as Protectionist Devices. In James Melvin, James Moore, and Ray Reisman, eds., *International Trade and Trade Policy*. Cambridge: MIT Press.

———. 1995. Free Trade Agreements versus Customs Unions. NBER Working Paper no. 5084. Cambridge, MA: National Bureau of Economic Research, April.

Krugman, Paul. 1991a. Is Bilateralism Bad? In Elhanan Helpman and Assaf Razin, eds., *International Trade and Trade Policy*. Cambridge: MIT Press.

———. 1991b. The Move toward Free Trade Zones. In Federal Reserve Bank of Kansas City, *Policy Implications of Trade and Currency Zones*, 7–42. Kansas City: Federal Reserve Bank.

———. 1993. Regionalism versus Multilateralism: Analytical Notes. In Jaime de Melo and Arvind Panagariya, eds., *New Dimensions in Regional Integration*, 58–79. New York: Cambridge University Press.

Kwan, C. H. 1994. *Economic Interdependence in the Asia-Pacific Region: Towards a Yen Bloc*. London: Routledge.

Lawrence, Robert. 1991. Emerging Regional Arrangements: Building Blocks or Stumbling Blocks? In R. O'Brien, ed., *Finance and the International Economy*, AMEX Bank Review Prize Essays, 24–36. Oxford: Oxford University Press.

Levy, Philip. 1993. A Political-Economic Analysis of Free Trade Agreements. Center for Economic Policy Research Publication no. 347. Stanford University, January.

Linneman, Hans. 1966. *An Econometric Study of International Trade Flows*. Amsterdam: North-Holland.

Oye, Kenneth. 1992. *Economic Discrimination and Political Exchange: World Political Economy in the 1930s and 1980s*. Princeton: Princeton University Press.

Panagariya, Arvind. 1994. East Asia and the New Regionalism. *World Economy* 17 (November): 817–39.

———. 1995. The Free Trade Area of the Americas: Good for Latin America? Center for International Economics Working Paper. College Park: University of Maryland.

Panagariya, Arvind, and Ronald Findlay. 1994. A Political-Economy Analysis of Free Trade Areas and Customs Unions. Working Papers in International Economics no. 2. University of Maryland.

Perroni, Carlo, and John Whalley. 1994. The New Regionalism: Trade Liberalization or Insurance? NBER Working Paper no. 4626. Cambridge, MA: National Bureau of Economic Research, January.

Petri, Peter. 1992. One Bloc, Two Blocs, or None? Political-Economic Factors in Pacific Trade Policy. In Kaoru Okuzumi, Kent Calder, and Gerrit Gong, eds., *The U.S.-Japan Economic Relationship in East and Southeast Asia: A Policy Framework for Asia-Pacific Economic Cooperation*, 39–70. Significant Issues Series, vol. 14, no. 1. Washington, DC: Center for Strategic and International Studies.

Richardson, Martin. 1993a. Endogenous Protection and Trade Diversion. *Journal of International Economics* 34 (May): 309–24.

———. 1993b. On Equilibrium in a Free Trade Area with Internal Trade. Georgetown University, May.

Saxonhouse, Gary. 1993. Pricing Strategies and Trading Blocks in East Asia. In Jeffrey Frankel and Miles Kahler, eds., *Regionalism and Rivalry: Japan and the U.S. in Pacific Asia*, 89–119. Chicago: University of Chicago Press.

Schott, Jeffrey. 1989. *Free Trade Areas and U.S. Trade Policy*. Washington, DC: Institute for International Economics.

————. 1991. Regional Trading Blocs. *World Economy.*

Sinclair, Peter, and David Vines. 1994. Do Fewer, Larger Trade Blocs Imply Greater Protection? The Good News and the Bad News about Regional Trading Blocs. University of Birmingham and Oxford University, June. Manuscript.

Stein, Ernesto. 1994. The Welfare Implications of Asymmetric Trading Blocs. In Essays on the Welfare Implications of Trading Blocs with Transportation Costs and Political Cycles of Inflation. Ph.D. diss., University of California, Berkeley.

Stein, Ernesto, and Jeffrey Frankel. 1994. The Welfare Implications of Continental Trading Blocs in a Model with Transport Costs. Pacific Basin Working Paper Series no. PB94-03. San Francisco: Federal Reserve Bank, May.

Summers, Lawrence. 1991. Regionalism and the World Trading System. In Federal Reserve Bank of Kansas City, *Policy Implications of Trade and Currency Zones,* 295–302. Kansas City: Federal Reserve Bank.

Thurow, Lester. 1992. *The Coming Economic Battle among Japan, Europe, and America.* New York: William Morrow.

Thursby, Jerry, and Marie Thursby. 1988. Bilateral Trade Flows, the Linder Hypothesis, and Exchange Risk. *Review of Economics and Statistics,* 488–95.

Viner, Jacob. 1950. *The Customs Union Issue.* New York: Carnegie Endowment for International Peace.

Wang, Zhen Kun, and L. Alan Winters. 1991. The Trading Potential of Eastern Europe. CEPR Discussion Paper no. 610. London: Centre for Economic Policy Research, November.

Wei, Shang-Jin. Forthcoming. Gradualism versus Big Bang: Speed and Sustainability of Reforms. *Canadian Journal of Economics.*

Wei, Shang-Jin, and Jeffrey Frankel. 1996. Can Regional Blocs Be Stepping Stones to Global Free Trade? *International Review of Economics and Finance* 5:339–47.

Winters, Alan. 1996. Regionalism and Multilateralism. Washington, DC: The World Bank. Manuscript.

Wonnacott, Paul, and Mark Lutz. 1989. Is There a Case for Free Trade Areas? In Jeffrey Schott, ed., *Free Trade Areas and U.S. Trade Policy,* 59–84. Washington, DC: Institute for International Economics.

World Trade Organization Secretariat. 1995. *Regionalism and the World Trading System.* Geneva: World Trade Organization.

Comment   David Hummels

In this paper the authors provide some empirical evidence on the nature of regional trading patterns, then develop a political-economy model of regionalization and trade liberalization. I will focus my comments entirely on the empirical sections of their paper.

The authors argue that the best way to understand the nature of regional blocs is to examine trade patterns directly, rather than to focus on legal arrangements that bring them into force. Accordingly, they present evidence of these patterns in the form of a bilateral gravity model of trade. The idea is that in the context of a complete specialization model of trade it is possible to provide a

David Hummels is assistant professor of economics at the University of Chicago Graduate School of Business.

"norm" of bilateral trade.[1] This norm is based on such variables as size, per capita incomes, and naturally occurring trade resistance factors like distance, adjacency, and language. Once established, the authors look for deviations from this "norm" that indicate intraregional biases. This is done by including intercepts for trading blocs, and by including measures of bilateral exchange rate variability.

In the context of a complete specialization model, empirical gravity estimates describe both how trade *is* and how trade *should be*. If one finds complete specialization to be a compelling description of international production and trade, the authors' approach is legitimate and informative. In this vein, I have only a few quibbles that I will present here. Below, I will address the theoretical foundations of this enterprise, and whether these inferences are appropriate.

The authors report that size, incomes, and a variety of trade resistance factors such as distance, adjacency, and language are significantly correlated with bilateral trade. This result is standard in the literature, and unsurprising here. They find that intraregional trade biases are significant, and that bilateral exchange rate variability diminishes trade somewhat. However, this relationship breaks down in later years. Several problems are evident.

First, the authors' pool data on trade from 1970 through 1992 in order to measure the effects of regionalism. The hypothesis implicit in the regional bloc intercepts is that regional trading arrangements cause deviations from the "norm" of bilateral trade. Of course, NAFTA did not exist until sometime after the sample period ends, so it is a bit mysterious how it could have caused these deviations. While one might argue that anticipation of the trading bloc might explain patterns in advance, inclusion of trade for 1970 stretches things a bit. The possibility this raises is simply that there is something unique about North American trade, or European or East Asian trade, that is not well captured in the included variables. Thus, omitted variables, and not the presence of regional trading arrangements, cause deviations from bilateral trade "norms."

Second, the authors justify inclusion of bilateral exchange rate variability as an explanatory variable by describing it as a kind of trade resistance, possibly one that regional currency areas may mitigate. They report that it has some diminishing effect on trade, and in table 7.6 present some upper-bound estimates of the effect of exchange rate stabilization in the European Union between 1980 and 1990. This table is misleading, even as an upper-bound estimate. The elasticity of trade with respect to volatility comes from 1980, easily the largest estimate. Further, the relationship between trade and volatility actually becomes significantly *positive* by 1990, a year in which volatility increases dramatically worldwide.

---

1. Complete specialization may be due to product differentiation as in familiar monopolistic competition models, but can also be found in perfect competition models. See Deardorff, chapter 1 in this volume.

Third, bilateral exchange rate variability lacks strong theoretical foundations for inclusion here. It is not clear, for example, why *bilateral* variability matters and not *overall* variability. Further, the general equilibrium effects on trade are poorly understood. If the peso begins to fluctuate wildly against the dollar, does it also fluctuate against other currencies? If so, doesn't this increase costs for all trading partners, resulting in price changes that offset the effects of the fluctuation?

On a related matter, there are a great many empirical gravity estimates in this literature, each with a partial listing of favorite variables that plausibly correlate with trade. In this regard, empirical gravity estimates closely resemble the literature on cross-country growth regressions. Like that literature, gravity empirics would benefit greatly from robustness checking in the style of Levine and Renelt (1992).

Above I suggested that, if one finds complete specialization a compelling description of production and trade, the authors' approach is legitimate and informative. In what follows, I want to reopen the question of the gravity model's theoretical foundations and ask if the inferences regarding intraregional trade biases drawn here are appropriate.

Theoretical foundations for gravity empirics employ complete specialization and identical preferences to generate the simple gravity equation with trade proportional to the bilateral partners' sizes and the distance between them. This paper (and most other empirical gravity work) studies the volume of *all* trade, including primary, intermediate, capital, and consumption goods. However, the theory addresses only trade in consumption goods, which comprise something on the order of one-third of all trade. For simple gravity predictions to go through in a model including all trade, one needs complete specialization in all goods, *and* a production analog of identical preferences. Derived demands for nonconsumption goods come from production functions; thus, production functions must be identical across countries. Further, because goods are completely specialized, it must be that the same production function applies for all countries *and for all goods*. This strains plausibility.

Nevertheless, the gravity equation fits the data quite well, leading naturally to the question, why? I will offer at least a partial explanation here.[2] Theoretical gravity models are fundamentally about the positive proportionality between country size (measured by partners' GDPs) and bilateral trade. This relationship is also very strong empirically. Theoretical models generating the equation imply that this relationship should hold exactly for every country pair. However, the econometric exercise does not impose such strong conditions. It asks if, on average, large countries have large bilateral trade volumes. What must be true for this to hold?

Proposition 1: If a country trades a lot with the world as a whole, it must be that, on average, it trades a lot with its bilateral partners.

2. See Haveman and Hummels (1997) for a more detailed exposition of the points that follow.

Proposition 2: If large countries trade more with the world as a whole, then large countries must, on average, trade more with their bilateral partners.

These propositions may seem obvious, coming as they do from a simple adding-up constraint, but their logic is important. Neither proposition says anything about individual partners; the volume of trade with any one partner could be greater or smaller than the sample mean. On average, however, a country with more trade overall must have more bilateral trade. So, the only thing that is necessary for the gravity equation to hold econometrically is for large countries to have more trade with the world. Though one can imagine specific models where there is no correlation between size and overall trade, it can be shown that this relationship is robust to a very wide class of trade models. It will be true of models in which production is completely specialized and trade is therefore bilaterally determinate. It will also be true of a broad class of models in which production is incompletely specialized and trade is therefore bilaterally indeterminate.

In the paper at hand, the authors wish to provide a "norm" of bilateral trade against which to measure deviations associated with intraregional trade biases. This suggests two problems. First, even if there is an overall tendency to trade more intraregionally, it is difficult to make normative statements about the bias. Second, regional trading bloc dummies are not necessarily evidence of intraregional bias.

To see the first point, consider the problem of a small country choosing to import wheat from among ten equal-sized exporter countries, each of which charges the same c.i.f. price for its wheat. The gravity equation predicts that this country will import one-tenth of the total amount from each country. Suppose instead that it buys all of its wheat from one country. It is getting the same amount of wheat at the same price, and so cannot be worse off. Indeed, any arbitrary combination of bilateral import volumes that adds up to its total import demand will give the same welfare. And, if overall import demand increases with the size of the importer, any arbitrary combination will still "fit" the gravity model econometrically. This illustrates that, with incomplete specialization, bilateral trade volumes can depart from gravity predictions in arbitrary ways that have absolutely no normative content.

Regarding evidence of intraregional bias in trading patterns, consider a neoclassical model with many homogeneous goods, many countries, and no barriers to trade. Trade is determined vis-à-vis the world and distributed in some indeterminate way among its bilateral partners. A regression of trade volume on country size indicates an average relationship between these variables for the sample. If a country's *total* trade is higher than its size predicts (it lies above the regression line), then the average trade of its bilateral pairs must also be higher than its size predicts. As a result, that country's bilateral pairs will tend to have a positive intercept in a bilateral trade estimate. For a given bilateral pair, if both countries have an above average tendency to trade overall, this bias in the intercept is reinforced. This is not to say that every one of the bilateral pairs will be above average, merely that there will be a bias in this direction.

To control for this effect, can one simply compare the within-bloc intercepts to intercepts indicating one partner is in the bloc and one out? The authors argue that if within-bloc dummies are positive and extrabloc dummies are negative, this is evidence of trade diversion. Assume that bloc members have a higher than average tendency to trade overall, and nonbloc members have a lower than average tendency. Then, intrabloc dummies will tend to be positive, and extrabloc dummies will be smaller or negative. This indicates that these countries' trade volumes deviate from overall averages, but says nothing about their bilateral relationships. Why would a bloc have a systematically higher overall trade volume than its size predicts? Well, perhaps because these blocs are trade creating, not trade diverting!

References

Haveman, Jon, and David Hummels. 1997. What Can We Learn from Bilateral Trade? Gravity and Beyond. Mimeo.
Levine, Ross, and David Renelt. 1992. A Sensitivity Analysis of Cross-Country Growth Regressions. *American Economic Review* 82:942–63.

Comment   Philip I. Levy

I very much enjoyed reading the Frankel and Wei paper. It deals with issues that are central to the normative discussion about regional trade liberalization and provides some provocative answers. I will confine my comments about the empirical section of the paper to a brief concluding thought. I would like to focus my discussion instead on the theoretical political-economy issues, since this is an area in which I have done some work. Frankel and Wei give a very useful summary of work on this front and extend it with a new model of their own.

Let me start by characterizing some of the challenges for anyone trying to make a theoretical argument in this area. The basic question is whether regional agreements are likely to lead toward or away from multilateral liberalization. Frankel and Wei take it as given that multilateral liberalization is the ultimate goal—the economist's nirvana, as they put it—an assertion with which I heartily concur.

For a regional agreement to *lead* anywhere, we must have in mind some idea of endogenous policy formation. Further, since regional agreements are "leading," we wish to have such a model where we start with some sort of regional decision and end with some sort of multilateral decision.

It makes some difference whether one starts by assuming that—absent any regional agreement—a multilateral agreement is politically feasible or not. I

Philip I. Levy is assistant professor of economics at Yale University.

have done some work in which multilateral free trade is politically feasible initially and regional agreements may render it infeasible (Levy 1994). In this median voter setting I also show that the effect could not work in reverse. The idea is that the median voter—or whoever is controlling the policy decision—will only allow his or her welfare to ratchet upward. If multilateral liberalization is preferred to an initial state, this is because the deciding actors would be better off under multilateral free trade. If they would prefer the initial state to multilateral free trade, why would they accept an intermediate state that made them worse off, so that multilateral free trade might then look appealing?

This type of reasoning makes me pessimistic about the effects of regional agreements. Since much of the world seems to be pursuing strategies of regional liberalization, however, I would like to be persuaded this could be a positive force that expands possibilities for broader liberalization.

There are a number of works in the literature that make arguments along these lines, but I think the new model presented by Frankel and Wei is as convincing as any of them, so let me discuss it in detail.

The authors set up a model in which we have two countries, A and B, and a rest-of-world (country C). There are three sectors. Countries A and B each have a comparative advantage in an industry all their own, but produce and protect in the other two sectors. To enliven the discussion, let's assume that A is efficient in agriculture and inefficient in textiles and in "other manufactures." B is efficient in "other manufactures" and inefficient in agriculture and textiles.

The argument is that, without a regional agreement, one can allocate people and switching costs within a country in such a way that workers in two of three sectors would constitute a majority and successfully oppose global liberalization, so multilateral free trade is initially not feasible. Thus, in country A a coalition of textile and manufacturing workers opposes multilateral free trade, while in B a coalition of agricultural and textile workers opposes multilateral free trade. (The Fernandez and Rodrik [1991] structure that the authors adopt explains why a majority might approve of a change ex post but not ex ante. I will continue my summary without this complication, however, as the central points are unchanged.)

When these agents are presented with a bilateral free trade agreement between A and B, it is favored by two out of three sectors in each of the countries, and the "other manufactures" workers in A and the agricultural workers in B are forced to switch into their countries' efficient sectors. After the switch, they become supporters of multilateral free trade. Now there are majorities in favor of multilateral liberalization.

The tenor of this argument seems similar to one put forward by Rachel McCulloch and Peter Petri (1994), who argued that certain industry lobbies that opposed multilateral trade might get wiped out by regional liberalization.

Frankel and Wei present two versions of this argument. In the first version, the opponents of multilateral free trade do not anticipate the effects of their vote on the multilateral free trade decision (or the multilateral decision is so far off in the future that the opponents of multilateral free trade don't care). I find this myopic case fairly unpersuasive as a predictor of world events. We see GATT liberalization and regional agreements proceeding concurrently and many of the opponents of multilateral liberalization—textiles workers and agricultural workers—are also opponents of the regional agreements. The unions in the United States that opposed NAFTA seemed to recognize the potential connection to multilateral free trade.

If the opponents of multilateral free trade are far-sighted, it seems that they should continue to be able to block multilateral free trade. Recognizing this, Frankel and Wei present a case in which myopia is not necessary. They show that, even though there was a majority opposed to multilateral free trade, through regional liberalization this coalition can be be undone. This approach is referred to in the paper as the "divide and conquer" approach. The government—for reasons unspecified, but presumably because it agrees with us that multilateral free trade would be nirvana—sets up a very specific agenda in which there are two votes. The first vote is on a bilateral agreement between A and B. The second is on a bilateral agreement with C.

The effect of this structure is to divide the coalition opposing multilateral free trade. Frankel and Wei solve backward: whatever the outcome of the first vote, the "other manufactures" sector and the efficient agriculture sector in A will want to take advantage of the lower prices on textiles offered by free trade with C. Assuming the "other manufactures" sector is still intact at this stage (and not merged with agriculture), it would be unthreatened by the possibility of trade with B, since that will never be offered again (by assumption). Thus, agriculture and "other manufactures" in A would join together to approve a free trade agreement with C in the second stage.

The other inefficient sector in A, textiles, would anticipate this and favor the bilateral agreement with B in the first stage, since it offers cheaper "other manufactures" and since there seems to be no hope of maintaining a coalition against multilateral liberalization. Thus, in the end, the world is joined in multilateral free trade.

This strikes me as a very curious argument—the path to multilateral liberalization runs through renouncing multilateral liberalization! It is absolutely essential to the model that there *not* be a vote on multilateral free trade in the future. If there were, then it is straightforward to argue that the coalition opposed to multilateral free trade would not break apart. It is crucial that at the second-stage vote, *if* the first bilateral agreement were rejected, it would never be introduced again.

I find it somewhat hard to imagine that a government could credibly commit to such a strategy, particularly the kind of government that would set up such a special structure as a means to achieve multilateral free trade. It would be an especially impressive feat in a country in which two-thirds of the voters are opposed to multilateral free trade. Thus, I am not left feeling confident about the beneficial impact of regional liberalizations.

Frankel and Wei are thorough in their analysis and demonstrate the possibility of regional agreements not leading to multilateral free trade (which I find more plausible, for reasons given above). However, if one accepts their contention that the theoretical arguments could go either way, this suggests that empirical evidence should be all the more valuable.

Yet, it seems to me, the kind of empirical evidence we would like to see would be a demonstration that one of the political-economy effects predicted by myself, by Frankel and Wei, or by others is occurring—that regional liberalization has weakened or strengthened the power of an opponent of multilateral free trade (or, equally, that it has weakened or strengthened the power of a proponent of multilateral liberalization). Among regional agreements—real or imagined—it seems to me that only the European Union is sufficiently advanced as a region to have experienced such effects. By casual observation (I think of French agriculture or European auto manufacturing) it is not at all clear that regional liberalization has strengthened the prospects for multilateral liberalization.

References

Fernandez, Raquel, and Dani Rodrik. 1991. Resistance to Reform: Status Quo Bias in the Presence of Individual-Specific Uncertainty. *American Economic Review* 81 (December): 1146–55.

Levy, Philip I. 1994. A Political-Economic Analysis of Free Trade Agreements. Economic Growth Center Discussion Paper no. 718. Yale University, June.

McCulloch, Rachel, and Peter Petri. 1994. Alternative Paths toward Open Global Markets. Paper presented at the conference in honor of Robert M. Stern, University of Michigan, 18–20 November.

8 Tariff Phase-Outs: Theory and Evidence from GATT and NAFTA

Carsten Kowalczyk and Donald Davis

8.1 Introduction

Regionalization is now so widespread that the World Trade Organization, in one of its first studies since its creation, can claim that "when the WTO was established on 1 January 1995, nearly all its members were parties to at least one agreement notified to GATT."[1] According to the same study this process has picked up speed in recent years with almost a third of the 109 agreements brought to the General Agreement on Tariffs and Trade (GATT) between 1948 and 1994 having been notified since 1990. Clearly nations perceive the process of regionalization to be one from which they cannot afford to be left out.[2]

The question of whether the process of "regionalization" is desirable or not is an important one. A related question is whether the form in which the world trading system permits preferential arrangements is beneficial, and if not, which types of arrangements would be. It is particularly interesting, and this is the topic of the present paper, that results from economic theory offer only

Carsten Kowalczyk is associate professor of international economics at the Fletcher School of Law and Diplomacy at Tufts University. Donald Davis is assistant professor of economics at Harvard University.

The comments of Jeffrey Frankel, Arvind Panagariya, Robert Staiger, and conference participants are gratefully acknowledged. The first author also thanks Mark Hooker for discussions, and Robert Hinkle, Rafael Docavo-Malvezzi, Philip Moremen, Jennifer Norberg, Richard Ponzio, Ricardo Tejada, and Todd Trabocco for assistance.

1. WTO 1995, 27. By "regionalization" we mean the creation or expansion of preferential trading areas. Whether world trade has become regionalized has been the subject of several studies, including Anderson and Norheim (1993) and Frankel (1993).

2. Indeed, and as pointed out in the WTO study, should current talks toward establishing preferential trade across the Pacific (and the Atlantic) lead to agreements, then every current WTO member would participate in at least one trading bloc and be the outsider relative to at least one. To complete the picture, it should be pointed out that the number of GATT contracting parties has increased substantially over the same period of time, suggesting that a simultaneous process of "multilateralism" is unfolding.

mixed support for article XXIV, the condition under which about 90 percent of all notifications of preferential agreements have been presented to GATT.

Article XXIV deems admissible customs unions and free trade areas that eliminate duties on "substantially all the trade" between the partners and that apply extraclub duties that are "not on the whole . . . higher or more restrictive" than the initial duties.[3] The latter of these conditions aims at preventing clubs from forming for the purpose of extracting better terms of trade from outsiders through the use of higher external tariffs by club members, a concern that has received some support in economic analysis. The former of the two conditions in article XXIV was intended as a price to be paid by the participants in a preferential arrangement for the exemption from the most-favored-nation principle. However, received wisdom, which derives from Richard Lipsey and Kelvin Lancaster's work (1956–57) on the second best, supports the optimality of intraclub free trade only under quite restrictive assumptions.

It could be argued that actual trade arrangements reflect this ambiguity. The restriction on extraclub duties does seem to have been relatively effective, as GATT reports no major increases in between-club tariffs even for clubs of substantial size in world markets.[4] The implementation of the condition that tariffs be eliminated on substantially all intraclub trade has been less effective. This is in part due to the inherent vagueness of the language, and in part due to the sizable loophole offered by paragraph 5(c) of article XXIV, which states that "any interim agreement [necessary for the formation of a customs union or a free trade area] shall include a plan and schedule for the formation of such . . . within a reasonable length of time" (Jackson, Davey, and Sykes 1995, 49). Agreements on customs unions and free trade areas presented to GATT have often left out important sectors, and tariff reductions have sometimes been at a leisurely pace.

Recent theoretical work on customs unions and free trade areas has primarily been concerned with their effect on interclub protection, and has taken the intraclub liberalization as given, comparing, most frequently, the initial situation with one of internal free trade. Instead, this paper takes a closer look at intraclub reform. Even after the completion of the European Community's internal market, the expansion of the European Union, and the passage of the North American Free Trade Agreement (NAFTA), the issue remains important as major undertakings are under consideration or negotiation, including the integration of the east European nations into the European Union, and the formation of an Asian-Pacific trading bloc. The WTO even points to the consequences of intraclub reform for globalism by stressing how European Community (EC) expansions or deepenings induced the Dillon, Kennedy, and Tokyo Rounds (WTO 1995, 53–54).

---

3. See, for example, Jackson, Davey, and Sykes (1995) for the full text.

4. Of course, increased protection can take other forms, such as increased use of anti-dumping duties or of various quantitative measures.

This paper discusses global and preferential tariff phase-outs from both a theoretical and an empirical perspective. In particular, the paper presents an analysis of the agreed U.S. and Mexican NAFTA phase-outs and discusses how they might be explained from the perspective of bargaining between two governments responding to different domestic pressures and environments.

Section 8.2 reviews briefly the theoretical literature with particular emphasis on results on world welfare. Section 8.3 presents a historical discussion of phase-outs both in the context of global trade negotiation rounds and with respect to article XXIV. Section 8.4 summarizes results from the empirical literature on tariff reductions. Section 8.5 considers U.S. and Mexican phase-outs in NAFTA. Section 8.6 concludes.

8.2 A Review of the Theoretical Literature

Theoretical work on reform of trade policy, including preferential arrangements such as customs unions and free trade areas, can usefully be separated into two, sometimes overlapping, literatures: one considering the welfare consequences from such reforms, and another investigating which coalition equilibria will emerge. The majority of this work has assumed that national governments are the decision makers and that each government's objective is to maximize national income.

Few general results have been established for tariff reforms that encompass all nations. Early work by Jaroslev Vanek (1964), later generalized to more than three countries by Tatsuo Hatta and Takashi Fukushima (1979), demonstrate that a reduction of the highest tariff rate to the next highest level raises global welfare when initial trade taxes are either positive or zero and the high-tariff good is a net substitute to all others.[5] Hatta and Fukushima (1979) show also that an equiproportionate reduction of all tariffs raises global income. Kowalczyk (1989) demonstrates that if there are trade subsidies in addition to tariffs then an equiproportionate rate reduction has an ambiguous effect on world welfare when rates are ad valorem, while Fukushima and Namdoo Kim (1989) show that no such ambiguity exists if rates are specific.[6]

As discussed in Kowalczyk (1992), work on the selective reduction of non-extreme tariffs leads directly to the literature on trading clubs. Drawing on earlier work by James Meade (1955) and S. A. Ozga (1955), Vanek (1964, 1965) shows that the reduction of a single tariff, which is not extreme, has an ambiguous effect on world income. If the tariff under consideration is between partners, and if the reform constitutes a complete elimination, this result exemplifies Jacob Viner's earlier proposition (1950) that a customs union has the potential to lower world welfare.

---

5. This literature assumes that international income transfers are feasible and hence applies the potential Pareto criterion as its world welfare indicator.

6. For a small country, Lopez and Panagariya (1992) show that reducing the highest tariff can lower welfare if intermediate goods are imported.

The theme that trading blocs may lead to suboptimally large trade between bloc members due to redirection of trade flows reappears in Paul Krugman's demonstration (1991a) that symmetric bloc enlargements may lower world welfare until three blocs exist in a world with strong preferences for variety in consumption.[7] In a comment on this work, T. N. Srinivasan (1993) generates an example where world welfare may decrease or increase from bloc enlargement due to the possibility of changing composition of blocs of different size. Alan Deardorff and Robert Stern (1994), in a related vein, argue that, if trade is due to comparative advantage rather than taste for varieties, then enlargement of even symmetric blocs may raise expected world welfare.[8]

Krugman (1991b, 1993) finds that introducing transport costs into his varieties model may reverse his initial negative finding, and that the formation of "natural blocs," that is, blocs between countries that can trade at low transport costs, will tend to raise global welfare. Jeffrey Frankel, Ernesto Stein, and Shang-Jin Wei (chap. 4 in this volume) demonstrate that a comparison of transport costs between bloc members and nonbloc countries is needed for a full assessment of whether such blocs are welfare improving or not. If the latter costs are relatively low, then it is possible that natural blocs will lower world welfare.[9]

Viner's result has also spurred research on the optimality properties of article XXIV's intraclub free trade requirement. Murray Kemp (1969) argues that free internal trade maximizes members' welfare if their external tariff is optimal, and Takashi Negishi (1972) shows that, if there are positive tariffs on extraunion trade, then world welfare maximization requires a positive intraunion tariff in a two-good world.[10] For the special case of a small union, John McMillan and Even McCann (1981) show that tariff elimination is optimal if the goods traded between club members are separable from those traded with the nonmember. Michihiro Ohyama (1972) and Kemp and Henry Wan (1976) demonstrate that a customs union setting its "compensating external tariff,"

---

7. The effect of country size on bloc formation is analyzed in Kennan and Riezman (1990).

8. Deardorff and Stern assume that blocs set prohibitive tariffs on trade with each other and that blocs are formed by random drawings of members and combinations of blocs. Haveman (1992) shows that, if extraclub tariffs are not assumed to be prohibitive, then Deardorff and Stern's model also generates Krugman's U-shaped world welfare curve.

Bond and Syropoulos (1996) suggest that a symmetric bloc equilibrium like Krugman's may be unstable since a country will have an incentive to switch blocs to join a (thereby) larger club. They show also that, if interbloc trade becomes relatively unimportant compared to intrabloc trade, then noncooperative Nash external tariffs will tend to fall, and welfare tend to rise, as symmetric blocs are enlarged. However, Krugman (1993) demonstrates that it is not the increase in optimal extraclub tariffs that drives the results in his first paper; rather it is the misallocation of goods across blocs.

9. Frankel (1993) labels the latter type of bloc as "super-natural." Frankel, Stein, and Wei argue that theirs is more than a theoretical anomaly: their preferred estimate of intercontinental transport costs is relatively low.

10. Frankel, Stein, and Wei (chap. 4 in this volume) and Stein (1994) present similar results for a world where asymmetric blocs can form and find that a positive intraclub tariff maximizes world welfare for all transport costs in the Krugman model.

that is, the external tariff that leaves trade with nonmembers unaffected, raises world welfare.[11]

With few exceptions, this work generally does not consider the individual nation's incentive to participate in the proposed reform, whether it is global or preferential. John Kennan and Raymond Riezman (1990) show that large countries and customs unions seeking improved terms of trade through tariffs may refuse to agree to global free trade. Kowalczyk (1990) argues that a similar result holds for a small country, which has the option of membership of multiple free trade areas. Kowalczyk and Tomas Sjöström (1994) derive an expression for side payments, and show how such payments must go from those with much to gain from cooperation to those with little to gain to eliminate all participants' objections to a global agreement whether nations act alone or as members of trading blocs.

Little work considers the dynamics of current rules for preferential trading agreements and their impact on global welfare. Martin Richardson (1995) shows that members of a free trade area may reduce their external tariffs to zero in a competition for tariff revenue. Support for the opposite and conventional view that customs unions are preferable is implied by Kyle Bagwell and Robert Staiger's work (1993a, 1993b), which demonstrates that free trade areas will tend to increase between-club tariffs before and during negotiation phases while customs unions have the opposite effect. Contrary to Richardson's work, which has implications for long-run equilibrium tariffs, their model has the special property that extraclub tariffs, once clubs have been fully implemented, return to their initial level.[12]

This focus on the dynamics of internal tariff reform is very apropos. As we will see shortly, actual trade liberalization, at both global and regional levels, has often been extended in time. We would like to know what determines these time paths, which industries will be liberalized more or less rapidly, and the welfare consequences of these paths.[13] These are the questions discussed in the remainder of the paper.

8.3 Gradualism in the World Trading System

The notion that agreed tariff reductions should happen over several years rather than precipitously is seen both in recent global negotiation results and

---

11. McMillan (1993) proposes that article XXIV be revised to deem all blocs that do not lower trade with nonmembers as GATT-admissible. Roessler (1993) discusses some difficulties associated with such a proposal. He suggests that it would make the international trading system results-rather than rules-oriented and require that negotiators were able to agree on a methodology for estimating the expected effects on trade flows from various proposals.

12. Ludema (1994) finds that the ability to propose and establish preferential trading areas can affect the distribution of income in a global agreement when bargaining is costly.

13. Bhagwati (1993) has stressed the importance of looking at the dynamics of the problem. Grossman and Helpman (1993) suggest that offering different rates of tariff adjustment or even exemptions may be necessary for gaining political support for a free trade area. Levy (1994) also presents a political-economy model of preferential trading arrangements.

in article XXIV agreements. However, while preferential trade and phase-outs have the same origin in the negotiations of the International Trade Organization, GATT policy and practice toward phase-outs in multilateral agreements have developed differently from those toward preferential phase-outs: global round phase-outs are a relatively recent phenomenon, and the lengths of phase-out periods have shown only limited variation; in contrast, phase-outs were included in the original article XXIV of GATT, and actual periods have varied greatly and have caused controversy.

When negotiating what later became GATT, the United States argued for lower tariffs and proposed, in particular, the elimination of all forms of discriminatory treatment—including a three-year freeze and a ten-year phase-out of Britain's Imperial Tariff Preferences. This was opposed by Britain, whereupon the United States modified its position to favor customs unions and, when article XXIV was under negotiation, free trade areas (Wilcox 1949, 71).

Following this attempt by the United States, the length of a substantive tariff-reduction period was not stated explicitly again until the Kennedy Round. Rather, tariff reductions in early GATT agreements tended to take force almost immediately upon a contracting party's signing of an agreement. Agreed tariffs from the 1947 Geneva Round thus went into effect the following year; the Annecy Round results, completed in 1949, entered into force by late April 1950; the Torquay Round tariffs, agreed to in 1950, were put in place by the end of 1951; and the Dillon Round reductions, negotiated by 1961, were implemented by July 1962 (Hudec 1990, 50; GATT 1949, 1951, 1962).

These early negotiation rounds were mostly over bindings of existing rates rather than over actual rate reductions.[14] With the 1962–67 Kennedy Round the focus shifted to negotiating reductions, with the parties agreeing to a general 50 percent cut in tariffs on nonprimary manufactured products.[15] The parties agreed also to permit members to choose between an immediate rate reduction and a five-year transition period of equal-sized cuts (GATT 1967). The latter period originated with the negotiating mandate in the United States Trade Expansion Act of 1962, and was relatively uncontroversial as a point of reference for the round (Preeg 1970, 199–200). Negotiations were then over exemptions to these two principles.

Participants in the Tokyo Round of 1973–79 agreed to implement cuts, effectively amounting to an average one-third tariff reduction with larger relative cuts of higher rates, in eight equal-sized annual installments beginning on 1 January 1980 (GATT 1979). The eight-year period was favored by the United States and the EC and was later accepted by other participants (Winham 1986, 201).

Finally, the 1986–94 Uruguay Round led to an agreement to implement most

---

14. Finger and Holmes (1987) present evidence to this effect.
15. Jackson (1989, 53) reports that, including exceptions, the effective average tariff reduction has been estimated to be about 35 percent.

tariff reductions fully with five equal annual rate reductions beginning on 1 January 1995. The five-year period was put forward by a group of developing countries following an earlier European Union proposal of eight years (Stewart 1994, 428).[16]

While early global rounds implemented the resulting reductions relatively rapidly, there was never such a presumption for the implementation of customs unions and free trade areas. Part of the rationale for the lack of discipline implied by article XXIV's vagueness on standards for interim agreements (as quoted in the introduction to this paper) could be that the alternative—specifying a maximum phase-out period—effectively would have prevented countries with particularly high initial tariffs or high adjustment costs from joining customs unions or free trade areas. In any event, actual agreements have differed greatly in their interpretation of what constituted a "reasonable length of time." Some relatively recent agreements have incorporated periods of adjustment of twenty-two years or even indefinite length while other agreements, including the 1960 agreement establishing the European Free Trade Association (EFTA) and the 1965 free trade agreement between Australia and New Zealand, provided for a maximum ten-year phase-out.[17] As a consequence, it has been a widely held view that article XXIV imposed little discipline on the formation of preferential trading areas.[18]

These difficulties led Japan and India to present proposals to the parties of the Uruguay Round to revisit article XXIV with particular concern for the effects of customs unions and free trade areas on nonmembers and, in Japan's case, to address "the lack of discipline on interim agreements." A draft proposal, supported by the United States and Japan but opposed by the EC, was presented by the chairman of the negotiation group in October 1990. It was included in the Dunkel draft in 1991, and was adopted in the final agreement (Stewart 1994, 1841–42). The resulting "Understanding on the Interpretation of Article XXIV of the General Agreement on Tariffs and Trade 1994" specifies that "any interim agreement . . . shall include a plan and schedule [that] should exceed 10 years only in exceptional cases."[19]

---

16. GATT (1994, 8–15) offers a discussion of the tariff concessions of the Uruguay Round. Schott (1994, 11, 61) estimates them to average 40 percent, with reductions by the United States and the European Union of about 33 and 37 percent, and reductions by Japan of about 56 percent.

17. Stewart 1994, 1837. Stewart also quotes the Latin American Free Trade Area agreement as stating that "it was impossible to indicate at present the products in respect of which customs duties would not have been abolished at the end of the transitional period."

18. The early test was the two-product European Coal and Steel Community, which obtained an article XXV waiver by GATT (Dam 1970, 290). The WTO (1995) reports that ninety-eight article XXIV arrangements had been notified to GATT by January 1995; six agreements had been stated as conforming with article XXIV, while for the remaining cases "the working parties have . . . never reached the conclusion that the legal requirements had *not* been met. . . . *making no pronouncement on the key matters they were charged to examine has been the rule for Article XXIV working parties*" (16–17, original emphasis).

19. The understanding provides also that "general incidence shall . . . be based upon . . . weighted tariff rates." See Jackson, Davey, and Sykes 1995.

The Canadian negotiator Michael Hart reports that both the 1960 EFTA agreement and the 1965 agreement between Australia and New Zealand were among the precedents and reasons presented in the Canada-U.S. free trade negotiations for a ten-year maximum phase-out. While ten years was eventually incorporated into the 1988 agreement, it did not happen without prior consideration of alternative proposals for more rapid reductions.[20] (The Canada-U.S. agreement provides also for immediate or five-year phase-out periods, as well as exceptional categories; the assignment of industries to phase-out categories was determined through consultation with industry and other potentially affected parties [Bello and Holmer 1992, 425–26].) It was on this background that negotiations of NAFTA—to which we turn in section 8.5—began two years later.

8.4   Some Empirical Results on Tariff Reform

Like theoretical work on tariff reductions, empirical work on the subject is scant. This literature has assumed that the evolution of tariffs responds primarily to distributive considerations and political influence, and it has sought proxies such as labor adjustment and firm concentration within industries to gauge the willingness to accept reform and the ability to oppose it.

An early contribution is John Cheh's study (1974) of U.S. duty reductions in the Kennedy Round. Participants agreed at the outset of the round that manufacturing tariffs would be cut by 50 percent across the board with subsequent bargaining over which sectors should be exempted from this cut and receive less or no reduction. Restricting the sample to the industries receiving exemptions, his dependent variable is industry percentage tariff reduction. Cheh finds that an industry's original level of protection, its growth rate, and its relative use of unskilled and relatively high-age labor significantly affect the size of its Kennedy Round tariff cut. He concludes that the rate reductions were aimed at reducing short-run labor adjustment.

Malcolm Bale (1977) presents further evidence for Cheh's explanation. Defining adjustment costs as lost wages during unemployment plus any wage cut from accepting a new job within one year, he considers 477 legally displaced U.S. workers in six industries and finds that the simple correlation between such costs and the size of the industry's Kennedy Round tariff reduction is negative 0.88.

Expanding on a study by Richard Caves (1976), G. K. Helleiner (1977) studies tariffs and their changes for eighty-seven Canadian manufacturing industries for 1961 and 1970. He finds that his variables seem to explain nominal

20. Hart (1994, 216) mentions how, at the outset, Canada suggested that the United States phase out tariffs immediately while permitting Canada a transition period. This proposal was turned down. Canada then argued that an adjustment period of seven years was "in line" with various precedents; the Tokyo Round cuts had, for example, been implemented over this period.

rather than effective levels, but effective rather than nominal changes. (The latter is in contrast to Cheh [1974], who finds nominal rates and changes in them to be better explained than effective rates.) Helleiner finds further that market concentration (market share of largest four firms) explains reduction (higher concentration implies less reduction), and that the higher the percentage of small firms in an industry the larger is reduction in protection over the period considered. He finds that unskilled labor intensity does not explain changes.[21]

In a study of U.S. Tokyo Round tariff cut offers, Robert Baldwin (1985) finds weak evidence that low tariff cuts tend to be in industries where import penetration (imports divided by the sum of production and net imports) is high (conditional on being a net import industry), and where workers are unskilled and hence earn low wages (share of labor costs to unskilled workers as a fraction of total labor costs); somewhat surprisingly, U.S. tariff levels are not significant. An alternative approach treating the difference between the original U.S. offers of duty cuts and the cuts implied by the round's agreed Swiss formula (which implied larger reductions of higher tariffs) does considerably better. For this specification Baldwin finds that tariff levels and average wage levels are significant, as are changes in industry conditions such as employment growth and import penetration.

Some of these authors mention that trade negotiations involve reciprocity and that rate reductions therefore are an outcome of bargaining between nations (see, e.g., Baldwin 1985, 145). Yet no study conditions one nation's concessions on those of its trading partners. Due to the vast complexity of global rounds, including the tying of seemingly unrelated issues, it could be quite difficult to establish reciprocity between individual nations for such negotiations. Michael Finger (1974), rather than focusing on individual nations, analyzes the results of the Dillon Round as the outcome of a bargain between two groups of countries, developed and developing. He argues that tariff cuts were not as deep for manufactured products in which developing countries might have potential for exporting as in other products since these countries did not have much market access to offer in return.

It seems that preferential trade agreements constitute a promising area for detecting reciprocity, at least at a first pass. The next section considers the recent NAFTA to investigate whether there is reciprocity in the sense that phase-out periods for products in one country can help explain the phase-out periods in the partner country. Admittedly, this takes a narrow view of what were in fact very broad negotiations involving a substantially wider set of issues including tariff snapbacks, domestic content rules, and the inclusion of

---

21. A study by Lee and Swagel (1994) considers industrial protection (tariffs and nontariff barriers) across forty-one countries. They find that value-added and share of industry output that is exported help explain protection, and that less protection goes to labor-intensive industries and more to capital- and skill-intensive ones.

new sectors such as services. Yet the analysis can still be useful, we hope, by casting some light on what may influence the outcome of a bilateral negotiation between nations.

8.5 A Preliminary Investigation of NAFTA Phase-Outs in the United States and Mexico

Negotiations toward establishing NAFTA began in June 1990 with a meeting of the trade ministers of Canada, Mexico, and the United States. The negotiating parties adopted the general principle of a ten-year maximum for tariff phase-outs, recognizing the ten-year rule in the Canada-U.S. agreement and the existence of a Uruguay Round proposal recommending a maximum phase-out period of ten years for article XXIV agreements. The countries also agreed to a fifteen-year phase-out period for exceptional cases.

An accord was signed in December 1992, and the agreement went into effect on 1 January 1994. It consists of eight parts covering, among other issues, trade in goods and services, technical barriers to trade, and government procurement. It specifies rules of origin, and has supplemental agreements on environmental and labor cooperation. Notwithstanding that Canada is a founding member of NAFTA, the following discussion of NAFTA tariff phase-outs focuses on Mexico and the United States. Their mutual trade is large and significant to both parties, while trade between Canada and Mexico is small.[22]

Some aspects of NAFTA, such as tightened content rules as compared to the Canada-U.S. agreement, constitute a setback for the world trading system. However, the NAFTA agreement also introduces discipline for new issues, including agriculture, textiles, and trade in services, that even GATT did not cover effectively at the time NAFTA was negotiated. The agreement also implies free trade of maquiladoras production into Mexico after a seven-year phase-out of the current 50 percent limit on the share of such production that can be sold in Mexico (Hufbauer and Schott 1993, 152). Finally, NAFTA constitutes itself as an open club with an accession clause stating that NAFTA can be acceded to by all countries in the Western Hemisphere.[23]

Article XXIV issues are addressed in annex 302.2 of the agreement and the associated tariff schedules. The annex identifies five general tariff phase-out categories specifying the number of equal-sized annual cuts to free trade (A, immediately; B, five stages; C, ten stages; C+, fifteen stages; D, continued duty free) and some exceptional categories (B+, seven stages; B6 and B1, five

---

22. In 1991, about 2 percent of Canada's imports came from Mexico while only 0.3 percent of its exports went to Mexico. For the same year, about 2 percent of Mexico's imports and exports originated in or went to Canada. (Calculations based on IMF 1995.)

23. Bhagwati (1991) has argued in favor of incorporating such a stipulation into the WTO rules. Given the findings of Frankel, Stein, and Wei (chap. 4 in this volume), however, this apparently attractive requirement could be welfare reducing even—or in particular—if customs unions or free trade areas are regional.

stages with small initial reductions versus large initial reductions; C10, nine stages).[24] The tariff schedules list products according to the harmonized system and associate with each product a phase-out category and its 1991 base tariff. Both for the United States and Mexico the base tariff most often quoted is an ad valorem rate; in particular there are few quotas listed for Mexico. This bears evidence of the extent of the tariffication program Mexico undertook in part associated with its 1986 accession to GATT.

Inspection of the schedules does not reveal any exception to the requirement that final tariffs be zero. The majority of tariffs are to be eliminated within ten years, and most fall within categories specifying equal-sized annual reductions of five, seven, or ten years. Citing a 1993 study by the U.S. International Trade Commission, Frederick Abbott (1995) reports that products accounting for less than 1 percent of 1990 U.S. imports from Mexico and about 1.5 percent of Mexican commodity imports from the United States obtained the fifteen-year phase-out. For U.S. imports from Mexico, the study anticipates that about 54 percent would be free on implementation (category A), 8.5 percent within five years (category B), 23 percent within ten years (category C), with about 14 percent of imports already being duty free at the time of the study. For Mexican imports the corresponding estimates in the study are 31 percent in category A, 17 percent in B, 32 percent in C, and 18 percent initially free. The same study estimates that the agreement covers all U.S. imports from Mexico while leaving less than 2 percent of Mexico's imports from the United States uncovered (Abbott 1995, 62).

We are interested in identifying some of the determinants of how products are assigned to different tariff phase-out categories. For that purpose we sampled commodities for Mexico and the United States at the five-digit standard international trade classification (SITC) level, which is the most disaggregate level of trade flows presented in the United Nations *Commodity Trade Statistics.* We sampled first the products that account for relatively large shares of total trade within two-digit categories based on 1991 export and import data for Mexico and the United States.[25] Then, to correct for any problems caused by the possibility that small initial trade flows might be due to trade barriers or the threat of such, we sampled five-digit commodities randomly within the two-digit categories that are not represented among the first set of products.[26] Using the United Nations (1986) concordance between the SITC and the harmonized system, we recorded the implied tariff and staging category—the former as an ad valorem tariff rate, the latter as the number of years equal to the

24. *North American Free Trade Agreement* (1993), annex 302.2, paragraph 2; *1993 North American Trade Guide* (1992), p. I-4.

25. We chose 1991, rather than a later year, to minimize any effects on trade flows from expectations of the free trade agreement.

26. Trefler (1993) demonstrates how accounting for endogeneity of 1983 U.S. manufacturing quotas raises the estimate of impeded imports by a factor of ten compared to when barriers are considered exogenous.

number of tariff reductions.[27] For most categories several tariff items correspond to the given harmonized code, making it necessary to go to six- or eight-digit harmonized code to obtain duty level and phase-out. In these cases five-digit values of base rates and phase-outs are found by unweighted averaging across all relevant six- and eight-digit duties and phase-outs.[28] The procedure resulted in 148 five-digit product lines for the United States and 685 lines for Mexico, with 56 common product categories. These commodities account for 34.6 percent of U.S. imports from Mexico and 15.4 percent of its imports from the world, and 38.5 and 40.1 percent of Mexico's imports from the United States and the world, respectively.

Table 8.1 summarizes the data by presenting overall and one-digit averages for Mexican and U.S. tariffs, *MET* and *UST*, and for phase-outs, *MEPOUT* and *USPOUT*. While Mexico undertook major trade reform in the eighties, it remains a relatively protected economy with its 18.59 percent average import duty. The 5.91 percent U.S. average overestimates U.S. protection on imports from Mexico for two reasons: imports from the maquiladoras are not taxed on full value but only on value-added, and much of Mexico's trade already qualified for duty-free entry under the Generalized System of Preferences.[29] In both countries, categories 0 and 1 (agriculture, and beverages and tobacco), receive high protection. High-tariff categories are also Mexico's category 4 (oils) and U.S. category 8 (miscellaneous manufacturing, which includes clothing and footwear). The table reveals further that, on average, Mexico takes 5.64 years to phase out protection compared to the United States' 1.38 years. At this very aggregate level there is also a tendency for high-duty sectors to receive longer phase-outs than low-duty ones in both countries.

As is the case for empirical work on protection, it would be difficult to distinguish between competing models of tariff phase-outs. The objective of the following analysis is, instead, to identify variables that can provide some explanation of the variation in phase-outs across product categories. Even though commodities at the eight-digit level fall neatly into predetermined phase-out categories, averaging to a lower-digit level usually leads to numbers of years of phase-out that do not correspond exactly to any category. Accordingly, the endogenous variables *USPOUT* and *MEPOUT* can take noninteger values.

Various consumer, producer, import, and export interests affect a govern-

27. Since the first NAFTA tariff reduction occurred when the agreement went into effect on 1 January 1994, this approach implies that the number of years of phase-outs are counted from 1 January 1993.

28. For Mexico, both imports and exports are stated f.o.b., for the United States exports are f.o.b. but imports c.i.f. A more significant difference between the two countries is that Mexico, until 1992, excluded maquiladoras trade from its merchandise trade and instead tabulated it as services trade, while U.S. exports and imports with Mexico include trade with the maquiladoras. The difference is marked: for example, Mexico listed 1991 merchandise imports from the United States to be $25 billion while the United States listed 1991 merchandise exports to Mexico as $32 billion.

29. On the other hand, since NAFTA invalidates Mexico's Generalized System of Preferences status in the United States, some Mexican products do face higher U.S. import duties during the NAFTA-transition period than they did before NAFTA went into effect.

Table 8.1   **Average Tariffs and Phase-Outs, Overall and for One-Digit SITC Codes**

Category	MET (%)	MEPOUT (years)	UST (%)	USPOUT (years)
All imports	18.59	5.64	5.91	1.38
0 Food and live animals	20.78	7.00	10.65	0.82
1 Beverages and tobacco	34.91	8.44	14.40	5.00
2 Crude materials, inedibles	5.48	3.38	0.60	0.26
3 Fuels, lubricants, etc.	7.45	2.00	0.00	0.00
4 Animal, vegetable oils, fats	43.00	10.00	3.72	0.00
5 Chemicals, related products	11.12	4.83	4.89	0.92
6 Manufactured goods	13.22	6.73	5.42	1.87
7 Machines, transport equipment	14.10	3.28	3.17	0.62
8 Miscellaneous manufacturing articles	17.25	5.11	10.32	2.92

Sources: Calculations based on *North American Free Trade Agreement* 1993 and United Nations 1992.

ment's bargaining stance, as do any preferences held by, in particular, the executive branch of government, which may not be reflected in those of any private group. From the earlier discussion of existing work on tariff phase-outs, we know that analysis of such effects would require industry-level data for, among other variables, labor-adjustment cost, unskilled-labor intensity, and industry concentration ratios. At this first pass we consider only exogenous variables that are directly implied by the tariff and trade data described earlier in this section. This is a serious limitation of the analysis. On the other hand, it does permit us to take full advantage of the highly disaggregate nature of the data at hand. We take, therefore, the approach of summarizing domestic import-competing and other pro-protection pressures by the initial tariff level and hypothesize that, for any level of commodity aggregation, higher values of *UST* are associated with higher values of *USPOUT* (similarly for *MET* and *MEPOUT*), as groups that have been successful at obtaining protection would like to see it extended.[30]

As stated in table 8.2, which lists the variables used in the empirical analysis, we define also (imperfect) measures of import and export interests, *USML(ME)* and *USXL(ME)*, given by U.S. imports from or exports to Mexico as a share of total U.S. trade, with *MEML(US)* and *MEXL(US)* being similar variables for Mexico. Our hypothesis is that a large import share may lead to resistance to rapid liberalization, while a large export share induces export interests to lobby their government for rapid opening of a foreign market.[31]

We calculate Grubel-Lloyd indexes of intraindustry trade between Mexico

30. Baldwin (1985) finds that R^2 consistently falls below 0.10 when the U.S. tariff level is excluded from equations explaining the U.S. Tokyo Round proposal.

31. More satisfactory measures of import penetration and export stance would divide imports from and exports to Mexico with U.S. domestic sales or U.S. production of the good.

Table 8.2   **List of Variables**

USPOUT	number of years before free trade is reached in the U.S.
UST	initial ad valorem tariff rate in the U.S.
C	constant
USX(j)	U.S. exports to region *j*, for *j* = Mexico, rest of world, or world
USM(j)	U.S. imports from region *j*, for *j* = Mexico, rest of world, or world
USIIT(j)	Grubel-Lloyd measure for U.S. intraindustry trade with region *j* = {*USX(j)* + *USM(j)* − |*USX(j)* − *USM(j)*|}/[*USX(j)* + *USM(j)*]
USXL(ME)	U.S. exports to Mexico relative to total U.S. trade = *USX(ME)*/[*USX(W)* + *USM(W)*]
USML(ME)	U.S. imports from Mexico relative to total U.S. trade = *USM(ME)*/[*USX(W)* + *USM(W)*]

Notes: All variables are at the five-digit SITC code level. Exchanging *ME* for *US* throughout defines the similar variables for Mexico.

and the United States, *USIIT(ME)* and *MEIIT(US)*, and for each country's trade relative to the rest of the world, *USIIT(ROW)* and *MEIIT(ROW)* (see Grubel and Lloyd 1975). The hypothesis for the former is that larger intraindustry trade between Mexico and the United States will lead to faster market opening in both countries as opportunities due to access to partner markets can offer some compensation even for import-competing firms. Regarding the latter variables, a member's large intraindustry trade relative to the rest of the world may be a sign of a strong industry, which would lobby for rapid access to partner markets. The free trade partner may, on the other hand, perceive this as a threat and try to extend the product's phase-out period. The net effect depends on the relative strength of these forces.

Table 8.3 presents results for the United States for all five-digit product categories combined, and for categories 5, 6, 7, and 8 separately. The coefficient on the initial tariff rate *(UST)* is positive and significant when all products are considered jointly and when they are considered separately, implying that commodities with higher duties, as hypothesized, tend to get longer periods of adjustment. Intraindustry trade with Mexico *(USIIT(ME))* and with the rest of the world *(USIIT(ROW))* enters significantly and is negative when all U.S. products are considered; however, eliminating it does not have much effect on R^2 except for category 8 (miscellaneous manufacturing), where intraindustry trade with Mexico becomes significant and the duty level does not when the two variables are considered jointly. (When *USIIT(ROW)* is dropped from the equation, the tariff level regains significance at the 1 percent level.) *USML(ME)* and *USXL(ME)*, both of which are correlated with the Grubel-Lloyd index, are never significant, and sometimes have the wrong sign.

Given our data, we are, unfortunately, not able to distinguish between the several political-economy models that might cause such results. Rather, our finding is the very limited one that some of the underlying forces explaining U.S. levels of protection and phase-outs in global negotiations also seem to be

Table 8.3 **Effects of U.S. Tariffs and Intraindustry Trade on U.S. Phase-Outs across Five-Digit Product Categories**

	C	UST	$USIIT(ME)$	$USIIT(ROW)$
Endogenous Variable: $USPOUT$ All Categories				
Observations	148			
Coefficient	1.91**	17.26**	−1.42*	−1.49*
Standard error	(0.61)	(2.92)	(0.65)	(0.74)
T-statistic	3.11	5.89	−2.16	−1.99
$R^2 = 0.26$; adjusted $R^2 = 0.24$				
Coefficient	0.28	18.6**		
Standard error	(0.29)	(2.94)		
T-statistic	0.96	6.31		
$R^2 = 0.21$; adjusted $R^2 = 0.20$				
Endogenous Variable: $USPOUT$ in Category 5				
Observations	31			
Coefficient	−0.67	40.96**	−0.29	−0.83
Standard error	(1.78)	(11.95)	(1.51)	(1.90)
T-statistic	−0.38	3.42	−0.19	−0.44
$R^2 = 0.34$; adjusted $R^2 = 0.27$				
Coefficient	−1.38	42.41**		
Standard error	(0.83)	(10.94)		
T-statistic	−1.66	3.87		
$R^2 = 0.34$; adjusted $R^2 = 0.31$				
Endogenous Variable: $USPOUT$ in Category 6				
Observations	37			
Coefficient	0.93	43.37**	−0.19	1.96
Standard error	(1.75)	(16.84)	(1.57)	(1.74)
T-statistic	0.53	2.57	−0.12	−1.13
$R^2 = 0.29$; adjusted $R^2 = 0.23$				
Coefficient	−0.77	52.05**		
Standard error	(0.94)	(14.74)		
T-statistic	−0.82	3.53		
$R^2 = 0.26$; adjusted $R^2 = 0.24$				
Endogenous Variable: $USPOUT$ in Category 7				
Observations	31			
Coefficient	−0.71	33.53**	−0.28	0.50
Standard error	(0.68)	(6.79)	(0.70)	(0.67)
T-statistic	−1.03	4.93	−0.39	0.75
$R^2 = 0.48$; adjusted $R^2 = 0.43$				
Coefficient	−0.50	33.34**		
Standard error	(0.28)	(6.51)		
T-statistic	−1.77	5.11		
$R^2 = 0.47$; adjusted $R^2 = 0.45$				

(*continued*)

Table 8.3   (continued)

	C	UST	USIIT(ME)	USIIT(ROW)
		Endogenous Variable: *USPOUT* in Category 8		
Observations	26			
Coefficient	4.46*	16.16	−6.21**	−1.65
Standard error	(2.13)	(8.56)	(2.31)	(2.45)
T-statistic	2.08	1.88	−2.68	−0.67
$R^2 = 0.46$; adjusted $R^2 = 0.38$				
Coefficient	0.10	24.68**		
Standard error	(0.96)	(8.28)		
T-statistic	0.10	2.98		
$R^2 = 0.27$; adjusted $R^2 = 0.23$				

Note: All variables are at the five-digit SITC code level.
*Significant at 5 percent level.
**Significant at 1 percent level.

at work in preferential negotiations.[32] (The important exception is the large product category "miscellaneous manufacturing" where tariff levels, somewhat surprisingly, do not explain phase-outs.) Recalling the theoretical results on reform, we also note that permitting high-duty industries long phase-outs might reduce or even disallow the welfare gains that could otherwise be accrued from harmonizing tariffs through, for example, cutting extreme rates the most. (It should be stressed that it need not—rate-cutting rules that raise world welfare when implemented across all the world's trading nations need not raise world welfare when implemented only across a subset of the world's countries.)

A different picture emerges for Mexico where the data do not, at the five-digit level, account for the variation in phase-outs, whether across all product categories or within categories 5, 6, and 7. (As will be discussed below, category 8 is different.) The correlation between phase-outs and tariffs across all products is only 0.03, and it is 0.06 between phase-outs and intraindustry trade with the United States; the correlation between the same variables for categories 5, 6, and 7 is also zero.[33] The variable most strongly correlated with Mexico's phase-outs is Mexico's exports to the United States as a fraction of Mexico's total trade *(MEXL(US))*. It does not, however, enter significantly in regressions, whether across or within categories.

It is remarkable that Mexico's tariffs do not help explain Mexico's phase-outs at the five-digit level. After all, our results for U.S. phase-outs, as well as the work summarized earlier in this paper on the Kennedy and Tokyo Rounds,

32. Such forces could stem from pressure from lobbying groups, or they could reflect social preferences over the distribution of income.
33. The correlation between phase-outs and tariffs for the United States is 0.46.

consistently establish a role for the initial duty level in explaining tariff reductions, at least for the United States. In the remainder of the paper we will investigate this finding for Mexico's five-digit duties and phase-outs. We will focus on two candidate explanations. One is that the Mexico-U.S. negotiations may have favored U.S. concerns regarding phase-outs either because of strong U.S. pressure or because phase-outs were not critical to Mexico's NAFTA strategy because of other objectives including ensuring access to the U.S. market and establishing credibility of policy reform through international commitment.[34] Another possibility is that the averaging of eight-digit rates and phase-outs required for five-digit values may obscure a correlation at the eight-digit level. These are not mutually exclusive explanations.

Concessions, and hence reciprocity, could be broad-based and could involve comparing overall duty reductions (Mexico's 18.59 percent versus the United States' 5.91 percent), imports covered ($24 billion for Mexico versus $31 billion for the United States), or tariff revenues ($5 billion for Mexico versus $1.8 billion for the United States). At the other extreme, reciprocity could be narrow. The tariff negotiations between Mexico and the United States could be conducted at the eight-digit level with the presumption that identical products in the two countries, at that level, would receive identical phase-outs.

Table 8.4 hints at the possibility that U.S. preferences may have affected Mexican phase-outs in a negotiation with narrow reciprocity. Category 8 is the only one where Mexican tariffs hold some explanation for phase-outs, and they do so significantly, at the 1 percent level. Intraindustry trade with the United States is not significant *(MEIIT(US))*; however, intraindustry trade with the rest of the world *(MEIIT(ROW))* is, sometimes at the 1 percent level. The positive sign of this coefficient implies that larger Mexican intraindustry trade with the rest of the world is associated with slower Mexican NAFTA phase-outs. One explanation for this could be that Mexico wanted to soften the impact from free trade with the United States for industries involved in these products. An alternative, and more plausible, explanation is that the United States may have desired slower U.S. phase-outs for products that Mexico trades extensively with the rest of the world. The United States would thereby delay Mexican producers' shifting sales from Mexico or from third markets to the United States. If narrow reciprocity was assumed, this would in turn imply slower Mexican phase-outs for these products.

To investigate further whether the U.S. stance influences Mexico's phase-outs, we consider the fifty-six five-digit categories that are common for the two countries in the data. Since U.S. and Mexican phase-outs are jointly determined in the NAFTA bargain, we approach the problem by two-stage least

---

34. Associated with this explanation is that Mexican tariffs may not be as strong indicators of strength of import-competing interests as are U.S. tariffs. Mexico undertook extensive reforms in the 1980s, and traditional import-competing interests may have lost influence in the process of implementing the associated tariff structure.

Table 8.4   **Effects of Mexico's Tariffs and Intraindustry Trade on Mexico's Phase-Outs for Five-Digit Products in Category 8**

	Endogenous Variable: $MEPOUT$ in Category 8			
C	−5.53**	−3.19**	−3.03**	−2.92**
	(2.24)	(1.35)	(1.37)	(1.36)
	−2.46	−2.35	−2.20	−2.14
MET	44.79**	41.28**	42.89**	43.80**
	(9.06)	(8.69)	(8.77)	(8.65)
	4.94	4.75	4.88	5.06
MEIIT(US)	0.68	−0.10	1.05	
	(1.73)	(1.62)	(1.54)	
	0.39	−0.06	0.68	
MEIIT(ROW)	4.24**	4.23**		
	(2.08)	(2.09)		
	2.03	2.02		
MEML(US)	2.83			
	(2.19)			
	(1.39			
R^2	0.23	0.22	0.19	0.19
Adjusted R^2	0.20	0.20	0.18	0.18
Observations		110		

Notes: Numbers in parentheses are standard errors; *t*-statistics are listed below.
**Significant at 1 percent level.

squares. Table 8.5 reports results from regressing Mexican phase-outs on a number of variables including the predicted value of U.S. phase-outs *(USPOUTF)* from stage 1 of the procedure. The table reveals that U.S. phase-outs enter significantly and with the expected sign.

Table 8.6 reports analogous results for U.S. phase-outs for the same fifty-six categories using Mexico's phase-out as instrument. The coefficient on the predicted value of Mexico's phase-out *(MEPOUTF)* is significant in only one specification. Also, the coefficient estimate is smaller than the coefficient estimate for the predicted value of the United States' phase-out *(USPOUTF)*.

Viewed together, these results suggest that Mexican phase-outs have less bearing on U.S. phase-outs than vice versa. They suggest also that reciprocity with respect to tariff phase-outs is at work. This, in turn, breaks the expected positive link between product tariff level and length of phase-out period for one of the participants unless the countries' initial duty levels happen to covary positively in a very particular pattern.

We investigate, finally, the fifty-six common five-digit categories for reciprocity at the eight-digit level, and follow two procedures: an exclusive one where we record a product as a concordance only if both countries' tariff schedules list identical eight-digit codes for the product; and an inclusive one where we add to this list products where we can assign one country's six-digit duty and phase-out to the other country's corresponding eight-digit categories.

Table 8.5   **Two-Stage Regressions of Mexico's Phase-Outs with the United States' Phase-Outs as Instrument**

Endogenous Variable: *MEPOUT* for Common Categories			
C	2.84	3.63*	2.69	3.70*
	(2.25)	(2.11)	(2.22)	(2.18)
	1.25	1.71	1.21	1.69
MET	2.93	6.03	2.88	6.16
	(13.76)	(13.54)	(13.67)	(13.69)
	0.21	0.44	0.21	0.45
MEIIT(US)	1.99	1.59	1.81	1.63
	(1.77)	(1.74)	(1.73)	(1.77)
	1.12	0.91	1.04	0.92
USPOUTF	0.68**	0.69**	0.74**	0.67**
	(0.26)	(0.24)	(0.24)	(0.26)
	2.58	2.88	3.06	2.53
MEML(US)	3.06		2.65	
	(2.19)		(2.06)	
	1.39		1.28	
USXL(ME)	−6.13			−1.51
	(10.43)			(9.98)
	−0.58			−0.15
R^2	0.24	0.21	0.24	0.21
Adjusted R^2	0.17	0.17	0.18	0.15
Observations		56		

Notes: Numbers in parentheses are standard errors; *t*-statistics are listed below.
*Significant at 5 percent level.
**Significant at 1 percent level.

The exclusive approach yields a correlation between *MEPOUT* and *MET* of 0.43, and between *MEPOUT* and *USPOUT* of 0.41. The inclusive approach implies correlation coefficients for the same pairs of variables of 0.35 and 0.27, respectively. For either approach, the correlation between *MET* and *UST* is only 0.16.

These findings lend some support to the view that there was an attempt at establishing narrow, that is within eight-digit category, reciprocity in the negotiations. They also suggest that averaging can make it difficult to detect political-economy effects from tariff levels to phase-outs as well as signs of narrow reciprocity.

8.6   Conclusion

This paper has discussed tariff phase-outs in both a multilateral and a preferential context. The theoretical literature demonstrates that reducing the dispersion of tariffs tends to be welfare-improving. Empirical work on U.S. tariff reductions shows, on the other hand, a tendency toward reducing high tariff rates by less, or more slowly, than would be implied from theory.

Table 8.6   **Two-Stage Regressions of the United States' Phase-Outs with Mexico's Phase-Outs as Instrument**

Endogenous Variable: *USPOUT* for Common Categories				
C	−0.91	−0.64	0.15	−1.36
	(2.04)	(1.75)	(1.80)	(2.07)
	−0.44	−0.37	0.08	−0.65
UST	8.23	11.88**	9.99*	11.05*
	(5.30)	(4.99)	(5.07)	(5.18)
	1.55	2.37	1.97	2.13
USIIT(ME)	−2.40*	−1.93*	−2.55*	−1.77
	(1.19)	(1.14)	(1.19)	(1.17)
	−2.00	−1.69	−2.13	−1.51
MEPOUTF	0.52*	0.37	0.39	0.44
	(0.29)	(0.27)	(0.26)	(0.29)
	1.80	1.38	1.48	1.52
USML(ME)	−5.20*		−4.39	
	(2.88)		(2.79)	
	−1.80		−1.57	
MEXL(US)	1.41			0.82
	(1.27)			(1.25)
	1.10			0.65
R^2	0.47	0.44	0.46	0.44
Adjusted R^2	0.42	0.40	0.42	0.40
Observations	56			

Notes: Numbers in parentheses are standard errors; *t*-statistics are listed below.
*Significant at 5 percent level.
**Significant at 1 percent level.

In a very preliminary investigation of the agreed tariff phase-outs between the United States and Mexico in NAFTA, we find evidence that U.S. phase-outs tend to be long for high-duty product categories. We find also that intraindustry trade between partners may induce shorter phase-outs, while a member's intraindustry trade with outside countries could slow tariff elimination.

Mexican tariff phase-outs do not seem to be explained by Mexican protection, at least not at the five-digit SITC level. For a subset of product categories we find, instead, that they are correlated with U.S. phase-outs. This may suggest some product-level reciprocity and that other issues, including the overriding one of obtaining free trade in the near future with its northern neighbors, were given higher priority by Mexican negotiators than the question of how to phase duties out. Furthermore, and as stressed in Kowalczyk 1990, since integration between a large and a small country implies gains in favor of the small country, our finding may also reflect an attempt by the parties to make the agreement more attractive for the United States, which otherwise might not stand to gain much from the agreement, at least in the short run.

As a final note, we stress again that this paper is only a first pass at starting to investigate empirical features of tariff bargaining. The analysis, as presented, has many serious limitations, including that we have focused exclusively on trade data and not included industry data that earlier contributions on political economy, both theoretical and empirical, have found to be potentially helpful in explaining protection and its changes.

References

Abbott, Frederick M. 1995. *Law and Policy of Regional Integration: The NAFTA and Western Hemispheric Integration in the World Trade Organization System.* Cambridge, MA: Kluwer.

Anderson, Kym, and Hege Norheim. 1993. History, Geography, and Regional Economic Integration. In Kym Anderson and Richard Blackhurst, eds., *Regional Integration and the Global Trading System,* 19–51. Hemel Hempstead, England: Harvester Wheatsheaf.

Bagwell, Kyle, and Robert W. Staiger. 1993a. Multilateral Tariff Cooperation during the Formation of Customs Unions. NBER Working Paper no. 4543. Cambridge, MA: National Bureau of Economic Research, November.

———. 1993b. Multilateral Tariff Cooperation during the Formation of Regional Free Trade Areas. NBER Working Paper no. 4364. Cambridge, MA: National Bureau of Economic Research, May.

Baldwin, Robert E. 1985. *The Political Economy of U.S. Import Policy.* Cambridge: MIT Press.

Bale, Malcolm. 1977. United States Concessions in the Kennedy Round and Short-Run Labour Adjustment Costs: Further Evidence. *Journal of International Economics* 7:145–48.

Bello, Judith H., and Alan F. Holmer. 1992. *Guide to the U.S.-Canada Free-Trade Agreement.* Englewood Cliffs: Prentice Hall.

Bhagwati, Jagdish. 1991. *The World Trading System at Risk.* Princeton: Princeton University Press.

———. 1993. Regionalism and Multilateralism: An Overview. In Jaime de Melo and Arvind Panagariya, eds., *New Dimensions in Regional Integration,* 22–51. Cambridge: Cambridge University Press.

Bond, Eric, and Costas Syropoulos. 1996. The Size of Trading Blocs: Market Power and World Welfare Effects. *Journal of International Economics* 40:411–37.

Caves, Richard. 1976. Economic Models of Political Choice: Canada's Tariff Structure. *Canadian Journal of Economics* 9:278–300.

Cheh, John H. 1974. United States Concessions in the Kennedy Round and Short-Run Labor Adjustment Costs. *Journal of International Economics* 4:323–40.

Dam, Kenneth. 1970. *The GATT: Law and International Economic Organization.* Chicago: University of Chicago Press.

Deardorff, Alan V., and Robert M. Stern. 1994. Multilateral Trade Negotiations and Preferential Trading Arrangements. In Alan V. Deardorff and Robert M. Stern, eds., *Analytical and Negotiating Issues in the Global Trading System,* 27–85. Ann Arbor: University of Michigan Press.

Finger, J. Michael. 1974. GATT Tariff Concessions and the Exports of Developing Countries. *Economic Journal* 84:566–75.

Finger, J. Michael, and Paula Holmes. 1987. Unilateral Liberalization and the MTNs.

In J. Michael Finger and Andrzej Olechowski, eds., *The Uruguay Round: A Handbook on the Multilateral Trade Negotiations,* 52–58. Washington, DC: World Bank.

Frankel, Jeffrey. 1993. Is Japan Creating a Yen Bloc in East Asia and the Pacific? In Jeffrey Frankel and Miles Kahler, eds., *Regionalism and Rivalry: Japan and the U.S. in Pacific Asia,* 53–85. Chicago: University of Chicago Press.

Fukushima, Takashi, and Namdoo Kim. 1989. Welfare Improving Tariff Changes: A Case of Many Goods and Countries. *Journal of International Economics* 26:383–88.

General Agreement on Tariffs and Trade. 1949. The Annecy Protocol of Terms of Accession to the General Agreement on Tariffs and Trade. Geneva: GATT.

———. 1951. The Torquay Protocol to the General Agreement on Tariffs and Trade. Geneva: GATT.

———. 1962. Protocol Embodying the Results of the 1960–1961 Tariff Conference. Geneva: GATT.

———. 1967. Geneva Protocol to the General Agreement on Tariffs and Trade. Geneva: GATT.

———. 1979. Geneva Protocol to the General Agreement on Tariffs and Trade. Geneva: GATT.

———. 1994. *The Results of the Uruguay Round of Multilateral Trade Negotiations: Market Access for Goods and Services: Overview of the Results.* Geneva: GATT.

Grossman, Gene, and Elhanan Helpman. 1993. The Politics of Free Trade Agreements. NBER Working Paper no. 4597. Cambridge, MA: National Bureau of Economic Research, December.

Grubel, Herbert G., and Peter J. Lloyd. 1975. *Intra-Industry Trade: The Theory and Measurement of International Trade in Differentiated Products.* New York: Wiley and Sons.

Hart, Michael. 1994. *Decision at Midnight: Inside the Canada-U.S. Free-Trade Negotiations.* Vancouver: University of British Columbia Press.

Hatta, Tatsuo, and Takashi Fukushima. 1979. The Welfare Effect of Tariff Rate Reductions in a Many Country World. *Journal of International Economics* 9:503–11.

Haveman, Jon. 1992. On the Consequences of Recent Changes in the Global Trading Environment. Department of Economics, Purdue University. Mimeo.

Helleiner, G. K. 1977. The Political Economy of Canada's Tariff Structure: An Alternative Model. *Canadian Journal of Economics* 4:318–26.

Hudec, Robert E. 1990. *The GATT Legal System and World Trade Diplomacy.* 2d ed. St. Paul: Butterworth Legal.

Hufbauer, Gary C., and Jeffrey J. Schott. 1993. *NAFTA: An Assessment.* Revised ed. Washington, DC: Institute for International Economics.

International Monetary Fund. 1995. *Direction of Trade Statistics Yearbook.* Washington, DC: International Monetary Fund.

Jackson, John. 1989. *The World Trading System.* Cambridge: MIT Press.

Jackson, John, William J. Davey, and Alan O. Sykes, Jr. 1995. *Legal Problems of International Economic Relations.* 3d ed. St. Paul: West.

Kemp, Murray C. 1969. *A Contribution to the General Equilibrium Theory of Preferential Trading.* Amsterdam: North-Holland.

Kemp, Murray C., and Henry Y. Wan, Jr. 1976. An Elementary Proposition concerning the Formation of Customs Unions. *Journal of International Economics* 6:95–97.

Kennan, John, and Raymond Riezman. 1990. Optimal Tariff Equilibria with Customs Unions. *Canadian Journal of Economics* 23:70–83.

Kowalczyk, Carsten. 1989. Trade Negotiations and World Welfare. *American Economic Review* 79:552–59.

———. 1990. Welfare and Customs Unions. NBER Working Paper no. 3476. Cambridge, MA: National Bureau of Economic Research, October.

———. 1992. Paradoxes in Integration Theory. *Open Economies Review* 3:51–59.

Kowalczyk, Carsten, and Tomas Sjöström. 1994. Bringing GATT into the Core. *Economica* 61:301–17.

Krugman, Paul. 1991a. Is Bilateralism Bad? In Elhanan Helpman and Assaf Razin, eds., *International Trade and Trade Policy,* 9–23. Cambridge: MIT Press.

———. 1991b. The Move toward Free Trade Zones. In Federal Reserve Bank of Kansas City, *Policy Implications of Trade and Currency Zones,* 7–41. Kansas City: Federal Reserve Bank.

———. 1993. Regionalism versus Multilateralism: Analytical Notes. In Jaime de Melo and Arvind Panagariya, eds., *New Dimensions in Regional Integration,* 58–79. Cambridge: Cambridge University Press.

Lee, Jong-Wha, and Phillip Swagel. 1994. Trade Barriers and Trade Flows across Countries and Industries. NBER Working Paper no. 4799. Cambridge, MA: National Bureau of Economic Research, July.

Levy, Philip. 1994. A Political-Economic Analysis of Free Trade Agreements. Econ Growth Ctr Div Paper 718, Department of Economics, Yale University, June.

Lipsey, Richard G., and Kelvin Lancaster. 1956–57. The General Theory of Second-Best. *Review of Economic Studies* 24:11–32.

Lopez, Ramon, and Arvind Panagariya. 1992. On the Theory of Piecemeal Tariff Reform: The Case of Pure Imported Intermediate Inputs. *American Economic Review* 82:615–25.

Ludema, Rodney. 1994. On the Value of Preferential Trade Agreements in Multilateral Negotiations. Department of Economics, University of Western Ontario. Mimeo.

McMillan, John. 1993. Does Regional Integration Foster Open Trade? In Kym Anderson and Richard Blackhurst, eds., *Regional Integration and the Global Trading System,* 292–310. Hemel Hempstead, England: Harvester Wheatsheaf.

McMillan, John, and Even McCann. 1981. Welfare Effects in Customs Unions. *Economic Journal* 91:697–703.

Meade, James. 1955. *Trade and Welfare.* London: Oxford University Press.

Negishi, Takashi. 1972. *General Equilibrium Theory and International Trade.* Amsterdam: North-Holland.

1993 North American Trade Guide. 1992. Philadelphia: North American.

North American Free Trade Agreement. 1993. Washington, DC: GPO.

Ohyama, Michihiro. 1972. Trade and Welfare in General Equilibrium. *Keio Economic Studies* 9:37–73.

Ozga, S. A. 1955. An Essay in the Theory of Tariffs. *Journal of Political Economy* 63:489–99.

Preeg, Ernest H. 1970. *Traders and Diplomats.* Washington, DC: Brookings Institution.

Richardson, Martin. 1995. Tariff Revenue Competition in a Free Trade Area. *European Economic Review.* 39:1429–37.

Roessler, Frieder. 1993. Regional Integration Agreements and Multilateral Trade Order. In Kym Anderson and Richard Blackhurst, eds., *Regional Integration and the Global Trading System,* 311–25. Hemel Hempstead, England: Harvester Wheatsheaf.

Schott, Jeffrey J. 1994. *The Uruguay Round: An Assessment.* Washington, DC: Institute for International Economics.

Srinivasan, T. N. 1993. Comment. In Jaime de Melo and Arvind Panagariya, eds., *New Dimensions in Regional Integration,* 84–89. Cambridge: Cambridge University Press.

Stein, Ernesto. 1994. Essays on the Welfare Implications of Trading Blocs with Transportation Costs and Political Cycles of Inflation. Ph.D. diss. Department of Economics, University of California, Berkeley.

Stewart, Terence P., ed. 1994. *The GATT Uruguay Round: A Negotiating History, 1986–1992.* Vol. 1. Boston: Kluwer.

Trefler, Daniel. 1993. Trade Liberalization and the Theory of Endogenous Protection:

An Econometric Study of U.S. Import Policy. *Journal of Political Economy* 101:138–60.

United Nations Statistical Office. 1986. Standard International Trade Classification Revision 3. Statistical Papers Series M, no. 34/Rev. 3.

———. 1992. *Commodity Trade Statistics 1990–91.* New York: United Nations.

Vanek, Jaroslev. 1964. Unilateral Trade Liberalization and Global World Income. *Quarterly Journal of Economics* 78:139–47.

———. 1965. *General Equilibrium of International Discrimination: The Case of Customs Unions.* Cambridge: Harvard University Press.

Viner, Jacob. 1950. *The Customs Union Issue.* New York: Carnegie Endowment for International Peace.

Wilcox, Clair. 1949. *A Charter for World Trade.* New York: Macmillan.

Winham, Gilbert R. 1986. *International Trade and the Tokyo Round Negotiation.* Princeton: Princeton University Press.

World Trade Organization Secretariat. 1995. *Regionalism and the World Trading System.* Geneva: World Trade Organization.

Comment   Arvind Panagariya

The first three substantive sections of this paper provide an extremely useful discussion of the relevant theory and past experience. From the relatively small size of the paper, it may not be immediately obvious, but the authors have encapsulated a vast amount of information on analytic results from the piecemeal-reforms literature, various GATT rounds, and the empirical literature on the determinants of tariff liberalization. In addition, in the last substantive section, they have managed to give us an original econometric analysis of the political economy of the tariff phase-out in NAFTA.

Because the empirical section is the most interesting part of the paper, I will concentrate my comments on that section. But before doing so, let me make one point that relates to the theoretical section of the paper. According to a large body of the literature reviewed in the paper, preferential trading has an ambiguous effect on welfare. Yet, during the NAFTA debate, the view gained ground—even among many well-informed economists—that *any* liberalization was a good thing and that free trade areas (FTAs) were essentially equivalent to nondiscriminatory free trade. The original version of this paper, by adopting the title "On Intrabloc Tariff Reform," which conveys the sense that intrabloc tariff elimination is necessarily a good thing, seemed to fall into the same trap. I am glad, however, that the authors have decided to adopt a more neutral title in the final version.

Let me take a moment to dispel the notion that preferential trading, in general, and NAFTA, in particular, is necessarily a good thing. Recently, Jagdish

Arvind Panagariya is professor of economics at the University of Maryland, College Park.
The author thanks Carsten Kowalczyk for suggestions on an earlier draft.

Bhagwati and I (Bhagwati and Panagariya 1996; Panagariya 1996) have argued that if a high-tariff country (Mexico) forms an FTA with a low-tariff country (the United States), the static welfare effect of the union on the former (Mexico) is likely to be negative. To explain, note that when Mexico eliminates tariffs on the United States but retains them on the outside world, unless imports from the outside world are eliminated entirely, a substantial part of the tariff revenue collected on imports from the United States is transferred to exporters in the United States in the form of better terms of trade. The larger the imports from the United States and the higher the initial tariffs in Mexico, the larger the transfer. Because tariffs in the United States are initially low, the tariff-revenue transfer to Mexican firms from the preferential access to the United States' market is low. Thus, the net tariff-revenue redistribution goes against Mexico. Moreover, because redistribution effects are rectangles whereas trade-creation and trade-diversion effects—the main focus of the traditional theory—are triangles, the presumption is that the static welfare effect of NAFTA on Mexico will be negative.

The empirical part of the paper carries out an econometric investigation of the determinants of tariff liberalization in different sectors in the United States and Mexico. At first glance, it may seem that, since all tariffs on within-union trade are to be eliminated, what intersectoral differences are there to explain? But here the authors bring in the important point that the timetable for tariff phase-out is not uniform across sectors. Tariffs in some sectors will be eliminated faster than others. Therefore, we can sensibly ask why some sectors got placed on the fast track while others were placed on a slow track.

To answer, the authors take the length of time allowed before the elimination of the intra-NAFTA tariff at the sectoral level as the dependent variable and initial U.S. and Mexican tariff rates and the extent of intraindustry trade in the sector as the main independent variables. Remarkably, the authors find that the United States' initial tariff rate is a statistically significant explanatory variable in the equation of not only the United States but also Mexico. Thus, the greater the initial tariff protection in a sector in the United States, the longer the time allowed for the removal of the tariff in that sector not only in the United States but also Mexico. Equally interestingly, initial tariffs in Mexico are not statistically significant even in its own equation.

I have three comments on this very interesting section. First, I found the average tariff of 5.9 percent on Mexican goods in the United States, estimated by the authors, to be on the high side. Imports of many goods from Mexico enjoyed preferential treatment under the Generalized System of Preferences (GSP) even prior to NAFTA. Moreover, the overall U.S. tariff averages 4 to 5 percent. Revenue collection on imports from Mexico is between 3 and 4 percent of the imports. Based on these facts, the average tariff rate applying to Mexico should be substantially lower than 5.9 percent.

Second, though the current tariff rates in Mexico do not explain the tariff phase-out under NAFTA, the rates imbedded in the GATT bindings may. Presumably, the structure of GATT bindings reflects better the structure of the current political power of producer interests than the actual tariff structure.[1]

Finally and most importantly, in their empirical work, the authors seem to take the view that whatever explains the nature of trade liberalization in a multilateral context (i.e., the GATT rounds) also explains trade liberalization in an FTA context. But one should expect the theory of preferential liberalization to be different from that of nondiscriminatory liberalization. I can think of at least three political-economy models of preferential liberalization.

Thus, casting the problem from Mexico's standpoint, we can first hypothesize that Mexican producer lobbies are the dominant force in Mexico. In this case, products likely to lead to trade diversion will be liberalized first and those leading to trade creation will be liberalized last. Domestic producers will accept tariff reductions affecting outside countries more readily than those affecting themselves. Second, we can imagine that the chosen sequencing of the phase-out was determined by a welfare-maximizing Mexican government. In this case, products associated with trade creation will be liberalized first while, among products leading to trade diversion, those likely to result in large tariff-revenue transfer to U.S. firms will be liberalized last. Finally, it is entirely possible that once Mexico agreed to go through NAFTA, given the large economic size of the United States, it lost all bargaining power. In this model, all shots will be called by the U.S. lobbies, and products whose liberalization serves U.S. export interests are likely to placed on the fast track.

Anecdotal evidence suggests that the phase-out of Mexico's tariff was indeed influenced by the U.S. producer interests.[2] If this is correct, the authors' finding that the higher the initial U.S. tariff in a sector the longer the time allowed for liberalization in Mexico has the implication that U.S. export interests in Mexico are represented by precisely those sectors that enjoy a high degree of protection within the U.S. market. That, in turn, implies that NAFTA may well have been an instrument of extending protection for U.S. firms to Mexico in sectors where they had to be protected domestically and, hence, did not enjoy a high degree of comparative advantage vis-à-vis outside countries. The likelihood of trade diversion in the Mexican market as a result of NAFTA then is high.

---

1. Mexico has undergone major tariff reforms in recent years, which may have led to a reconfiguration of political power of producer interests. GATT bindings rather than actual tariff rates may better represent this new configuration of political power.

2. For example, some U.S. auto manufacturers were already manufacturing automobiles in Mexico and faster tariff reduction on automobiles imported from the United States would have affected their operation in Mexico adversely. Therefore, liberalization of auto imports was placed on a slow track.

References

Bhagwati, Jagdish, and Arvind Panagariya. 1996. Preferential Trading Areas and Multilateralism: Strangers, Friends, or Foes. In Jagdish Bhagwati and Arvind Panagariya, eds., *The Economics of Preferential Trade Agreements,* 1–78. Washington, DC: AEI Press.
Panagariya, Arvind. 1996. The Free Trade Area of the Americas: Good for Latin America? *World Economy* 19 (5): 485–515.

Comment   Robert W. Staiger

Introduction

Carsten Kowalczyk and Donald Davis have written a paper that asks two largely separable but very important questions. First, can the form in which the world trading system permits preferential trading arrangements, as embodied in GATT's article XXIV and now incorporated in its successor, the World Trade Organization (WTO), be explained by economic theory? And second, do the staging rules that determine the speed with which the United States and Mexico eliminate tariffs on their bilateral trade under NAFTA reflect some notion of "reciprocity"?

To provide an answer to the first question, the authors survey recent theoretical arguments and conclude that economic theory at present provides only mixed support for article XXIV. To provide an answer to the second question, the authors examine whether either country's product-level staging decisions help predict those of its trading partner. They find that U.S. staging decisions help to predict the staging decisions of Mexico but not vice versa. They interpret this as evidence of "narrow reciprocity," in the sense that Mexico appears to have adjusted its own staging decisions to achieve a degree of product-by-product reciprocity with the staging decisions of the United States.

The first portion of their paper provides a useful synthesis of existing work on the theory of preferential trade agreements. However, the original contribution of the paper lies mainly in the authors' attempt to utilize data on NAFTA staging decisions to study the importance of reciprocity in trade negotiations, and it is to this portion of their paper that I will direct my comments.

Reciprocity

While much has been written about the principle of *reciprocity* as a pillar of GATT, the authors rightly point out that there is little in the way of hard empiri-

Robert W. Staiger is professor of economics at the University of Wisconsin, Madison, and a research associate of the National Bureau of Economic Research.

cal evidence as to whether any notion of reciprocity is actually borne out in the negotiated outcomes under GATT.[1] This is not to say that reciprocity as a negotiating principle of GATT is in doubt: there is ample evidence that achieving an overall balance of offers is an important goal of negotiators.[2] But how close negotiators come to achieving their goal of reciprocity in any given negotiation is still an open empirical issue. After making this point, the authors then observe that the staging rules under which preferential agreements are phased in may be a good place to look for evidence of reciprocity, and the staging rules adopted by the United States and Mexico in implementing NAFTA become the focus of their empirical exercise.

But is the same reciprocity principle that forms a pillar of GATT likely to be reflected in the staging rules of a preferential agreement such as NAFTA? I am skeptical that it is. My doubts are based on two observations. My first observation concerns the theoretical underpinnings of reciprocity under GATT, and whether we should *expect* the logic of reciprocity to extend to preferential agreements negotiated within the context of a broader multilateral agreement such as GATT. My second observation concerns the actual implementation of GATT's principle of reciprocity and, if it *did* extend to preferential agreements, how it would apply in the specific case of two countries of vastly different size such as the United States and Mexico. I will elaborate on each observation in turn.

Should we expect the same principle of reciprocity to be applied consistently across multilateral and preferential settings? To begin to answer this, I first need a theoretical framework that can explain the role of reciprocity in a multilateral agreement such as GATT. Only then can I assess whether the logic of reciprocity is likely to extend to a preferential agreement negotiated within the context of the broader multilateral agreement.

The very notion of reciprocity suggests that governments consider reductions in their own tariffs a price to be paid for increased access to foreign markets. Indeed, this mercantilist orientation is imbedded in the language of GATT itself, where a government's decision to open its markets to imports is viewed as a "concession" that is deemed worthy only for the export benefits that a reciprocal concession from a trading partner would generate. This perspective is hard to reconcile with standard economic arguments, which hold that free trade is the best *unilateral* trade policy.

Nevertheless, theoretical underpinnings can be given to the principle of reci-

---

1. Throughout my comments I will follow Kowalczyk and Davis in referring to reciprocity as the balance of concessions that governments seek to obtain through negotiations. For further analysis of the meaning of reciprocity in GATT and its economic interpretation, see Bagwell and Staiger (1997a).

2. Even in GATT negotiating rounds where formula cuts were adopted, as in the Kennedy Round, a great deal of effort was put into developing adequate measures to define and judge the "balance of advantages" or "reciprocity" resulting from the negotiations (see, for example, Preeg 1970, 130–34).

procity in multilateral negotiations if one adopts the view, as in Bagwell and Staiger (1996), that GATT's central purpose is to prevent governments from exploiting their ability to shift costs of trade intervention onto trading partners when making trade-policy decisions in pursuit of domestic objectives. Observing that such cost shifting will occur through the terms-of-trade implications of intervention, we find that the terms-of-trade implications of trade-policy intervention imply that governments face less than the full cost of protecting their import competing sectors and exaggerated costs of stimulating their export sectors. As a result, whatever governments might seek to achieve through the national price effects of their trade policies—whether acting as national income maximizers or as agents for politically powerful interest groups, and whether motivated by complex distributional concerns or simply by the desire to create jobs in certain sectors—they will have a tendency to oversupply policies directed toward import protection and undersupply policies directed toward export promotion relative to the efficient intervention levels given their objectives. The principle of reciprocity can be readily interpreted within this framework as the desire of governments to exchange reductions in trade restrictions, so that more efficient outcomes may be realized: under reciprocity and the balance of concessions that it demands, the terms-of-trade implications of each country's own liberalization are neutralized, thereby removing an obstacle that prevented each country from unilaterally liberalizing in the first place. Therefore, *reciprocity facilitates the removal of inefficient trade restrictions that arise as a consequence of terms-of-trade motivations.*

Could reciprocity in the staging decisions of a preferential agreement negotiated within the context of a broader multilateral agreement also be explained on the grounds that it facilitates the removal of inefficient trade restrictions that arise as a consequence of terms-of-trade motivations? It seems unlikely. First, staging rules are by nature transitory, and their determination is more likely to be driven by a desire on the part of governments to mitigate the adjustment costs of achieving regional integration than by the efficiency concerns that can explain the principle of reciprocity in GATT. Second, explaining reciprocity in a preferential agreement on efficiency grounds is made difficult by a simple observation: any set of national prices achieved through the discriminatory tariffs associated with a preferential trade agreement could be achieved in the absence of the preferential trade agreement by a set of nondiscriminatory most-favored-nation (MFN) tariffs that generate the same country-by-country pattern of *multilateral* trade flows.[3] Hence, the desire of countries to negotiate preferential trade agreements within the broader context of GATT (and GATT's willingness to accommodate these desires under certain circum-

---

3. Strictly speaking, this statement is only valid in a partial equilibrium setting where income effects are absent. More generally, the income effect in moving from discriminatory tariffs might require changes in multilateral trade flows to maintain constant national prices (see Bagwell and Staiger 1996).

stances) is not easily explained as the result of a search for trading arrangements that yield more efficient outcomes.[4] Instead, regional integration initiatives are more likely to reflect broader objectives such as military security or political stability (and GATT's acknowledgment that such objectives can be served by deeper integration among a subset of its members).[5]

This suggests to me that the central purpose of preferential agreements within a multilateral framework is likely to be fundamentally different than the purpose of the multilateral agreement itself, and therefore that the logic of reciprocity in the multilateral context will not generally apply to preferential agreements negotiated within the broader multilateral framework. As a consequence, I am skeptical that we can learn much about the reciprocity principle that forms a pillar of GATT by looking at the staging rules under which preferential agreements are phased in.

Nevertheless, suppose the same principle of reciprocity that is found in GATT *did* extend to the staging rules for the United States and Mexico in implementing NAFTA. What would we expect to see in the data? If the principle of reciprocity as found in GATT were applied consistently to preferential agreements, I would expect to find *very little* evidence of reciprocity in the staging rules that implement a free trade agreement between a large and small country such as the United States and Mexico under NAFTA.[6] This is because the reciprocity principle of GATT is effectively applied only among the major industrialized countries. Small countries are extended the tariff reductions negotiated among their larger trading partners on an unconditional MFN basis, and are therefore not required to reciprocate with tariff reductions of their own. This is true in GATT rounds in which negotiations have proceeded under a *principal supplier* rule (whereby requests for concessions on a particular product are made only by the exporter of the largest volume of that product, with the negotiated outcomes then extended to all GATT member countries on an unconditional MFN basis), an approach that was used explicitly in the GATT rounds prior to the Kennedy Round (see, for example, Dam 1970, 61–62) and partially returned to in the most recent Uruguay Round. But it is also true of rounds such as the Kennedy Round and the Tokyo Round, where negotiators adopted a common tariff-cutting rule.[7]

The fact that small countries have generally not been asked to offer recipro-

---

4. A qualification to this statement is warranted. Weak enforcement mechanisms at the multilateral level may prevent countries from achieving efficient policies under GATT, in which case stronger enforcement possibilities among a subset of GATT-member countries could allow further preferential liberalization toward efficient policies. (See Bagwell and Staiger 1997b, 1997c, 1997d; Bond and Syropoulos 1996a, 1996b; Bond, Syropoulos, and Winters 1996.)

5. Or, in the case of customs union formation, an enhanced negotiating position within GATT (see, for example, Ludema 1992).

6. For my argument, what is relevant is that Mexico is small in the sense of its ability to affect world prices.

7. See Dam (1970, 68–78) and Preeg (1970, 130). For example, in assessing the implications of adopting a common ("linear") tariff-cutting rule for the principle of reciprocity in the Kennedy Round, Dam observes:

cal concessions to large countries in GATT negotiations suggests to me that, if there *is* strong evidence of reciprocity in the particular staging decisions of the United States and Mexico under NAFTA, it is *not* driven by the same underlying forces that have made the reciprocity principle a pillar of GATT.

Conclusion

What, then, does looking for evidence of reciprocity in the staging rules of preferential agreements mean? I am not exactly sure. Yet the authors do find some evidence of reciprocity in the staging rules of NAFTA, in the sense that U.S. staging decisions help to predict the staging decisions of Mexico but not vice versa. They interpret this as evidence of "narrow reciprocity," in the sense that Mexico appears to have adjusted its own staging decisions to achieve a degree of *product-by-product* (five-digit SITC level) reciprocity with the staging decisions of the United States. While this reciprocity appears to be operative in only one direction, it is nevertheless noteworthy that it holds product by product: compared to the traditional notion of an *overall* balance of concessions that characterizes the reciprocity principle under GATT, this is a particularly strong form of reciprocity (see, for example, Dam 1970, 58–61).

The authors have therefore provided an interesting empirical finding, but for the reasons given above I am not convinced that it reflects reciprocity in action. What could it reflect, if not reciprocity? I can think of at least one possibility. It seems plausible that the pattern of political support and/or the degree of adjustment cost across sectors is an important determinant of the staging rules in each country. It also seems plausible that these variables would be highly correlated across countries, that is, the lists of industries that enjoy strong political support or suffer major adjustment costs are likely to look very similar across countries. And finally, the existing tariff structure in the United States is likely to strongly reflect these industry characteristics (see, for example, the empirical evidence in Baldwin 1985) but, as a result of the major liberalization of Mexico's trade policy that has occurred in the context of broader reforms instituted since the mid-1980s, the existing tariff structure in Mexico may well not. Under this interpretation, U.S. tariff levels would help predict U.S. staging patterns while Mexican tariff levels would not predict Mexican staging patterns (as the authors find) and, by serving as a proxy for measures of the pattern

---

Interestingly enough, the shift from the product-by-product method to the linear method was not accompanied by a deemphasis of the principle of reciprocity. The first principle in the 1963 Resolution was:

> A significant liberalization of world trade is desirable, and . . . for this purpose, comprehensive trade negotiations, to be conducted . . . on the principle of reciprocity, shall begin at Geneva on 4 May 1964, with the widest possible participation. (Basic Instruments, 12th Supplement, 1964, p. 47.)

Only in the fourth principle was the linear method mentioned for the first time. (69)

Later, Dam writes: "The Kennedy Round experience suggests that rules alone cannot determine the content of tariff negotiations, particularly so long as the principle of reciprocity exercises such a powerful influence on negotiators" (77).

of political support and/or adjustment costs across sectors of the Mexican economy, U.S. staging patterns would help predict Mexican staging patterns as well.

References

Bagwell, Kyle, and Robert W. Staiger. 1996. Reciprocal Trade Liberalization. NBER Working Paper no. 5488. Cambridge, MA: National Bureau of Economic Research, March.

———. 1997a. Reciprocity, Non-Discrimination, and Preferential Agreements in the Multilateral Trading System. NBER Working Paper no. 5932. Cambridge, MA: National Bureau of Economic Research, February.

———. 1997b. Regionalism and Multilateral Tariff Cooperation. In *International Trade Policy and the Pacific Rim,* ed. John Piggott and Alan Woodland. London: Macmillan.

———. 1997c. Multilateral Tariff Cooperation during the Formation of Customs Unions. *Journal of International Economics* 42:91–123.

———. 1997d. Multilateral Tariff Cooperation during the Formation of Regional Free Trade Areas. *International Economic Review* 38:291–319.

Baldwin, Robert E. 1985. *The Political Economy of U.S. Import Policy.* Cambridge: MIT Press.

Bond, Eric W., and Costas Syropoulos. 1996a. The Size of Trading Blocs: Market Power and World Welfare Effects. *Journal of International Economics* 40:411–37.

———. 1996b. Trading Blocs and the Sustainability of Inter-Regional Cooperation. In M. Canzoneri, W. Ethier, and V. Grilli, eds., *The New Transatlantic Economy.* Cambridge: Cambridge University Press.

Bond, Eric W., Costas Syropoulos, and Alan A. Winters. 1996. Deepening of Regional Integration and External Trade Relations. CEPR Discussion Paper no. 1317. London: Centre for Economic Policy Research.

Dam, Kenneth W. 1970. *The GATT: Law and International Economic Organization.* Chicago: University of Chicago Press.

Ludema, Rodney. 1992. On the Value of Preferential Trade Agreements in Multilateral Negotiations. Manuscript.

Preeg, Ernest H. 1970. *Traders and Diplomats: An Analysis of the Kennedy Round of Negotiations under the General Agreement of Tariffs and Trade.* Washington, DC: Brookings Institution.

9   Overview

Anne O. Krueger

9.1   Introduction

Until the postwar era, most-favored-nation (MFN) treatment was far from universal. The United States, for example, negotiated separate treaties governing trade with a large number of countries and, until the 1920s, differentiated preferences were the norm.[1] With the passage of the Reciprocal Trade Agreements Act in 1934, the United States shifted to an MFN policy for countries with whom a treaty was negotiated and, in the postwar years, strongly supported MFN through the General Agreement on Tariffs and Trade (GATT), explicitly rejecting preferential arrangements. Adoption of MFN implied the absence of discrimination among countries in tariff rates although, as Taussig noted, it is always possible to specify a tariff as specific as the one that was levied on milk originating from cows grazing at a height in excess of 15,000 feet for more than two months of the year. One can thus at least in principle often achieve geographic discrimination through a sufficiently pointed structure of tariffs.

With the notable exception of the European experience,[2] the first forty years

Anne O. Krueger is the Herald L. and Caroline L. Ritch Professor of Humanities and Sciences in the Economics Department at Stanford University. She is also director of Stanford's Center for Research in Economic Development and Policy Reform and a research associate of the National Bureau of Economic Research.

1. Taussig (1931). Taussig reported the plethora of bilateral trading agreements—with individually specified tariff treatment—in the late 1800s and noted that their complexity gradually drove countries to consider more uniformity across countries. He dates the American move toward inclusion of MFNs in commercial treaties as starting in 1924.

2. The European Union (EU) began life as the European Common Market, with six founding members: Belgium, France, Germany, Italy, Luxembourg, and the Netherlands. It expanded to twelve members as Denmark, Greece, Ireland, Portugal, Spain, and the United Kingdom acceded in the 1970s and 1980s. During that period, it was also renamed the European Community. In the 1990s the name once again changed, to European Union, to connote the move toward a "single market." Additional countries (including Austria, Sweden, the Czech Republic, Poland, and Hun-

of the postwar era were marked by trade liberalization in a multilateral context. Such preferential arrangements as there were (East African Common Market, Latin American Free Trade Association, and so on) were either disbanded or largely ineffectual, again with the notable exception of the European Union (EU). Even Commonwealth preferences were abandoned as Britain joined the European Common Market.

The EU itself seemed "different." First and most important, integration of the European economies took place, at least through the 1970s, in the context of liberalization of trade with the rest of the world. Second, motives for European integration seemed more political than economic ("strategic" in Whalley's words); several EU "crises" would most likely have resulted in the dissolution of the arrangement had it not been for overriding political concerns. Third, the direction of the EU was clearly toward much greater integration than a preferential trading arrangement (PTA) alone would have implied.

The initial proposals for a European Common Market spurred considerable thought regarding PTAs in the 1940s and 1950s. Out of that literature, which included most prominently Meade (1953) and Viner (1950),[3] came the classic distinction between trade creation and trade diversion, which has been in one way or another central to the analysis of the effects of PTAs ever since.

For, while the initial instinct of economists and others was to assume that formation of a PTA meant the lowering of trade barriers and must therefore be a movement toward freer trade and hence welfare-enhancing, the Vinerian distinction between trade creation and trade diversion vividly demonstrated that analysis of PTAs was in the domain of second best. That is, comparison is not between a first-best policy (free trade, in the absence of monopoly power in trade[4]) and a policy in which first-best conditions are violated, but between two policies in each of which first-best conditions are violated but in different ways.

Whereas first-best policy is for the domestic marginal rates of transformation (DMRTs) among commodities to equal the international marginal rates of transformation (IMRTs), a country entering a PTA is typically moving from a situation in which DMRTs are unequal to the IMRTs (because of the presence of tariffs pre-PTA) to a situation in which the DMRTs become equal to the

---

gary) are now seeking membership. In partial reaction to the Common Market, a European Free Trade Association (EFTA) was formed among a number of countries (including the United Kingdom and others who subsequently joined the EU). EFTA countries entered into free trade agreements with each other, and had free trade in manufactured goods with the countries in the EU. I shall use the term European Union (EU) when reference is to current practices or practices that still continue. When reference is to a specific time in the past, I shall use the name applicable at the time.

3. See Lipsey (1960) for a survey of the literature to that date.

4. Unless there is a divergence between domestic and international marginal rates of transformation, free trade is always a first-best policy for a country: domestic distortions in a first-best world are corrected through the appropriate domestic interventions. From a global perspective, of course, free trade is optimal even when individual countries have monopoly power in trade.

marginal rates of transformation in some trading partners, but where the marginal rates of transformation in those trading partners are then unequal to those in other countries. The distortion is moved from the domestic border vis-à-vis all other countries to the domestic border and PTA partner countries vis-à-vis all other countries, and there is no a priori means for specifying which distortion is closer or farther from a Pareto-optimal outcome. As a result, trade may be diverted from low-cost sources (outside the PTA) to higher-cost sources (within the PTA), or it may be created, as sources shift from high-cost domestic production to lower-cost PTA-partner production.[5]

After the initial spurt of interest in PTAs in the 1950s, the apparent ascendancy of the multilateral system over PTAs led to a loss of interest in the latter, and economists' research focused almost entirely on issues associated with individual countries' trade policies vis-à-vis the world economy or with the properties of the open multilateral system itself. Analysis of PTAs was a virtually forgotten domain.

In the 1980s and 1990s, however, PTAs have once again been ascending in importance (see WTO 1995). In 1982, the United States formally renounced its earlier support for the multilateral system to the exclusion of PTAs and stated that it would welcome PTAs with "like-minded" countries seeking to go beyond GATT in removing barriers to trade between them.[6] It followed up with free trade arrangements (FTAs) negotiated with Israel, Canada (the Canada-U.S. Free Trade Agreement), and then with Canada and Mexico (North American Free Trade Agreement [NAFTA]). It is already the stated intent of the group of countries associated in the Asia-Pacific Economic Cooperation group (APEC) to form a region of free trade by the year 2010 for developed countries and 2020 for less developed countries.[7] The countries of the Western Hemisphere likewise declared their intent of reaching a hemisphere-wide FTA. Some countries have indicated their intent to join more than one preferential grouping.[8] Immediate challenges for the EU relate to the applications for entry of a variety of countries to the east and south of the existing borders. In the

5. Note, however, that lower-cost partner production need not be the low-cost world source. Trade creation may enhance welfare, but may nonetheless be Pareto-inferior to multilateral free trade. Once a PTA has been formed, those producers gaining through trade creation in either partner country may become opponents of multilateral liberalization in order to avoid losing their PTA-induced markets.

6. The first departure from MFN for the United States for members of GATT was the acceptance (after much resistance) of the Generalized System of Preferences for developing countries, which was authorized under GATT. Even before the official announcement of the "two-track" policy in the early 1980s, however, the United States unilaterally extended preferences to countries eligible for the Caribbean Basin Initiative.

7. The APEC wording is ambiguous as to whether the countries in the region intend to practice global free trade by the years specified or whether they contemplate a PTA in the region.

8. The United States itself would be in the Western Hemisphere Free Trade Association (the presumed successor to NAFTA) and the APEC grouping. Chile is negotiating for entry into NAFTA, already has an FTA with some Latin American countries including Mexico, is in APEC, and is seeking an FTA with the EU.

somewhat more distant future, the United States and EU have officially expressed an interest in the formation of the Trans-Atlantic Free Trade Area (TAFTA).

In these circumstances, it is natural for economists to revisit the questions that arise out of PTAs, and the papers at this conference address some key aspects of those questions. Analysis is difficult for several reasons. In large part, this is because of the second-best aspect of PTAs. What we would ideally like to know is the level of economic efficiency (for the world as a whole and for individual trading nations) and welfare associated with worldwide free trade contrasted with that of individual nations under their existing tariffs, compared in turn with welfare under preferential arrangements. But even that very ambitious specification is not enough: to determine welfare under existing tariffs, is it legitimate to compare a country's tariff situation with that under free trade, assuming that other countries retain their existing tariff structure? Or should it instead be recognized that if, for example, India went to free trade, there might follow some adjustment of tariffs in other countries? And, as if these questions were not difficult enough, questions arise as to the determinants of tariff levels under preferential arrangements contrasted with the determinants of tariffs of individual countries.[9]

Moreover, given that global free trade represents a Pareto optimum from the viewpoint of the world as a whole,[10] determinants of tariff structures remain a puzzle to economists. Moreover, a central question is whether formation of PTAs is conducive to leading the world closer to multilateral free trade or, instead, is likely to lead to larger trade barriers between PTA groupings as trade barriers within PTAs are dismantled. Indeed, in an important sense, the extent to which formation of PTAs is conducive to further liberalization of world trade in the future is *the* key question for analysts.

Even if we did have an accepted theory of the political economy of tariff determination, we would still need a theory and methodology for estimating what bilateral trade flows would be under each of the hypothesized circumstances. Whereas theory offers a good guide at least to the economic cost of a tariff or the tariff equivalent of other trade barriers, there is little in theory to help in ascertaining what "optimal" bilateral trade flows are.

9. An interesting set of questions is which countries might gain by aligning themselves with which trading partners in any preferential arrangement.

10. One of the difficult questions that has not been satisfactorily addressed in the literature on the political economy of trade policy is why compensation mechanisms cannot be created between countries (and, for that matter, within countries that lack monopoly power in trade) so that free trade is a reality. After all, even if there is monopoly power in trade, the rest of the world could afford to bribe the monopolist to practice free trade, leaving both the monopolist and the rest of the world better off. In light of Becker's argument (1983) that wealth transfers will be effected in the cheapest possible way, this puzzle compels attention. None of the papers at this conference (or elsewhere, to my knowledge) seriously addresses this issue, so it is ignored here.

9.2 Motives for Forming Preferential Trading Arrangements

The papers at this conference all represent significant steps forward in addressing these questions. John Whalley addresses two of the key questions: the welfare costs that might be associated with a world of PTAs with large trade barriers between groupings, and the motives for small countries in entering PTAs. He notes that there are a variety of motives for forming PTAs, and then develops a model in which small countries need to defend themselves against potential losses should large countries with monopoly power in trade exercise that power by forming trading blocs and imposing optimal tariffs. To examine this question, Whalley formulates a computable general equilibrium model, following Krugman (1991) in assuming that individual nations in the absence of PTAs and trading blocs levy optimal tariffs on each other. Assuming that countries levy optimal tariffs provides an analytical framework within which tariff levels can be endogenously determined and, as such, has a great deal to be said for it. Whalley's estimates of the magnitudes of potential gains (resulting from terms of trade changes) are interesting and useful.

A first part of the exercise examines the welfare impact of individual countries' and groups of countries' impositions of optimal tariffs. One of the fears about PTAs has been that they might ultimately result in the division of the world into trading blocs: as trade relations become more and more open among PTA members, it is possible that barriers to trade with the outside increase. Whalley's model provides a basis for estimating how large the gains and losses under such a scenario might be.

In Whalley's model, since large countries have most monopoly power in trade, they lose if they are bound under a PTA not to use that power against their PTA partners. Small countries, however, seek insurance against the eventuality of the exercise of monopoly power by large countries, which is their motive for entering a PTA with a large country. This, in turn, implies that large countries should receive a static benefit from PTA membership to offset the costs of forgone future monopoly power against them.

Because of the complexity of Whalley's model, there are some key simplifying assumptions and estimates to which the results are highly sensitive.[11] The numbers need, therefore, to be taken as a first approximation. In a country-specific model of optimum-tariff-ridden Nash equilibrium, for example, Whalley's estimates suggest that the United States and Europe would come out as net gainers (1.2 percent and 3.7 percent of national income, respectively) while Japan would emerge a loser (5.2 percent of income).[12] But the really big losers

11. Chief among these appear to be the two-good assumption with each region producing only one good for export and importing the other good, and the use of Armington elasticities. These latter clearly drive the estimates in an optimal-tariff and retaliation framework.

12. That the elasticities may be suspect is illustrated by examination of Whalley's individual numbers. For example, in a postretaliation equilibrium, U.S. tariffs against the EU product is over

are the smaller countries, as illustrated by the estimated losses of 25.5 percent and 8.5 percent for Canada and Mexico, respectively, if they were to go into a tariff war alone. The rest of the world is estimated to suffer a welfare loss equivalent to 10.6 percent of national income.

The rest of the world, consisting of unaligned countries sufficiently small so that they cannot individually affect their terms of trade, has the most to lose if the world divides into trading blocs. As such, small countries may feel impelled to align themselves with large countries (as Canada and Chile) in order to avoid being left out. This is an important insight, and one that probably follows even if PTAs do not precisely formulate optimal tariffs.[13]

One must, however, question the assumption that optimal tariffs would be formulated when countries setting their individual tariffs have set tariff rates far below the estimated optimum in the Whalley model. To be sure, this raises the issue of the role of GATT/WTO (World Trade Organization) in determining or constraining tariff levels, which in turn is a function of the extent to which PTAs are a step toward multilateral liberalization or instead represent a move toward trading blocs with relatively high walls of protection between them.

In discussions of the EU, NAFTA, and other regional arrangements, one question has been whether there is anything special about regional PTAs, as contrasted with PTAs among geographically dispersed countries. Spilimbergo and Stein address the welfare effects of PTAs when factor endowments, variety, and transport costs all influence trade flows. They consider countries producing agricultural goods (subject to constant returns to scale) and manufactures (in which variety is important), and examine possible PTAs in light of relative factor endowments (rich countries are assumed to have relatively more resources in manufactures because they are relatively well endowed with capital) and transport costs.

Not surprisingly, they find that, the more weight attached to product variety, the greater the gains from forming a PTA among rich countries (that produce varietal goods). This leaves open, of course, the question of why rich countries would impose tariffs on the importation of varietal goods from other rich countries and not resort unilaterally to zero tariffs for these items. In their model, when trade is predominantly comparative-advantage-based, the welfare benefits to rich countries from forming a PTA with a poor country increase and

---

400 percent and the EU tariff against the American product is over 900 percent. This results in a shrinkage of trade volumes to 5 percent or less of initial trade flows. It is difficult to believe that the gains from improved terms of trade could offset losses in the quantity of trade of this magnitude without extraordinarily small (in absolute value) elasticities of demand. It may be noted that Whalley's estimated optimal tariff postretaliation for the United States is over 400 percent for all regions, while that of the EU is over 800 percent.

13. The model also has interesting insights to the sequence in which bargaining with respect to entry into a PTA takes place. Clearly, in Whalley's model small countries are better off bargaining jointly for a PTA than they are bargaining sequentially, as they must give up less to the large country to obtain insurance. However, the last to enter a sequential bargain may be better off than the first, as Whalley finds that Canada would have been better off to bargain after Mexico (because of Mexico's larger size).

those associated with a PTA among rich countries diminish. Spilimbergo and Stein also find that poor countries will always be better off integrating with a rich country, and will always be worse off when entirely left out of any trading bloc. Finally, in the absence of transport costs, their model yields the result that consolidation of the world into a few PTAs would result in reduced welfare.

They then turn to the role of distance in the formation of PTAs. Earlier, Krugman (1991) and Summers (1991) had pointed to "natural trading partners" as being geographically proximate. They then argued that the formation of PTAs was likely to be beneficial. Spilimbergo and Stein attempt to test this in the context of their model by adding distance and transport costs explicitly. Adding transport costs is similar to increasing the importance of comparative-advantage-based trade (because of the lower elasticity of substitution among such goods than among varieties of the same product).

They use this framework to simulate several possible PTA scenarios. In an interesting one, they examine whether Chile would be better off in NAFTA or in Mercosur: the latter would dominate only if transport costs were very high (which would greatly reduce the potential trade between Chile and northern members of NAFTA). In general, as transport costs increase, the welfare gains from regional PTAs increase, and, in the limit as transport costs become prohibitive, regional PTAs capture all the potential gains from trade with no further gains accruing from a multilateral trading system.

Spilimbergo and Stein's results provoke a number of questions. If, as their model indicates and as seems reasonable, the gains to multilateral trade increase as transport costs fall, why should regional PTAs emerge in the 1990s when transport costs are far lower than they were several decades ago? Why, too, should resistance in developed countries to PTAs between developed and developing countries appear to be so much greater than to PTAs between developed countries if, as their model suggests, welfare gains to developed countries are greater in the latter case? Does this suggest the predominance of comparative-advantage-based trade?

The conclusions of the Whalley and the Spilimbergo-Stein models point to the centrality of the determinants of the structure of protection pre- and post-FTA. Those issues, in turn, divide into the political economy of tariff determination and into the determinants of the form (FTA or customs union) of PTA. These issues are dealt with in part of the paper by Frankel and Wei.[14] Turning first to tariff determination, they consider the optimal tariff case, covered by Whalley, and political-economy models where other considerations are involved. Trade diversion resulting from a customs union or free trade area, for example, is likely to lead to more opposition to multilateral trade liberalization because those benefiting from the PTA would lose their gains to third countries in a multilateral framework. This is the outcome, for example, of the

---

14. Whalley also has some results pertaining to differences between FTAs and customs unions in the context of his model.

Grossman-Helpman (1995) median voter model, and also Levy's model (forthcoming) in which support for trade liberalization arises from increased varietal trade while opposition emerges when trade is factor-endowment-based. Once a PTA has been formed, support for further trade liberalization is diminished, as part of the variety-based gains from trade are already achieved.

A critical question in the "stumbling bloc or building bloc?" analysis focuses on the terms on which new members may accede to the PTA. If any country seeking membership may join,[15] an attractive PTA could eventually include all countries as members and thus automatically transform into multilateral liberalization. However, issues arise if blocs form for motives such as those suggested by Whalley. For, as new members seek to join, the gains to the original members diminish. At some point, it is likely (and inevitable in some models) that further membership will diminish welfare and PTAs would then, if maximizing their individual welfare, refuse further members.

However, there are also mechanisms by which PTAs may increase support for multilateral trade liberalization. These include the locking-in of trade opening (as exemplified by Mexico), the ability of governments to insulate themselves more from protectionist pressures under a PTA than unilaterally, and the efficiency of negotiating with larger units such as the EU rather than with 100+ individual countries.

Frankel and Wei also sketch their own model, in which a single move to multilateral free trade would be opposed by workers in two of three industries (each of which employs an equal number of workers), but in which a move to an FTA would arouse opposition only from those in one of the two industries (as the FTA partner is not a threat in one industry and the price of the second imported product might be lower). Once the PTA is in place, however, workers in the industry that already faced import competition from the PTA partner will, along with those in the export industry, support a further move to multilateral free trade.

While this sequence would lead to further trade liberalization,[16] that is not inevitable, as Frankel and Wei recognize. If sufficient trade diversion occurs under a PTA, it could result in a majority's blocking further multilateral liberalization, even in circumstances where an initial majority might have supported it.

In this regard, nothing in economic theory suggests that preferences should be either 100 percent or zero. Indeed, the economic logic of trade creation and trade diversion suggests that partial preferences might be optimal, although GATT/WTO rules permit PTAs only when preferences are 100 percent. It has been suggested, however, that keeping preferential arrangements within low

15. As noted by Frankel and Wei, a number of models have been developed in which nonmember countries do find it in their interest to join a PTA.

16. Other arguments that an PTA would lead to further liberalization have not been modeled. It has been argued, for example, that firms that are not currently trading internationally may gain experience in a regional PTA that will then reduce their fears of further trade opening.

limits (22 percent reduction below multilateral tariffs is the number reported in Frankel-Wei from Stein) would maintain incentives for PTAs to accept new members, or to move to multilateral free trade.

There are also contrasts between customs unions and FTAs, and the choice may be based on political-economy considerations. FTAs may be more amenable to capture by special-interest groups, through exploitation of rules of origin. Accession of new members to an FTA will be more difficult and less automatic than under a customs union, because differences in external tariffs will drive negotiations over rules of origin applicable to the new member in an FTA, and not in a customs union where the external tariff is given. Frankel and Wei also note that sectoral exclusions are far easier in FTAs than in customs unions (and are, at least in principle, illegal under WTO and GATT). However, FTAs may be more conducive to further multilateral trade liberalization, as there will be pressure on producers importing inputs into the higher-tariff countries to seek tariff reductions.

9.3   Empirical Evidence

The papers discussed so far have examined the welfare effects of PTAs, and have shed light on certain aspects of the issue, but also raise a number of questions, many of whose answers depend on the relative orders of magnitude of different effects. In light of these results, it is natural that considerable research efforts should go into empirical work, estimating quantitatively the effects of PTAs on trade flows.

Researchers attempting to understand bilateral trade flows early on turned to econometric estimates of the determinants of trade, starting with a gravity model in which bilateral flows are a function of their size (as reflected by GDP and population) and the costs of transacting business between them (usually taken to be a function of distance). When interest turned to the effects of PTAs, dummy variables for the presence of PTAs were introduced into gravity models to test for the quantitative effects of preferential arrangements.

Before interest focused on the effects of PTAs, the gravity model was already found to do a good job of explaining bilateral trade flows, and economists began developing theories consistent with these models.[17] Deardorff's paper represents a contribution to the theoretical foundation for these models, showing that they are consistent with virtually any model of trade in which different countries specialize in different groups of commodities.[18] Deardorff starts by positing an international price vector, in response to which in the absence of transport costs countries' production takes place. Demands (at the

---

17. See Deardorff's paper for a brief overview of the evolution of the literature.

18. If two countries specialized in precisely the same commodities, of course, they would not export to each other. In Deardorff's model, however, there are no transport costs, and domestic production is treated as being thrown on the world market and then randomly assigned to importing countries, including the producer.

same international price vector) from each country are then randomly matched by supplies and, since transport costs don't matter, a home country's buyers of the good it exports may nonetheless satisfy their demands from a foreign source while the country's exports are greater than domestic production less domestic demand.

Deardorff then proceeds to introduce transport costs, which insure that factor price equalization will not obtain, and, in a world with many more commodities than countries, he argues that it is likely that most goods will be supplied by only one country. In that circumstance, a gravity equation for bilateral trade flows would be justified even in a Heckscher-Ohlin world. Thus, the gravity model would appear to be consistent with virtually any trade model in which specialization obtains.

Frankel and Wei use a gravity-model specification in their paper and augment it with a number of variables that can plausibly be thought to influence bilateral trade flows. These include distance between each pair of countries (which may influence not only transport costs but interest charges and other user costs), contiguous borders, and a common language between a pair of countries. They then add dummy variables for regional groupings. They estimate the model using data for sixty-three countries (which gives 1,953 bilateral trade observations), for four years between 1970 and 1992.

Frankel and Wei's data show that the "affinity" variables are significant and that there are intraregional trade biases. Western European countries are estimated to have traded 17 percent more than the unaugmented model would have predicted, and the trade of Western Hemisphere countries, APEC, and the Association of Southeast Asian Nations (ASEAN) was about 40, 215, and 145 percent higher than predicted.

But they then proceed to examine the extent to which intraregional trade was higher because the pair of countries in question traded more overall, and were thus more open than average, as contrasted with a circumstance in which greater trade between a country pair might arise at the expense of third countries (outside the PTA). The Western European and East Asian groups were found to have such high coefficients because they were trading more overall, relative to their size. An East Asian country, for example, traded about twice as much with a country outside the region than two random countries outside East Asia even after account was taken of distance and the other variables mentioned above. Frankel and Wei interpret these results to imply that intraregional trade in East Asia and Western Europe has not grown at the expense of trade with third countries, and thus has been predominantly trade-creating.

Interestingly, both APEC and the Western Hemisphere countries trade less than predicted; once that is taken into account, the larger-than-predicted trade within each group is taken as a sign of trade diversion. As a next step, Frankel and Wei take into account the trend over time in "openness" and in greater-than-predicted intraregional trade. In the Western European case, countries were trading more outside the region than predicted in 1970, and gradually shifted toward more trade within the region; by the end of the period, their extra-European trade was still larger than predicted, but less so than it had been in earlier years.

When Frankel and Wei turn to formal regional groupings, they find that the EC, Mercosur, and ASEAN all exhibited "openness" in the sense defined above. By contrast, the European Free Trade Association (EFTA) and NAFTA show evidence of trade diversion. Their interpretation is that most countries that choose to liberalize their trade with neighbors are also more able to liberalize internationally, but that either result can happen.

Finally, Frankel and Wei investigate the extent to which currency blocs and currency stability seem to follow regional trading blocs and to influence the volume of trade between country pairs. They find evidence of a European currency bloc (around the mark) and a dollar bloc in the Pacific, with no evidence of a yen bloc. They also find some evidence supporting the view that exchange rate volatility has suppressed trade flows.

Frankel, Stein, and Wei obtain yet further results with the gravity model. They include many of the same variables as in Frankel and Wei and add a number of variables such as per capita income levels to reflect the "affinity" between countries. They then estimate their model with data for sixty-three countries (1,953 bilateral trade observations) for three years, 1970, 1980, and 1990.

In this paper, they are concerned with the importance of "affinity" variables and again focus on the extent to which trade flows deviate from predicted levels because of these and other factors. Western European countries are estimated to have traded 36 percent more than the unaugmented gravity model would have predicted.

They then examine the extent to which intraregional trade was higher because the pair of countries in question was more open than average, as well as trends in intraregional trade in these regions over time. Intra-EU trade increases over time, but not at a statistically significant rate once the other variables are taken into account. Intra-Asian trade is high, but shows no trend. Frankel, Stein, and Wei interpret these results to imply that intraregional trade grew rapidly, and then turn to the question of whether the growth was trade-creating or at the expense of trade with the rest of the world.

They augment their model with transport costs and imperfect competition, and show that for reasonable values of the transport parameter, regional preferential groupings are welfare-improving contrasted with geographically removed partner preferences. However, overall they conclude that the extent of preferences among regional partners has probably significantly exceeded the optimal amount.

The improved theoretical grounding for gravity models provided by Deardorff and the fact that Frankel and Wei, and Frankel, Stein, and Wei, can obtain such significant and interpretable relationships between the gravity-equation dummy variables appears to lend credence to the use of these techniques for interpretation of the impact of PTAs and other variables of interest.

Eichengreen and Irwin, however, implicitly challenge the gravity model and its results. They note, first, that intraregional flows are higher than predicted before, as well as when, a PTA is in force. Second, they point to a number of reasons why "history should matter." That it should matter has been demonstrated in the hysteresis literature: once an exporter has developed a distribution network in another country, he is likely to continue using it unless there is a large decrease in profitability. There can be several reasons for this. It may be because fixed costs are sunk and only variable costs need be covered; it may result simply from acquaintance with the market. To be sure, exogenous events such as war or depression may significantly shift historical trading patterns, but Eichengreen and Irwin expect the influence of historical trading ties to be important much of the time.

Eichengreen and Irwin note that failure to include lagged variables in a gravity model will significantly bias estimates of effects of PTAs if PTAs are formed among countries with unusually close trading ties pre-PTA. That there might be unusually strong motivation to form a PTA with countries with which there are unusually strong trade ties seems plausible. Eichengreen and Irwin point to the possibility that countries might form a PTA to insulate their trade with important trading partners from shocks.

Eichengreen and Irwin use their data set (thirty-four countries for 1928 and 1938; thirty-eight countries for 1949, 1954, and 1964) to examine whether "history matters." They test the extent to which deviations of trade patterns from the straightforward gravity predictions in one period are explained at least in part by deviations in preceding periods.

In their specification, the usual gravity-model variables are significant and surprisingly stable for the various years for which they provide estimates. When they add lagged trade as another variable, however, the magnitude of coefficients on current incomes and distance is reduced. Trade in 1949 (after the disruption of the Second World War) is significantly influenced by trade patterns in 1928 and 1938, with 1938 trade being twice as important as 1928 trade. By 1964, however, the impact of prewar trade patterns has disappeared.

One interesting result that arises from their specification is that, despite the smaller estimated "direct" income coefficients in their equations, one can estimate a "long-run" elasticity of trade with respect to income, taking into account, for example, the effect on trade in 1954 of additional income in 1949 when it is recognized that the increased trade in 1949 increases trade in 1954. These estimated "long-run" trade elasticities are higher than those obtained in a gravity model without lagged variables.

Having estimated their model and demonstrated the importance of lagged variables, Eichengreen and Irwin then proceed to introduce dummy variables: a first dummy variable is when both countries are members of the same PTA, a second when only one country is. The coefficient on the first dummy, if positive, would indicate positive trade creation between the PTA partners; the second, if negative, would indicate trade diversion from third countries.

There are a number of interesting findings: GATT members traded more with one another (positive first dummy) than predicted in 1949 after the conclusion of the first round of multilateral tariff reductions, but this effect had disappeared by the 1950s.[19] Countries that had been British colonies traded more with Britain and less with the rest of the world in 1949 than predicted; by the 1950s, however, these countries traded less with the rest of the world and no more than predicted with Britain.

Eichengreen and Irwin's demonstration that history does indeed matter is convincing. Nonetheless, it raises the question of whether history itself, or some characteristics of trading partners that are correlated over time, are the variables yielding their results. Interestingly, none of the discussion of gravity models in the conference explicitly addressed the role of trade barriers in influencing bilateral flows. Although the presence of a regional arrangement implicitly represents the absence (or at least the greatly reduced presence) of trade barriers, one would anticipate that the average height of protection of PTA members toward trade with nonpartners would be a significant variable. Perhaps for lack of the requisite data, such a specification has not been attempted.

Nonetheless, a number of findings suggest that variables with serial correlation may be at work. Commonwealth preferences, after all, were extended for a long time and reflected lower trade barriers among Commonwealth countries than between those countries and other trading partners. Likewise, the high coefficients found on openness in East Asia and Western Europe both in Frankel and Wei and in Eichengreen and Irwin may reflect the fact that the countries in those groupings had relatively low external trade barriers. By contrast, most countries in the Western Hemisphere (with the exception of the United States) had relatively high trade barriers for the periods covered by the various data sets, and trade among Western Hemisphere countries may have been less than average for the world over several time periods for that reason. The same phenomenon may have been at work in the ASEAN region. Certainly, if one estimated the average tariff equivalent of trade barriers for the postwar years included in the two studies, it seems clear that Europe, the United States, and probably Japan after 1970 had lower trade barriers in general than did other countries of Asia, all of Latin America, the Middle East, and Africa. All else equal, countries with higher trade barriers would be expected to trade less than countries with lower ones.

Other empirical aspects of PTAs are examined in chapters 7 and 8. Kowalczyk and Davis analyze intrabloc tariff reform, while Engel and Rogers examine the law of one price, and the difference borders (and regional groupings) make to its functioning.

Kowalczyk and Davis examine the time- and industry-specific patterns of phase-outs in regional PTAS in order to attempt to assess whether the pattern

---

19. To be sure, the fact that trade among GATT members had increased in 1949 influences the historical values used in the later regression estimates.

of phase-outs was welfare improving (if higher tariffs were reduced sooner) or not (if tariff dispersion increased during the phase-out period). In doing so, they are not examining trade creation versus trade diversion in the traditional sense, and are examining only the period of transition en route to full PTA status. They find that higher-duty imports into the United States tended to have longer tariff phase-out periods under NAFTA than did lower-duty items, but there was no similar pattern for Mexico. As discussed with respect to other papers, the absence of a satisfactory explanation of existing tariff levels forms a major difficulty in interpreting their results. The simplest explanation for the finding might be that industries in the United States with high tariffs are the ones that have the most political influence over bargaining processes, and that they were able to use that influence in NAFTA negotiations (to slow down phase-out) as they had earlier used it to obtain high tariffs.

But, as in all such analyses, the more fundamental question arises: how were U.S. and Mexican authorities able to set the agenda for NAFTA in such a way that only the timing of tariff phase-out could be affected? To be sure, rules of origin and other side measures were also used, but the fundamental proposition remains: the political power of various groups was seriously eroded once the commitment to NAFTA was made: all that could be done was to slow it down (through slow phase-outs) and to seek other protectionist devices (rules of origin) as partial replacements.

These considerations raise one important set of issues for research with which this conference did not deal: that is, the role of institutional arrangements in constraining the choices of various actors in seeking or granting protection. The papers assuming the use of optimal tariffs for PTAs did so on the implicit assumption that GATT/WTO rules would not apply (because tariffs are bound under WTO). Yet those rules have clearly been an important factor in the liberalization of the world economy over the past half century. Likewise, the existence of multilateral tariff negotiations under GATT enabled export interests in various countries to restrain politicians in granting protection to import-competing interests. In considering whether PTAs are likely to be conducive or a hindrance to further liberalization of the multilateral trading system, issues such as their role in tariff negotiating processes need to be considered.

Even more broadly, there are important questions as to the sorts of institutional design or constraints on PTAs (customs union only?) that would increase the likelihood of further liberalization multilaterally. While a cynic might respond that the level of protection is determined by national governments in their own self-interest, he would have to answer difficult questions as to why such governments enter into PTAS, and whether institutional arrangements might not be found that altered self-interest. But those issues constitute a research agenda for one or more conferences in the future.

Finally, Engel and Rogers examine deviations from the law of one price between regions and across national borders. In an important sense, their methodology represents an alternative to gravity models as a mechanism for examining the effects of PTAs. In particular, they use observations of prices of commodities in different locations at the same point in time, and then attempt to estimate the determinants of price differences. They find that nominal exchange rate variability and distance both account for a significant portion of the failure of the law of one price to hold.

Further, they find that prices of the same commodity diverge more between regions (holding other variables constant) than they do within a regional (North America, EU) preferential grouping, but that divergence is not reduced within Asia. This tends to reinforce findings of others that Asia is less integrated as a region than is Western Europe.

Examination of price patterns is a valuable methodology for increasing our understanding of the role of borders and other factors in preventing the law of one price from obtaining. But, as Kenneth Froot noted in discussion, ascertaining what an identical commodity is is difficult. For example, goods sold in upscale shops differ from those sold in discount stores. Efforts to make price comparisons must confront the challenge that problems such as this present.

9.4   Conclusions: What Have We Learned and What Do We Need to Know?

The papers presented at this conference all add to knowledge and understanding concerning trade patterns in a world in which PTAs are formed. If one turns to the "big questions" posed at the beginning, one would have to conclude that, to date, the evidence is that PTAs have on balance more likely been trade-creating than trade-diverting. In part, this is probably a natural consequence of falling transport and communications costs and of the successive rounds of multilateral tariff reductions under GATT. After all, the lower the average level of protection, the less meaningful are tariff preferences.

The fact of multilateral trade liberalization meant that increased integration within PTAs (notably the EU) took place concurrently with increased openness of most economies. The evidence from the empirical research reported at this conference suggests that, for the most part, increasing regional integration was taking place, but at a faster rate than increasing global integration, which was nonetheless occurring.

For the future, a number of questions arise. Clearly, the long-term impact of PTAs depends on whether they are accompanied by continued multilateral liberalization or instead they substitute for it. Assessing the impact of PTAs on future multilateral trade relations is exceptionally difficult. In part, it depends on how influential the GATT institutional role is thought to have been in the past. It depends as well on the sorts of political-economy considerations discussed above, including especially the extent to which PTAs now in the process of formation represent trade creation or trade diversion. Perhaps most important of all, it depends very much on the costs of disintegration of the world trading system into regional groupings along the lines discussed by Whalley.

On all of these issues, a great deal remains to be learned. Based on the evidence in this conference, however, there are at least weak grounds for optimism that PTAs may contribute to, rather than substitute for, continued multilateral trade liberalization.

References

Becker, Gary. 1983. A Theory of Competition among Pressure Groups for Political Influence. *Quarterly Journal of Economics* 98 (August): 371–400.

Grossman, Gene, and Elhanan Helpman. 1995. The Politics of Free Trade Agreements. *American Economic Review* 85 (September): 667–90.

Krugman, Paul. 1991. Is Bilateralism Bad? In Elhanan Helpman and Assaf Razin, eds., *International Trade and Trade Policy.* Cambridge: MIT Press.

Levy, Philip. Forthcoming. A Political-Economic Analysis of Free Trade Agreements. *American Economic Review.*

Lipsey, Richard. 1960. The Theory of Customs Unions: A General Survey. *Economic Journal* 70 (September): 496–513.

Meade, James. 1953. *Problems of Economic Union.* Chicago: University of Chicago Press.

Summers, Lawrence. 1991. Regionalism and the World Trading System. In Federal Reserve Bank of Kansas City, *Policy Implications of the Trade and Currency Zones,* 295–302. Kansas City: Federal Reserve Bank.

Taussig, Frank. 1931. *A Tariff History of the United States.* New York: Putnam and Sons.

Viner, Jacob. 1950. *The Customs Union Issue.* New York: Carnegie Endowment for International Peace.

World Trade Organization Secretariat. 1995. *Regionalism and the World Trading System.* Geneva: World Trade Organization.

Contributors

Jeffrey H. Bergstrand
Department of Finance and Business
College of Business
University of Notre Dame
Notre Dame, IN 46556

Eric W. Bond
Department of Economics
Pennsylvania State University
University Park, PA 16802

Donald Davis
Department of Economics
111 Littauer Center
Harvard University
Cambridge, MA 02138

Alan V. Deardorff
Department of Economics
University of Michigan
Ann Arbor, MI 48109

Barry Eichengreen
Department of Economics
University of California
549 Evans Hall
Berkeley, CA 94720

Charles Engel
Department of Economics
University of Washington
Seattle, WA 98195

Jeffrey A. Frankel
Member
Council of Economic Advisers
Room 315, OEOB
Washington, DC 20502

Kenneth A. Froot
Graduate School of Business
Harvard University
Soldiers Field
Boston, MA 02163

Gene M. Grossman
Woodrow Wilson School
Robertson Hall
Princeton University
Princeton, NJ 08544

Jon Haveman
Department of Economics
Purdue University
1310 Krannert Building
West Lafayette, IN 47907

David Hummels
Graduate School of Business
University of Chicago
1101 East 58th Street
Chicago, IL 60637

Douglas A. Irwin
Department of Economics
Dartmouth College
Hanover, NH 03775

Michael Knetter
Department of Economics
Dartmouth College
Hanover, NH 03755

Carsten Kowalczyk
Fletcher School of Law and Diplomacy
Tufts University
Medford, MA 02155

Anne O. Krueger
Department of Economics
Stanford University
Stanford, CA 94305

Paul Krugman
Department of Economics
MIT, E52-383A
Cambridge, MA 02139

Robert Z. Lawrence
Kennedy School of Government
Harvard University
79 JFK Street
Cambridge, MA 02138

Edward E. Leamer
Anderson Graduate School of
    Management
University of California
PO Box 951481
Los Angeles, CA 90095

Philip I. Levy
Department of Economics
Yale University
PO Box 208269
New Haven, CT 06520

Arvind Panagariya
Department of Economics
University of Maryland
3105 Tydings
College Park, MD 20742

Dani Rodrik
Kennedy School of Government
Harvard University
79 JFK Street
Cambridge, MA 02138

John H. Rogers
Federal Reserve Board
M.S. 22
Washington, DC 20551

Antonio Spilimbergo
STOP W-0436
Inter-American Development Bank
1300 New York Avenue NW
Washington, DC 20577

T. N. Srinivasan
Economic Growth Center
Yale University
27 Hillhouse Avenue
New Haven, CT 06520

Robert W. Staiger
Department of Economics
University of Wisconsin
1180 Observatory Drive
Madison, WI 53706

Ernesto Stein
STOP W-0436
Inter-American Development Bank
1300 New York Avenue NW
Washington, DC 20577

Shang-Jin Wei
Kennedy School of Government
Harvard University
79 JFK Street
Cambridge, MA 02138

John Whalley
Department of Economics
Social Science Centre
University of Western Ontario
London, Ontario N6A 5C2
Canada

Paul Wonnacott
Department of Economics
Middlebury College
Middlebury, VT 05753

Author Index

Subject Index